The self concept

WITHDRAWN

The self concept

in theory, measurement, development and behaviour

R. B. Burns

Longman
London and New York

To P., H. and R.

Longman Group Limited
Longman House
Burnt Mill, Harlow
Essex CM20 2JE, England
Associated companies throughout the world

*Published in the United States of America
by Longman Inc., New York*

© Longman Group Limited 1979

First published 1979
Third impression 1984

British Library Cataloging in Publication Data

Burns, R B
  The self concept.
  1. Self-perception
  I. Title
  155.2   BF697   78–40864

ISBN 0–582–48951–2

Printed in Singapore by Selector Printing Co Pte Ltd

Contents

Introduction

The subject of this book is the self concept, that individual and exceedingly personal, dynamic and evaluative picture which each person develops in his transactions with his psychological environment and which he carries round with him on life's journey. The self concept is a composite image of what we think we are, what we think we can achieve, what we think others think of us and what we would like to be. This book is an attempt to collate into a comprehensive primer, much of the existing knowledge about the theoretical rationale, growth, measurement and behavioural expression of the self concept, knowledge which for the most part lies scattered in a variety of learned journals, mainly American; yet such knowledge could be of immense value to a wide range of professionals in the 'helping services' both trainee and trained.

The emphasis on family influences and on the effect of the self concept in the teaching–learning situation is a function of the writer's own interests in child development, educational psychology and teaching, yet this text has been written for a wider readership than those solely concerned directly with the rearing and education of children. It should prove of immense value to students and researchers requiring a ready source of test instruments and research references, as well as all those interested in understanding a little more about human behaviour and interpersonal relationships. This small volume is not meant to be an aid to 'self analysis' or 'self help', though there is no doubt it will help to guide the thinking reader to clarify and refine his answers to those searching questions each of us poses to ourselves about who we are and how we become the individuals we do.

The theoretical frame of reference within which the writer places the self concept is variously known as the 'perceptual', 'phenomenological' or 'humanistic' approach. This implies a consideration of human behaviour not solely through the eye of some external observer, but also and more importantly, from the subjective point of view, that of the individual doing the behaving. This approach is a concern with the way the individual perceives and construes his environment, of which his self concept constitutes a central and all-pervasive focal point, into a uniquely meaningful construction. Our quest, not only as psychologists but also as fellow human beings, is an attempt to understand why others perceive themselves as they do and what consequent effects this has on their behaviour.

Section A of this book provides some historical background and overview of major theories about the self concept, including an attempt to clarify the semantic confusions which surround apparently synonymous self-referent terminologies. This leads to an exploration of the contemporary setting of self-concept study within the ambit of phenomenology, with an attempt to provide, as a conclusion to the section, a personal conceptualisation and interpretation of the self concept as a constellation of attitudes held towards all facets of the individual by the individual himself.

In section B consideration is given to the theoretical problems involved in measuring the self concept. A review of particular techniques and scales of practical utility is provided. This collection of 39 instruments for indexing the self concept, some of which are reproduced in their entirety, should prove a goldmine for anyone needing a scale for some research project.

Section C details the development of the self concept in the individual, emphasising the role of physical growth and change, feedback from significant others, sex role learning, child-rearing practices, and the adolescent self concept. The final section (section D) explores some of the important behavioural effects of the self concept with particular reference to therapy, interpersonal relationships, minority groups, delinquency and academic performance. Both sections C and D are based on summaries of major investigations in the specific aspects covered, with an attempt to convey results and implications without burdening the reader with statistical and technical detail. However, full references are provided for every piece of research/measuring instrument discussed so that any particular interests can be followed up in detail by the reader. The bibliography at the conclusion of the book is perhaps the largest set of references on the self concept currently found in a British text.

Since experimental studies of the role of the self concept on behaviour have only been conducted to any extent over the last two decades, there is still much that is to be discovered, and the present volume can only be regarded as an introductory text providing a summary of what psychologists have been able to discover up to the present. No final comprehensive prescriptive document about the self concept is yet possible. But consideration of the existing body of research knowledge and theoretical postulations even at this juncture demands confident support for regarding the self concept as a major factor in the control and direction of human behaviour and performance. The purpose of this book is essentially to convey that message to those with a

concern for understanding and modifying the behaviour of those
for whom they have responsibility whether as teachers, parents,
social workers, probation officers, counsellors of various types and
the like. After reading this book, I hope that like me, each reader
will agree that the self concept can no longer be relatively ignored
and denied its justifiable presence in the contemporary and future
study of human behaviour.

I am deeply indebted to a great many students and colleagues
who in tutorials, lectures and informal conversation have helped
me to formulate and reformulate, clarify and refine my
understanding of and perspective on the self concept. Grateful
thanks go also to Gladys Claridge, Judy Breedon and Jennifer
Kenyon, the typists who struggled to read my illegible hand with
speed and accuracy.

Leeds, 1978

Acknowledgements

We are grateful to the following for permission to reproduce
copyright material:

James Battle for Form B – *The Canadian Self-Esteem Inventory for
Children* © 1976, James Battle; E. M. Berger for scale *Expressed
Acceptance of Self and Expressed Acceptance of Others*; J. C.
Bledsoe for *The Bledsoe Self Concept Scale*; Counselor Recordings
and Tests for the *Piers-Harris Children's Self Concept Scale*; Helen
Davidson and Judith King (The City University of New York) for
Self-Appraisal Scale; McGraw-Hill Book Company for exhibits 9.5,
pp. 429–431 and 9.6 pp. 433–436 *Scales for the Measurement of
Attitudes* by Shaw and Wright. Reprinted by permission of the
publishers; Princeton University Press for Scale D-1 'Self Esteem'
in Appendix D, *Society and Adolescent Self-Image* by Morris
Rosenberg, Princeton Univ. Press 1965, Princeton Paperback
1968. Reprinted by permission of the publishers; Walter B.
Waetjen for items from the test *Self-Concept As A Learner*
(SCAL) © 1963 Walter B. Waetjen.

The history and theory of the self concept

Chapter 1

The self concept in psychological theory

You may already be asking:

'What is this self concept thing he is writing about?'
'How is it defined?'
'Is it all that important to merit me reading this book?'

and asking quite rightly too!

Since many of you will not have met the concept previously it would seem logical to commence this book

(a) by outlining briefly why the self concept is invested with such importance as to require a book written about it though I hope the reasons will become obvious as readers work their way through the book;

(b) by discussing in some detail the place of the self concept in psychological theory; and

(c) by developing a clear conceptualisation of the self concept and other 'self' terms.

There is no doubt that one of the most significant and recent interpretations of human personality is located in self-concept theory. Many contemporary psychologists, as we shall see in detail in this and the next chapter, ascribe to the self concept a key role as a factor in the integration of personality, in motivating behaviour and in achieving mental health. Perhaps, of all the reasons for the current surge of interest in the study of human behaviour none is more compelling than the desire of individuals to know more about themselves, to understand what makes them tick. The psychologists' construct of the self concept is the operational approach to the perennial philosophic question 'Who am I?'. We have all posed ourselves this question many times and while sometimes we feel we really do know who we are, there are times when we have felt confused and at a loss to determine the issue. We can be quite shocked to discover that other people may not agree with our self perceptions. Occasionally we learn rather suddenly things about ourselves that we never thought were there – as when we give vent to a fit of anger or consider deceiving the Inland Revenue in our tax returns. In physical and mental illness the patient may feel that he is unreal or distorted. The role of psychotherapy is often to reveal aspects and levels of self perception of which the patient was unaware. The Delphic admonition 'know thyself' has been echoed down the ages in many forms such as Chaucer's,

> 'Ful wys is he that kan hym selven knowe'
>
> (Monkes Tale)

and Robert Burns' plea,

> 'Oh wad some pow'r the giftie gie us
> to see oursels as ithers see us,
> It wad frae monie a blunder free us,
> An foolish notion.'

Though no psychologist worth his salt could logically put his faith in emotive, poetic outpourings to justify and validate psychological truths, such material derived from insightful geniuses may and often can provide clues worthy of more rigorous investigation. It is apparent that the search for identity is currently an even more real and pressing need for many individuals involved in the rapid flux of the contemporary technological and impersonal era. From earliest recorded times there is evidence that man has sought to understand the causes of his behaviour and create a sense of identity. Kelly (1955) has indicated that every man in his own particular way is a layman psychologist continually trying to predict and control the course of events in which he is involved. The aspirations of the scientist are in fact the aspirations of all men. Each one of us puts forward theories, tests hypotheses, evaluates evidence and derives conclusions in an attempt to make sense of ourselves and of the environment. The context of primitive religions provided the earliest attempts of man to understand himself, and generally proposed a view of man as a physical body possessing some internal agent or non-physical counterpart which regulated his destiny. Various conjectures such as 'soul', 'nature', 'breath', 'will' and 'spirit' were formulated. Such metaphysical elements are rejected by psychologists since they are not amenable to experimental methodology, only to speculation. The self concept which we shall formulate later as the evaluated beliefs a person holds about himself, is accepted by most psychologists as a far more worthy and respectable subject for study since it is amenable to scientific investigation. Self-concept theorists promote the self concept as the most important and focal object within the experience of each individual because of its primacy, centrality, continuity and ubiquity in all aspects of behaviour, mediating as it does both stimulus and response.

Although language has often been claimed to be the sole attribute that is unique to man, the self concept is possibly a stronger claimant for that role of distinguishing man from the rest of living matter. Fromm (1964) sees man as transcending all other forms of life since only he is life actually aware of itself. Bidney (1953) was also prompted to acknowledge that only man has the ability to objectify himself, to stand apart from himself and consider what he is and what he would like to do and become. Dobzhansky (1967), the famous geneticist, also claims self awareness as the fundamental characteristic and evolutionary novelty of *Homo sapiens*. This self awareness places considerable implications on human experience since it involves a search for the meaning of life itself. To know one's identity permits the comprehension of one's past, of the potentialities of one's future, and of one's place in the order of things. Man's conception of himself influences his choice of behaviours and his expectations from life. Hilgard (1949) claims that defence mechanisms can only be understood in terms of a self system to which feelings of guilt can be attached.

The importance of self reference has been demonstrated in verbal material for non-clinical groups by Buhler (1935), Goodenough (1938) and Gesell and Ilg (1949), and for clinical groups by Rogers (1951). In 1934, Fisher's work indicated that 33 per cent of children's remarks had the self as subject. Records of adult verbal conversations also demonstrate a similar high frequency of self-referring items, for example Henle and Hubble (1938) recorded a 40 per cent frequency. Self-referent constructs are seen as a fruitful way of explaining diverse and sometimes paradoxical behaviour at an individual level.

Despite the obvious importance of a concept so integrally a part of each human's development and behaviour, three major controversies have denied the self concept of its recognition as the *sine qua non* in the explanation of human behaviour until the second half of this century. These controversies concern:

(*a*) the lack of agreement over definitions of the plethora of self-referent terms;
(*b*) the encounter between rival approaches in methodology to the study of psychology, namely that between the behaviourist and cognitive schools of psychology; and
(*c*) the problems of measuring such an apparently subjective experiential element.

The first two issues will form a major concern of Chapters 1–3 inclusive, while the third will be the subject of Chapter 4.

The development of the self concept in psychological theory

The pre-psychological period

The term 'self concept' is only of twentieth-century origin. Writings on the individuality of the behaving organism up to this century concerned themselves with a very imprecisely defined and vague Self which was equated with such metaphysical concepts as 'soul', 'will' and 'spirit'. Thus most pre-twentieth-century discussion of self was embedded in a morass of philosophy and religious dogma, with self regarded as some non-physical incumbent of a physical body. Such views are apparent in Homeric writings and Plato's *Phaedo.* Aristotle and his contemporaries speculated on the nature of soul, but it was within the ambit of Christianity that the distinction between body and soul was most marked and promoted. When the physical body died, its tenant, the soul, mind or person, vacated it to continue an existence in Heaven. However, this sort of account restricts the self to unscientific speculation in theological and philosophic terms. It was not until the seventeenth century in Western Europe, a relatively stimulating intellectual era, that the dawning of a new dualism occurred different from the existing dichotomy; this was a dualism of consciousness and content which has developed into an acceptable distinction between the concept of self and the self concept. Descartes made the original contribution. His *cogito ergo sum* (I think, therefore I am) emphasised the centrality of the self in consciousness. Locke and Hume developed this notion and introduced the other side of the equation in emphasising the content of sensory experience. Locke (1960) conceived of man as a 'thinking intelligent being, that has reason and reflection and can consider self as itself' (p. 188). Hume (1928), too, argued in favour of sense-based identity, claiming, 'for my part when I enter most intimately into what I call myself I always stumble on some particular perception or other . . ., I never can catch myself at any time without a perception and never can observe anything but the perception' (p. 252).

Across the Channel, Kant (1934), in his *Critique of Pure Reason,* developed this dualism further by specifying the distinction between the self as subject and self as object. Schopenhauer (1948) also elaborated on this dualism of the subject–object, labelling these aspects as the Knower and Known respectively. Some attempt was made in the nineteenth century by the phrenologists to isolate the physical location of self and Viney (1969) quotes a delightful description of the physical organ of self esteem taken from an English publication of 1815.

Gall first found this organ in a beggar: in examining the head of this person, he observed in the midst of the upper posterior part of the head an elevation which he had not before observed in so high a degree: he asked him the cause of his mendicity; and the beggar accused his pride as the cause of his mental state . . . We have a great number of proofs as to this organ, and can establish its existence. Proud persons, and those who, alienated by pride, imagine themselves to be emperors, kings, ministers, generals, etc. possess it in a high degree.

However humorous such an account is, like the derivations of philosophic analysis, it was speculative and unscientific, though by the nineteenth century philosophy analysis had produced that notion of a global self which was differentiated into subject and object. This differentiation was a ready-made seedbed for more rigorous investigation and theorising by psychology when it developed towards the end of the nineteenth century.

William James

William James (1890) was the first psychologist to elaborate in a most cogent fashion on this necessary subject–objection distinction. The chapter on Self in his monumental work *The Principles of Psychology* (1890) was one of the longest in that two-volume book, and his contributions to theorising about the self concept cannot be overestimated. He gave it deeper coverage than any of his predecessors, and his writing marks the change between older and newer ways of thinking about it. He was strikingly objective in his treatment of the problem and hurled stinging criticism at earlier philosophic notions. 'Altogether,' wrote James (1890) 'the Soul is an outbirth of that sort of philosophizing whose great maxim, according to Dr Hodgson, is: "Whatever you are totally ignorant of, assert to be the explanation of everything else." ' (p. 347)

He assumed that everything, self or not-self was objective. In his development of Kant's thesis, James (1890) categorised two aspects of the global self, 'personality implies the incessant presence of two elements, an objective person, known by a passing subjective thought and recognised as continuing in time. Hereafter let us use the words Me and I for the empirical person and the judging thought.' (p. 371) James considered the global self as simultaneously Me and I. They were discriminated aspects of the same entity, a discrimination between pure experience (I), and the contents of that experience (Me); between a Self as Subject (I), and a Self as Object (Me). This difference is quite apparent in the linguistic sense and it probably appears to be emphasising the obvious to state that we all recognise that humans have the characteristic of consciousness and this permits our awareness of environmental elements. However, common-sense this distinction may seem, it does pose difficulties at a psychological level since the self-reflexive act involved in identifying the Me, at the same time indissolubly links and integrates the Knower and the Known. Each cannot exist without the other; the Self is simultaneously Me and I. So it is impossible to imagine either consciousness in an abstract form lacking any content, or content existing apart from the consciousness that permits awareness of it. Experience must involve experience of something. James was aware of this criticism and noted that while language allows us to categorise in terms of

Knower and the Known, they are only discriminated aspects of the
singularity of the process of experience, a global self which is no
less than the person himself. The Self as Known or Me is in the
broadest sense everything that a man can call his. James claims
that this empirical self comprises four components which are
classed in descending order of their implications for self esteem as
spiritual self, material self, social self and bodily self.

By 'spiritual self' James meant thinking and feeling, i.e. what we
most truly seem to be. 'We take a purer self-satisfaction when we
think of our ability to argue and discriminate, or our moral
sensibility and conscience, or our indomitable will, than when we
survey any of our other possessions. Only when these are altered is
a man said to be *alienatus a se*.' (James, 1890, p. 296.) A certain
part of the stream of consciousness is abstracted from the
remainder and identified with self to a considerable degree. This is
the centre around which all other aspects of the empirical self
cluster; it is the source of interest, effort, attention, will and choice,
a composite of all one's intellectual, religious and moral
aspirations. From it can arise a sense of moral or mental
superiority or conversely a sense of inferiority or guilt.

James made no claims as to whether the material selves or the
social selves were the more important, merely that both were
intermediate between the bodily self and the spiritual self in
importance. A person has as many different social selves as there
are individuals and groups about whose opinions he cares. There
may be conflict between some of these social selves. The most
important of them relates to the person we love. One's family
belong to the social selves only because they are human beings;
otherwise they are part of the material selves which are one's
possessions, e.g. house and lands, car and bank account. Our social
and material selves are concerned with enhancing self esteem and
serve social ends, involved as they are with obtaining admiration,
notice of others, influence, power, etc. Our various acquisitions are
more or less intimately ours because they are saturated with our
involvement.

The material self consists of the clothing and material
possessions we see as part of us. The importance of clothes to
many people is obvious. Some find it necessary to always 'dress to
the hilt'; with many present college students, it seems that their
clothes are not important to them. Yet even dungarees and denims
can be considered a vital part of the student uniform which enables
one to be tagged as a student. A child extends his self concept by
identifying with material possessions; give a boy a gun, and cowboy
outfit and he becomes a cowboy. Give a girl a dolls' house,
complete with furniture and dolls, and she becomes a mother.

For some people, the material aspects of their lives are so
prominent that the material self is a significant portion of their

entire self concept. The individual who buys things because of their 'image' is simply saying that he wants you, as well as himself, to conceive of him in a particular way. The portly man of 48 who buys a Lotus Elan may be trying to change his self concept. He may actually become young and sporty (in his eyes) by the purchase. Many people do define themselves by what they own rather than by what they do. After all, if you possess a costly tent, a pair of expensive hiking boots and appropriately faded cut-off jeans, you must be an experienced hiker. Most of us, whether we go to the extent described above or not, can find material objects we own that are central to our material self. Whether it be a professor's book, a director's Rolls or a student's scarf, we all have a material self which is part of our overall self concept.

The bodily self is placed last in importance, but children and adolescents are very concerned with their body images as will be shown in Chapter 6, and James was possibly in error in his ranking on this point. Even adults spend considerable time and expense in nourishing, maintaining and adorning their bodies to produce a favourable image, e.g. muscle men; hair styling. The fact that the human body can readily be set off as an organic unit prompts us to be aware of it. However, some people work to suppress the sense of their body. For example sexual relations are regarded not as an expression of themselves but only as an act their body performs. Achieving an awareness of the self begins with experiencing one's body and feelings, often accomplished through the reactions of others. The point is that the more bodily self awareness one has, the more 'alive' one is.

These four selves combine in unique ways to constitute each person's view of himself and in many respects cannot be neatly split up. For instance, clothing, so much a part of material self, enhances bodily self and satisfy social ends by gaining others' attention.

One thing about a complex society is that we can choose between several goals. We each can set our own goals, each one related to different components of the self, and evaluate our success at them. This leads us to James' 'law' (1890). It all depends on what you see yourself as being. James elaborated on the determinant of the level of a person's self evaluation (James used 'self-feeling' and 'self-regard' as synonyms for this). He argued that it is the position a person holds in the world contingent on his success or failure that determines self esteem. Though we want to maximise all of our various selves, limitations of talent and time prevent this so each of us has to choose particular selves 'on which to stake his salvation' (James, 1890, p. 310). Having chosen, our level of self regard can be reduced only by deficiencies (or raised only by achievements) which are relevant to our 'pretensions'. In a very famous passage James (1890) explained in a personal example the principle of self esteem, culminating in what can only be dubbed as 'James'' law.

> I, who for the time have staked my all on being a psychologist, am mortified if others know much more psychology than I. But I am content to wallow in the grossest ignorance of Greek. My deficiencies there give me no sense of personal humiliation at all. Had I 'pretensions' to be a linguist, it would have been just the reverse. So we have the paradox of a man shamed to death because he is only the second pugilist or the second oarsman in the world. That he is able to beat the whole population of the globe minus one is nothing; he has 'pitted' himself to beat that one; and as long as he doesn't do that nothing else counts. He is to his own regard as if he were not, indeed he *is* not.
>
> Yonder puny fellow, however, whom everyone can beat, suffers no chagrin about it, for he has long ago abandoned the attempt to 'carry that line', as the merchants say, of self at all. With no attempt there can be no failure; with no failure no humiliation. So our self-feeling in this world depends entirely on what we *back* ourselves to be and do. It is determined by the ratio of our actualities to our supposed potentialities; a fraction of which our pretensions are the denominator and the numerator our success: thus,

$$\text{Self-esteem} = \frac{\text{Success}}{\text{pretensions} \dots}$$

> To give up pretensions is as blessed a relief as to get them gratified; and where disappointment is incessant and the struggle unending, this is what men will always do. (pp. 310–12)

It is clear that how James felt about himself depended, in large measure, on how he saw himself in relation to others who also backed themselves to be psychologists. Our feelings of self worth and self esteem derive partially from our perceptions of where we see ourselves standing in relation to others whose skills and abilities are similar to our own on particular self images. For example, if a person 'backs' himself to be a first-rate footballer, but is relegated to the reserves, then he will have to do one of three things: (*a*) rationalise his sub-par performances; or (*b*) lower his expectations; or (*c*) do something else in which greater success is more possible. Expectations are self imposed and refer to our personal levels of aspirations, for what is a success or enhancing experience for one can be a failure or deflating experience for another.

James thus produced an extremely rich and comprehensive formulation of the objective Me. It included feelings, evaluations and attitudes as well as descriptive categories, a view that anticipated future conceptions. He had detected the integrative aspects of the self concept.

The encounter with Behaviourism

Although, as we have already noted, James had amplified in psychological terms the philosophic dualism of I and Me at the turn of the century, apart from a few theorists, most psychologists avoided the self and its multitude of hyphenated elaborations until the middle of this century as though such constructs were 'unclean' and would contaminate them. The reason for this lay in the ascendance and dominance of the Behaviourist rationale during the second, third and fourth decades of this century as propounded by Watson, Thorndike, Hull and Skinner. Behaviourism, with its overriding emphasis on the scientific method as a cardinal tenet of its faith, directed psychology to a rigorous study of only those aspects of behaviour which were observable and measurable, i.e. stimuli and responses defined operationally. Armchair theorising, introspection and subjectivity were denigrated and attacked as unscientific and impossible to validate. If theoretical concepts were not capable of being tested, then, argued the Behaviourists, there was no place for them within the ambit of psychology. Only by adopting a rigorous behaviourist stance, it was maintained, could psychology cease to be the handmaiden of philosophy and range itself respectably alongside other sciences. Anything to do with 'mind' or mental events such as purpose, expectations, thoughts and sensation had to be banished from the lexicon of psychology; no interpretation the organism might make of stimuli was acceptable.

This rigid dogma placed self-concept study under considerable pressure since self-referent constructs necessarily imply a central focus on internal experience, subjective interpretation and self report. As a result of this methodological clash, in which the early battles were won by the Behaviourists, a relative neglect of psychological study of the self concept occurred. Behaviourism was very attractive, it must be faced, with its offering of reliable, replicable, statistical results relating overt measurable stimuli, responses and reinforcement together under controlled experimental conditions, contrasting so starkly with the ambiguities of self terminology, and dearth of empirical evidence on the self. Only a few brave souls continued to discuss the 'self' during the first half of this century, and their views will be considered in the following chapter.

But eventually even purists among the Behaviourists were compelled to modify their rigorous tenets of faith. Firstly, it became obvious that such an approach seriously limited the possible range of psychological study, and it was appearing rather incredible that major concerns of individuals such as hopes, expectations, beliefs, thoughts, which provide man with his most distinctive human behaviour, were ruled out of order, and, as a corollary, so too was any comprehensive account of human behaviour. Secondly, evidence began to accumulate which could not be explained without recourse to internal processes. For example animals could learn and retain information without reinforcement being applied (Blodgett, 1929). A retreat from the hard-line position commenced in the late 1930s and both Hull and Tolman were led to postulate the hypothetical construct of the intervening variable that interpolates itself between stimulus and response. These intervening variables are used to explain internal states that prompt behaviour. This admitting of the importance of events internal to the organism that were not observable enables, as a corollary, a more respectable place to be found for the phenomenal self concept within the ambit of psychological study. No longer was it tainted with the flavour of scientific obscenity. Other developments noted by Wylie (1961) which helped to carry self constructs back into the mainstream of psychology were firstly the increasing importance attached to ego development and function by neo-Freudians (e.g. Hartmann 1958; Erikson 1963), coupled with the needs of clinical psychology for a less restrictive theorising than the Behaviourists could provide to account for findings and to promote investigations in that field. Secondly, the infusion of phenomenological theory and method with Lewin, Snygg and Combs, and Rogers as its champions into the life blood of psychology has firmly established the self concept as an important construct in the study of human behaviour. During the last 20 years a deluge of experimentation and theorising on the self concept has flooded the pages of psychological journals.

Behaviourism and phenomenological self theory do pose two different and distinct models of man and a methodology associated with each model, which all suggests that acceptance of one orientation implies the exclusion of the other. But to make self theory and Behaviourism mutually exclusive is erroneous. Both approaches are necessary in order to understand in full the complexity of human behaviour, and in fact they support each other. Self-concept theory and research indicates that attitudes to self influence behaviour and provide insights into individual perceptions, needs and goals. What self-concept theory lacks is an explanation of how change in self concept, perception and behaviour can occur. This is where Behaviourist theory and principles can be employed and integrated with self-concept theory. For example, a diet of positive reinforcement contingencies is the best way to provide a person previously a failure with feelings of success which will lead to increasing self esteem and alter his perception of himself, of others and of the environment. Thus, behaviour modification and self conception are closely related processes, as will be shown in more detail in Chapter 8.

Behaviourism did have beneficial effects for the study of the self. Investigators began to study more clearly defined aspects of the global self which could be operationally defined; for instance, self esteem or evaluation is the extent to which a person feels positive or negative about certain specified characteristics of himself. It became possible to postulate hypotheses capable of being tested, using such specific and measurable delineations of the self, e.g. persons with negative self evaluation are likely to report more frequently than those with positive self evaluation that they feel inferior to others. Such predictions can be tested using appropriate sampling procedures and statistical techniques. Thus, the study of the self in its various manifestations became more precise, experimental and systematic as a result of the injection of the Behaviourist approach into the mainstream of psychological methodology.

The criticism by the Behaviourists that self-concept theory could not be and was not capable of being validated experimentally was erroneous even in the early days of self-concept theory. By 1915 Cogan and his colleagues, prior to the development of Behaviourism, had studied the relationship between self ratings and ratings given by others, with the conclusion that agreement on desirable traits was far greater than on undesirable traits. Todd (1916) studied the descriptions that various ethnic groups, e.g. Kaffirs, and Maoris, included in their self pictures. Other early empirical studies were conducted in Germany where Stern (1922) examined the delinquent self concept, and in Japan where Kubo (1933) assessed self concepts by adjectival checklists. Thus, the collection of evidence concerning the self concept, rather than mere speculation, began earlier than Behaviourists would have us believe.

The self concept and symbolic interactionism

The relationship between an individual and his fellow men had been, until the writings of James and Freud, an assumption that individuals existing prior to the relationship met and entered into the relationship. But a new view pointed clearly to the human infant's long period of dependency on adults with the consequent opportunities of learning society's standards and values. This view linked to the inclusion of self conception into sociological theory produced a new approach to the individual–society relationship.

Symbolic interactionism involves three basic premises. Firstly, humans respond to the environment on the basis of the meanings that elements of the environment have for them as individuals. Secondly, such meanings are a product of social interaction, and thirdly these societal/cultural meanings are modified through individual interpretation within the ambit of this shared interaction. Self and others form an inseparable unit since society, constructed out of the sum of the behaviours of the humans composing that

society, then places social limits on individual behaviour. W.
is possible to separate self and society analytically, the
interactionist assumption is that a full understanding of one
demands a full understanding of the other, in terms of a mutually
interdependent relationship. Cooley and Mead provided the basic
ideas.

(a) C. H. Cooley

Cooley's original view was that individuals are prior to society, but
he soon modified his beliefs and laid a heavier emphasis on society
to the extent that 'self and society are twin born . . . and the notion
of a separate and independent ego is an illusion' (p. 5). Individual
acts and social pressures mutually modify each other. A further
shift in emphasis was to come later when Mead argued that self
actually arises from social conditions. Cooley (1902) defined the
self as 'that which is designated in common speech by the
pronouns of the first person singular, "I", "me", "mine" and
"myself" ' (p. 136). He noted that what is labelled by an individual
as self evokes stronger emotions than what is tagged as 'non-self',
and that it is only through subjective feelings that self can be
identified.

It can be demonstrated experimentally that a major perspective
if the self concept is the 'other self', or how you think others think
of you. The content of the 'self as others see you' and the self as
you believe you are, have been shown repeatedly (e.g. Sheerer,
1949; Burns, 1975) to be very similar. It was Cooley who first
pointed out the importance of subjectively interpreted feedback
from others as a main source of data about the self. In 1902,
Cooley introduced the theory of the 'looking-glass self', reasoning
that one's self concept is significantly influenced by what the
individual believes others think of him. The looking glass reflects
the imagined evaluations of others about one.

Each to each a looking glass,
reflects the other that doth pass

(1902, p. 152).

There must be few people who have never been placed in a
situation where they have been acutely conscious of their existence
and appearance, in essence an extremely heightened sense of self.
A person who faces an 'audience' of any sort, or who has to
interact with others may fidget, sense tenseness, have 'butterflies in
the tummy' and perspire. This is more concern with 'what are they
thinking of me?' 'how do I look?' 'what sort of impression am I
making?', than with the real concerns of the interaction. This
concentration with imagining how one is evaluated can have quite
a serious effect on the performance of such groups as teachers,
actors, interviewers and the like. When Cooley coined his phrase,
'the looking-glass self' he had this connection between self

...ed opinions of others about one in mind.
...ollows (Cooley, 1902):

14 . . . our face, figure, and dress in the glass, and are interested in
...em because they are ours, and pleased or otherwise with them according
as they do or do not answer to what we should like them to be; so in
imagination we perceive in another's mind some thought of our
appearance, manners, aims, deeds, character, friends, and so on, and are
variously affected by it. A self-idea of this sort seems to have three
principal elements: the imagination of our appearance to the other person;
the imagination of his judgement of that appearance; and some sort of
self-feeling, such as pride or mortification. The comparison with a
looking-glass hardly suggests the second element, the imagined judgement,
which is quite essential. (p. 159)

This looking-glass self arises out of symbolic interaction between
an individual and his various primary groups. Such a group
characterised by face-to-face association, relative permanence and
a high degree of intimacy between a small number of members
produces an integration of individuality and group. The
face-to-face relationships within the group serve to produce
feedback for the individual to evaluate and relate to his own
person. Hence the self concept is formed by a trial-and-error
learning process by which values, attitudes, roles and identities are
learned.

Cooley (1902) provides an account of how self feeling is
developed in relation to the individual's interpretation of physical
and social reality. The objects within this reality include the
physical body opinions, purposes, possessions, ambitions, in fact
'any idea or system of ideas drawn from the communicative life
that the mind cherishes as it's own' (p. 68). This account does tend
to neglect those aspects of a person felt to be an integral part but
not likely to be cherished, e.g. a handicap, or failure. He saw the
objects appropriated by self feeling as social in two senses. Firstly,
their meaning was furnished by the common language and culture.
Secondly, self conceptions and their associated evaluations were
derived from the person's subjective construction of the
judgements that significant others held regarding his actions and
attributes. Self and society mutually define each other, acting as
points of reference one for the other, so that 'self and society are
twin born' (Cooley, 1902, p. 5).

(b) G. H. Mead

Mead elaborated on James' social self in a development of
Cooley's theory and produced a more extensive theory of self
development. Like Cooley he saw no other birthplace for self than
society. The self of any individual develops as a result of his
relations to the processes of social activity and experience and to

other individuals within those processes. For Mead (1934) the self concept as an object arises in social interaction as an outgrowth of the individual's concern about how others react to him. So that he can anticipate other people's reactions in order to behave appropriately, the individual learns to interpret the environment as the others do. The incorporation of such estimates as to how this 'generalised other' would respond provides the major origin of internal regulation that eventually comes to guide and maintain behaviour, even if external forces are no longer present. In this way the community exercises control over the behaviour of each individual, as it is in the form of the generalised other that the social process and culture pattern are assimilated into the individual. Self then is a social structure arising out of social experience. Once formed it can provide social experience for itself. But, more importantly, Mead saw language as the connection between self and society. Since man has the symbol of language, it is indifferent whether meaning is communicated between two individuals or between an individual and himself. In this latter situation the individual is putting himself in the place of the other and can take, 'the attitudes of another and act towards himself as others act' (Mead, 1934, p. 171). By combining many instances of this the individual integrates the attitudes of others towards himself into the 'generalised other'. In this way Mead claims that the problem of how an individual can be an object to himself has been solved. He differentiated between Me and I by giving them different contexts in which to operate. In situations of group membership, status, roles and interaction with others the emphasis is on Me. In situations where a person is distinguishing himself from others by his unique capacities or asserting himself against a situation, then the I is emphasised as he realises himself in the process of preserving the self. Mead insisted throughout his writings that whatever we mean by self it clearly belongs to the reflexive mode where the agent is the object of his own activities.

But the 'I–Me' dichotomy specified by Mead is different in one major way from James' initial formulation. Mead's 'I' is the impulsive tendency, the unorganised, undisciplined, undifferentiated activity of the individual (almost a parallel to the Freudian id). Every behaviour commences as an 'I', but develops and ends as a 'Me' as it comes under the influence of societal constraints. 'I' provides the propulsion; 'Me' provides direction. The development of self is thus based on the emergence of 'Me'. Mead characterises this emergence in children through two stages. Firstly, play, a spontaneous activity, enables the development of elementary role taking. Game, on the other hand, results from an internalisation of the roles of others, as the self assumes the generalised attitude of a member of the group to which the self belongs.

In this way the individual comes to respond to himself and develop self attitudes consistent with those expressed by others in his world. He values himself as they value him; he demeans himself to the extent that they reject, ignore or demean him. The end result is the conclusion Cooley had already argued in a very similar theory, that the individual will conceive of himself as having the characteristics and values that others attribute to him.

Mead's writings suggest that the self is composed of numerous 'elementary selves' which mirror aspects of the structure of the social process. A reflection of the entire social process is contained in the structure of a complete self. Mead's analysis of the elementary self as a means whereby self is enabled to fit social order is in reality the notion of social identity. Each person has many social identities which provide a major link between self and society, e.g. a person can be a son, father, husband, wage-earner, etc.

So as Cooley had done before him, Mead emphatically expressed the inseparability of Self and Society with the latter as the mechanism through which the person receives his statement of account, with its credits and debits. To Mead, 'no man is an island' and psychology showed repeated acceptance of the fact that society gives shape and meaning to individual self conceptualisation.

Goffman and the presentation of self

Goffman (1959; 1967) offers an extension of symbolic interactionism into a dramaturgical metaphor, claiming that the individual puts on a 'show' for others by managing the impressions he gives others about himself. He scrutinises dispassionately the techniques used daily by each of us in order to create our individual identities.

Goffman (1959) explains the generation of self through social interaction as follows:

In analysing the self, then we are drawn from its possessor, from the person who will profit or lose most by it, for he and his body merely provide the peg on which something of a collaborative manufacture will be hung for a time. And the means for producing and maintaining selves do not reside inside the peg; in fact, these means are often bolted down in social establishments. There will be a back region with its fixed props. There will be a team of persons whose activity on stage in conjunction with available props will constitute the scene from which the performed character's self will emerge, and another team, the audience, whose interpretive activity will be necessary for this emergence. The self is a produce of all these arrangements, and in all of its parts bears the marks of this genesis. (p. 253)

Goffman's dramaturgical analysis of society offers a useful way of examining society in which men are not trying to do but to be.

The task of image projection is seen as part of the socialisation process. These social identities are used as the basis of behaviour in specific contexts, providing cues for others to facilitate the task of communicating to others just 'who' he is at that particular time and place. While Mead presents the development of self in society with a stable and continued presentation of self, Goffman presents short-term selves focusing now in this role and now in that in the management of impression and of personal front. For Mead self and society are twinborn; with Goffman self and society interact in short episodes in which the script is followed to the end, but when the 'play' is over the individual sheds one costume and dresses himself up in another. It is not a con game; it is the adaptation of self to different roles to facilitate social processes wherein each knows what the others are performing. However, this self presentation involves the totality of the person and provides such an all-embracing concept of self that self comes to mean the total person rather than solely an objective Me. Moreover, Goffman's analysis presents a rather sordid, cynical view of human interaction characterised by duplicity, hypocrisy and opportunism.

So despite the seminal ideas propagated by the symbolic interactionists, a critical review would suggest that they failed to produce a consensual and operational definition of their core concept, the self. They also tended to ignore the affective and unconscious elements in their explanation of human behaviour. But their message is clear as far as self-concept formation and its relation to subjectively interpreted environmental reality is concerned. If we fail to organise our feelings and behaviour into compatability with the normative order then society disintegrates. Each person must develop considerable skill in reading the symbolic cues which give meaning and definition to the situation so that the correct social identity is chosen. The construction of self through learning in the early years within primary groups and later within secondary groups allows for the presentation of the self with its specific identity matching the specific context. In this sense then social order and self are inseparable; the self learned within social order and social order preserved by the interaction of appropriate aspects of self by the participants. Social reality and self integrity demand that we orchestrate our identity with the situation.

Freudian, neo-Freudian theory and the self concept

(a) Freud

A concept of self is implied in the work of Freud, but with the emphasis being laid on id functioning at the expense of the ego, the self construct never became sufficiently explicit. Freud's ego (1923, 1946) represents all that is sane and rational in mental life in contrast to the impulsive irrational id. The ego is a set of processes such as perceiving, and thinking; it determines the content of consciousness, and distinguishes between reality and imagination. Such an element, then, is the same as the global self, that totality of psychological processes which control the speed and direction of the flow of consciousness, intimately concerned with purposive motivated behaviour. The Freudian ego sometimes seemed to mean 'person', at others it was the process involved in attaining psychic balance between id and superego, and at other times it was ascribed executive powers that went far beyond cognitive processes. Such confusions are highlighted as Wylie (1961) points out in the defence mechanisms where the ego (agent?) appraises events in terms of their threat to the ego (person?). Then the ego (agent?) learns to avoid this threat by the use of, say, rationalisation (ego process?). Thus, in the Freudian sense ego refers to the core of personality that controls impulses and drives from the id and superego in conformity with the requirements of reality. However, this ego has roots in unconscious dynamics while the self concept, especially as emphasised in phenomenological theory, is anchored in conscious awareness and subjective experience. Freud certainly promoted a view of rational conscious control of human behaviour, but his material allowed him to see more clearly than others that irrational unconscious determiners of behaviour had to be reckoned with.

(b) Jung

Jung (1960) echoed Freud in believing that the ego was the conscious part of the personality. His ego was 'The complex of representations which constitutes the centrum of my field of consciousness and appears to possess a high degree of continuity and identity' (p. 540). However, the self became all-inclusive, being the total of unconscious and conscious aspects. It was an archetype representing man's striving for unity and wholeness. Jung claimed the self did not emerge until the various components of personality were fully developed and individuated, and this could only occur in middle age. The self represents an equilibrium between the conscious (the ego) and the unconscious levels. This view of striving towards the single goal of self development has much similarity with phenomenological views on self actualisation and the process of becoming.

The work of neo-Freudians bears some relationship to the self, especially from a developmental point of view, but again the self does not appear central to their theories. They clearly perceived the importance of self attitudes, but were more concerned with its implications for therapy than for self theory as such.

Adler, Sullivan and Horney all appear to emphasise sociocultural situations and interpersonal relationships as significant in the development of self-as-object. Inherent in all their views is that the

self is learned through accumulated social contacts and
experiences, with a negative self concept and a distorted
relationships with people being reciprocal. The individual
seen as striving to actualise and maintain the integrity of h.
personality. Even the ideal self is learned through interpers
relationships, for the giving and withholding of love is a maj
source of learning the ideal self concept.

(c) Adler

The basic feature of Adlerian psychology is his conception of 'life
style' which determines behaviour. Adler's self is a highly
personalised, subjective system through which a person interprets
and gives meaning to his experiences. Unlike Freud, who
emphasised unconscious motivation, Adler stressed consciousness
as the centre of personality. He saw man as a conscious being,
usually aware of his reasons for behaviour, capable of organising
and guiding his actions with complete awareness of their
implication for his own self realisation (Adler, 1927).

For Adler every person has the same goal, that of self assertion.
Adler believed each human was born into the world feeling
incomplete and inferior, hence the origin of the drive to attain
superiority or self assertion was the motivation of the fear of
inferiority. He saw that there were innumerable possible 'life
styles' for achieving that goal. For example, one person may try to
become superior through academic success, another may aim to be
an athlete, and still another tries to achieve a body rippling with
muscles. Each has an individual life style, and arranges his life in
order to achieve the end of being more or less superior to those
seeking similar goals, just as James had previously argued.

A person's life style is created largely by the inferiorities, either
fancied or real, that a person has. An individual who is, let's say,
diminutive and feels unnoticed may organise his whole life in terms
of this deficiency. How many 'musclemen' have in fact originally
been weaklings? Likewise, a physical handicap (Douglas Bader),
speech defect (Demosthenes; King George VI), etc. is an immense
influence on the life style of the individual. This life plan aims
either to overcome the defect or compensate for it. This
establishment of a goal or direction in life gives meaning to events
which might not make sense otherwise. Thus, for Adler the self
system originates and develops out of the behaviour employed to
manipulate feelings of superiority out of feelings of inferiority.

(d) Sullivan

Sullivan (1953) was quite dogmatic that he knew what the 'self'
was, but he found it quite elusive to produce an adequate
definition. He asserted, 'when I talk about the self system I want it
clearly understood that I am talking about a dynamism' (p. 167).

Sullivan's self dynamisms sometimes appears to mean certain habits utilised to avoid anxiety, and sometimes to mean one's view of oneself.

Sullivan (1953) claimed that the self system was 'an organisation of educative experience called into being by the necessity to avoid or to minimise incidents of anxiety' (p. 165). Hence, it is the need to avoid unpleasant emotions that motivates the self system. Early reward–punishment contingencies operated by the mother-figure enables the child to internalise values, prohibitions, events, etc. into organised subsystems of the 'good' and 'bad' me. Sullivan claims that children classify experiences as pertaining to the 'good me', 'bad me' and the 'not me'. These categories involve respectively acts that are approved, disapproved and dissociated. The last two occur from the existence of anxiety associated with the act. The child attempts to maximise positive reinforcement from the mother-figure by behaving in ways that will provide pleasure for the mother-figure. Sullivan argues that the mother-figure's pleasure/displeasure is communicated to the child through empathy.

Thus, according to Sullivan the self system is purely a result of interpersonal experience arising out of anxiety encountered in the pursuit of need satisfaction. But the interaction emphasises the role of the mother-figure and not society at large.

(e) Horney

Like Sullivan and Adler, Horney reacted against Freud's concentration on instinctive forces. Like Sullivan too, Horney saw the self system arising out of anxiety. Her ideas derive from her primary concept of basic anxiety, which she defined as:

. . . the feeling a child has of being isolated and helpless in a potentially hostile world. A wide range of adverse factors in the environment can produce this insecurity in a child; direct or indirect domination, indifference, erratic behavior, lack of respect for the child's individual needs, lack of real guidance, disparaging attitudes, too much admiration or the absence of it, lack of reliable warmth, having to take sides in parental disagreements, too much or too little responsibility, overprotection, isolation from other children, injustice, discrimination, unkept promises, hostile atmosphere so on and so on. (Horney, 1945, p. 41)

She argued that any one or combination of these experiences could lead a person to adopt certain strategies to satisfy a neurotic need or needs growing from disturbed human relationships. Horney originally proposed ten needs, any one of which could be acquired as a result of trying to solve the problem of disturbed human relationships. Horney later classified these ten neurotic needs under three headings: (1) moving towards people; (2) moving away from people; and (3) moving against people.

Each of these represents a basic orientation toward others and oneself.

A person whose predominant interpersonal trait is one of moving towards people wants affection, approval and especially a partner, and obtains safety through dependence. A person who moves against people interprets the world as a rough place where only the fittest survive and everyone else is hostile. The callous pursuit of personal interest with excellence, prestige and success is the sole aim for this makes him safe from others. The person who moves away from people maintains privacy and independence. He fears attachment or obligation and aims to avoid being hurt by others.

Horney claims that the essential difference between a normal and a neurotic conflict is one of degree. She states that everyone has these conflicts to some degree, but some people usually because of early experiences with rejection, neglect, overprotection and other expressions of unfortunate parental treatment, possess theirs in exaggerated form. Horney considers that in order for each person to achieve self realisation a model of an idealised self image must be erected, but an unrealistic ideal self image results from using these needs to escape from basic anxiety. Such an ideal image feeds feelings of superiority and pride which are threatened by neurotic problems.

Thus the genuine goal of self realisation is bypassed with behaviour patterned on the idealised self. This search for the ideal is an unobtainable goal, and attempts to gain this illusory goal results in inner conflict which augments the neurotic behaviour. But Horney fails to clarify whether the individual is unaware of this ideal self or whether he is unaware of how unrealistic it is. Horney (1950) also appears to feel that the child is extremely sensitive to expressions of love and hostility, and his behaviour is positively reinforced not only by setting up ideals but also for controlling himself by them. The reinforcement of his behaviour through these perceived indications, gives him to understand that he is fulfilling expectations for his own development and therefore pleasing parents and friends.

Ego and self

During the 1940s and 1950s the indiscriminate use of the somewhat parallel concepts of ego and self caused considerable controversy. Allport (1943) claimed at one point that ego and self were the same thing. Dissatisfied at this fusing of two terms with different origins, both Chein (1944) and Bertocci (1945) attempted to differentiate between ego and self. Chein restricted self to object as the content of awareness, and employed ego as the motivational–cognitive processes built around the self. It is the ego that enhances, defends and preserves the self. This dichotomy reflecting the division by William James into self as object and self (ego) as process was not to remain long, and most later writers fuse the two selves and allow ego to lapse back into a more ego-oriented psychoanalytic field.

The approach of Bertocci (1945), abetting the confusion, was to switch round Chein's application of the two terms. Bertocci employs the term 'self' for the ego-as-process while the self-as-object becomes, in his terminology, the ego.

Sherif and Cantril (1947) present a developmental picture of the self, giving clear evidence of the developing awareness of status that occurs in *social maturation*. They tended to use ego not in terms of psychoanalytic theory but as the object self, a constellation of attitudes reflecting what I think about myself, what is mine, what I identify with. This developmental picture of the ego is the same as that which earlier and later writers detailed as self as object. However, they developed this ego into a motivating force which energises and directs behaviour, so blurring, as is now current in phenomenological circles, the distinction between object and process.

It was left to Symonds (1951), following Chein's (1944) distinction, to emphasise clearly the difference between ego and self. He defined ego as a group of processes, such as perceiving, remembering, thinking, whose role is to take responsibility for 'developing and executing a plan of action for attaining satisfaction in response to inner drives. It is that phase of personality which determines adjustments to the outside world.' (Symonds, 1951, p. 4.)

He restricted the term 'self' to the way in which the individual perceives, conceives, values and responds to himself. To use Symonds' own words, it 'refers to bodily and mental processes as they are observed and reacted to by the individual' (p. 4). While the ego and self are distinct aspects of personality, Symonds believed there was considerable interaction between them. When the ego processes effectively cope with inner drives and external reality the individual thinks well of himself. Likewise, a confident self held in high regard enables the ego to function more effectively. But essentially, effective ego functioning is the prerequisite before high self esteem and self confidence can be achieved.

The proprium of Allport

Renewed consideration of the confusing application of self terminology led Allport (1955) to attempt a fresh start on the problem of what 'self' was so he coined a new term 'proprium' to add to the escalating list. The noun form 'proprium' he saw as 'all the regions of our life that we regard as intimately and essentially ours' (p. 38). This appears to be very similar to what has been regarded as ego involvement. This proprium consists of seven aspects:

(a) bodily sense – sensation;
(b) self identity through time – continuous existence;
(c) self enhancement – assertion and love of self;
(d) self extension – identification with others and other things – mine;
(e) rationality – planning, coping;
(f) self image;
(g) propriate striving – motivated behaviour to enhance the self image.

The difficulty here is that one cannot identify the proprium until what people regard as essentially theirs is identified. He had originally conceived of eight propriate functions, but in his later writing (Allport, 1961) he relegated the troublesome 'knower' to the realms of philosophy from where it had come. His other seven propriate functions are all objects of knowledge and summate to what James had identified as the empirical 'me'. By 'propriate', Allport (1955) meant 'central to our state of existence' (p. 38).

The seven aspects of the proprium of an individual are what makes him different from all other individuals. Allport agrees with Jung that a man does not have a full-blown self until middle age at least. Allport considered the mature person a true extension of all the self concepts he has gained in attaining adulthood. He designated a developmental sequence for the growth of the proprium (Allport, 1961). During the first 3 years of life a sense of bodily self, a sense of continuing identity, and a sense of self esteem make their appearance. By adolescence the child develops self awareness to enable him to cope with his problems by means of reason and thought. Intention, long-term proposals and distant goals emerge during adolescence.

Allport hoped that by describing the self as an aggregate of propriate functions a factotum view of self as a homunculus (little man in the brain who does the organising and pulls the strings of personality) is avoided.

Cattell

Cattell (1950) accepted the notion of self as a keystone in personality and tried to tie it into his imposing set of factors. He distinguishes a Felt Self, which is introspective, a Contemplated Self, and a Structural Self. The Contemplated Self comprises both the real and ideal aspects, the totality of what a person believes he is and of what he would like to be. This ideal is composed of both wishes and oughts. In short, the Contemplated Self is inferred from behaviour and reported by introspection. Cattell claimed that it has a strong interest in social reputation.

The Structural Self is a descriptive, theoretical concept postulated to explain the data of the self. It is to Cattell (1950) the fourth factor in the economy of the personality integrating ego, id and superego into 'one dynamic structure or unified sentiment' (p. 230). This sentiment of self causes the individual to 'pay attention to certain objects, or class of objects, and to feel and react in a certain way with regard to them' (p. 231). Here Cattell intimates for the first time the importance of selective perception as it relates to the self concept. His conception then is of a self that is both object and process as James and Allport had held before. While James had given the self a dynamic quality of self esteem, and Allport had attributed to it the 'propriate' function of striving activity, Cattell stresses its role of integrating personality. Like McDougall's master sentiment of self regard, so too is Cattell's self sentiment, the unifying thread on which all other sentiments are fixed.

Erikson and identity

Of the neo-Freudians only Erikson really paid much attention to the self as object. Adler had suggested that what is frequently labelled 'ego' is nothing more than the style of the individual. Life style for Adler included all phenomena of a psychological nature. Any adequate psychology is a psychology of the ego. Erikson in his views on identity took up this distinction, continuing the accepted division of regarding ego as the subject, that central organising agency, and self as object so that self identity emerges from experience. Erikson provides an extension of Freudian theory emphasising ego development in the cultural context. He demonstrates (1965) how cultures elaborate out of a biologically given basis an identity which is appropriate to the culture in question and manageable by the individual. Erikson indicates that identity is obtained from 'achievement that has meaning in the culture' (p. 228). Identity arises out of a gradual integration of all identifications. Therefore, it is important for children to come into contact with adults with whom they can identify. Erikson generates an eight-stage developmental sequence of identity growth. He details the particular conflicts which are characteristic of different stages and the qualities that emerge on the resolution of these conflicts. Identity is a particular problem in adolescence and Erikson pays considerable attention to the crisis and diffusion of identity at that stage. He defines identity as a 'subjective sense of an invigorating sameness and continuity' (1968, p. 19). He is somewhat reluctant to provide a tight definition of identity which is not solely the sum of roles assumed by the person, but includes emerging configurations of identifications and capacities, a function of direct experience of self and the world and perceptions of the reactions of others to self. It is psychosocial in that it also involves an individual's relationships with his cultural context.

In psychological terms, identity formation employs a process of simultaneous reflection and observation, a process taking place on all levels of mental functioning, by which the individual judges himself in the light of what he perceives to be the way in which others judge him in comparison of themselves and to a typology significant to them; while he judges their way of judging him in the light of how he perceives himself in comparison to them and to types that have become relevant to him. (Erikson, 1968, p. 22)

This process of identity formation is similar to the Cooley-Mead formulation concerning the role of the generalised other. But Erikson sees these processes as for the most part unconscious. He criticises other terms such as self conceptualisation, self image and self esteem, which provide a static view of what he considers is an evolving process 'for identity is never established as an achievement in the form of a personality armour, or of anything static and unchangeable' (1968, p. 24). Identity formation, like the ideas of Goldstein, Maslow and Rogers on self actualisation is a continuing process of progressive differentiations and crystallisations which expand self awareness and exploration of self. A sudden awareness of the inadequacy of existing identity as life advances generates initial confusion followed by exploration of new identities and new ways of being. Erikson claims that an optimal sense of identity is a sense of knowing where one is going and inner assuredness. Erikson's developmental views will be considered more closely in Chapter 6 where the problems of adolescent self conceptualisation is discussed.

Organismic theory and the drive of self actualisation

Maslow, Lecky, Angyal and Goldstein each espouse similar theories within the province of the organismic approach to psychology. Organismic theory stresses that the person:

(a) is an organised system and cannot be studied in an atomistic fashion, isolating particular elements; and

(b) is assumed to be motivated by only one basic drive, that of self actualisation, a singleness of purpose to realise inherent potentialities.

What appears to be different drives such as hunger, self esteem, achievement, power are interpreted solely as manifestations of the supreme purpose to actualise oneself.

(a) Goldstein
Goldstein claims that the satisfaction of any particular need comes

to the foreground when it becomes a prerequisite for the self realisation of the whole being. He regards self actualisation as a creative trend. Although self actualisation is seen as universal it takes different forms from person to person. This is because there are differences between innate potentialities as well as different environments to which to adjust. Goldstein argues that a person's potentialities can be assessed by discovering what he prefers to do and what he does best. Here he is making a somewhat dubious assumption that preferences correspond to potentialities. Conscious motivation is stressed, with the person obtaining self actualisation by coming to terms with the environment since the environment provides the means to the end as well as the obstructions which may cause hindrance.

Goldstein (1939) informs us that a healthy organism is one 'in which the tendency towards self actualisation is acting from within and overcomes the disturbance arising from the clash with the world not out of anxiety but out of the joy of conquest' (p. 305). Thus, for the self system to come to terms with the environment involves either the mastery of it, or the accepting of difficulties with consequent adjustment to make the best of it. If the discrepancy between the goals of the self system and the realities of the environment is too wide then goals must be lowered to permit actualisation at that level. This formulation has affinities with the self-esteem equation of James (1890).

(b) Angyal

Angyal (1941) postulates a symbolic self which is the aggregate of all the self conceptions a person has. He warns, however, that such a symbolic self is not a reliable indicator, for what a person thinks about himself is rarely a true picture of reality. Hence, if a person behaves in accordance with the image he holds of himself then his behaviour can be inappropriate to the reality of the situation on occasions. He attributes two basic trends to the self, those of self determination and its opposite, self surrender. These arise from tensions between environment pulling one way and the organism in another way. This leads to two patterns of self, one healthy, the other neurotic. The former feeds on feelings of confidence while the latter grows out of feelings of incompetence, doubt, and weakness. Angyal argues that both of these patterns of self evaluation exist in each person, but one is usually dominant.

(c) Maslow

Maslow's (1954) contribution was to emphasize the master drive of self actualisation within a theory of human motivation. He felt that psychology ought to concentrate on 'healthy' rather than 'sick' people, focusing on man's strengths and virtues, rather than his frailties and sins. Maslow (1967), writing from the 'organismic' approach, claims like Goldstein that 'in practically every human being and certainly in almost every new born baby, there is an active will towards health, an impulse towards growth or towards the actualisation of human potentialities' (p. 168). He regards the self as innately good, so that environment is unmasked as the source of neurotic behaviour, misery and ignorance. He also feels that some people are afraid of and draw back from becoming fully human. The self actualisation drive is there to be unfolded in a benign environment by active efforts of the person.

His proposed self actualisation need effects a striving to develop one's capacities, self understanding and self acceptance along lines set out along one's 'inner nature'. Since self actualisation is the pinnacle of the human needs, more basic needs such as survival come first as the bedrock on which the rest can be established. Then, and only then, can the individual aim for self actualisation. That is, when the needs that have greatest potency and priority are satisfied, the next need in the hierarchy emerges and presses for satisfaction. He assumes that each person has five basic needs, which are arranged in hierarchical order from the most potent to the least potent as follows:

1. The physiological needs, i.e. hunger and thirst.
2. The safety needs.
3. The love and belongingness needs.
4. The esteem needs.
5. The self-actualization needs, i.e. the desire for self fulfilment, for becoming what one has the potential to become.

Maslow made intensive clinical studies of people whom he judged to be self actualising in the sense of moving in the direction of achieving and reaching their highest potential. Such people are rare, as he discovered. In his group he included, Lincoln, Jefferson, Walt Whitman, Beethoven, William James, F. D. Roosevelt, Einstein, Eleanor Roosevelt, Albert Schweitzer, along with some personal acquaintances of his own.

Maslow discerned some basic personality characteristics which distinguished such self-actualising persons from 'ordinary' mortals. This is not to suggest that each person he studied reflected all the characteristics, but each did, however, exhibit a greater number of these and to a greater degree than might be expected in a less 'self-actualising' person. Such identifying characteristics included a realistic orientation to life, positive self acceptance, positive acceptance of others in general, spontaneity of thinking and emotions, a lack of self centredness, independence of thought – democratic, ethical, creative – and a sense of identity with the whole of mankind. Maslow's survey provides the most detailed conception of self actualisation yet developed.

(d) Lecky

Lecky (1945) like Cattell also appears to restate McDougall's conception of a master sentiment of self regard. His basic premise is that all the values of an individual organised into a single system, the nucleus of which is his conception of himself. As the person undergoes new experiences he accepts or rejects them in terms of their compatibility with his present conception of himself, and hence maintains consistency in behaviour and in self conception. He believed each person has to define for himself the nature of that totality which he is, so that all experiences can be assimilated to maintain the unity and integrity of the organism and the achievement of self consistency. This self consistency is both the sole drive and the sole goal. Like all the organismic theorists Lecky placed great faith in the potentialities of the human being and his powers of self growth.

Summary

The first chapter has taken a brief look at the history of the self concept in psychological theory. Self conceptualisation is regarded as a major facet and determinant of every individual's behaviour by many psychologists. Writings from classical Greek times to the present reveal a shift in emphasis from a philosophic and subjective experiencing 'I' to a psychological, and empirical 'Me', a move from the self as knower to the self as known, a discrimination most cogently established by William James. Despite the introduction of a rigorous Behaviourist stance by Watson the self concept was kept alive and made a central feature in many theorists' postulations. From the review in this chapter of a variety of theoretical positions on the nature of the self concept, it is obvious that conceptions of the self system are often considerably vague, occasionally mutually contradictory (especially with regard to terminology), and lacking any definitive or complete statement. Ideas rather than facts dominate the scene. However, whether self, self concept, proprium, self esteem, ego, or identity is the particular term favoured by a theorist it is apparent that most theories are concerned with individual self evaluation and the manner in which such appraisal motivates and directs behaviour, a theme taken to its ultimate by the organismic theorists who reduced all motivation to one basic drive, that of self actualisation. This theme also blurs the distinction between the self as known as the self as knower or doer since the data cognised about the self is behaviour influencing. Elements which consistently emerge from the theoretical approaches are that:

(*a*) two basic aspects of a global self can be discriminated;
  (i) I or self as knower/process/doer;
  (ii) Me or self as known which can include a variety of
   subselves, e.g. physical, social, other, ideal;
(*b*) a person as an entity separate from others and existing over
  time is experienced;
(*c*) both knowledge (self image) and evaluation (self esteem)
  appear as two basic elements of any self concept;
(*d*) self knowledge and evaluation are learned through experience,
  essentially that of social interaction with significant others.

Further reading

Gordon C. and **Gergen, K. J.** (eds). *The Self in Social Interaction,* Vol. 1, New
  York: Wiley, 1968. This book contains a selection of original and classic articles
  on the self concept written by many of the theorists mentioned in Ch. 1.

Hall, C. S. and **Lindzey, G.** *Theories of Personality* (2nd edn), New York: Wiley,
  1970. This book surveys in some depth all major personality theories which
  involve to varying degrees a commitment to some form of self conceptualisation
  (Chs 4, 7, 8 and 13).

enomenological approach
self concept

The most recent theorising about, and studies of the self concept have taken place within the ambit of phenomenology, which Wylie (1961) has so succinctly defined as 'the study of direct awareness' (p. 6). As we have already seen, at one level the assertion that a 'self' exists may involve no more than the fact that human beings are consciously aware of themselves and environment. To proceed beyond this point and describe at an objective level the characteristics and attributes of a given individual not only involves methodological and measurement problems but also the selection of a frame of reference, since a given individual could be described from the point of view of innumerable observers, including that of the individual himself.

A fundamental thesis of the phenomenological approach is that behaviour is not only influenced by past and current experiences but by the personal meanings each individual attaches to his perception of those experiences. This fluid organisation of personal meanings that exist for any person at any moment of time is the perceptual or phenomenal field. It is this private personal world of the individual that strongly influences behaviour. So behaviour is more than merely a function of what happens to us from outside but also how we feel about ourselves. As we shall see in Chapter 8, therapy facilitates the individual towards new perceptions of his problems so they can be coped with more effectively. The term 'phenomenal' has its origin in the Greek word *phainesthai* which means 'to appear so' or 'as it appears'. Thus, phenomenology is concerned with a person's perception of reality not in reality itself.

No one can ever observe a Self, his own or someone else's, directly. It can be approached through the perceptions of someone, perceptions based on inference and interpretations of observed behaviour. It is sufficient that the ways in which the individual is perceived can be studied, since it is these perceptions that are among the most important determinants of behaviour and places the self concept and its study in the realm of phenomenology.

Perceptions from the external world are the basic ingredients from which the self concept is developed, and maintained. In an attempt to avoid conflict from incompatible ideas and situations, the individual tends to perceive only those elements he wants to.

Perceptions are selective and are often definitely ɛ
result of the distortions engendered by motives, go.
and defence mechanisms (e.g. Bruner and Goodmar
Vinacke, 1952; Judson and Cofer, 1956). The old ac
believing' is perhaps closer to the truth when expresse
'Believing is seeing'. Our views and attitudes, the mosι
basic of which are those relating to our self as a person
the raw sensory input into idiosyncratic perceptions, the
determining the kind and quality of experiences.

The self concept acts as a selective screen, the permeability of
which is determined by individual developmental history and the
nature of the environment relative to the person. In stressful
conditions the screen becomes a barrier which isolates the
individual who becomes a prisoner of his own ego defences.
Eventual inadequacy becomes the inevitable result of closing off
avenues of communication with the outside world. The few
avenues that are left promote a rigidity in approach. This 'tunnel
vision' effect narrows the perceptual field, promoting stereotyped
thinking, thereby preventing the individual seeing or trying
anything new (Lazarus *et al.*, 1952). As Jersild (1952) points out,
whenever a person resists learning that would be beneficial to him,
we may suspect that he is trying to safeguard his picture of himself.
His picture may be false and inadequate, but it is the only one he
knows. Only under conditions of great security can he afford to
drop the screen in order to accommodate to new experiences.

Selective attention to the wealth of stimuli that impinge on the
person is also involved. A person cannot simultaneously register
everything. He has to focus on a few stimuli. It would involve too
much cognitive strain to attend to every aspect of our total
environment. The directions in which perceptions are oriented are
not the sole function of the relative arousal value of available
stimuli but depend on individual past experience, expectation,
present needs and current self conceptions. Again the work of
Vinacke (1952), Judson and Cofer (1956), and Bruner and
Goodman (1947) are relevant. Perception is thus selective in terms
of both quality and quantity, with the concept one has of oneself
expanding or limiting the richness and variety of perception.
Rogers (1951) states: 'As experiences occur in the life of an
individual they are either symbolised, perceived and organised in
some relationship to the self; ignored because there is no perceived
relationship to the self structure; denied symbolisation or given a
distorted symbolisation because the experience is inconsistent with
the structure of the self.' (p. 503) In other words, then, it is the
individual's concept of himself that determines the kind and quality
of the experiences perceived. Shaffer and Shoben (1957) also
support the proposition that the self concept limits openness to
experience. 'Because the self concept shapes new experiences to

to its already established pattern, much behaviour can be erstood as a person's attempt to maintain the consistency of his self concept, a kind of homeostasis at a higher psychological level.' (p. 103)

A basic tenet of both cognitive psychology and phenomenology, then, is that behaviour is the result of the individual's perception of the situation, not as it actually exists but rather as it appears to him at the moment of behaviour. Perception is other than what is physically out there. Yet what is perceived is 'reality' to the perceiver, the only reality by which he can guide his behaviour. The phenomenological approach to behaviour, into the principles of which the modern theory of self conception has became cemented, interprets behaviour in terms of the phenomenal field of the subject, and not in terms of analytical categories imposed by an observer. That is to say that behaviour can best be understood as growing out of the individual subject's frame of reference.

Lewin's field theory

Lewin (1936), the precursor of this phenomenal field approach, conceptualised an explanation of behaviour in terms of field theory. In brief, this suggests all behaviour arises from a total field which is not the 'real' field but the field as the behaving individual sees it. The individual himself is one aspect of the behavioural field and is always subject to field forces, never free to act independently of those impinging forces. So the self concept lies within the life space region, as a core area in the individual's psychological universe. The life space includes the individual's universe of personal experiences such as goals, evaluations, ideas, perceptions, etc. All the variables that determine the direction of behaviour lie in the life space of the individual. To predict behaviour it is necessary to know the life space of the person at the time the behaviour is to be predicted. Lewin's self closely resembles that of Mead as an objectified self, but Lewin gives it a functional process of causality that is dynamically active through the mechanism of life space, giving continuity to personality.

Raimy

Raimy (1948) extended this self concept from a perceptual frame of reference into the clinical field. He defined the self concept as, 'a learned perceptual system which functions as an object in the perceptual field' (p. 154). His study consisted of a six-category checklist to classify patients' statements in terms of self reference. Three of the categories related to approval of self, disapproval of self and ambivalence towards self. Reliability of the classification was determined by reclassifying the statements 6 months later. A frequency count of the number of times the same response was reclassified in the same category revealed over 80 per cent of the 874 client responses were reclassified in the same category. Four other judges also carried out this procedure with an 81.8 per cent agreement on reclassification. High validity was shown by comparing the results with independent analyses of two counselling cases by two other methods.

When this category checklist was applied to 14 counselling cases for which data from 111 recorded interviews existed, consistent differences were found between cases judged to have been counselled successfully and those which had been unsuccessful. In the successful ones there was a marked shift from a preponderance of self-disparaging and ambivalent statements at the outset to a strong emphasis on self approval at the conclusion. This shift was not in evidence in the unsuccessful cases. Successful counselling seems to involve a change in the patient's concept of himself.

Raimy emphasised that a person's notion of himself is a complex and significant factor in his behaviour. He further suggests that what a person believes about himself is a factor in his social comprehension of others. As a more or less organised perceptual object, Raimy (1948) held that self perception was more than the activation of internal or distance receptors. It 'involves situational and memorial factors as well as sense data' (p. 154). Raimy's work prepared the self concept for inclusion into phenomenology. He made it subject to the general laws and processes of perception so that the self concept is built up by compounding an infinite number of perceptual impressions.

Snygg and Combs

Snygg and Combs (1949) offer a perceptual view of behaviour similar to Maslow's observations which is a perspective considerably different from Skinner's behaviourist model. Skinner they claim, . . .

sees man as the victim of his environment. He is what he is because of what has happened to him. Unfortunately, this point of view, while making possible great strides in some aspects of human living, has, at the same time, made it difficult for us to understand some of our most pressing problems. It has given rise to a mechanistic conception of human beings as physical objects whose behaviour is the result of forces acting upon them. It has largely dehumanized psychology, making of human beings little more than objects to be manipulated at will. . . . Such a view of behavior places the responsibility quite outside the individual himself. The implications of this view are widespread throughout all phases of our society. (pp. 309–10)

As an alternative to this conception, Combs and Snygg (1949) propose this view:

[Man] is part controlled by and in part controlling his destiny . . . [this view] provides us with an understanding of man deeply and intimately affected by his environment but capable also of molding and shaping his destiny in important ways. . . . If the [perceptual] view of human behavior . . . is accurate, it calls for a very different approach to human problems. How people perceive themselves and the world in which they live is an internal, personal matter. What people believe about themselves and their environment is not directly open to manipulation. A man's perceptions arise within himself. We cannot make people perceive. Effective, satisfying human relationships can only be developed through helping ourselves and others to perceive more freely and accurately. Man is not a puppet bandied about at the mercy of the forces exerted upon him. On the contrary, he is a creature of discretion who selects his perceptions from the world he lives in. He is not the victim of events but is capable of perceiving, interpreting, even creating events. The perceptual view sees man as a growing, dynamic, creative being continuously in search of adequacy. Instead of an object at the mercy of environment, he is, himself, a purposive agent engaged in a never-ending business of becoming. People in this sense are processes rather than objects, growing rather than static, and call for the same kind of treatment we accord other growing things. . . . The perceptual view leads to methods of dealing with people which recognize the internal character of perception and seek to affect behavior through processes of facilitation, helping, assisting, or aiding the normal growth strivings of the organism itself. (pp. 309–12)

In essence they are contending that the locus of psychological causation lies entirely within the phenomenal field of conscious experience. Thus, the self concept, the central and sovereign feature of the phenomenal field must be studied from the standpoint of the perceiving individual. Snygg and Combs (1949) developed even further this phenomenological orientation because of the central role they accord to conscious feelings, cognitions and perceptions, so that, 'all behaviour without exception is completely determined by and pertinent to the phenomenal field of the behaving organism' (p. 15).

The phenomenal field is the totality of experiences that a person is aware of at any instant. While this awareness can by definition never be at an unconscious level, it can vary in level and intensity. This approach states that how a person behaves is a result of how he perceives the situation and himself at the moment of his action. Awareness is the cause of behaviour. The phenomenal self is differentiated out of the phenomenal field, and has significance only within this totality of experience. This phenomenal self, 'includes all those parts of the phenomenal field which the individual experiences as part of characteristic of himself' (1949, p. 58).

Snygg and Combs have thus provided a self which fuses the roles of self-as-object, and self-as-process. It is an object since it consists of self experiences. It is a process since it is an aspect of the phenomenal field which determines all behaviour. This self which is both an object and a process avoids the arbitrary distinctions, previous confusions, and semantic difficulties that plagued many previous conceptions. Combs makes this dual capacity apparent in a personal communication to Hall and Lindzey which they quote. 'The self is composed of perceptions concerning the individual, and this organisation of perceptions in turn has vital and important effects on the behaviour of the individual.' (Hall and Lindzey, 1957, p. 470.)

A person's self concept is then himself from his own point of view. It is not a mere conglomeration of isolated concepts about the person but a patterned interrelationship or *Gestalt* of all these (Raimy, 1948). Like many of the concepts of which it is composed, the self concept has a degree of stability and consistency which gives predictability to the individual and his behaviour. Lecky (1945) had already foreshadowed these phenomenological points, suggesting that the drive within the individual to maintain his integrity and balance is always in terms of that individual's perception of the world around him. 'Behaviour expresses the effort to maintain the integrity and unity of the organisation. . . . The nucleus of the system, around which the rest of the system revolves, is the individual's idea or conception of himself.' (Lecky, 1945, p. 29.)

The phenomenal field of Snygg and Combs appears to possess three constituents (Fig. 2.1). The total perceptual field which includes all the individual's perceptions may be represented by the largest circle, A. Within this field there is a smaller area, B, which

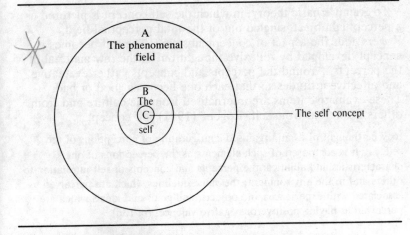

Fig. 2.1 The phenomenal field (adapted from Snygg and Combs, 1949).

includes all those perceptions which a person holds about himself, irrespective of their clarity or their importance at any particular moment. This is the phenomenal self. The heart of both the field and the self consists of a still smaller area which Snygg and Combs suggest includes only those aspects which are important or vital to the person. This is the self concept. It is a stable, important and characteristic organisation composed of those perceptions which seem to the individual to be basically him (Snygg and Combs, 1949).

Rogers' self theory

Carl Rogers, though born into a stable conservative Protestant family, changed his career orientation several times before qualifying in clinical psychology. He tried agriculture, history and religion before his exposure to psychology. He concentrated on child psychotherapy, using pragmatic and eclectic approaches. He later came to focus his psychotherapeutic interests more on adults. He has played a key role in developing therapeutic techniques, encounter groups in an attempt to increase self awareness, self understanding and expression of feeling. In a recent poll conducted by the American Psychological Association, he was ranked third after Freud and Skinner as the theorist whose ideas have most influenced contemporary psychology.

Phenomenology, with the perceived self concept as its core, was appropriated by Rogers to underpin his developing client-centred approach to psychotherapy. Like Raimy, he was able to describe therapeutic change in terms of a perceptual frame of reference. The present state and formulation of self-concept theory owes much to Rogers' work, and developed out of his experiences with clinical cases.

To Raimy's basic theory, in which the self concept is pictured as a perceptual object, singled out of the total perceptual field, Rogers adds the aspect of conceptualisation. The self becomes a concept developed by reflexive thought out of the raw material of the percepts. Around the percepts and concepts gather evaluative and affective attitudes so that each one becomes good or bad. These evaluative items are internalised from the culture and from others, as well as from self. Rogers' (1951) self concept

may be thought of as an organised configuration of perceptions of the self. . . . It is composed of such elements as the perceptions of one's characteristics and abilities; the percepts and concepts of self in relation to others and to the environment; the value qualities which are perceived as associated with experiences and objects; and goals and ideals which are perceived as having positive or negative valence. (p. 136)

It is apparent even from the above quotation that Rogers is inclined to use the term 'self' in ambiguous ways. The 'self' in lines 2 and 4 of the above quotation seems to be a synonym for 'person'. Again he uses 'self' as 'person' when he claims (1951, p. 40) 'there are many elements of experience which the self cannot face'.

Patterson (1961) provides a succinct sketch of the place of the self concept in early Rogerian theory. He saw it as the core concept from the inception of Rogers' formulation in 1947 when Rogers claims that the self is a basic factor in the formation of personality and in the determination of behaviour. This thesis was amplified and extended (Rogers, 1951) with the addition of 19 propositions about the self concept. In 1959 Rogers produced his most detailed and systematic formulation in which self actualisation became the sole motive, with the self concept defined as 'the organised, consistent conceptual Gestalt composed of characteristics of the "I" or "me" and the perceptions of the relationships of the "I" or "me" to others and to various aspects of life, together with the value attached to these perceptions' (1959, p. 200). The ideal self is introduced into the theory as 'the self-concept which the individual would most like to possess, upon which he places the highest value for himself' (1959, p. 200).

Several concepts having to do with regard are included. Rogers postulates a basic, though secondary or learned, need for positive regard from others – that is for warmth, liking, respect, sympathy and acceptance – and a need for positive self regard, which is related to or dependent upon positive regard from others. Positive self regard is synonymous with self esteem.

Unconditional self regard is a state of general positive self regard, irrespective of conditions. However, positive self regard may be conditional when the individual 'values an experience positively or negatively solely because of conditions of worth which he has taken over from others, not because the experience enhances or fails to enhance his organism' (1959, p. 209). In this case the individual is vulnerable to threat and anxiety.

The central points of Rogers' theory are:

1. The theory of the self, as part of the general personality theory, is phenomenological. The essence of phenomenology is that 'man lives essentially in his own personal and subjective world' (1959, p. 191).

2. The self becomes differentiated as part of the actualising tendency, from the environment, through transactions with the environment – particularly the social environment. The process by which this occurs is not detailed by Rogers, but is presumably along the lines described by Cooley and Mead.

3. The self concept is the organisation of the perceptions of the

self. It is the self concept, rather than any 'real' self, which is of significance in personality and behaviour. As Snygg and Combs (1949, p. 123) noted earlier the existence of a 'real' self is a philosophical question, since it cannot be observed directly.

4. The self concept becomes the most significant determinant of response to the environment. It governs the perceptions of meanings attributed to the environment.

5. Whether learned or inherent, a need for positive regard from others develops or emerges with the self concept. While Rogers leans towards attributing this need to learning, it seems appropriate to include it as an element of the self-actualising tendency.

6. A need for positive self regard, or self esteem, according to Rogers, likewise is learned through internalisation or introjection of experiences of positive regard by others. But, alternatively, it may be considered an aspect of the self-actualising tendency.

7. When positive self regard depends on evaluations by others, discrepancies may develop between the needs of the organism and the needs of the self concept for positive self concept for positive self regard. There is thus incongruence between the self and experience, or in other words psychological maladjustment. Maladjustment is the result of attempting to preserve the existing self concept from the threat of experiences which are inconsistent with it, leading to selective perception and distortion or denial of experience by incorrectly interpreting those experiences.

8. The organism is an integrated whole, to which he attributes, like the organismic theorists, one dynamic drive – that of self actualisation – a basic tendency to 'actualise, maintain and enhance the experiencing organism' (1951, p. 487).

9. The development of self concept is not just the slow accretion of experiences, conditionings and imposed definitions by others. The self concept is a configuration. Alteration of one aspect can completely alter the nature of the whole. Thus, Rogers is using the term 'self concept' to refer to the way a person sees and feels about himself. But, as he goes on to develop his theory, his usage of the concept also incorporates the second sense – of a process controlling and integrating behaviour. But in Rogers' theory the self concept is not an executive or doer. There is no need for positing such a role. The organism is by nature continually active, seeking its goal of actualisation, and the self concept as part of the organism is also seeking actualisation through its constant activity. The self concept thus influences the direction of activity, rather than initiating it and directing it entirely. Thus, Rogers avoids the problem of reification and the ambiguousness of the concept of the 'I' or the ego as an executive. In this way the self as known and the self as knower are fused. Behaviour is 'the goal directed attempt of the organism to satisfy its needs as experienced in the field as perceived' (1951, p. 491).

10. In his formulation of the concept of the ideal self, Rogers indicates that the perception of the ideal self becomes more realistic, and the self becomes more congruent with the ideal self, as an outcome of therapy. This suggests that personality disturbance is characterised by an unrealistic self ideal, and/or incongruence between the self concept and the self ideal. This formulation has been the basis of some research by the client-centred school, e.g. Butler and Haigh (1954). Rogers' theory does not emphasise conflict between the self concept and the self ideal as a source of disturbance, but stresses the conflict between the self concept and organismic experiences as its source. This is in contrast to some other theories in which the self ideal is a central concept and an important factor in psychological adjustment or maladjustment, e.g. Horney (1950).

11. The notion of the self as used by Rogers is broader than the self concept. It includes the self concept and the ideal self. What else it includes, is not clear. Rogers considers the self concept to be in the person's awareness, consisting of data about the individual which are evaluated, whereas his use of 'self' sometimes appears to mean 'person' as has already been indicated or may include aspects of the individual not permitted to enter awareness.

His theory has stimulated much empirical work by his colleagues (e.g. Stock 1949; Butler and Haigh, 1954; Chodorkoff, 1954; Omwake, 1954). He presented the theory to the public in 1951. It is formulated out of a series of 19 propositions. The first seven propositions refer to the organism and the phenomenological character of the environment, the eighth introduces the concept of self, which the remaining propositions elaborate into an essay on self psychology.

Rogers views the perception of self as following the general laws of perception. It represents an organised and consistent conceptual *Gestalt*, a pattern of related perceptions, rather than an aggregate of unrelated parts. Despite its fluid and changing character it retains its coherent, integrated, and organised qualities. Following Snygg and Combs, Rogers fuses the self into both a conceptual object and a process guiding behaviour. The organism functions so as to maintain consistency and congruence between the self and experiences. 'Most of the ways of behaving which are adopted by the organism are those which are consistent with the concept of Self.' (1951, p. 507.) This concept of self consistency was originally Lecky's (1945). The individual develops a value system, the nucleus of which is the individual's valuation of himself. Behaviour is an attempt to maintain the integrity of the system.

In response to a state of incongruence, that is, a threat presented by recognition of experiences that are in conflict with the self concept, the individual uses two defensive processes. Distortion is employed to alter the meaning of the experience; denial removes the existence of the experience. Rogers emphasises the former technique since if denial leaves an experience completely unsymbolised how can a phenomenological approach ever deal with such a process? Distortion is in the direction of making the experience consistent with self. Meaning is given to events, not in and of themselves, but by individuals with past experiences concerned about the maintenance of their self concepts. Rogers developed client-centred therapy (Ch. 8) as a technique to modify self conception, thereby facilitating congruence between experience and self conception, a state of psychological adjustment.

Once the self concept has developed, all interpretations and motivations are channelled through it. It resists all efforts at disruption. The individual interprets the want for self maintenance as the need to maintain a picture of the self as known. Some sort of picture will be preserved at all costs. This inertia or resistance to change is essential to allow the self concept to fulfil its function of giving stability to personality, permitting the individual and others to predict behaviour. Change is also difficult since the individual develops strategies, the various defences known to all psychologists and utilised in Rogers' theory, to maintain this self as known. These are strategies which:

(*a*) 'have a high probability of giving us evidence that we are who we think we are; or
(*b*) cover up or redefine evidence that we might be something we think we are not' (Babladelis and Adams, 1967, p. 265).

Hence, behaviour is consistent with the organised hypothesis and concepts of the self structure. But in defending itself against incongruent experiences the individual becomes a captive in his own fortifications, limited to certain predictable manoeuvres.

Maladjustment develops when experiences are denied awareness by blocking or distortion and are prevented from being adequately assimilated into the self concept. Thus, Rogers views maladjustment as a state of incongruence, the most serious source of incongruence being between self and organism. This can arise when a person's concept of self is heavily dependent on values and definitions internalised from others. So, incongruence would occur where an individual's self concept heavily stressed love and concern for others, and that person found himself in a situation where strong feelings of aggression towards others were aroused as a result of frustration. These feelings might then be denied awareness as his self concept could not assimilate the idea that he could hate. Incongruence between self and organism would result. Rogers gives as an example a rejecting mother who cannot admit to herself her feelings of aggression towards her child. She therefore perceives his behaviour as bad and deserving punishment. She can then be aggressive towards him without disturbing her self concept of 'good and loving mother' because he is seen as worthy of punishment. The origins of such incongruence between self concept and organismic feelings often lie early in life. Parental affection and 'positive regard' are often conditional on a child disowning his true feelings. If he really does want to smack Mummy then he is a 'bad boy' – a person of no merit. Rogers argues that it is important in bringing up children not to demand that they disown or distort their own feelings as a condition of their worth and acceptance, even though, of course, they may be required to inhibit the actual expression of their feelings. Rogers urges that parents should preferably indicate to the child that although they understand his feelings he is not allowed to act on them because of the damage or distress such behaviour would cause, rather than express disapproval at the possession of the feelings themselves. This later ploy merely tells the child he is disapproved of and 'bad'. The child should thus be encouraged to inhibit the expression of certain feelings rather than disown them. This obviates considerably the possibility of organism–self incongruity and ensuing later maladjustment.

Rogers admits to an unconscious element in his theory, an aspect Snygg and Combs would never countenance. This inclusion enables Rogers to place a greater emphasis on previous learning and experience, making the individual appear less like driftwood in a sea of consciousness, but it is never clearly specified how such non-phenomenological constructs as unconscious motivation, repression and denial, for example, can be articulated into a phenomenological system that is theoretically based on direct awareness and experience.

Snygg and Combs (1949) were being logically consistent in ignoring and denying that aspects below the level of awareness have no bearing on behaviour, hence their extravagant claim, 'all behaviour without exception is completely determined by and pertinent to the phenomenal field of the behaving organism' (p. 15). Field theory has provided psychology with new insights, especially that of making us aware of the validity of other people's 'fields' yet there is a lack of a complete explanation of human behaviour, since there is no place for behaviour causation other than consciousness.

Rogers (1951) attempts to maintain his phenomenological position by implying that only when information about self and environment from the unconscious reservoir comes at least dimly into awareness does it influence behaviour. The self concept is thus 'an organised configuration of perceptions of the self that are admissible to awareness' (p. 136). However, in other places there is tacit assumption that unconscious elements do influence behaviour. For example, Rogers (1951) claims, 'He may have some experiences which are inconsistent with this perception, but he either denies these experiences to awareness, or symbolises them in such a way that they are consistent with his general picture' (p. 321). And again, 'While these concepts are non-verbal, and may not be present in consciousness, this is no barrier to their functioning as guiding principles' (p. 498). Rogers attempts to extricate himself from this dilemma posed by a phenomenological framework by suggesting there are levels of discrimination below the level of conscious recognition and that, for example, threats may be unconsciously perceived or 'subcepted' (McCleary and Lazarus, 1949) before they are perceived. A threatening object or situation may produce visceral reactions, e.g. a pounding heart, which may be experienced as feelings of anxiety without any identification as to the cause of the disturbance. Denial or repression may then be invoked to prevent the experience becoming conscious. This is still far from satisfactory and it would appear that a totally phenomenological approach is impossible since conscious awareness is not the sole arbiter of behaviour. Rogers' use of the symbolism appears different from the usual established use in mathematics and science. He follows Angyal (1941) in viewing symbolisation as the bringing of experiences to the conscious level.

Another dilemma that Rogers solves by leaving the conceptual foundations of pure phenomenology is that created by accepting that behaviour is based on the individual's experiences, and yet also accepting that the individual can and does have a dependable knowledge of the world most of the time so that he is able to behave realistically. Rogers suggests that this is possible because the person tends to check his experiences of the environment against the environment as it really is. Those perceptions that are inadequately, or not, tested, may cause unrealistic behaviour. It is obvious that while Rogers does not deal with the philosophical issue of what is 'true reality', he accepts that a person tests his experiences, which at the outset are no more than tentative hypotheses about reality, and through this comes to separate fact from fiction in his subjective world. Much of this testing, Rogers suggests, is the checking of the correctness of experiences against information derived from other contexts, situations and experiences. Present experience is construed and interpreted on the basis of previous experiences, the interpretation of which led to successful behaviour and outcomes. This approach appears analogous with Kelly's (1955) later innovation, the personal construct system with its model of man-the-scientist. Rogers (1951) similarly looks on the self structure as 'an organisation of hypotheses for meeting life' (p. 191).

Rogers views man's nature as essentially positive, moving basically towards maturity, socialisation and self actualisation. He contends that Freud has presented us with a picture of man who at heart is irrational, unsocialised and destructive of self and others. Rogers accepts that a person may at times function like this, but at such times he is neurotic and least functioning as a fully human being. When man is functioning freely, he is open to experience, and free to act in a positive, trustworthy and constructive manner. 'One of the most refreshing and invigorating parts of my experience is to work with such individuals and to discover the strongly positive directional tendencies which exist in them, as in all of us at the deepest levels.' (Rogers, 1961, p. 27.) Rogers' tone and spirit does not assume inherent destructive drives but posits a natural growth towards a healthy, self-actualising, self-realising personality. The individual is always in a state of becoming. Change is the result of maturation and learning and the direction of change is movement towards the 'true Self'. This 'true Self' is not a static tensionless existence since such changes and growth uncovers further possibilities for what the person can truly become. Given understanding in the individual of the real issues and choices, the decision is always to move forward. The self structure is revised to assimilate new experiences, which are inconsistent with the existing structure in conditions of complete absence of threat.

The phenomenological approach has been part of a significant effort by some psychologists to come to terms with human experience. It seeks to take behaviour as it is. But it has two potential major limitations. It may exclude from investigation certain critical variables, and it can lead to unscientific speculation. As Smith (1950) has argued, a psychology of consciousness has limits, and unconscious strivings and defensive techniques of adjustment of which we are unaware do warp our behaviour.

To develop a scientific psychology, the psychologist must employ constructs that are abstractions and that go beyond the phenomenal field of the individual. McLeod (1964), himself a phenomenologist, observes that to build a science of psychology, one must transcend the phenomenal world by developing constructs and by anchoring observations to non-phenomenological controls. However, Rogers (1963) does not believe that the phenomenological approach is the only one for psychology, and he acknowledges the importance of unsymbolised experiences, i.e. those not made conscious, especially over the rigid defensive efforts of the self to protect itself. Even the decision to frame an approach in terms appropriate to the 'private world' of the behaving person does not necessarily imply a commitment to the exclusive use of phenomenal concepts. Lewin, whose psychological life space provided the solution to the dilemma posed by non-phenomenal bases to behaviour. Lewin (1936) argues that,

'It is likewise doubtful whether one can use consciousness as the sole criterion of what belongs to the psychological life space at a given moment. . . . For example, the little child playing in the garden behaves differently when he knows his mother is at home than when he knows she is out. One cannot assume this fact is continually in the child's consciousness. Also a prohibition or a goal can play an essential role in the psychological situation without being clearly present in consciousness. . . . Here as in many other cases it is clear that one must distinguish between 'appearance' and the 'underlying reality' in a dynamic sense. In other words the phenomenal properties are to be distinguished from the conditional–genetic characteristics of objects and events, that is from the properties that determine their causal relationships. . . . 'As far as the conceptual derivation is concerned one may use effectiveness as the criterion for existence: what is real is what has effects.' (p. 19)

Lewin's life space then is not merely the phenomenal field. It is not immediately given in the concreteness of experience; it is an abstract hypothetical construct inferred by the observer to account for the individual's behaviour. But it is still formulated in terms of what is behaviourally real to the individual and not in terms of what is physically observable to the scientist. Hence it is anchored in a subjective frame of reference, and yet accepts that some behaviour is motivated unconsciously. As has been indicated, Rogers reverts, without acknowledging it, to this less restrictive concept. Rogers' concept of self is similar to Erikson's identity in that it fuses evaluated self image and the consequent pattern of organised integrative behaviour. Similarly, both are configurations based on direct experience and the internalised values of significant others and society. One important difference is that Rogers restricts the self concept to a conscious *Gestalt*, whereas a major part of identity is unconscious. Other differences can be noted, too. Rogers places far less emphasis on unconscious processes and more on the phenomenal world of conscious experience. He also adopts a less developmental approach than Erikson. Although he considers that infantile residues may affect adult functioning, for Rogers the important moment is 'here and now'. Both theorists use psychotherapy as the source of their material. But Rogers, influenced by his scientific background, in contrast to Erikson's impressionistic and informally exploratory approach, seeks to formulate his theory in terms of specific propositions and, where possible, to subject them to more formal research investigation. Such drives as self actualisation as postulated by Maslow, Goldstein and Rogers appears to deny the basic idiographic approach of such humanistic psychologists, who at the same time as deploring the limitations of nomothetic laws when applied to the uniqueness of each person, in practice accept nomological principles in asserting the general process of self actualisation as a property of all individuals.

Personal construct theory (Kelly, 1955)

Since this theory does not have the self concept as its core like
Rogers', only a brief overview will be given. The self is involved in
that central constructs are usually those formed about self.

Kelly puts forward the view that an individual's behaviour and
personality can be explained in terms of the individual and unique
complex of constructs and cognitions he possesses, and by means
of which he adapts to the world as he perceives it to be. He
suggests that as a result of experience each individual develops a
complex of personal constructs, a network and hierarchy of
cognitive structures by means of which he comes to decisions about
the most appropriate behaviour to use to meet present and future
situations.

His main thesis is that in everyday life all people are constantly
engaged in problem solving, and that their personal constructs are
an important means of bringing order to their universe. He
suggests that each individual constructs his own hypotheses to
explain his past and present experiences; to discriminate between
experiences and events as he perceives them to be; to categorise
them; and to plan his present and future actions. The cognitive
categories a person has available provide the dimensions and range
of his ability to discriminate between experiences and to deal with
them intellectually. Thus, one of the major intellectual functions of
cognitive structures is to provide the basis for the individual's plans
and decisions regarding the choice of appropriate behaviour to
meet familiar or unfamiliar situations. The information and
knowledge gained by categorising an event provides the basis for
action. For example, if we think a child's crying is due to pain, we
seek the source of pain. If the child is flushed and has a high
temperature we may conclude that his pain is due to sickness and
send for a doctor. If on the other hand we think that the child is
crying with frustration and annoyance because he has dropped his
ice cream on to the ground and it is no longer fit to eat, then we
may choose to comfort him, ignore him, or buy him another ice
cream. If we classify events usefully and accurately we can behave
appropriately. However, if we classify events wrongly we may
make serious or even fatal mistakes.

Kelly's emphasis upon the individual as a problem solver, a
generator of hypotheses and theories to predict, control and
understand himself and others, provides us with a model of man as
a scientist. Although every individual is not indeed a scientist, all
individuals may perhaps be considered to apply scientific
principles, however crudely, to the problems they encounter in
everyday life. A person must interpret his own behaviour as well as
that of others. Since one's own behaviour is so important the
individual applies many different constructs to his own actions. The
placement and classification of his own behaviour and actions

within his personal construct system comes to define the self; thus the individual evaluates who and what he is against the background of his own construct system. Kelly regards the self as another construct. It is a construct that enables self to be an individual differentiated from others. Constructs are templates or patterns, ways of categorising similarities and differences which we perceive in our environment. Kelly provides a valuable technique for eliciting constructs about self and environment (Ch. 5). Constructs are regarded as bipolar and are consistent ways an individual will construe his world. For example a person may always construe the elements in his environment on a moral–immoral basis or on a radical–reactionary basis.

The term 'constructive alternativism' has been applied to the philosophical assumption behind the theory and refers to the belief that everything we perceive and experience is open to as many different interpretations as humans who experience it. For example, to say to a student, 'You can do better than that' may mean to one student that the teacher sees him as an able student and he feels motivated to reach the standard the teacher thinks him capable of. Another student may interpret the comment as a damning criticism and feel a failure.

Personal construct theory is stated in a very formal way with one fundamental postulate and eleven corollaries. The fundamental postulate states: 'A person's processes are psychologically channelised by the ways in which he anticipates events.' This suggests that behaviour is a function of individual meaning; man is an active interpreter.

A person develops a set of constructs for construing himself out of past experience, e.g. feedback from others, and utilises these to regulate his behaviour so that he maximises the likelihood of the predicted outcome occurring. Of course the construct about self may be wrong and lead the subject into the production of neurotic behaviour to maintain the construct in a disconfirming environment. It takes a major act of therapy to modify constructs or ways of interpreting self and environment. Anxiety is seen as an awareness that the events with which a man is confronted lie mostly outside the range of convenience of his construct system. Guilt is the displacement of self from core constructs, i.e. the present perception of self is incongruent with the personal construct system. The individual may attempt to deal with guilt by revising some of his basic constructs. However, such basic and important constructs are not easily changed, and hence considerable threat and anxiety may be generated. The person who experiences such feeling may perhaps strive to change his behaviour, attempt to revise his personal constructs regarding the self, or if efforts in these directions are too difficult he may form constructs which will 'rationalise' the discrepancies between his behaviour and his construct system. The theory has been criticised as placing too great an emphasis on cognition and intellect at the expense of emotions. It is a theory of cognition extrapolated into a theory of personality.

Epstein's self theory

Without a superstructure of postulates and corollaries, Epstein's (1973) theory is similar to Kelly's Role Construct Theory but is limited to the self. Epstein argues that the self concept is more properly identified as a self theory constructed by the individual about himself as a functioning, experiencing person who copes with the nature of his psychological environment. A self theory for Epstein, like the constructs of Kelly (1955) enables the individual to organise and interpret experience without which it would be impossible to function effectively in the face of complex environmental stimulation. Although Kelly did articulate extensively on a self concept, it can be argued that such is a universal higher order postulate in an individual's total conceptual system whereby all other constructs are classified into a self system and a non-self system.

He suggests that by recognising the implicit theories that individuals have about themselves very much as Kelly had postulated, it becomes possible to assimilate the views of phenomenologists on the nature of the self concept into a wider conceptualisation that is acceptable to all psychologists. The recognition of the self concept as a self theory reunites the known and the knower as the phenomenologists attempted to. This obviates any banishment of the executive self or the processes from the domain of the objective self. The concept of inherent growth and self actualisation postulated almost as an act of faith by phenomenologists becomes acceptable once it is recognised that individuals have self theories, Epstein adds. He is able to incorporate emotion into self theory since such a theory has as its general function a hedonistic purpose, maximising the pleasure–pain balance to ensure that life is liveable and emotionally satisfying, facilitating the maintenance of self esteem and organising the data of experience to that end. Epstein claims that the need for people to defend so desperately certain concepts or values irrespective of their validity is understandable in the context of functioning with an individualised self theory. Consistency and continuity of behaviour is largely a result of the self theory. Experience that would radically distort it tends to be denied, as for example when a person states, 'I wasn't myself' or 'It can't be true', or to be distorted and subjectively interpreted in a way favourable to the individual. This view of consistency and the

of the self as known is quite similar to Sullivan's claim that
mism is constructed out of experiences of approval and
val which influences self evaluation establishing the basic
d 'bad' me, which prevents the experience of anything
discordant or corrective.

Summary

The phenomonological approach continues the trend initiated by
the organismic theorists in blurring the distinction between self as
known and self as knower by postulating self actualisation as the
sole human drive. The private world of the individual, that
organisation of personal measurings which environmental
stimulation offers, of which self perception is a major element, is
regarded as the determiner of behaviour. Rogers develops previous
theorising by Snygg, Combs and Raimy, erecting a
phenomenological theory of behaviour and of counselling
techniques with the self concept as their core.

The basic premises of the phenomenological approach as
developed by Rogers are that:

(*a*) behaviour is the product of one's perceptions;

(*b*) these perceptions are phenomenological rather than 'real';

(*c*) perceptions have to be related to the existing organisation of
the field, the pivotal point of which is the self concept;

(*d*) the self concept is both a percept and a concept round which
gather values introjected from the cultural pattern;

(*e*) behaviour is then regulated by the self concept;

(*f*) the self concept is relatively consistent through time and
situation, and produces relatively consistent behaviour
patterns;

(*g*) defence strategies are utilised to prevent incongruities
occurring between experience and the cognised self concept;

(*h*) there is one basic drive, that of self actualisation.

Both Kelly and Epstein argue that each person is concerned with
making sense of themselves by construing patterns of events
involving self. The individual's behaviour is the outcome of his
unique interpretation of his environment the focus of which is
himself.

Further reading

Bannister, D. and **Mair, J. M.** *The Evaluation of Personal Constructs,* London:
Academic Press, 1968. This book details Kelly's Personal Construct Theory and
the Rep Test.

Gordon, C. and **Gergen, J. K.** (eds). *The Self in Social Interaction,* Vol. 1, New York: Wiley, 1968. Ch. 44 is a paper by Rogers.

Hall, C. S. and **Lindzey, G.** *Theories of Personality* (2nd edn), New York: Wiley, 1970. Ch. 13 deals in depth with Rogers' Self Theory.

Pervin, L. A. *Personality,* New York: Wiley, 1970. Ch. 6 is a detailed account of Rogers' theory.

Chapter 3

The self concept as an organisation of self attitudes

The first two chapters have demonstrated that a large number of psychologists have elaborated on the self concept or other similar self-referential terms as a major element in their theorising about human behaviour and personality. But it is equally apparent that in the field of psychology which is generally distinguished by the imprecision of its terminology and by an incapacity to even agree on definitions, self-referent constructs stand foremost in the ranks of this confusion. A wide range of self terms are employed by different psychologists in inconsistent and ambiguous ways. The application of other concepts such as 'ego', 'identity' and 'proprium', creates further confusion. Numerous other terms using 'self' as an adjective also abound. These various terms have been employed interchangeably and synonymously by some writers while others use them to discriminate different aspects of self conception. There is no intention to impose a long list of tedious definitions of each term on the reader. But it seems appropriate at this juncture to present a discussion conveying my interpretation and conceptualisation of these terms in order to clarify what exactly is implied by the 'self concept'. Other psychologists and readers may not necessarily agree with the arguments presented since they reflect my own bias and approach. Providing such disagreements give rise to critical constructive thinking then a valuable purpose will have been served.

We can best envisage the theoretical structure of the self that this book is attempting to convey by considering it as a hierarchical structure. Figure 3.1 is an attempt to clarify in a hierarchical manner what in most psychological writings is a very unclear set of terms. At the summit the superordinate construct is that of the Global Self, that sense of continuity, or what James termed the 'stream of consciousness' which is the totality and singularity of the Person. This Global Self includes so much that it ceases to have any value or meaning since the study of it would be no less than the study of the experiencing agent and his entire psychological processes. It is composed of the two aspects first differentiated by the philosophers:

(a) the Self as Knower, or I, i.e. the process of active experiencing; and (*b*) the Self as Known or Me, i.e. the content of that experiencing.

It does not, on initial consideration appear unreasonable to consider the Self as Knower or the experiencing subject as the aspect of major concern. It is this basic human capacity for awareness that makes us each acknowledge our self identity. That well-known saying of Descartes, *'cogito ergo sum'* or 'I think therefore I am', is the essence compelling each of us towards an intellectual and emotional commitment to the existence of Self. However, such an approach restricts study to unscientific speculation in theological and philosophical terms. Another

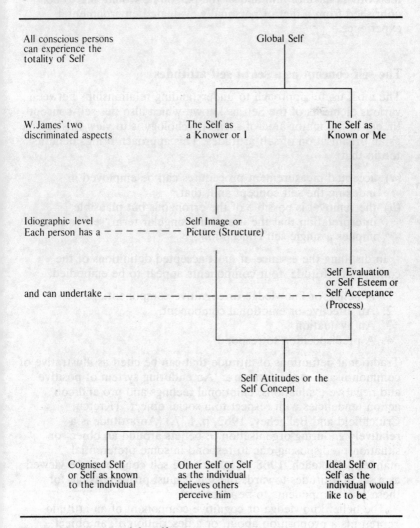

Fig. 3.1 The structure of the self.

difficulty is that this concept of Self as Knower is a nomothetic concept, i.e. of universal application since every person has the capacity for undertaking active experiencing and self awareness.

The content of the experiencing or the Self as Known is on the other hand an idiographic concept, i.e. person specific. In other words, while everyone is an experiencing 'I', in Raimy's (1943) pithy phrase, the self concept is, 'the individual as known to the individual' (p. 18) a unique configuration. This aspect of the Global Self, the self concept, or Me, is the individual's percepts, concepts and evaluations about himself, including the image he feels others have of him and of the person he would like to be, nourished from a diet of personally evaluated environmental experience.

The self concept as a set of self attitudes

The most useful approach to understanding relationships between various elements of the Self as known which also ties self-concept theory into a major area of social psychology is to view this collage as an organisation of self attitudes. This approach brings benefits too in that:

(a) accepted measurement procedures can be employed in indexing the self concept and; that
(b) the removal is possible of the erroneous but plausible interpretation that the use of the singular term 'self concept' implies a single self conception.

In distilling the essence of most accepted definitions of the concept of 'attitude' four components appear to be embodied.

1. A belief, or knowledge or cognitive component.
2. An affective or emotional component.
3. An evaluation.
4. A predisposition to respond.

Traditional definitions of attitude that can be cited as illustrative of common usage of the term are: 'An enduring system of positive and negative evaluations, emotional feelings and pro and con action tendencies with respect to a social object.' (Kretch, Crutchfield and Ballachey, 1962, p. 177.) 'An attitude is a relatively enduring organisation of beliefs around an object or situation predisposing one to respond in some preferential manner.' (Rokeach, 1968.) Thus for the self concept to be viewed as a set of attitudes towards the self it must prove possible for these four components to be identified.

The belief knowledge or cognitive component of an attitude represents a proposition about, or a description of, an object irrespective of whether the knowledge is true or false, based on either objective evidence or subjective opinion. Thus, if the object is myself I could state that I am short in stature. Hence the beliefs component of the self concept are the practically limitless ways in which each person perceives himself. Why not pick up a pen and write down a list of descriptions and attributes relevant to yourself, about what you are, and how you see yourself. My list, when I tried this task, contained elements such as these: Male, white, married, lecturer, house owner, car owner, psychologist, teacher, ambitious, not tall, bespectacled, enjoys classical music. There is little doubt your list would contain similar items and categories of beliefs and knowledge about yourself.

This sort of listing can continue *ad infinitum* as the list can conceivably contain all one's attributes, self conceptualisations, role and status characteristics, possessions and goals. All these elements can be ranked in order of personal importance since some self conceptions are central and others more peripheral to our sense of well-being and these may change rank depending on context, experience or momentary feelings. With only 16 elements in a global self concept, the possible permutations of ordering by importance are 20,923,000,000,000,000 individual configurations!

Former President Lyndon Johnson once labelled himself as 'a free man, an American, a United States senator, a Democrat, a liberal, a conservative, a Texan, a taxpayer, a rancher and not as young as I used to be nor as old as I expect to be'. Such descriptions serve to distinguish the person as unique from all other persons. But equally important such self descriptions and beliefs are all invested with emotive and evaluative overtones. A dogmatic statement like this will probably be rejected by some of you as an over-generalisation. For it could well be contested that while there are strong attitudinal components to the self concept, not all the beliefs a person holds about himself are evaluated. Hence the term 'self concept' might well not be fully equivalent to self attitudes. However, even seemingly affectively neutral beliefs about one's own self carry implicit evaluative overtones. For instance, part of my self concept includes the facts that I live at a certain address, and possess a certain model of car. Superficially there is no evaluation or affective component present, but implicitly, perhaps at a barely conscious level, there is. This arises because the possession of that address or car can be good or bad. For example, I live in X road (and that is good because it is a high-class district); I have a Z car (and that is good because it emphasises my wealth and masculinity). Of course, these aspects might well have been evaluated negatively. Think about some of your self descriptions. Are there any that convey no emotive evaluative overtone whatsoever? To be male or female, white or coloured, a success or a failure, hardworking or lazy, a sportsman or spectator, tall or short, or any other attribute, involves some loading with evaluative connotations derived from subjectively interpreted feedback from others and from comparison with subjectively interpreted cultural, group and individual standards and values. The affective component of an attitude exists because the cognitive component arouses emotional and evaluative discharge of varying intensity depending on context and cognitive content. This arousal centres on either the object itself or around other objects, i.e. persons reflecting positive or negative positions with respect to the object. Taken from my personal listing of attributes for instance, my shortness in stature evoked a strong emotional feeling and negative self evaluative since lack of height doesn't fit with the cultural stereotype of a male and prevented my development as a good rugby footballer, a sport I enjoyed as a youth. Finally, evaluated knowledge about the person whether subjectively inferred or objectively factual predisposes the individual to respond or behave in one way rather than another. To continue my personal example, my lack of height in late adolescence led me to avoid playing rugby as I become less able to compete and shine any more among, at that time, faster-growing youths. This led me to take up other activities such as athletics and academic pursuits as compensation. Consider some of the elements in your own list of beliefs and attributes. How does your standing in them in relation to societal, group and your own values affect your behaviour; do your conceptions of yourself influence your pattern of behaviour? Without knowing anything about any of you, I can, with some confidence, answer the question and say on your behalf, 'Yes, quite considerably!'

This evaluative loading of the self concept is learned, and since it is learned it can alter in direction and weighting as other learning experiences are encountered. For example a person may have a concept of himself as a bright student deriving from his performance in school examinations and the feedback he receives from teacher and peers. This brings pleasure and satisfaction, since being a bright student has positive connotations within society and at home where the achievement motive and success have been positively reinforced. However, this positive self evaluation may fluctuate as increasingly harder work brings poorer examination results or as significant others in the peer group begin to evaluate other behaviours, e.g. athletic, as more important. Again as time passes the bright student might find in adulthood that academic success is not the sole criterion of happiness or getting on in life, so that a lowering of the weighting will occur though it will still remain positive. So self evaluation is not fixed; it relates to each particular context. The evaluative significance of most concepts is taken from the surrounding culture in that many evaluations have become normative. Dull, fat, immature all have negative evaluations for instance, while clever, muscular and dependable possess positive overtones. Not only are the evaluative overtones learned from the culture, but by self observation and by feedback from social interaction such evaluative concepts come to be applied to the individual.

The terms 'self image' and 'self picture' have frequently appeared in the literature with the implication that they are synonymous with the term 'self concept'. The writer prefers to avoid these two terms as they give a rather static and neutral appearance to what it has been argued is a dynamic, evaluative and considerably emotively charged concept. They fail to convey the attitudinal content of the self concept. So the self image of self picture is only one of two elements of the self concept; the other component is the value which the individual attributes to particular descriptions (Fig. 3.1). Most writers employ 'self esteem' to designate this self-evaluation component. By self esteem, Coopersmith (1967) refers to 'the evaluation that the individual makes and customarily maintains with regard to himself; it expresses an attitude of approval or disapproval and indicates the extent to which the individual believes himself to be capable, significant, successful and worthy. In short, self-esteem is a personal judgement of worthiness that is expressed in the attitudes the individual holds'. (p. 4) Rosenberg (1965) defines self esteem in similar vein as 'a positive or negative attitude towards a particular object, namely, the Self' (p. 30). Self esteem seems to imply simply that the individual feels he is a person of worth, respecting himself for what he is, not condemning himself for what he is not, and the extent to which he feels positively about himself. Low self esteem suggests self rejection, self derogation and negative self evaluation.

Self esteem according to Brisset (1972) encompasses two basic psychological processes, (*a*) the process of self evaluation and (*b*) the process of self worth. Each is complementary to the other and Brisset (1972) argues that self worth is more fundamental to the human being than self evaluation, though both elements of self esteem necessarily involve putting what one is or what one is doing into context or providing oneself and one's activities with a reference.

Self esteem in terms of self evaluation refers to the making of a conscious judgement regarding the significance, and importance of oneself or of facets of oneself. Anything related to the person, as has been argued, is liable for such evaluations on the basis of criteria and standards involving any one or combinations of consensual goals (e.g. wealth, prestige), levels of achievement, moral precepts and norms of behaviour. Three principal reference points appear pertinent in self evaluation. Firstly the comparison of the self image as known with the ideal self image or the picture of the kind of person one would wish to be. This sort of comparison has been a dominant theme in numerous approaches to psychotherapy (e.g. Horney; Rogers) whereby congruence of these two selves is an important indicator of mental health. Even James' (1890) classic view of self esteem (see p. 9) as the ratio between actual accomplishments and aspirations is a statement of this major reference point in self evaluation, the actualisation of ideals. Those who are fortunate to be able to live up to their standards and realise their aspirations develop on this model a strong sense of self esteem. Those who find that they do not measure up to their own ideals are likely to possess low self esteem. Sadly, the help they are frequently proferred amounts to little more than persuasive advice to adjust their goals by lowering their sights. In other words there is an attempt to resocialise them by making them aware of their capabilities, adjusting ideals to reality.

The second reference point involves the internalisation of society's judgement. This assumes that self evaluation is determined by the individual's beliefs as to how others evaluate him. This conceptualisation of self esteem was promoted by Cooley (1912) and Mead (1934) initially.

The third and final reference point involves the individual evaluating himself as a relative success or relative failure in doing what his identity entails. It involves not the judgement that what one does is good in itself but that one is good at what one does. The pattern that emerges is of individuals fitting into an ongoing social structure as best they can. If roles are played properly then collective purposes are served and individual esteem satisfied. Society provides the opportunities for developing self esteem, but to ensure this at an individual level it can only be achieved by adjustment to what is provided.

Self worth is the feeling that the 'self' is important and effective, and involves the person being aware of himself. Whereas notions of self evaluation suggest that a person's sense of self esteem derived from measuring up to certain standards, reward for meeting his own and others' aspirations for him is self esteem. On the other hand self worth is more fundamental, involving a view of oneself as being master of one's actions, a sense of competence which is intrinsic rather than depending on extrinsic support. Thus, self worth becomes a rather nebulous concept, falling more within the ambit of the self as knower or experiencer. Hence self esteem to be operationalised for measurement purposes is best regarded as self evaluation, with a phenomenological orientation implied, the evaluation being subjective whether involving one's own assessment of performance or one's interpretation of the assessment of oneself made by others, both in relation to self-pointed ideals and culturally learned standards.

Osgood's investigation (Osgood, Suci and Tannenbaum, 1957) into connotative meaning showed the consistent appearance of 'evaluation' as the major judgemental dimension. Hence taking self pictures as central features of the individual's psychological self meaning, it is not unreasonable to accept the pervasive nature of evaluation of such pictures since evaluation is a basic and normal approach to any psychological object. Another factorial approach that again demonstrates the attitudinal organisation of the self concept stems from the recent work on the factorial structure of motivation (Cattell and Child, 1975). They demonstrate the consistent appearance of what they call the 'self sentiment'. This pervading self sentiment they describe as a 'collection of attitudes all of which have to do with that self-concept which the human level of intelligent abstraction makes possible and which we all possess' (p. 97). Their analysis suggests that this dynamic self concept is composed of attitudes concerned with the preservation of the physical self, the control of self, and the need for self esteem. This objective finding of a consistent and ubiquitous motivational and attitudinal structure is additional support for viewing the self concept as an attitude with all its evaluative and predisposing behavioural implications. Thus, from a variety of independent sources the view promoted in this book that the self concept is best regarded as a dynamic complex of attitudes is given consistent support.

A positive self concept can thus be equated with positive self evaluation, self respect, self esteem, self acceptance; a negative self concept becomes synonymous with negative self evaluation, self hatred, inferiority and a lack of feelings of personal worthiness and self acceptance. Each of these terms carries connotations of the others and have been used interchangeably by various writers (Wylie, 1961; Coopersmith, 1967, etc). Persons with high self appraisal and self esteem are generally accepting of themselves; those who attribute negative values to themselves have little self esteem, self respect or self acceptance. The terms 'self concept', 'self attitudes' and 'self esteem' will be regarded henceforth as synonymous in this book. They are all evaluated beliefs about the person which can range along a positive–negative continuum.

Two major writers on the self concept have produced extended definitions of the construct which accord with the conceptualisation being conveyed in this chapter. Rogers (1951) states that the self concept

is composed of such elements as the perceptions of one's characteristics and abilities; the percepts and concepts of the self in relation to others and to the environment; the value qualities which are perceived as associated with experiences and objects; and the goals and ideas which are perceived as having positive or negative valence. It is then the organised picture, existing in awareness either as figure or ground, of the self and the self-in-relationship, together with the positive and negative values which are associated with those qualities and relationships as they are perceived as existing in the past, present, or future. (p. 138)

Similarly, Staines (1954) provides a definition which places the self concept into the realm of attitude study. He states that it is a conscious system of percepts, concepts, and evaluations of the individual as he appears to the individual. It includes a cognition of the evaluative responses made by the individual to perceived and conceived aspects of himself; an understanding of the picture that others are presumed to hold of him; and an awareness of an evaluated self which is his notion of the person as he would like to be and the way in which he ought to behave. (p. 87)

Are attitudes to self similar to attitudes towards other objects?

Rosenberg (1965) considers this question in considerable detail and concludes that 'there is no qualitative difference in the characteristics of attitudes towards the self, and attitudes towards soup, soap, cereal or suburbia' (p. 6). This argument takes as its point of departure the reality that we have attitudes towards objects, that some of these objects are people, of which the most important is the individual himself. It has been shown above that the basic components of an attitude are similarly revealed in self attitudes so that the self concept combines:

(*a*) self image – what the person sees when he looks at himself;
(*b*) affective intensity – how strongly the person feels about these various facets;
(*c*) self evaluation – whether the person has a favourable/unfavourable opinion of various facets of that image;
(*d*) behavioural predisposition – what the person is likely to do in response to his evaluation of himself.

Rosenberg adds several other components common to all attitudes, such as the importance of self attitudes relative to other attitude objects, the consistency of facets of the attitude, the temporal stability of the attitude and the clarity of the attitude.

However, there are aspects of the self concept which differentiate self attitudes from attitudes to any other object. These distinctive qualities are:

1. Lack of a common reference object: with attitudes in general, studies can be made of many people's attitudes to a common reference object. In self attitudes people are perceiving absolutely different objects – themselves. The referent is not commonly

available; only the person who formulates the abstraction is in a position to define and evaluate its characteristics. As Rosenberg (1965) points out, 'if one man thinks Picasso is superb whereas another considers him abysmal, then these men disagree. But if one man considers himself intelligent, and another considers himself stupid, these men do not disagree. They are looking at different objects.' (p. 28) A study of self attitudes deals with as many different objects as there are members in the sample. Though this feature of self attitudes appears to distinguish it from other attitudes, it can be claimed (Watts, 1964) that the distinction is one of degree rather than of kind, since all perceptions and reports are selective and interpretative, and this holds true for external as well as internal objects. Again, even though the object of consideration differs in each self perception, the dimension applied to each (e.g. evaluation) is the same. By focusing on the end product of the judgement process or self appraisal, it becomes possible to compare individuals who differ in particulars.

2. All persons are motivated to hold the same attitude towards the self. This is essentially towards the favourable or positive pole. 'Self-love and pride are universal in human nature, even though in mature personalities they are not necessarily sovereign' claimed Allport (1961, p. 155). Of the many sentiments proposed by McDougall (1908) the sentiment of self regard was the master one to which the remainder of the sentiments were subordinated. One thing that Murphy (1947) believed was common from culture to culture was the phenomenon of self love. People do not hold negative self concepts, feelings of low self esteem, and low self acceptance with equanimity and contentment. Rosenberg (1965) demonstrated a strikingly consistent appearance of a highly depressed state alongside low self esteem, while Star (1950) showed that those of low self esteem were eight times more likely than those of high self esteem to manifest a large number of psychosomatic symptoms that have been shown to be closely related to neuroticism. This seems to be a most important feature of self attitudes that almost everyone would prefer to have positive or favourable ones.

3. The object is important to everyone: although there is a wide variation in the importance attached to various objectives by different individuals, the self concept is central to every person's psychosocial existence. One can hardly imagine a person who is totally indifferent to himself. As Murphy (1947) has observed, 'Whatever the Self is, it becomes a centre, and anchorage point, a standard of comparison, an ultimate real. Inevitably it takes its place as a supreme value.' (p. 498) Therapy protocols reveal a focus on the self concept with a significant proportion of verbal material relating to it. Even in everyday conversation both 'I' and 'Me' references are considerable. Most people are eager to talk

about themselves when given the opportunity, some boringly and tediously so.

4. The self is reflexive: since the self is reflexive, the person holding the attitude and the object towards which the attitude is held, are one and the same. Such statements as 'I wash myself' and 'I dislike myself' demonstrate the point that the person is both subject and object, the two discriminated aspects of the global self. This provides a unique perspective; no one else can say how we feel or perceive ourselves, and it is the basic tenet of faith of the phenomenologists.

5. Emotional commitment: as Cooley (1902) suggested certain emotions such as pride, conceit, shame, despair and mortification are only aroused in relation to self or ego-involved objects. These emotions largely explain why self attitudes are of great importance for mental health.

6. Sources of influence: there are differences between the kind of influences that affect self attitudes and those that affect attitudes to many other objects. Interpersonal communication rather than mass communications systems influence self attitudes, whereas newspapers, TV and radio, help to define more clearly our attitudes to other objects. As will be demonstrated in Chapter 6 self evaluation depends to a considerable extent on the individual's interpretation of what he believes others think of him. Evaluation is always effected with reference to criteria. These are usually the standards of society, group and family, both objectively and subjectively derived. The selectivity of standards and values which limit the possible range of self evaluation operates according to Rosenberg (1965) through the principle of psychological selectivity.

Psychological selectivity

James (1890) initially pointed the way with his ingenious formula:

$$\text{Self-esteem} = \frac{\text{Success}}{\text{pretensions} \ldots}$$

It is fairly simple to demonstrate that the individual can maintain, or enhance, his self esteem by either reducing the denominator or increasing the numerator. It is the subjective assessment of success in relation to what he wants to be that counts. As James (1890) so wisely understood, 'our self feeling in this world depends entirely on what we back ourselves to be or do' (p. 64). Certain roles, statuses, attributes, etc are not selected as important by the individual, hence evaluation on these aspects is not relevant on most occasions. The selection of certain standards by which success may be subjectively attained is open to all individuals on many facets of life. Thus, this apparently free selectivity of salient issues and standards provides a weighting which pushes the balance of evaluation well over to the positive side. But the freedom to select the issues and the standards they are judged from is not without limitation, since certain objective facts cannot be evaded. Students with consistently low marks are less likely to consider themselves good students than those with higher averages; a poor man cannot consider himself wealthy; a short man cannot consider himself tall – not as long as he is in contact with reality, at any rate. Again, self values might have been chosen before any opportunity has presented itself to allow them to be tested adequately. It might only become apparent later that the individual had an insufficiency of the necessary qualities or expertise. Many 'star' pupils from small primary schools have found this to their cost on moving on to a large secondary school.

Another limitation which can reduce the chances of a positive self concept is that many self values established early under the influence of significant others have been so strongly reinforced that it becomes difficult to change them at a later time, even when it is in the individual's interest so to do. Such a change may represent a major act of therapy.

Finally, since man is a social animal and lives in society, he cannot avoid the social and cultural roles, values and norms stemming from this environment. He finds himself judged by the criteria of his society and relevant subgroups, not merely those criteria of his own making. If he seeks his own approval and that of the group's he must excel in terms of their values. Certainly it is possible to enhance the self concept by renouncing society's values, ultimately by abandoning society, but even subgroups outside 'normal' society have certain values and standards of their own, e.g. hippy groups. Self values cannot easily be manipulated to suit the individual's psychological convenience, but the selection of self values does have wide latitude because of the huge range of alternatives available and the private nature of self values.

Interpersonal selectivity is highly limited in childhood. Most communications about oneself at that period of life come from parents with whom the child is stuck for better or for worse. If they love him, he is given at the outset a decisive basis for thinking well of himself; if he perceives disparagement and rejection, then it is difficult for the child to avoid the conclusion that he is unworthy. With no options there can be no selectivity.

The work of Hovland, Lumsdaine and Sheffield (1949) like that of Sherif and Sherif (1956), clearly demonstrates that the attitudes that are easiest to change or form are those that are least structured. Sherif and Cantril (1947) have shown that attitudes once formed tend to maintain themselves. It is precisely in childhood that the self concept is most unformed and unstructured.

Hence, with parents holding the monopoly of interpersonal communications at the same time as the child is emerging into self consciousness with nothing to base a self estimate on, their attitudes have a powerful significance at this time of life.

Thus, there are important limits on the selectivity of values and standards on which self attitudes come to be based. Several of these limits obtain in childhood when interpersonal communications are most decisive in developing self attitudes. So that despite the theoretical assumption that the individual could lower his pretensions to obtain more self esteem, the real limitations of living within a particular culture pattern in which evaluations against objective standards are frequently made, make it easy to see why some people do possess negative self attitudes despite individual preference to 'accentuate the positive'.

The predisposition to respond

As is well documented and observed in attitude study, individuals do not necessarily behave in a way that is consistent with their evaluated beliefs. However, self attitudes do on the whole tend to influence behaviour, because as Ziller (1973) argues a person with high esteem tends to evaluate information in terms of its relevance and meaning to the self concept, tending to assimilate the information to the self concept rather than restructuring the self concept. He is not a victim of events. The self concept mediates between organism and environment, and as a corollary it is proposed that self esteem controls the consistency of the organism's response to environment. However, there is less consistency of behaviour with the person of low self esteem. He is more 'field dependent' in that he tends to conform to the influence of the context, so that behaviour is directly related to the immediate environment. This leads to inconsistent behaviour and short-term adaptation characterised by S-R learning. The individual with positive self attitudes demonstrates consistency of behaviour as he is not under the sway of immediate stimulation but has a firmer basis for action with stimulation being interpreted and mediated by the organism. He can stand apart from the immediate environment firm in his belief in himself, behaviour governed by a well-ordered, ubiquitous and competent body of self perceptions. Thus, consistency arises from high self esteem establishing an internal guidance mechanism, an abstract self, whereas low self esteem with its lack of self confidence leads to a need to satisfy a wide variety of others, monitoring the behaviour of others before possessing a basis for action. But even with the individual of low self esteem a considerable consistency of behaviour can still be noted because he, like anyone else, wishes to preserve his self as known, and by invoking the use of defence mechanisms it is possible to obtain some sense of worth and modify environmental experience incongruous with the self as known.

The preservation of self attitudes, self esteem and personal worth

While the concept of defence mechanism is one of Freud's most significant contributions, Anna Freud (1946) provides the fullest authoritative discussion of the subject detailing 10 specific defence mechanisms. Rogers was concerned with defence too, but he did not discriminate so finely between particular defences, simply elaborating on three tactics – ignoring, denying or distorting experiences which are inconsistent with the self concept. But whatever the differences in nomenclature the general principle is the same, that of helping the individual to preserve his integrity, sense of personal worth and self evaluation when he finds himself in ego-involved stress situations which none of us can completely avoid in life's journey. For example the football fan who proudly announces, 'my team won today', may find some measure of importance by identifying himself with a successful team, the student who fails an exam may project the blame for his performance on to the teacher's lack of fairness or the poor construction of the test; the returning tourist who cheats the 'customs men' by not revealing the extra bottle may rationalise that everyone else cheats and he might as well too. The protection of self esteem from possible devaluation and thus from anxiety is the very essence of the defensive functions of these mechanisms.

The use of defence mechanisms is a normal human reaction, unless they are used to such an extreme that they begin to interfere with the maintenance of self esteem rather than aiding it. They are not usually adaptive in the sense of realistically coping with problems. For example, a person who continually rationalises away his blunders is not likely to profit from his mistakes on subsequent occasions. Defence mechanisms involve a fair degree of self deception and reality distortion. Furthermore, they often function on relatively unconscious levels and therefore are not subject to the usual checks and balances of more conscious processes. In fact, we usually resent having someone call our attention to them because once they become conscious they become less adequate in serving their purposes. Defence mechanisms can be best understood in view of the objective they serve, which is to safeguard the integrity and worth of the self. Thus, it is only as we conceive of an active dynamic self concept which struggles to maintain a certain stability that they make sense (Hilgard, 1949).

Perspectives of the self concept

This evaluated set of beliefs combines several perspectives, which can be separated in measurement procedures. Strang (1957) postulated four main perspectives after analysing unstructured compositions of adolescents on self themes:

1. The basic self concept, or the individual's perception of his abilities, status and roles in the outside world. It is his concept of the person he thinks he is.
2. The transitory self which the individual holds at the present time influenced by the mood of the moment.
3. The social self. This is the self as the individual believes others see and evaluate him.
4. The ideal self. This is the kind of person the individual hopes to be or would like to be.

Staines (1954) in his theoretical exposition, proposed only three aspects, omitting the transitory self concept. Most workers have followed this approach and accept a triad comprising cognised, other (social) and ideal selves (Fig. 3.1). The basic self, the concept of the person as he thinks he is, is generally termed the cognised self. Strang's social self was renamed by Staines as the other self, a self derived from the reflected appraisals of significant others *à la* Mead and Cooley. It is a major point of entry of data about the person. These impressions and inferences from statements, actions, subtle gestures of others towards the individual gradually establishes a self concept as the person believes he is seen by others and will come to include a point of view on all aspects of the cognised self. As will be indicated on the developmental aspects of the self concept (Ch. 6) it is apparent that the other and cognised selves must contain similarity of content. In contrast, various degrees of discrepancy are usually measurable between the content of the ideal and cognised selves.

The ideal self is a set of interpretations about the individual when he is revealing his most personal wants and aspirations, part wish and part ought. It may not be in touch with reality at all. Horney (1945) has shown that it may be so far away from our cognised self that its unhappy possessor is borne down with depression through its unattainability. She indicates that to abandon a striving to attain an unrealistic ideal self is 'one of the great reliefs of therapy' (p. 136). Murray (1953) describes the idealised picture of the self as a set of ambitions leading to a goal conceived by the person as himself at his highest hope. For Erikson (1956), the ego is a set of 'to be strived for but for ever not quite attainable ideal goals for the self' (p. 76). According to Allport (1961) the ideal self concept defines one's goals for the future. 'Every mature personality may be said to travel towards a port of destination, selected in advance, or to several related ports in succession, their ideal always serving to hold the course in view' (p. 285). Combs and Soper (1957) regard this ideal self as the kind of person the individual would like or hope to be, 'the aggregate of those characteristics of Self which the person feels are necessary to attain adequacy (sometimes unfortunately perfection)' (p. 140). It would seem that for many self-concept theorists the ideal self is an important aspect, and through reinforced social learning, a person accepts the cultural ideal or norm with respect to a specified characteristic or behaviour as his own personal idea. It is always there, so much part of the person, yet often leading on imperiously to varying degrees of condemnation when attempts to meet its demands fail.

Why a 'concept'?

Why do we call the self concept a concept? To answer this we need to outline what psychologists imply by the term 'concept'. Psychologists consider concepts as essential for human thinking. When we perceive a familiar stimulus we tend not to pay attention to its idiosyncratic features but immediately classify it as an 'X' or a 'Y'. That is, when we see a car we can state at once that it belongs to the class or concept of car, even though it may be a new model which we have never seen before with several unique features. If we had to attend to every stimulus and remember its exact qualities so that we would know it the next time the cognitive strain would be enormous. Concepts enable us to sort and classify stimuli, to recognise that some stimuli are similar yet different from other stimuli. The use of concepts facilitates the emission of a consistent response to a particular group of stimuli. Such classification enables the individual to gain control of his environment by cataloguing into discrete units the plethora of stimuli that impinge on his various sense organs. The ability to form concepts also facilitates the generalisation of learning from others. Self conception facilitates social interaction so that the individual can anticipate the expected reactions of others. It permits self evaluation to be carried out on the basis of which future behaviour can be based. For example, a concept of one's intellectual prowess would be invaluable in deciding whether to follow certain intellectual pursuits and a concept of one's physical ability would aid decisions about joining in various types of sporting activities.

   Such self conceptions, being fairly stable and enduring, provide the person with firmly based generalisations about himself so that his decision making, his behaviour and the expected reactions from others are consistent, whereas inability to predict outcomes and indecision about the appropriate behaviour repertoire to display generates stress and anxiety. The availability of a range of self concepts relevant to a particular context as a brief personal summary which the individual can communicate to others has an extremely functional value in society. By this others know what to expect from one behaviourally, and placement in formal institutions such as industry and higher education, requires instant, succinct self labels. To tell another, irrespective of the subjectivity of the message, that you are industrious, sociable, kind and cooperative permits both parties to interact in a socially meaningful way. Self conception and its communication within social interaction is perhaps carried to the *n*th degree in the computerised dating systems that demand the input of a brief self description. Inability to formulate a set of self labels appears to be anxiety provoking and this identity crisis has been seen to be particularly pertinent during adolescence (Erikson, 1968) when old self definitions are no longer appropriate and need replacing. But in one aspect the self concept is different from other concepts; it is not merely a naming or classifying technique. Because of its personal nature it has been argued that emotive and evaluative connotations of varying degrees are indissolubly linked to it.

The self concept is a hypothetical construct

The self concept is a hypothetical construct. In other words it is a useful way of predicting human behaviour, but we must be careful not to reify a hypothetical construct, viewing it as though it actually does exist like a real-world object. It is very easy to talk about the self concept, self esteem, self acceptance and the like as though they were physically real and tangible. Such terms as 'self picture' and 'self image' refer to this structural and static homunculus of self characteristics. It seems more appropriate, as we have done, to consider the self concept as a process, dynamic and subtly changing. Such terms as 'self esteem', 'self evaluation' and 'self acceptance' belong to this dynamic process of conceptualising experience and the ways in which this influences behaviour. However, these two approaches are not mutually exclusive and in the measurement procedures adopted in studying the self concept we momentarily freeze the evaluative dynamism to frame a static evaluated self picture. Self constructs are solely explanatory concepts with hypothetical properties. For example, if teachers convince a pupil that he has the ability and competence to do well academically and at some later date we note that the pupil will not shirk from tackling difficult material and has high achievement drives, then the self concept acts as an intervening variable or hypothetical construct to explain the relationship between the two observations. The self concept is acceptable because it permits us to understand behaviour. In the above example we can suggest that the pupil had developed a belief derived from teacher feedback that he was capable of achieving success at difficult tasks.

The plurality of self conception

The term 'self concept' is usually used in the singular when referring to a person's conception of himself. However, when a person is asked to describe himself a large number of different characteristics are generated as we found in our own listings, e.g. husband, father, Protestant, lawyer, honest, tall. Because of this many psychologists find it more fruitful to speak of multiple self conceptions. But since, as we have argued, each description or attribute is evaluated and possesses behavioural implications it would seem far more appropriate and in line with common sense to view the self concept as a constellation of attitudes towards the self. The self concept can remain singular as the sum of the self attitudes. However, the existence of multiple conceptions of the person means that some of these conceptions may be incompatible and inconsistent with one another. This is very likely since self attitudes are learned and the learning can occur in a wide variety of contexts. The rationale of dissonance theory (Festinger, 1957) is that inconsistent cognitions are intolerable and individuals will adopt strategies to eliminate such discrepancies, e.g. rationalising so that the negative opinion of another about ourselves which runs counter to our own opinion about ourselves, is judged as an incompetent assessor or one whose opinion matters little. But discrepancies between different self conceptions will, for the most part, not give rise to stress since they may be the result of realistic appraisals in different context, and additionally the functional value of some of the self conceptions may be of a very low order. For example, a teacher may see himself as an impersonal autocrat in the classroom yet as a tender, caring democrat within the home. The separate conditions under which these conceptions are generated make it unlikely that dissonance will be experienced. On the other hand, a youth who generally conceptualises himself as a 'hard' man may have on occasions to regard himself as the babysitter for a younger sibling. This latter role may engender considerable dissonance in producing a contrast between his interpretation of how his peer group will now perceive him, of how his parent still regard him and of his own desire to consider himself tough and independent. Whether or not inconsistency occurs depends on the ability to differentiate between particular self images.

In the above examples the teacher can separate his self conceptions of teacher and parent, but the youth cannot

differentiate his various roles. His view of himself as hard, tough
and masculine is demeaned by his babysitting role. The ability to
differentiate between particular self images contains the failure or
criticism of one image to that image, rather than tarnishing many
others besides. A man may possess a dominant image of himself as
husband. This image can be differentiated into numerous other
images and behaviours such as wage earner, father, 'odd job about
the house' man, bill-payer, gardener, etc. Evaluation on any one of
these perceived subjectively as negative may not affect subjectively
perceived evaluations of other aspects. Incompetence at mending a
fuse is not likely to have devastating effects on his opinion of
himself on other elements of his self concept, say as wage earner,
or gardener. This relates back to 'James' Law' on self esteem, in
that it all depends on what one backs oneself to be. The two
situations where subjectively interpreted criticism causes general
loss of self esteem are firstly when little or no differentiation
between various images occurs, that is when being able to do jobs
around the house is regarded as synonymous with being a
competent husband. Secondly, when the negatively evaluated
image is central to the person's whole being as with our babysitting
youth, since the degree of positive or negative feeling an image
evokes depends on the image's centrality. This is really another
aspect of differentiation between various self perceptions, in that
some are core beliefs; others are less significant, and yet others are
so peripheral to the essence of self that low evaluation of them is
not of any great concern. Those central and important self images
are cherished and highly resistant to change. From her
psychoanalytic work Horney (1939) discerned that most people
cling to their essential beliefs about themselves like a drowning
man holding tight to a straw.

Summary

The self concept, the conceptualisation by the individual of his
own person, is regarded as being invested with potent emotional
and evaluative connotations since the subjective beliefs and factual
knowledge the individual ascribes to himself are in varying degrees
so personal, intense and central to his unique identity. The fact
that the self image is the primary source of many satisfactions must
inevitably lead to it becoming heavily charged with emotion and
value. Self esteem or self evaluation is the process in which the
individual examines his performance, capacities and attributes
according to his personal standards and values, which have been
internalised from society and significant others. These evaluations
promote behaviour consistent with the self knowledge. This
conceptualisation of the self concept places it firmly within the

ambit of attitude study. Such an approach is quite fruitful since firstly it allows the accepted and well-tried methods used to index attitudes to be applied to the measurement of the self concept. Secondly, it draws attention to the fact that the self concept isn't a single element. Each individual possesses a large array of self concepts relating to specific perceptions. Hence, utilising self attitudes rather than self concept emphasises that there are many ways in which each person may conceive of himself.

Attitudes directed towards the person himself can be defined in the same way as attitudes directed to any other objects, as a relatively enduring organisation of affective and evaluative beliefs about oneself predisposing one to respond with greater probability in one way rather than in another.

So the self concept is presented here as an abstraction that all humans develop about the attributes, capacities, objects and activities that they possess and pursue, around which, derived from social experiences, values cluster. This abstraction 'me', is formed in the course of experience by the same processes of abstraction that are employed in other areas of experience. There is no *a priori* abstraction made by the individual about himself which exists apart from the preceding personal experiences and awareness.

Further reading

Diggory, J. C. *Self Evaluation: Concepts and Studies,* New York: Wiley, 1966.

Measurement of
the self concept

Chapter 4

Methodological problems

Much of the evidence and material presented in the succeeding chapters is based on research conducted on the self concept. Such research is of immense value because the results form knowledge and become the bases for action by professionals in various fields. It is necessary to take a hard look at the measurement of the self concept and the problems that are involved, not only in general terms but also with particular techniques. This chapter will concern itself with general methodological problems while Chapter 5 will review a range of specific self-concept assessment instruments.

Consideration of research literature covering studies conducted on the self concept reveals quite starkly the considerable variation in measurement procedures utilised by investigators who differ widely in theoretical orientation and in the meaning they each apply to the particular self-construct term they are attempting to study. Brookover, Erikson and Joiner (1967) make an important point when they note that sometimes the only similarity found in the literature between one study and another is the use of the term 'self-concept'. Wylie's (1961) close examination of 463 studies reveals an amazing array of hypotheses, research designs and measuring instruments. Many researchers have developed their own instruments which have been poorly checked for reliability and validity; they are often inadequately described and impossible to locate. This prevents opportunities for replication, and many of the instruments applied in self-concept studies have been used once only. In any case, as the opening chapters have revealed, the inadequate and conflicting theoretical conceptualisations of the plethora of self-referent constructs entails that studies employing such terms as 'self concept,' 'self acceptance', 'the self' or 'self esteem' may, or may not, be investigating the same phenomenon. The empirical study of the self concept is understandably in a parlous state and presents any investigator with untold difficulty in attempting to synthesise and collate reliable and valid information about the self concept.

Another problem encountered in working with the self concept which Wylie (1961) points to derives from the fact that each subject is his own best vantage point. This phenomenological perspective is different from that of the typical psychology experiment which provides every subject with a stimulus, the properties of which can be agreed upon by a body of independent observers, the response to the stimulus then being recorded. Since the experimenter's knowledge of the stimulus is independent of that of the subject's, an external criterion is available against which to measure the subject's response. If the subject emits an unexpected response then the experimenter might assume that the subject missed something or experienced something different from that expected. Or he might infer that the subject is deliberately withholding what he perceives or simply lacks the verbal skills to communicate his perceptions accurately.

Research in the field of the self concept must operate without the advantage of an external criterion. Interest is located simply in the stimulus as the subject interprets it. The stimulus is inferred from the subject's report of it. The researcher is unable to check the report independently since there is often no immediate stimulus, and no body of external observers can ever claim to pronounce on what the subject should presumably have experienced. This follows from the phenomenological approach adopted towards the self concept. The self concept must necessarily be inferred from the behaviour of the subject, and for research purposes this is essentially what the subject has to say about himself based on his private subjectively interpreted experiences. Allport (1955) has argued that the individual has a right to be believed when he reports on himself.

Since phenomenological theory appears inappropriate for the usual 'if-then' or stimulus-response experimental design in which observable behaviour, the dependent variable, is predicted as a function of the independent variable, research on the self concept employs essentially correlational designs. This limitation implies that cause–effect laws can never be unequivocally demonstrated. However, Verplanck (1954) has analysed quite revealingly the stimulus in Behaviourist learning theories, which shows clearly that the phenomenologist is not unique in the difficulty of defining his antecedents. Stimuli are seemingly response-inferred constructs in several theories, e.g. Skinner's (1938, 1953) 'stimulus' term; the hypothetical or inferential stimuli of Guthrie (1952). As Verplanck (1954) remarks, 'such inference backward to quasi-independent variables seems to be characteristic of the work of many behaviour theorists' (p. 286). So, in essence, self-concept investigations imply no fundamentally new methodological problems, because the operations used to define subject antecedents are essentially the same for both the phenomenologist and the Behaviourist. Wylie (1968) concludes, 'It does not seem to imply that a fundamental difference must obtain between behaviouristic and phenomenological research.' (p. 766)

The particular items included in a self-concept assessment

technique will affect the sort of score obtained. If the items concentrate on an area of life in which the individual displays little competence, say academic pursuits, then his self concept may appear rather negative; if the items relate to athletic activities in which he has considerable success then the evaluations will be far more positive. Therefore, a fairly broad range of items is necessary for the assessment of the general self concept, though this is not to deny that a sample of items from a specific category of behaviour can provide valuable information about a particular aspect of the individual's self concept. The use of questionnaire techniques to index self evaluation have provided an inaccurate impression that it can be viewed as global and fixed, i.e. that some people view themselves negatively *in toto* and others see themselves positively or anywhere in between. It is clear from the earlier discussion that such a global conception is erroneous and that individuals do possess many self conceptions, e.g. academic, physical, social, etc. Brookover, Thomas and Patterson (1964) and Barker Lunn's (1970) developments of academic self-concept scales are notable advances in this respect, as is the Body Cathexis Scale of Jourard and Secord (1954).

While many self-report techniques do circumscribe the range of aspects that subjects respond to, there is no way of knowing to what extent the limits of the measuring instrument imposed by the test's constructor prevents the subject from providing an accurate and full report of his self concept. However, open-ended techniques do not apparently solve this problem of restriction. Spitzer et al. (1966) asked subjects which of a range of self-concept measures they had taken allowed them to provide the most and least accurate descriptions of themselves. Forty per cent felt the open-ended instrument ('Who Are You?' Test) was the least accurate. Reasons given were that it strained their powers of introspection and that it lacked structure.

Self-report techniques and their limitations

'You never really understand a person until you consider things from his point of view – until you climb into his skin and walk around in it.' (*To Kill a Mockingbird*: Harper and Lee.)

This is an impossible counsel of perfection. Psychologists have to infer the self concept in other ways (*a*) by self-report techniques, i.e. what a person is willing to reveal about himself, and (*b*) by observation of the individual's behaviour. In other words we are faced with the inherent necessity of basing knowledge about the individual's self concept on the vagaries of introspection and/or of unknown bias in the observation and interpretation of overt behaviour. Combs, Soper and Courson (1963) have argued that most of the studies purporting to measure the self concept are not studies of the self concept at all; they are studies of the self report. These terms are not synonymous. Combs and Soper (1957) differentiate them clearly by emphasising that the self concept is how the individual sees himself, while the self report is what the individual is willing to say about himself to an outsider. How closely they will approximate would appear to depend on such factors as:

(*a*) the clarity of the individual's awareness;
(*b*) the availability of adequate symbols for expression;
(*c*) the willingness of the individual to cooperate;
(*d*) social expectancy;
(*e*) the individual's feeling of personal adequacy;
(*f*) his feelings of freedom from threat.

Similarly, Cattell (1946) indicates the following factors:

(*a*) 'lack of self knowledge . . .;
(*b*) distortion of responses by such factors as dishonesty, carelessness or ulterior motivation;
(*c*) lack of true measurement continuum;
(*d*) lack of understanding of what the question means.' (p. 342)

Firstly, lack of self knowledge will depend on the clarity of the subject's awareness, for some aspects of the self concept stand out in clear figure while others are immersed in ground. Whether or not they will be reported depends on whether they can be called into clear figure at that particular moment. Lack of clarity may also be of a more permanent character. Some aspects of the self concept may exist at minimal levels of awareness most of our lives, a shadowy, veiled penumbra of self ignorance. Degree of self insight does appear to be related to levels of education and intelligence (Vernon, 1963).

This leads to the second factor, the closely related question of the possession of the necessary symbols with which adequately to express the self concept. Self descriptions can only be reported in words. The individual may not possess a vocabulary of sufficient quantity and quality with which to express his self concept. Words may be inadequate in any case to convey the richness and subtleties inherent in human description. Again, words may not mean the same thing to one person as they mean to another – in essence a phenomenological problem. Self report is open to all the errors of human communication. Not only is verbal response a problem, especially in interviews but on rating scales too, where the meaning and interpretation of items causes difficulty. When faced with items such as, 'I have strange and peculiar thoughts' or 'I enjoy social situations' the subject's response is determined by his interpretation of 'strange', 'peculiar' and 'social situations'. For example, do 'social situations' refer to parties and functions, to working alongside others on tasks or to both? Responses may differ if the 'social situation' is seen as involving friends or mainly interaction with strangers. Even one-word trait – descriptive adjectives create situations where subjects differ in their interpretation. The description 'aggressive' may mean any of the following:

> inclined to start fights and quarrels;
> full of enterprise and initiative;
> pushing, energetic pursuit of one's ends;
> desire to dominate.

In short, for an individual to indicate that 'aggressive' is 'very much like me' may imply a wide range of things to different subjects. Another favourite term 'ambitious' can imply anything from 'hard-working', through 'wanting to advance' to 'disregarding the rights of others'. These examples are perhaps more than sufficient to suggest that any subject who should have the audacity to keep a dictionary by them while they complete a self-rating form will be thoroughly confused as to which particular definition is to be responded to! Hamid (1969) showed that anchoring procedures based on behavioural definitions of terms resulted in considerable agreement in concept meaning. This suggests that variation in individual interpretation of traits can be controlled to a great extent by adequate pre-chosen and stated definitions of the term used.

Thirdly, in society it is customary, and even sometimes necessary for the individual to hide his true beliefs. We are often well aware of the expectancies of others, and the things we say about ourselves are very much affected by this. Social expectancy will tend to distort self reports. Reference will be made later in this chapter to a major element in this problem, namely the social desirability response set.

Fourthly, the accuracy of the self report depends on the cooperation and motivation of the subject. If he wishes to deceive he can do so. He does not even have to reveal his lack of cooperation, if indeed he is even aware of it sometimes. Freedom from threat will decrease the necessity to defend the self, and reduce the need to resort to ego defence mechanisms in an attempt to obviate self knowledge.

Various attempts have been made to circumvent the difficulties of the self report by methods of forced choice or making subjects categorise statements about themselves. Notable among these methods is the Q technique of Stevenson (1953) which requires the subject to sort out a large number of self-referent statements into a series of piles to form a normal distribution. While such techniques force the subject to consider a number of self descriptions which he might otherwise avoid, many of the other variables still operate uncontrolled. Sophisticated statistical manipulation can never redress the built-in error.

Freeman (1950) looks at the positive side of self reports and claims that they are of inestimable value 'in so far as inventories actually get at aspects of personality that are beyond impressions made upon observers . . . they are the more valuable instruments' (p. 68). Self-report techniques are literally the only method available for measuring the self concept, and if they are to be rejected then psychology would be seriously limited. Psychology must concern itself with covert feelings in order to explain behaviour more adequately. At least the limitations and possibilities of such assessment techniques are known.

Other problems of self-concept measurement are the sort of problems that affect the measurement of any construct in the social sciences and relate to the basic rationale of the theory of measurement itself and the technical requirements of any research instrument. The essential demand is for acceptable levels of reliability and validity. While making no attempt to be too technical a brief consideration of reliability and validity is essential.

Reliability

No measurement instrument is perfect. The degree of error involved affects the dependability, consistency and accuracy of the instrument. Reliability is a measure of the accuracy and stability of a test. If a subject is given the same test on several occasions with a short time lapse between, say a couple of months, but obtains widely differing results from one occasion to another, then how are we to know which is the 'true' score? This test would be very unreliable. Only if very similar scores emerge would we accept the test as sufficiently reliable, accurate and stable. The simplest definition of reliability is the degree to which the testing instrument yields consistent scores when the test is applied a number of times to the same subjects. There are three empirical methods of estimating reliability:

(a) the correlation between scores on the same test given at different times (test–retest method);

(b) the correlation between two parallel forms of the same test given on the same occasion (alternate forms method);

(c) the correlation between comparable parts of the same test (the split-half method).

Each method has particular advantages and disadvantages. The test–retest method is affected by memory of specific items, by loss of motivation, by subjects missing the retest and by actual changes in the subject over the time interval. The usual time interval range is 1–3 months. The equivalent forms method is disadvantageous as it necessitates two forms of the same test and assumes that they are parallel. But they can be given on one sitting, thus eliminating many of the disadvantages of the test–retest method. The final approach has been to split the test in half after it has been taken, usually dividing it into odd- and even-numbered items. The scores from these halves are correlated as though they were two separate tests to demonstrate the degree of internal consistency, but this provides no measure of temporal consistency.

When the reliability of self-concept rating scales is reported at all, it is usually this split-half variety, so that time-associated errors indexed by the test–retest method are unmeasured. Only two longitudinal studies have become available, both of which suggest that the self concept can be measured reliably. Engel (1959) retested a group of adolescents 2 years after the original test. The overall correlation between these two occasions after legitimate statistical corrections was 0.78. Constantinople (1969) in her attempt to measure status and change in the self concept, categorised according to Erikson's psychosocial adolescent stage characteristics, found a 6-week test–retest correlation as high as 0.81 for intimacy with a median correlation of 0.70 for all the various measures. For personality measures these levels of reliability are fairly high!

Validity

Validity is simply the ability of the test to measure what it purports to measure. This immediately brings us face to face again with the difficulty of defining the self concept. The result is usually that the operational definition provided by the individual researcher becomes the major starting point in deciding what is actually being measured. There are a number of different types of validity. Content validity is concerned with whether the test possesses relevant content. As far as a self-concept test is concerned this is almost equivalent to face validity in that all the test need contain are items which require the elicitation of self-evaluative responses from subjects. Strong and Feder (1961) claim that every evaluative statement made by a person about himself can be considered a sample of his self concept. So this criterion for content and face validity appears easily met. Another type of validity is predictive validity which is the ability of the test to predict future behaviour or performance. For example, a reported positive academic self concept should be demonstrated by future high levels of academic motivation and success. Concurrent validity is a special case of predictive validity where the prediction is not for the future but in the here and now. For instance an adolescent with negative attitudes to his physical appearance is observed not to attend socials, dances or deliberately associate with peer-group members of the opposite sex. The lack of heterosexual and social behaviour validates concurrently the negative ratings made by the subject about body size, body shape and how he believes others perceive his physical attributes. All forms of predictive validity require an external criterion against which to validate the test. In the above examples these are academic success and avoidance or normal late-adolescent social behaviour.

It has been popular to try and demonstrate concurrent validity for self-concept scales by relating them to present levels of adjustment. Positive results are numerous in proving this relationship with an established variable. Calvin, Wayne and Holtzman (1953) had college students rank themselves on seven personality traits and found that self depreciation was related to high scores on the MMPI, which indicates a disturbed personality tending to the neurotic and even psychotic levels. Taylor and Combs (1952) tested the hypothesis that 12-year-olds found to be well adjusted on the California Test of Personality would more often admit statements of self reference that though unflattering were universally true. Hanlon, Hofstaetter and O'Connor (1954) compared the results of high school juniors on the California Test of Personality with the degree of congruence between the ratings of the cognised and ideal self, and found that the more congruence the greater the adjustment. Smith (1958) compared congruence between Q sorts for cognised self and ideal self with scores from the Edwards PPS and from Cattell's 16 FP. After making over 300 correlations he concluded that having a positive self concept is directly related to adjustment.

Attempts have been made to validate the self-concept scales concurrently against projective tests. Bills made several attempts to validate his scale by the Rorschach technique. However, the results were ambiguous and leave two observers, Cowen and Tongas (1959) rather dissatisfied. The TAT was used by Friedman (1955), to compare the Q-sort discrepancy of cognised self with the self as projected on to the TAT pictures. His normal subjects were the only group to project positive self qualities; neurotics and paranoids both projected negatively.

A different approach to concurrent validation of self-concept measures uses behaviour in a social situation as the criterion. The most sweeping results in this type of study are reported by Turner and Vanderlippe (1958) who found that Q-sort congruence between cognised self and the ideal self is greater in those college students who are more active in extra-curricular activities, who have higher scholastic averages and who are given higher sociometric rankings by fellow students. Eastman (1958) found

that the self ratings given on Bills' self-concept index positively
related to ratings for marital happiness. Chase (1957) discovered
that among maladjusted patients there was greater discrepancy
between Q sorts for cognised self and ideal self than between sorts
for average other person and ideal self. Another approach in
validating self-concept measures against adjustment arose out of
the collection of psychotherapy research studies reported by
Rogers and Dymond (1954). Change in self concept was found to
occur concurrently with improvement during psychotherapy. So,
overall, despite the varying forms of self-concept measures, it does
appear that the self concept has substantial concurrent validity
against a variety of other instruments.

Construct validity implies that the test supports theoretical
relationships. For instance, it is known that anxiety and
self-concept levels are related (e.g. Rosenberg, 1965). If a new
self-concept scale also demonstrates this same relationship to
anxiety then the test has construct validity as a measure of the self
concept. In order to prove construct validity one could use this
'known groups' technique where, in the above example, one would
look for minimum overlap of self-concept scores from neurotic and
non-neurotic groups.

A second approach to construct validity suggests that if various
self-concept scales are measuring the self concept then they should
all produce virtually the same results, i.e. intercorrelate highly,
because they are underlain by the same hypothetical construct. For
instance, self acceptance has been regarded as a synonym for self
esteem or evaluated self concept as measured by ratings scales, e.g.
Berger (1952). Self acceptance has also been indexed as the
discrepancy between cognised self and ideal self, e.g. Bills, Vance
and McLean (1951). To what extent these approaches provide
equivalent measures of self acceptance is doubtful for studies by
Bills (1958), Omwake (1954) and Cowen (1956) found
correlations varying from zero to +0.56 between a range of tests
all supposedly measuring the same concept, that of self acceptance.
Crowne, Stephens and Kelly (1961) intercorrelated six tests used
as self-acceptance indices by their various authors. The mean
intercorrelation was +0.52 ranging from +0.13 to +0.90. But
correlations with the Social Desirability Scale of Edwards (1957)
was as high and on occasions higher than correlations between
other self-acceptance measures. Thus the consistency between the
self-acceptance measures was due in considerable part to the
influence of social desirability. Wylie (1974) reports that of 93
cross-instrument correlations she examined only 7 which reached
as high as 0.80. All this evidence suggests that only very limited
construct validity exists for many self-concept tests. Of course this
is not unexpected with tests that attempt to assess a global or

overall self concept derived from varying theoretical formulations. But even where a more limited aspect of self perception is involved intercorrelations between scales still suggests that slightly different elements of the same aspect are being measured. In an unpublished study using 118 primary school pupils to compare four academic self-image scales, Reid (1976) found that the highest correlation for the whole sample was +0.7 between the Self Concept of Academic Ability Scale of Brookover, Erikson and Joiner (1967) and the Academic Self Image Scale of Barker Lunn (1970). Of all the other intercorrelations, which involved a subscale from the Self Esteem Inventory of Coopersmith (1967) and the Position in Class Scale of Willig (1973), none exceeded +0.34. Again, this suggests that construct validity is not too convincing, for the several scales are not equivalent in measuring academic self concept. If they were all measuring this single construct, intercorrelations would be much closer to unity.

Self presentation and disclosure

It has become recognised over the last 15 years that psychological research is a social interaction situation, and in order to interpret the obtained data a thorough investigation of the social interactions that permeated the research milieu ought to be performed. There is for example a 'demand characteristic' in psychological experiments whereby the subject tries to be a 'model' subject by behaving in the way he thinks the experimenter wants him to behave (Orne, 1962). This cooperative intent is unlikely to increase the chance of the subject responding more honestly on self-report instruments, for the subject's hunch as to what the experimenter is attempting to accomplish will bias his responses in unknown ways. Rosenberg (1969) has argued that subjects are motivated to present themselves as having favourable traits in order to gain approval from the experimenter. But this positive self presentation is not a universal systematic bias, for when trying to ingratiate themselves with lower-status persons, high-status subjects provide more modest self presentations than might be expected (Jones, 1964). Wylie (1974) notes, too, that it is commonly accepted that emphasising shortcomings is frequent in persons seeking counselling. Schneider (1969) demonstrates that when the experimental situation is manipulated to increase the subject's need for approval from other people, his self presentation increases in level of favourability. Such self-presentation variables creating various distortions in self-report instruments are at present unquantifiable but of vital importance. Some of these distorting variables have been catalogued as response sets.

Response sets

Response sets are consistent styles of responding to measurement instruments which have an undue influence on scores, distorting them in various and often unknown ways. Individual subjects tend to display the same response style across a wide variety of tests which creates positive correlations between tests due to this rather than to any real relationship between the variables being measured. While there are a considerable number of identifiable response styles (Fredericksen and Messick, 1959), the most pervasive in self-report techniques would seem to be acquiescence, and social desirability.

1. Acquiescence

This is a very important factor in self-report techniques where the respondent allocates his answer to an item, along a scale running from, for example, 'strongly agree' to 'strongly disagree', or 'mostly like me' to 'mostly unlike me'. Acquiescence is the tendency to agree so that if all statements are presented in a positive direction the subject's tendency to agree with items irrespective of their content may be represented in the total score to a high degree. This tends to cause spuriously high reliabilities as it is a systematic bias focused in one direction. On the other hand, acquiescence lowers validity since it is irrelevant to the criterion being measured and enables a subject to earn a different score from that he would have earned if the items had been presented with negative and positive statements in random order.

Studies on the acquiescence response set, or what Guilford (1954) called 'the error of the yes-man' (p. 231), show that up to 25 per cent of the variance, a sizeable component in other words, of test scores of scales whose statements are all worded in a single direction is due to acquiescence (Jackson and Messick, 1957; Couch and Kenniston, 1960). The best way of eliminating acquiescence is to include positively and negatively worded items in random order to prevent a subject merely ticking down the same column. This means that a subject has to indicate 'yes' to some items and 'no' to others in order to obtain a high score. But as there are only low correlations between a positive version of an item and its reversed form, the suggestion exists that reversed items are not necessarily the logical opposites of the original statement.

2. Social desirability

This is the tendency of subjects to attribute to themselves traits or characteristics which social consensus would indicate are socially desirable while rejecting those that are socially undesirable. For example, the statement 'I am an intelligent person' would be judged as socially desirable, whereas the statement, 'I resort to temper tantrums when I don't get my own way' would almost certainly be rated as socially undesirable by an independent group of judges. Hence, most subjects will endorse the former item but few would admit to the latter. This response set plagues the majority of personality investigations and is particularly active as a major source of error in self-report techniques. Though, as Mednick (1960) indicates, this is not always the case for some subjects go to the other extreme, attempting to paint themselves 'worse' or 'sicker' than they really are, e.g. neurotics are prone to exaggerate their defects. It is extremely easy to falsify responses so that a positive or good 'picture' is presented on a self-report test. This occurs especially when there is any incentive, for example to make a good impression on a superior, or gain selection, or when, as with self-concept studies, the evaluation is of the core area of the individual. Of course when items are subtle and ambiguous (in the sense that their meaning and relevance is not obvious) it is extremely difficult for the subject deliberately to present a particular picture of himself. However, with statements concerning the self concept it is exceedingly difficult to disguise their meaning and relevance.

While Edwards (1957; 1959) has shown there is a strong degree of correspondence between the independently judged social desirability of an item and the frequency of its endorsement by a group of subjects, this overall relationship hides big individual differences that exist in the influence of the social desirability of the items. Edwards offers no explanation on this point. The significance of such differences for personality have never been considered. When a subject scores highly on socially desirable items does this represent faking, self deception, or is he genuinely above average on socially desirable traits, or is it a combination of all these reasons? But in terms of the phenomenological approach to the self concept it is tempting to ask whether there is a problem here at all, for what a person believes about himself might not be objectively correct as judged by external observers but it is nonetheless true for him and motivates his behaviour. Thus, it can be argued that social desirability is a factor that is part of one's attitude to oneself. As Wylie (1961) admits, 'No way has been worked out to determine in what cases and under what circumstances the social desirability variable distorts individual self reports away from validity in reflecting S's phenomenal field.' (p. 28)

Vernon (1963), however, indicates that many more 'unpleasant' symptoms are admitted when self-report tests are answered anonymously and also claims that, 'highly educated persons such as students are often self analytic and introspective, more self depreciatory than non-academics' (p. 202). This same observation was interpreted by Loevinger and Ossorio (1959) as indicating that the better-educated person is more aware of himself. Counselling conditions also tend to reduce social desirability where subjects voluntarily attend with strong motivation to be candid to facilitate their 'recovery'. More subjects also respond 'no' to an undesirable item than 'yes' to its reversed form where it then describes desirable and acceptable behaviour.

The most effective way to counter social desirability is to apply the forced choice technique as adopted by Edwards in his Personal Preference Schedule, in which alternative answers to each item are equated for social desirability or frequency of endorsement as assessed by a body of independent judges. Total scores will still contain some element of social desirability, but it is considerably reduced.

The discrepancy score

Many studies investigating self conception and its correlates have made use of a data-manipulation technique which results in what has been termed a 'discrepancy score'. For example, a potentially fruitful and commonly accepted clinical hypothesis is the formulation that a discrepancy between an individual's conception of his cognised self and his ideal self is indicative of maladjustment and that as psychotherapy proceeds the discrepancy between the two selves should decrease, e.g. Bills, Vance and McLean (1951), Rosen (1956) and Worchel (1957). To obtain a discrepancy index between the cognised and ideal selves two similar methodological procedures have been commonly employed. One method consists in having an individual rate a number of personality traits on, say, a seven-point rating scale, under two instructional conditions. The person is asked first to rate his conception of his self as he is, and secondly to rate his notion of his self as he would like to be. The discrepancy measure is provided by the absolute sum of the differences between the pairs of trait items on the cognised self and ideal self ratings. Another procedure for obtaining an operational index of discrepancy has been through the Q technique in which the individual performs two Q sorts, a real self sort and an ideal self sort. The correlation between these two Q sorts provides the index of discrepancy. The lower the correlation, the greater the degree of maladjustment implied. That is, there is claimed to be an inverse relationship between maladjustment and self acceptance. After reviewing the literature in detail, McCandless (1967) concluded:

most research evidence indicates that people who are highly self-critical – that is who show a large discrepancy in the way they actually see themselves and the way they ideally would like to be – are less well adjusted than those who are at least moderately satisfied with themselves . . . evidence indicates that people experience conflict about the traits on which they have the greatest self-ideal discrepancy and that this conflict is strong enough to interfere with learning involving such areas. (p 280)

But there is some question whether the discrepancy is satisfactory from a measurement point of view and whether it is really all that different from the topic of positive and negative self concepts. Firstly, it is not known how much variance is contributed by each part to the variance in scores on this dual index. Secondly, there is considerable evidence (Bills, Vance and McLean, 1951; Jourard and Secord, 1955b; Rapaport, 1958) that there is very little intersubject variability on ideal self-concept ratings. This evidence of stereotyping, found in ideal ratings and ideal Q sorts, implies that the ideal self contributes very much less variance to discrepancy scores and correlations than actual self responses. If this is the case, such a measure then merely demonstrates a discrepancy between the subject's concept of himself as he is and the cultural norm. Wylie (1961) argues strongly that this is so and therefore the indexing of self acceptance and possible areas of inadequate adjustment can be reliably inferred from a subject's attitudes to himself as he is. Other difficulties can be noted in the use of two-part indices. A discrepancy score or an r of any value can be composed of innumerable combinations of item discrepancies. If absolute summing, i.e. irrespective of discrepancy direction, has been performed, it is impossible to know whether the subject's idea is above or below his actual self on particular items. Such summing without regard to sign is questionable.

   In view of these doubts and difficulties it would appear that a single index is preferable and even superior to a dual index. Actual self concepts distribute themselves on a normal curve while ideal self concepts produce an extremely negative skew (McCandless, 1967), as would be fully expected since the ideal self reflects the culturally desirable. It is not unsurprising to find that everyone ideally wants to be intelligent, physically attractive, good, happy, etc. Thus, most of the information to be gained from computing such a discrepancy score is already present in the variation of the cognised self scores (Schuldermann and Schuldermann, 1969). McCandless (1967) shows that the distribution of the discrepancy scores follows fairly faithfully the distribution of the original cognised self scores. All that appears to be happening is the subtracting of a wide range of self-concept scores from a relatively homogeneous constant. This lack of variation in ideal self judgements between individuals is an effect of the social desirability response set which has less of an influence on cognised self ratings.

Some of the inconsistencies between various studies relating maladjustment to self-ideal self discrepancies is shown by Kenny (1956) to be the result of failure to control this obtrusive variable of social desirability. For instance while studies by Bills (1953) and Roberts (1952) offer some positive support for the hypothesis that a discrepancy between cognised and ideal self is an index of personality disturbance, Zimmer's (1954) investigation yielded negative results. Kenny (1956) demonstrated that social desirability operates in a significant fashion across a range of personality evaluation techniques including rating scales and Q sorts, with correlations averaging around +0.82 between social desirability of an item and the probability of its endorsement. Similar high correlations between cognised self and ideal self must also reflect the intrusion of the social-desirability variable. So unless the social-desirability variable is controlled, the specific variance in the difference score between cognised self and ideal self will be negligible because social desirability will cancel out any reliable difference between the two selves. The net effect of an inflated correlation between the two selves is to reduce specific variance and to increase error variance in the discrepancy score. Thus, it becomes fruitless to investigate whether or not a discrepancy index is related to personality maladjustment if social desirability produced a high correlation between real self and ideal self.

Since control of social desirability is indispensable in these discrepancy indices, it might be better in view of the other arguments raised against them by Wylie to avoid their use completely. Additionally, Judd and Smith (1974) found that factor analyses of cognised self concepts and ideal self concepts of 445 students revealed different factors underlying the two selves. This raises serious questions about the appropriateness of computing discrepancy scores unless both concepts can be shown to possess similar factor structures.

Assessment of the self concept

There are two general methods that can be employed to measure the self concept of individuals.

1. By enabling the individual to report on himself in responding to test items, his self concept or some specific element of it can be indexed, usually in the form of a score. This paper and pencil method is applicable to individual and group administration.
2. The individual self concept can be inferred from behaviour observed by a single or set of external observers. This approach is usually limited to individual assessment.

(a) Self-report methods of assessing the self concept

Of the many possible self-report methods that could be utilised to elicit an individual's self description six methods, described below, dominate the research literature on the self concept.

1. Ratings scales:
These can be in the form of questionnaires, inventories and attitude to self scales. In general this method consists of providing a set of statements such as:

> I am a lazy person.
> I always get good marks in tests.
> I am easily irritated by people who argue with me.
> I don't question my worth as a person.

The subject responds to each statement by endorsing the degree to which the item applies to or characterises him along a defined scale with usually three, five or even more points on it. These points are usually labelled from 'never' or 'seldom' at one end of the scalar continuum to 'very often' or 'most of the time'. The values of the ratings are then used as numerical weights to arrive at a total score for all the items, for example:

	1	2	3	4	5
I feel worthless	Never	Rarely	Sometimes	Frequently	Always

	5	4	3	2	1
I am tolerant	Strongly agree	Agree	Neither agree nor disagree	Disagree	Strongly disagree

The most frequently used approach in measuring the self concept has been this rating scale technique adopting usually a Likert model which is entirely appropriate to and concordant with the argument posited in Chapter 3 that placed the self concept within the ambit of attitude study. Regarded as a set of attitudes towards the self, what techniques could be regarded as more apropos for assessment purposes than recognised and acceptable attitude scale techniques? Wylie (1961; 1968) has provided thorough surveys of published research on the self concept utilising rating scales, and has indicated that most of these studies have been inconclusive because of flaws in design. She described (1961) 80 instruments of the rating scale and questionnaire type, most of which were used once only, and for which published reliability information exists for only one-third of them. Many were clinical samples containing very small numbers of cases, and have been one-shot affairs without replication or cross-validation of instruments.

The rating scale produces a total score which is usually obtained by summing the rating assigned to each item. This summation process tends to obliterate the uniqueness of individual item responses and thus obscure important clues to certain elements of self perception. Inherent in the ratings process is the assumption that all the items on the questionnaire are equal in importance in the calculation of the total score. This technique is contaminated more than others by response sets such as acquiescence and social desirability. The 'halo' effect or the carryover effect from one item to the other is also prevalent.

2. The check list.
By this method the individual merely checks the appropriate adjectives or statements that describe himself. Only those items are checked that apply to the subject. It is essentially a yes/no response scale. The all or none checking prevents any determining of the degree of involvement that the items have for the individual. Thus the Likert-type rating scale is preferable as it provides more data.

3. Q sorts.
The sorting of statements about the self concept on cards has had considerable vogue. It is an easy, interesting and motivating task which has been used with children (Staines, 1954) and clinical cases (Butler and Haigh, 1954). This sorting technique developed by Stevenson(1953) is called the Q sort. The most extensively used set of Q-sort items for indexing the self concept is the group of 100 self-referent items derived from therapeutic protocols and used by Butler and Haigh (1954). These personality descriptive items which tend to be very general assertions and not situationally specific, e.g. 'I am shy', are sorted by the subject into nine piles which are arranged on a continuum according to the degree to which the subject claims they are characteristic of himself. The subject is forced by the instructions to place a specified number of items into each pile so as to yield a quasi-normal distribution of items. These items can be sorted again into nine piles on a continuum according to the degree to which they are characteristic of his ideal for himself, or of how he believes others view him. Each item in the sort can be assigned a value of from one to nine depending on the pile in which the subject has placed it. It is essentially a nine-point rating scale with items forced into a normal distribution. With 150 statements each on a card the subject would be requested to sort the 150 cards into the following distribution:

	Most like me ◄───────────► Least like me							
No. of cards	4	9	16	26	40	26	19	9	4
Scale value	9	8	7	6	5	4	3	2	1

An individual may do several sorts under different instructions, e.g. self concept, ideal self, mother's self concept, wife's self concept, etc. Rapid calculation of correlation coefficients are possible between several sortings of one individual or between one sorting each by several subjects. If correlations between subjects are close to +1.0 then they have highly similar self concepts; a low or negative correlation identifies differences in self concept which can be considered in detail by inspecting the distribution of the cards. The problem is that many sets of Q sorts have been used once only. For 20 out of 22 sets described by Wylie (1961) no information regarding validity is available and for 16 of the sets no published reliability data is presented. As an individual technique it is a lengthy and time-consuming one.

4. Unstructured and free response methods.
In these the subject is required to provide material about himself, usually by completing sentences or writing an essay. In the former the subject is presented with a number of incomplete statements which he is requested to complete. For example he might be given:

I am . . .
When I am with other adolescents I . . .
I cannot . . .
I am always happy when . . .
I am afraid when . . . .

In the unstructured composition the subject is asked to write an essay on 'Myself'. Both these approaches provide problems in the analysis and quantification of the data. Jersild (1952) and Strang (1957) have both based their major researches on the unstructured essay.

The value of free response or unstructured techniques lies in the removal of the restriction imposed by the rating scale technique where the subject is forced to choose among limited alternatives to circumscribed questions causing the subject to provide a response that doesn't accurately reflect his feelings. But the freedom to respond brings with it the corollary that classification of responses becomes very difficult. The projective quality of the obtained responses means that the scoring procedure rests for the most part on the subjective judgement of the scorer himself despite the application of pre-selected categories. The scorer must still decide if a response fits into one category or another. Validity is difficult to ascertain and face validity is often the only form advanced.

5. Projective techniques.
Some researchers have attempted to use projective techniques to measure the unconscious self concept, e.g. Friedman, 1955; Mussen and Jones, 1957; Linton and Graham, 1959. They use this

approach because they believe unconscious aspects are pertinent to self theories. They reason that a range of measures from the phenomenal field provides an incomplete inventory of relevant variables on which the subject's behaviour is based and some important characteristics of the subject are unavailable to his awareness. Theorists point out that much important learning occurs preverbally, and the need to maintain a positive self concept might lead to denial and repression.

Although research on unconscious self attitudes is quite limited, it does indicate that most people evaluate themselves more highly unconsciously than consciously. Epstein (1955) for instance found severely disturbed mental patients revealed more favourable unconscious self concepts than did normal subjects, though the latter possessed more favourable conscious self concepts. But it will take imaginative research work to probe beneath what a person is willing and able to communicate directly. Such projective approaches pose a unique problem. To prove a certain projective response or score represents an unconscious attitude towards the self; it is necessary to prove not only that the subject holds this attitude but also that he is unaware of it. No researcher appears to have checked to see if the same attitude might be consciously present. Only if inferences from self report and the projective measures differ, are there any grounds for exploring the more complex assumption that the latter is exposing an unconscious self attitude. In any case, projective techniques are in a far more parlous state than the more commonly used ratings and attitude scales for indexing self attitudes in respect of reliability, validity and interpretation.

6. Interviews.
This method is very apparent in counselling and in psychotherapeutic studies of the self concept and self-concept change. The client-centred approach of Carl Rogers with its open-ended encounter is a typical example. This aspect of self-concept assessment will be detailed in Chapter 8 where client-centred therapy is discussed.

(b) Assessment of self concept by observation

The rationale for the observation of human behaviour has been traditionally to ensure the observer is passive, uninvolved and as detached as possible to prevent the observed person being disrupted and being too aware of the observation process which might cause him to display different behaviour from that if no observer had been present. The aim was to attain objective perception of the individual's typical behaviour. The observer was a camera impersonally making a faithful record of human events.

More recently Combs (1965) has argued that this classical approach to observation is restrictive and frustrating in self-concept investigation because 'of a mistaken belief that observation must be made objectively' (p. 64). He would substitute sensitivity as the major criterion with the observer looking for reasons for behaviour rather than at behaviour itself. Combs (1965) continues by explaining,

I have given up asking my students to make coldly factual detailed reports. I now ask them to do what I do myself when I watch a child behaving or a teacher teaching – to get the feel of what's going on, to see if they can get inside the skin of the person being observed to understand how things look from his point of view. I ask them, 'what do you think he is trying to do?' 'how do you suppose he feels?', 'how would you have to feel to behave like that?' and so on. (p. 66)

It seems that Combs' approach strives to maximise exploration, involvement and sensitivity to the individual. The optimum approach to observing behaviour is to aim for objectivity in observation then allow sensitivity, experience and empathy to play a larger part in forming more subjective inferences. Complete objectivity by an observer is impossible. Every observer brings to bear on his observations meanings and inferences derived from his own past experiences, expectations and attitudes, some of the last being his attitudes towards the person being observed. Before drawing inferences about anyone it is always advisable to pose this question to yourself, 'how do I feel about this person?'

Observations invariably commence with appearance. We can become aware very readily of the subject's height, weight, posture, grooming, cleanliness, physical disabilities and the clothes he wears. Next we can take note of his speech, movement, habits, facial expressions, reactions and manners. We must be particularly on the qui vive for subtle, often fleeting clues which tell us how he relates to his peer group and to other groups, watching for the things he seeks to avoid as well as the things he seeks out, his reactions to success, failure, approval, disapproval. This evidence is the raw material from which inferences are drawn. But it is essential to remember that it is the subject's perception and evaluation of these elements rather than any objective statement of observations by an outsider which is necessary for our understanding of him since it is the former which influence the subject's behaviour.

Observations can be structured by providing the observer with a checklist and rating scale covering various attributes and behaviours. But this technique can blind the observer to other characteristics and behaviours which are important for that subject but which have not been included in the observer's tasks. Once behaviour and appearance have been observed then inference is possible. Inference has been demonstrated by Courson (1965) to be a valuable scientific tool with high inter-observer reliability. On the basis of observations, one can then ask 'are the subject's beliefs about himself generally positive or negative?', 'what are some of the main beliefs he holds about himself?', 'which beliefs are central, most value laden, most resistant to change?' 'what problems does he have and what is his most pressing problem now?. The answers to such questions as these will lead us to an inferred self concept. Such inferences from behaviour may lead to a better understanding of a subject's self concept since behaviour constitutes a larger sample of human performance than a restricted list of self-report statements provided by the research worker. This approach uses the observer as the test instrument. The inferred self concept obtained in this way is based on the assumption that if behaviour is a function of perception by observing behaviour it should prove possible to infer the characteristics of the perceptions that produced the behaviour.

This 'reading behaviour backward' escapes most of the sources of error indicated for the introspective self report but, of course, it does not produce a perfect relationship to the self concept either. Such inferences have been the stock-in-trade of the clinical psychologist. Their accuracy as self-concept descriptions will be dependent upon the sensitivity and skill of the observer. Such skill and sensitivity, however, are subject to training and so lie far more within the control of the experimenter than does the subjects' self reports. It may therefore be presumed on logical grounds that the inferred self concept is probably a much more accurate measure of the self concept than the subject's self report.

That there is only a slight relationship between self report and inferred self concepts has been demonstrated by Combs, Soper and Courson (1963) who obtained a mean correlation of only +0.114 for 18 test items. However, their self-report scale was created specifically for the study and no reliability and validity coefficients are reported. The sample was small, consisting of only 59 children. Parker (1966) also studied the differences between self reports made by children and their self concepts as inferred from their behaviour. His results support the earlier claims of Combs and Soper (1957), for even under conditions of anonymity a correlation of only +0.25 between the two methods was found. However, the sample was only 30 strong and the rating scale used was devised solely for the study and had no reported reliability or validity. It is difficult to know how much faith can be placed in the findings of these two studies.

This chapter has been aimed at cautioning readers not to be over-enthusiastic in seizing an instrument to measure the self concept without due regard to limitations inherent in self-report techniques. Certainly the self-report technique is a much simpler

and more direct device than inference. It also lends itself to
accepted research designs and to the application of well-tried
statistical techniques. But despite such advantages self reports may
obscure understanding since they may not give valid reflections of
subjects' self concepts. We must continually be alive to the possible
masquerade of the self concept, disguised in a fanciful outfit of
defence mechanisms, social acceptability, lack of insightfulness,
ulterior motivation and downright deceit. Scores must be
interpreted in a guarded manner. Because of different theoretical
stances and definitions, research studies test instruments may be
looking at subtly different elements of self conception without
readers being made aware of the particular interpretation implicit
in the study. The degree of confidence that can be given to many
of the instruments used is questionable, with many 'one-shot'
efforts lacking acceptable validity and reliability indices, if reported
at all!

It is pointless, however, to argue over what is a person's 'real'
self concept since we have to depend on operational definitions.
The validity of any approach is governed by its utility as a
predictor of behaviour. Personal meaning and interpretation are far
more fundamental to self-concept investigation than truthfulness.
By recognising such limitations associated with self reporting, we
are also recognising that self-concept assessment is not an exact
and precise science and must imply approximation. But this is no
different from assessment of most psychological constructs. For
example, no psychologist now accepts that an intelligence score is
precise; it registers an approximate level of academic aptitude. This
approximation in self-concept assessment allows, as with other
constructs, the practitioner to make use of the information as a
guide rather than as a prescriptive device, and employ sensitivity
and caution in judging complex individuals rather than jumping to
erroneous conclusions.

Summary

A survey of assessment techniques for measuring the self concept
reveals:

(a) a general picture of inadequate research designs and testing
instruments most without any reported reliability and validity
indices;
(b) a necessary basis in self-report techniques with weaknesses in
the data in that it requires the subject to report truthfully and
willingly;
(c) self-report techniques employed are:
(i) rating scales – the most frequently used technique,

    (ii) Q sorts,
   (iii) projective methods,
   (iv) unstructured essays and sentence completion,
   (v) interviews;
(*d*) reliability (temporal) where reported is consistently above
    0.70;
(*e*) cognised self-ideal, self-discrepancy index is regarded as
    statistically questionable and redundant;
(*f*) social desirability and acquiescence are recognised as pervasive
    sources of error which can be reduced to a minimum by
    employing suitable techniques;
(*g*) concurrent validation of self-concept measures where reported
    is satisfactory against other measures of maladjustment.

Further reading

Wylie, R. *The Self Concept,* Lincoln: Univ. of Nebraska Press, 1961. This
book provides an extremely detailed but rather technical account of the
problems of self-concept measurement.

Chapter 5

A survey of specific instruments

This chapter presents and reviews a variety of specific instruments which have been employed in self-concept studies. While each instrument is described in brief, for full details readers must consult the original sources. In appraising these instruments readers must also continually bear in mind the backcloth of measurement problems considered in the preceding chapter.

The following instruments have been chosen on the basis of several criteria.

1. They should be suitable for and reflect the full age range from pre-school children to adults.
2. A range of techniques, i.e. self report, projective, pictorial, topological and direct observation should be represented.
3. They should have been designed with the so-called 'normal' population in mind rather than a psychopathological population.
4. They have enough information accompanying them to enable investigators to find the sources, judge their value and use them effectively.

However, a few have been included which need to be applied with caution until more research and development is carried out on them. Moreover, nearly all the scales need standardising and even rewording for British subjects. *Caveat emptor* should be the watchword of any social scientist choosing a self-concept measuring instrument.

A. General self-concept/self-esteem measures

1. Self-esteem inventory

Source: Coopersmith (1967)
Type of measure: Rating scale (2-point)
Age range: 10–16 year olds

Description.
The scale was specifically devised for a research study (Coopersmith, 1967). The full form of the scale contains 58 items

and has a test–retest reliability over a 5-week period with 10-year-old children of 0.88 and over a 3-year interval with a different sample of 55 students a reliability of 0.70 was recorded. A shortened version of 25 items correlates 0.86 with the full version (Argyle and Lee, 1972). The full scale can be divided into four subscales, viz. social, peers, parents, academic.

Some items were derived from the Butler–Haigh Q sort (1954) reworded for children; other items were devised by the author. All the items in the scale were agreed upon by expert judges as reflecting either high or low self esteem, and then were pre-tested for comprehensibility on a small sample of children.

In an analysis of the SEI, Edgar et al. (1974) using 816 12–14-year-old children, the four subscales (social self, peers, home–parents, academic) were found to be internally consistent (alpha coefficients ranging from 0.58 to 0.89). An alpha coefficient of 0.87 was reported for the total scale. A factor analysis revealed one dominant factor which suggests that a global self-esteem measure can be obtained quite validly from the inventory. Test–retest reliability of full and subscales appeared quite high, but were only reported in mean score terms. Thus the four subscales appear justifiable. Using another 107 13–14 year olds, the high internal consistency of the four subscales and total scale was demonstrated again.

The subjects are requested to tick each statement either as 'like me' or 'unlike me'. The statements tap a wide area of self conception and are written in positive and negative forms to obviate the acquiescence response set. Connell and Johnson (1970) found that for early adolescent males high sex role identification was related to high self-esteem scores. Boshier (1968) reports correlations around +0.8 between self-esteem scores and liking one's first name. Trowbridge (1970) confirmed her prediction that pupils taught by teachers who had undertaken a training programme to sensitise them to individuals would have higher self-esteem scores. On the same lines Purkey, Graves and Zelner (1970) found higher self-esteem scores in 'humanistic' than in 'traditional' schools. The short form was used by Hawkins (1972) in an investigation of career aspirations of small samples of English and West Indian 14–16-year-old Nottingham pupils. He was able to discern that his English schoolboys had a significantly higher mean level of self esteem than the West Indian boys ($p < 0.001$). The full scale may be consulted in Coopersmith (1967).

2. Self-social symbols task

Source: Long, Ziller and Henderson (1968); Long, Henderson and Ziller (1967); Ziller et al. (1969); Ziller (1973)
Type of measure: Non-verbal topological representation
Age range: 3 years to adult

Description.
This topological approach was employed as a non-verbal test to remove the restrictions imposed by verbal problems associated with the subjects' understanding of statements and trait lists, especially where children are concerned. Many subjects are not necessarily articulate about their conception of themselves or their environment, and the subjects' labels for their constructs mean what the examiner interprets them to mean. Moreover, such non-verbal techniques obviate the social desirability response set. In the non-verbal method designed by Long and her colleagues, the subject selects and arranges symbols to represent himself in relation to other salient people. The assumption is made that individuals are able to communicate various aspects of their self concepts and their self–social interactions by topological representation. The Self–Social Symbols Task provides the following measures:

1. Self esteem – this is defined as the value or importance attributed to the self in comparison with others. This dimension was conceived of as a rank-ordering of persons, in which the self may assume a position ranging from first to last. The measure of self esteem consisted of a row of eight circles representing individuals. The subject is asked to select one of the circles to represent himself. Positions to the left were assumed to represent a higher degree of self esteem. This assumption was supported by a finding of Morgan (1944) that the stimulus to the left in a row of stimuli was ranked as more important than those appearing further to the right.

Evidence supporting the validity of this task was found in an earlier study (Henderson, Long and Ziller, 1965) in which children arranged various arrays of people into rows. To a significant degree ($p < 0.001$) the 'smartest' child was placed to the left, and the 'dumbest' and 'bad' child to the right. In a second array, mother and father were placed to the left and teacher and neighbour to the right ($p < 0.001$). In the third group 'home' and 'school' were placed to the left, 'pencil' and 'game' to the right ($p < 0.001$). Further evidence of validity was provided by a sample of 48 children who placed the self significantly ($p < 0.02$) further left among a group of children than they did among a group of adults. The findings that neuropsychiatric patients placed the self significantly further to the right than did normals ($p < 0.001$) (Ziller, Megas and De Cenio, 1964), and that sociometric isolates placed the self significantly ($p < 0.005$) further to the right than did sociometric stars (Ziller, Megas and De Cenio, 1964) also supported the validity of this task.

2. Power – this is in relation to certain authority figures, and measures self as superior, equal or inferior to the other person. In the measures of power, a higher position on the vertical plane was assumed to represent greater power. This assumption was supported by the findings of Osgood, Suci and Tannenbaum (1957) that ratings on a 'high–low' dimension had a high loading on a 'power' factor. It was also consistent with a cultural metaphor associating power with a 'high' position. In this task, subjects are given a circle representing the self which is surrounded by a semicircle of other circles. The subjects are asked to select a circle to represent another person (father or teacher, in the present study), (1) directly above, (2) diagonally above, (3) even with, (4) diagonally below, or (5) directly below the circle representing the self. The responses were scored from one to five, with a higher score indicating a lower position for the other person. Evidence supporting the validity of this task was found in an earlier study in which three samples of eighth-graders ($Ns = 83, 60, 76$, respectively) placed teacher in a significantly higher position ($p<0.01$ in all cases) than friend (Ziller and Long, 1964.)

3. Individuation – this is defined as the degree to which a person differentiates himself from his peers. The extremes of this dimension were considered to be 'like' and 'different from' others. Our measure of individuation included a large circular area containing a randomly placed array of small circles, representing 'other children'. The subject was asked to select one of two circles at the bottom of the page to represent himself. The choice of a circle 'different' from those representing peers (i.e. shaded) was interpreted as a higher degree of individuation.

Evidence supportive of validity was found in an unpublished study in which 27 pairs of twins chose significantly fewer ($p<0.05$) of the 'different' circles to represent the self than did a control group of non-twins matched for sex, age and class in school. Children who had moved frequently were also found to represent the self significantly ($p<0.05$) more often as 'different' than those who had lived in a single community all their lives (Ziller and Long, 1964).

4. Identification – identification of the self with particular other persons was defined as the placement of the self in a 'we' category with the other person. Heider (1958) has suggested that when a person indicates that two objects 'belong together', it may be assumed that a concept relates them. Thus, placing the self in close proximity to the other person was assumed to indicate a high degree of identification with him.

Two kinds of tasks measuring identification were included in this study. In the first, the subject was presented with two gummed circles (a red one for the self, and a green one for friend). He was asked to paste them on a blank sheet of paper in any way he likes.

The distance between the circles was measured in centimetres, with less distance assumed to represent more identification. In a second task, the subject is presented with a row of circles with another person (mother, father, teacher) located on the circle to the extreme left. He is then asked to select one of the remaining circles to represent the self. In this task, distance is measured by counting the number of circles intervening between the self and other, with less distance again assumed to indicate more identification.

Evidence supporting the validity of this latter task has been found. Children living in fatherless homes were found to be significantly less identified with father ($p<0.02$) than children of the same age and socioeconomic class whose fathers were present in the home. A second finding was that children rated by their teachers as being 'shy with teacher' were significantly less identified with teacher ($p<0.05$) than those rated as 'friendly with teacher'.

5. *Social dependency* – this is the degree to which the person perceives himself as a part of a group of others, as opposed to a perception of the self as a separate entity. It was thought that tendencies towards the group may reflect either succorant or affiliative motives. In the measure of social dependency, the subject is presented with a paper containing three circles (representing parents, teachers and friends) arranged as the apexes of an equilateral triangle. He is then given a gummed circle representing self and asked to paste it anywhere on the paper – only not on top of any of the other circles. Location of the self within, rather than outside of the triangular area is assumed to reflect a perception of the self as dependent upon, or as part of, the group of others.

6. *Centrality* – this is the degree to which the person adopts an inward rather than an outward orientation. The subject is asked to draw a circle to represent the self and one to represent a friend within a large circle, labelling each appropriately. The placement of the self closer than the other to the centre of the circle is assumed to represent greater self centrality, perhaps partly because the circle nearest the centre is ordinarily the one drawn first. Supporting the validity of these assumptions are the findings that both adult neuropsychiatric patients and emotionally disturbed children placed the self more often in the central position ($p = 0.05$ and 0.001, respectively) than did normal controls, as did sociometric isolates in comparison with sociometric stars ($p = 0.005$), and children who had moved frequently from community to community as compared with those who had lived in but a single community ($p = 0.01$).

7. *Complexity* – this is the degree of differentiation of the self concept. In the 10 complexity items, arrays of three figures varying in complexity, are presented to the subject. He selects one of the figures to represent the self, with a higher score associated with more complex figures. This item is relatively new. One recent finding is that, among a sample of high-achieving fifth graders, the 'good' readers (on the basis of the Iowa Tests of Basic Skills) represented the self as more complex than did the 'poor' readers ($p=0.001$).

All these tasks involve non-verbal responses and oral instructions. The test is designed for group administration and takes around 30 minutes to complete. The test comes in four variants, adult, student, adolescent and pre-school to 10 years. The latter variant involves the young child sticking on gummed shapes or pointing to a circle. Reliability of the adolescent form for self esteem = 0.08; identification = 0.78; social interest = 0.84; power = 0.65; centrality = 0.58.

The value of this test is that it is non-verbal and capable of being used with young children. But it may only be valid for cultures that read and order their qualities in a left to right and an up to down sequence.

A major disadvantage of this set of tasks is that the authors allude to many diverse theories in incomplete ways to provide a theoretical rationale to underpin the tasks. This produces somewhat of a ragbag of ideas without any explicit stand being taken on any theory. Neither is there any evidence to suggest that responses on non-verbal tasks are any less influenced by various distorting influences than are verbal tasks. There is in fact some overlap and confusion between the tasks. For instance a horizontal row of circles is presented to measure both self esteem and identification. In the former task the left–right dimension indexes self esteem, with the circle on the far left being the index of highest self esteem, self esteem decreasing with each circle next on the right. In the latter task, however, the far left circle is designated as say 'Father', with identification measured in terms of the subject's choice of 'self' circle to 'Father' circle. Hence, two interpretations are derived from the same layout.

However, it is an unusual, simple and ingenious method, and its potential warrants its being investigated and refined further. Wylie (1974) has already reported on a large number of validity studies supporting the tasks' rationales as well as noting satisfactory reliability indices.

3. Perception score sheet

Source: Combs and Soper (1963)
Type of measure: Observation schedule
Age range: 4–7 year olds

Description

It is designed for use by trained personnel to evaluate the self perceptions of children and their perceptions of other significant persons in their environment. There are 39 items or areas on which each child is rated, using a five-point scale. Most items are described and clarified, as in the following example of perceptions of self.

Adequate–inadequate: This category refers to the child's overall feeling of adequacy. It represents a global feeling of being fulfilled, enough, sufficient, as contrasted to feeling ineffectual, lacking, or the like. It should be recognised that it is possible for a child to feel generally adequate while at the same time possibly feeling inadequate with respect to some individual items on our checklist.

The items are grouped as follows: perception of self, self as instrument, self with other children, self with adults, self with teachers, self and the school curriculum, perceptions of others, perception of children, perception of adults, perception of teachers, perception of school. This observation schedule seems appropriate for most primary school children, although Combs and Soper used it only with kindergarten pupils.

Scores of the kindergarten group were factor analysed. Only 6 of the 39 items showed communalities of less than 0.70, indicating a high level of reliability for the scales. The strongest factor included 37 of the 39 items on the schedule, and accounts for 67 per cent of the total variance of the 39 items. The next strongest factor accounts for only 9 per cent of the variance.

4. Self-concept report scale

Source: Combs, Soper and Courson (1963)
Type of measure: Rating scale
Age range: Adolescent

Description

It is a simple scale of 18 pairs of positive and negative statements about self, arranged on a five-point scale. Examples of the 18 statements are:

People like to have me around, People don't care if I'm there or not. Teachers like me pretty well. Teachers don't like me much. I don't think I'm brave, I think I'm a brave person.
I'm not much good at sports and games. I'm good at sports and games.

Scale items are randomised so that positive and negative statements do not always run in the same direction. No labels or descriptions are placed on the five-point digit spread so that the values invested in the scale are more likely to be personal than externally suggested. No reliability is reported. Validity assessed in terms of concurrent validity against the criterion of inferred self concept (by teachers) was not statistically significant. The scale requires further research work before it is suitable for general application.

5. Self-concept scale

Source: Lipsitt (1958)
Type of measure: Adjective rating scale
Age Range: 9–16 year olds

Description
Lipsitt's instrument contains 22 adjectives describing personal attributes which are prefaced with 'I am'. This scale in terms of word difficulty and instructions would seem appropriate for older primary school children and lower secondary age levels. Each trait-descriptive adjective is rated on a five-point scale. Adjectives such as 'friendly', 'honest' and 'lazy' were employed. The rating categories scored from 1 to 5 were respectively 'not at all', 'not very often', 'some of the time', 'most of the time' and 'all of the time'. Three negative traits were scored in the reverse order. The score was obtained by summing the ratings with lower scores reflecting a degree of self disparagement. Lipsitt used this scale to measure ideal as well as cognised self by altering the preface to 'I would like to be'. In his work Lipsitt employed the much-criticised discrepancy index to provide a measure of adjustment, which he correlated with anxiety scores to demonstrate a relationship between self disparagement and anxiety. He found that actual self scores provided a stronger correlation with anxiety (i.e. low self–high anxiety) than did the discrepancy scores. Lipsitt computed test–retest reliabilities for his scale over a 2-week interval of between 0.73 and 0.91 depending on age and sex of the children. This scale has been a popular one because of its easy vocabulary and administration. For example, Lewis (1971) applied the scale with adaptation to adolescent educationally-subnormal boys. He obtained a split-half reliability of 0.88. To obviate the verbal problem Lewis transformed the Lipsitt verbal rating into a pictorial form of five buckets filled to decreasing levels with the particular quality to be rated. The middle bucket was to be regarded as typical of most ordinary boys. Four practice items were worked through by the subjects with the researcher to ensure familiarity with the requirements. For example, 'how tough are you? If you think you are as tough as most other boys put a ring round this middle bucket. If you think you are tougher – this bucket, and if you are much tougher – this end bucket', etc.

6. Self-esteem scale

Source: Rosenberg (1965)
Type of measure: Rating Scale
Age Range: Adolescents and students

Description
This scale was specifically designed by the author for the study
reported in his book *Society and the Adolescent Self Image* (1965).
The scale is an attempt to achieve a unidimensional index of global
self esteem based on the Guttman model, and has a reproducibility
index of 0.93 and an item scalability of 0.73. Silber and Tippett
(1965) obtained a 2-week test–retest reliability of 0.85. It consists
of 10 statements, 5 of which are phrased in a positive direction,
with the other 5 in a negative direction to control for acquiescence.
These are rated on a four-point scale ranging from strongly agree,
to strongly disagree. In general terms items score if positive ones
are disagreed with and negative ones agreed with so that high
scores reflect low self esteem. It does have the merits of ease and
economy of time which derive from administering a short scale.
This scale is reproduced on p. 104 by permission of Princeton
University Press, and is taken from Rosenberg (1965) *Society and
the Adolescent Self Image,* Scale D1 (Self Esteem), Appendix D.
   The scoring is somewhat confusing and care must be taken.
Cohen (1976) suggests and presents a cardboard cut-out marking
key to facilitate the scoring which is based on combinations of
responses. Rosenberg used the scale in a major study of over 5,000
American adolescents of both sexes, in order to investigate the
relationships between self concept and a substantial number of
psychological and sociological variables. This study will be
discussed in detail in Chapter 7. Hensley and Roberts (1976) in a
factorial analysis of the scale identified two factors – the first
loaded on positive self-appraisal items, the second on the negative
items. This is indicative of a response set and strongly suggests that
the scale is tridimensional. However, the scale is worthy of high
recommendation in view of its very acceptable reliability
coefficients attained on only 10 items and considerable evidence
for its construct validity derived from the many theoretical
relationships studied and shown to be significant in Rosenberg's
(1965) study.

7. How I see myself scale

Source: Gordon (1966)
Type of measure: Rating scale
Age range: 8–17 years

Put a tick in the appropriate box to show how you feel about yourself

	Strongly agree	Agree	Disagree	Strongly disagree
1. I feel that I am a person of worth, at least on an equal plane with others				
2. All in all, I am inclined to feel that I am a failure				
3. I feel that I have a number of good qualities				
4. I am able to do things as well as most other people				
5. I feel I do not have much to be proud of				
6. I take a positive attitude toward myself				
7. On the whole, I am satisfied with myself				
8. I wish I could have more respect for myself				
9. I certainly feel useless at times				
10. At times I think I am no good at all				

Description

The scale was devised from categories used by Jersild (1952) in classifying children's compositions on themselves. It assesses attitudes towards physical body, emotions, peers and school. But factor analysis shows that the structure isn't as simple as that with different sets of items assuming different degrees of importance at different ages and for the two sexes. The pre-adolescent form of the scale contains 40 items and the adolescent form 42 items, all rated on a five-point scale. The subjects complete the first two items on the scale under the direction of the teacher. Full instructions and list of scale items can be obtained from Gordon (1966). Norms (USA) are available for 8–17 year olds by sex, race and social class. The inventory was developed by testing students (grades 3–12) in a laboratory school at the University of Florida. The factor analytic study resulted from collecting data from a total of 8,979 school children in a north-central public school system.

Three separate test–retest reliability studies were done on the basis of the factor scores and total scores. One included a group of 'disadvantaged' mothers. Interval between testing ranged from 9 days to 2 weeks. Reliability coefficients using total score ranged from 0.87 to 0.89. Studies using factor scores had coefficients for factors ranging from 0.45 to 0.82. Content validity was established by the use of a model and material from Jersild (1952) who used an open-ended composition approach and then categorised the responses of children and adolescents. The items on the inventory were based on these categories. Studies were undertaken to assess other aspects of validity. Inventory scores were correlated with scores from an inferential technique – an observer used a mixture of interview, projective techniques and observation and quantified inferences on a seven-point rating scale. Correlations were positive and non-zero, but generally low. Ratings from classroom behaviour observations were correlated with inventory scores. Even though the observations covered a variety of topics and procedures, there were low but significant correlations between all parts of the scale and observed classroom behaviour. Other studies included comparison of student scores with adult scores, obtained from the sample of mothers used in the reliability study.

The author admits that further work in comparing this scale with other instruments, observed behaviour, and with environmental and developmental variables is necessary. However, more than the average amount of care and time have been taken in the development and study of the instrument since its inception in 1959. It is one of the few self-concept inventories that comes with a manual and a rationale. The manual is published by Florida Educational Research and Development Council, Gainesville, Florida.

8. The children's self-concept index

Source: Westinghouse Learning Corporation, 100 Park Avenue, New York.
Type of measure: Pictorial
Age range: 5–8 year olds

Description
The CSCI is a 26-item inventory designed for Project Headstart to assess the degree of positive self concept of children in grades 1–3. Peer acceptance and a positive reinforcement in the home and school are the major areas of emphasis in the index. Each item is composed of two sentences. One pertains to a balloon child, the other a flag child represented by a pair of stick figures. The child representing the socially desirable attribute is represented at alternate times by the two stick figures, so that neither the balloon child nor the flag child is the good child throughout the 26 items. The problem of numbering items is eliminated by using different coloured pages for each item.

The administrator says, 'I'm going to tell you a story. Listen carefully and mark an X in the little square under the child who is more like you, e.g.

"Most grown-ups don't care about the balloon-child."

"Grown-ups like to help the flag-child."

The test can be given without training to individuals or classroom groups. For larger groups an aide may be necessary, especially when dealing with first graders. Directions for administration and instructions for the children are easily understood. The entire test is read to the subjects with two sample items preceding the test to help the subjects understand the format.

The instrument was standardised on a sample of 1,900 disadvantaged children in grades 1–3 from nine geographic areas. Test–retest reliability after a 2-week interval was 0.66, computed on a sample of 100 second-grade students. The coefficient for internal consistency was 0.80. Rank-order correlations of scores with teacher ratings of the child's self concept ranged from 0.20 to 0.60 for four different classrooms. The low test–retest reliability may be due to personality instability in the primary years. Correlations between the CSCI and other measures of self concept would add evidence towards determining validity. The use of the test with 'middle-class' samples also would be of interest. Despite these drawbacks, the CSCI represents a creative attempt to evaluate the self concept of the very young and less verbally competent pupil.

9. Primary self-concept scale

Source: Muller and Leonetti (1972)
Type of measure: Non-verbal
Age range: 7–10 year olds

Description
This scale was specifically constructed for use with bilingual
children in the USA, and may, after appropriate adaptation and
research, be of value with immigrant and bilingual children in
Britain. Muller and Leonetti (1972) have demonstrated that the
test is quite appropriate for monolingual white children too. It is a
24-item test in pictorial form with each item depicting at least one
child in a positive role and at least one child in a negative role.
After being told a simple descriptive story about each of the
illustrations, the subject is requested to draw a circle round the
child that is most like himself. Each item scores one point for a
socially acceptable choice and zero if a negative role is chosen.
Eight factors are represented in the scale with two to four items
per factor. Each factor score is simply the number of points earned
which can vary between zero and four. For any factor Muller and
Leonetti (1972) considered a score of two or more to reflect a
positive self image. Examples of factors with pictorial item
descriptions are given below. Jensen, Michael and Michael
(1975) in a study of the scale report test–retest correlations (phi
coefficients) and concurrent validity indices measured against

	Item no. and description of picture
Factor 3 Child's view of himself as a pupil; like and dislike of school.	2. Reading–bothering a child reading 4. Looking out of window–reading 10. Doing school work well–not doing well. 19. Reading – playing in classroom
Factor 5 Child's view of physiological self	13. Small child – big child 15. Small child playing – big child playing 21. Strong child – weak child 23. White child – coloured child.

teacher ratings (see below). These results indicate that while the
scale has initial promise more developmental work is required,
especially in adding more new items to each factor and in
improving reliability and validity coefficients. Little is known about
the difficulties children, especially those from non-indigenous

Factor	Test-retest r	concurrent validity
Child's relationship with peers	0.69	0.27
Child's view of his acceptance by peers	0.55	0.49
Intellectual self image	0.25	0.16
Child's view of himself as competent to help	0.34	−0.19
Psysiological self	0.29	0.24
Child's view of himself as accepted by adults	0.57	0.57
Emotional Self	0.00	0.00
Child's view of self as a success	−0.02	−0.04

groups, may have in interpreting pictorial material. Of course, even in this type of test material social desirability is likely to intrude.

10. 'I feel – me feel' inventory

Source: Yeatts and Bentley (1968)
Type of measure: Non-verbal pictorial
Age range: Pre-school

Description
This is a 40-item inventory which measures five dimensions of the self concept: general adequacy, peer, school, physical and academic. Each item is a silhouetted picture of an event related to a young child's life. Underneath each picture are five faces which represent a five-point gradation between very sad and very happy. The subject puts an X on the face that shows how he feels about the picture. The test is administered individually. The captions that explain each picture are read to the child who is asked to look at the picture and put a cross on one of the five faces that best describes how the item makes him feel. White and Human (1976) report an internal consistency of 0.73, but concurrent validity against parental and teacher inferences of the child's self concept was quite low. One general factor has emerged from several studies, though (White and Bashaw 1970; White and Simmons, 1974). This scale would seem worthwhile for research and development, since there are so few non-verbal pre-school self-concept measures.

11. Index of adjustment and values

Source: Bills, Vance and McLean (1951)
Type of measure: Rating scale
Age range: Student and adult

Description
To develop this index 124 words were taken from Allport and Odbert's (1936) list of traits. An effort was made to choose those items which occur frequently in counselling interviews and which appear to present clear examples of self-concept characteristics. These trait adjectives were rated highly on a five-point scale ranging from 'seldom' to 'most of the time' to measure the self concept; secondly on a five-point scale ranging from 'I very much dislike being as I am in this respect' to 'I very much like being as I am in this respect' to indicate self acceptance, i.e. how the subject felt about himself as described on the self concept; and thirdly how much each subject would like each trait to be characteristic of them, i.e. the ideal self. Test–retest reliability over 3 weeks with 44

subjects was 0.67 for self acceptance and 0.68 for self-ideal discrepancy score. Item analysis resulted in the removal of unreliable items and the final scale contains 49 items, e.g. ambitious, calm, efficient, stubborn. This final form produced an odd–even reliability of 0.91 for self-acceptance scores, and 0.88 for the self-ideal discrepancy. Test–retest reliability over 6-weeks with 237 students was 0.83 for self acceptance and 0.87 for the discrepancy measure. The authors report three validity studies which provide strong evidence of the index's validity, viz. 14 neurotics as measured on Rorschach all fell below mean of self-acceptance scores, therapy produced changes in self-acceptance scores in the predicted direction, and low self-acceptance subjects reported that they were more threatened by others. The use of the discrepancy index is not advised (see Chapter 4). Since 40 of the 49 trait adjectives are 'desirable', the acquiescence response set is inadequately controlled. Wylie (1974) reports that self-concept and self-acceptance scores from this index correlate moderately with a wide range of other verbal self-report instruments purporting to measure the self concept. Since it is shorter and less cumbersome than other general self-concept instruments and has high reliability the index is of considerable value.

12. Interpersonal check list

Source: Leary (1957)
Type of measure: Check list
Age range: Adult

Description
It was developed by LaForge and Suczek (1955) to provide a multilevel diagnosis of personality and interpersonal structure of a group. It measures 'description' and 'values'. The inventory consists of 128 descriptive words and phrases. It provides a self description, an ideal self description and a measure of self acceptance (in terms of the discrepancy between self and ideal self descriptions).

In the Interpersonal Personal Personality System, Leary (1957, pp. 81–82) distinguishes five 'levels' of personality, which are identified thus: Level I = Public Communication (interpersonal impact of the subject on others); Level II = Conscious Descriptions (subject's view of self and world); Level III = Preconscious Symbolisation (subject's autistic and projective fantasy productions); Level IV = Unexpressed Unconscious; Level V = Ego Ideal (subject's view of his ideal self and his standards). Level II appears to refer to the phenomenal self concept, and Level V to the phenomenal ideal for self. However, Leary (1957) specifically denied that he was measuring 'level of consciousness'.

He preferred to say that Levels II and V are 'conscious descriptions' of self and ideal self, because measures at these levels reflect how the subject chooses to present himself, rather than how he actually sees himself.

In its most recent form, the Interpersonal Check List contains 128 items, 8 for each of the 16 variables in the theory's classification scheme. The 8 items for any variable include 1 of least 'intensity,' 3 for each of 2 intermediate intensity levels, and 1 of highest intensity. Items are serially listed on the sheet which the subject uses, with those from the 16 categories intermingled within the list. The subject describes his actual self and then his ideal self by checking as many items as he wishes.

The ICL has undergone successive revisions, involving 'several thousands' of subjects. Clarity of meaning was a consideration in choosing adjectives (or brief phrases) to be included in the successive revisions. In the final form of the ICL, intensity values were assigned on the basis of a combination of two criteria:

(a) whether psychologists had judged the item to be good, neutral, or bad from the viewpoint of the subject's culture;
(b) the frequency with which subjects had checked the item in earlier forms (for example, the lowest intensity value was assigned to an item checked by 90 per cent of persons, the highest intensity value to an item checked by 10 per cent of persons).

Intensity then appears to be no more than a synonym for social desirability!

The scoring is rather complicated and readers are urged to consult LaForge (1963) for a detailed explanation about the technique of scoring. Test–retest correlations from 0.73 to 0.78 have been reported (LaForge and Suczek, 1955). A reliability study by Armstrong (1958) indicates that the check list has high internal consistency with coefficients ranging from 0.95 to 0.97.

13. Children's self-concept scale

Source: Piers and Harris (1964)
Type of measure: Rating scale
Age range: 8–16 year olds

Description
This scale is built out of a pool of items derived from Jersild's (1952) collection of children's statements. The items were written as simple declarative statements. The final scale was reduced to 80 yes–no items after several pilot studies. Examples of these items are 'I am unpopular', 'I am a happy person', 'I cry easily'. It is a wide-ranging scale covering physical appearance, social behaviour,

academic status, depreciation, dissatisfaction and contentment with
self, with statements equally divided between positive and negative
forms and between high and low reflections of the self concept. A
high score (negative items reversed) indicates a more positive self
concept. Thus, there is an attempt to control the acquiescence
response set.

Reliability over both a 2-month and a 4-month period produced
a test–retest coefficient of 0.77. Internal consistency for 8-, 11-,
and 15-year-old groups ranged from 0.78 to 0.93. Correlations
with intelligence are low but positive, and the figure of 0.32 is
comparable with the correlation of 0.36 reported by Coopersmith
(1967) with his scale. A substantial inverse relationship is shown
between self concept and anxiety (-0.69). No constant sex
differences have been discerned. With regard to validity,
institutionalised female 'retardates' score significantly lower than
normal persons of the same chronological age. The Piers–Harris
scale correlates 0.68 with Lipsitt's scale. Several factorial analyses
have been made of the scale. Six interpretable factors constantly
appear, viz. happiness and satisfaction, social behaviour, anxiety,
popularity, academic competence and physical appearance. No
general factor appears though the test is intended to reflect the
general self concept. This scale has been carefully developed and is
widely used in the USA. It is now published commercially by
Counsellor Recordings and Tests, Acklen Station, Nashville,
Tennessee, who have permitted the reproduction of the test in full
below. The expansion of the scale from a dichotomous yes–no to a
five-point one would seem to be a sensible development for the
future.

	Yes	No

1. My classmates make fun of me . . .
2. I am a happy person
3. It is hard for me to make friends
4. I am often sad
5. I am clever
6. I am shy
7. I get nervous when teacher calls on me
8. My looks bother me
9. When I grow up, I will be an important person
10. I get worried when we have tests at school
11. I am unpopular
12. I am well behaved at school
13. It is usually my fault when something goes wrong
14. I cause trouble to my family
15. I am strong
16. I have good ideas

Yes   No

17. I am an important member of my family
18. I usually want my own way
19. I am good at making things with my hands
20. I give up easily
21. I am good in my school work
22. I am ashamed of many things I do
23. I can draw well
24. I am good in music
25. I behave badly at home
26. I am slow in finishing my school work
27. I am an important member of my class
28. I am nervous
29. I have attractive eyes
30. I speak well in front of the class
31. In school I am a dreamer
32. I am unkind to my brother(s) and sister(s)
33. My friends like my ideas
34. I often get into trouble
35. I am obedient at home
36. I am lucky
37. I worry a lot
38. My parents expect too much of me
39. I like being the way I am
40. I feel left out of things
41. I have nice hair
42. I often volunteer in school
43. I wish I were different
44. I sleep well at night
45. I hate school
46. I am among the last to be chosen for games
47. I am sick a lot
48. I am often mean to other people
49. My classmates in school think I have good ideas
50. I am unhappy
51. I have many friends
52. I am cheerful
53. I am stupid about most things
54. I am good at most things
55. I have lots of energy
56. I get into a lot of fights
57. I am popular with boys
58. People pick on me
59. My family is disappointed in me
60. I have a pleasant face

Yes No

61. When I try to make something, everything seems to
    go wrong
62. I am picked on at home
63. I am a leader in games and sports
64. I am clumsy
65. In games and sports, I watch instead of play
66. I forget what I learn
67. I am easy to get along with
68. I lose my temper easily
69. I am popular with girls
70. I am a good reader
71. I would rather work alone than with a group
72. I like my brothers (sisters)
73. I have a good physique
74. I am often afraid
75. I am always dropping or breaking things
76. I can be trusted
77. I am different from other people
78. I think bad thoughts
79. I cry easily
80. I am a good person

14. Tennessee self-concept scale

Source: Fitts (1955) Tennessee Department of Mental Health,
    Nashville, Tennessee. Now published commercially and obtainable
    from Counsellor Recording and Tests, Box 6184, Acklen
    Station, Nashville, Tennessee, complete with answer, score and
    profile sheets and a manual.
Type of measure: Five-point rating scale
Age range: 12 years of age upwards

Description
This scale consists of 100 self-descriptive items in booklet form.
The items were culled from a vague pool of unpublished sources.
There are no time limits, but most subjects complete it within 20
minutes. Half the items are phrased negatively to obviate
acquiescence. The scale is appropriate for both group and
individual administration and the vocabulary enables its use with
persons from 12 years of age upwards. Two scoring systems have
been devised for the scale, a counselling form and a clinical
research form. The counselling form is designed for use with
counsellors in schools, colleges and various community agencies. It
is quicker and easier to score since it deals with lower variables,

can be used for self interpretation and requires less sophistication in psychometrics and psychopathology than the clinical and research variant.

The scale contains two subscales.

1. Self Criticism. This subscale is composed of 10 items taken from the L scale of the MMPI. They are all mildly derogatory statements that most people admit as being true for them. Those who deny most of these statements are being defensive and deliberately attempting to create a favourable image of themselves. High scores indicate a healthy openness and capacity for self criticism. Low scores suggest that the scores on the other subscale are artificially high, elevated by this defensiveness.

2. Positive Subscale. This subscale consists of 90 items equally divided between positive and negative items. It provides the overall level of self esteem, with high scores designating persons who, like themselves, feel they are of value and worth and have confidence. Low scores indicate doubt about self worth, with the subjects being anxious, depressed, unhappy and lacking confidence. Further subdividing of the Positive Subscale score provides measures of:

    (*a*) identity – what I am;
    (*b*) self satisfaction – how the individual feels about the self he perceives;
    (*c*) behaviour – how the individual perceives his own behaviour;
    (*d*) physical self – how the individual views his health, body, appearance;
    (*e*) moral–ethical self – how the individual sees his moral worth;
    (*f*) personal self – how the individual assesses his adequacy as a person;
    (*g*) family self – how the individual perceives himself with reference to his closest and most immediate 'others';
    (*h*) social self – how the individual perceives himself as adequate in his social interaction with a wide range of others.

Two other scores are computed. The Variability score is a measure of the consistency of self perception across the various areas (*a*)–(*h*) above. High scores reflect high variability, suggesting little unity or integration of various self perspectives, a compartmentalisation of the various elements. The Distribution score is a reflection of the way the subject distributes his responses across the five-point scale. Low scores indicate defensiveness by responding frequently in the middle category. Extremely high scores from exclusive use of 5 or 1 are characteristics of schizophrenia. For the other scales which are used on the clinical form the reader is advised to consult the manual. Scoring procedures for both forms of the scale are detailed on the score sheets.

The standardisation group from which norms were developed was a sample of 626 persons, aged 12–68, with equal numbers of both sexes, representing a broad range of socioeconomic intellectual and ethnic groupings. Test–retest reliabilities over a 2-week period for the subscales on the counselling form ranged from 0.75 for Self Criticism to 0.92 for the total Positive Subscale with subelements of the latter running from 0.80 to 0.90. Validity measured on the basis of discrimination between groups representing 'normal' and psychiatric groups reveals an array of highly significant differences mostly at the 0.001 level. The interested reader is urged to consult the manual for the wealth of reliability and validity data.

15. 'Where are you' game

Source: Engel and Raine (1963)
Type of measure: Ladder rating scale
Age range: 8–9 year olds

Description
It is composed of seven bipolar dimensions, each thought to be important in the child's self concept, on which the subject is asked to rate himself on a five-point scale in the form of a vertical ladder. The seven dimensions are:

(*a*) seeing oneself as intellectually gifted, versus seeing oneself as lacking in such capacities;
(*b*) seeing oneself as happy, as opposed to considering oneself unhappy;
(*c*) considering oneself well liked by peers, versus seeing oneself as unpopular;
(*d*) seeing oneself as brave, as opposed to considering oneself easily frightened;
(*e*) conceiving of oneself as physically attractive, or unattractive;
(*f*) considering oneself strong or weak physically;
(*g*) seeing oneself as doing what one should, versus seeing oneself as being disobedient.

Each of these dimensions was allotted a page with five line spaces, vertically arranged, representing the five-point rating scale. Next to the top and the bottom space there was an extra space for demonstration purposes.

These dimensions were chosen on an *a priori* basis as representing salient features of the concerns of children at this age.

The test is administered individually as a game. The examiner demonstrates the use of the ladder by drawing a child of the same sex as the subject between various rungs verbally describing the characteristics of the child drawn. When the principle is understood, the subject is then taken through each of the dimensions and asked to put a check mark on the ladder. The child is asked why he placed the check mark where he did and the response is recorded.

Internal reliability is recorded as 0.60. A factor analysis suggests that each scale is a separate factor, but two factors explained 50 per cent of the variance, viz. interpersonal relationships and personal attributes (bravery, strength and attractiveness).

It would appear to be a simple instrument, making minimal demands on the subjects. But more evidence of reliability and validity would enhance it.

16 Bledsoe self-concept scale

Source: Bledsoe (1964, 1967)
Type of measure: Three-point rating scale
Age range: 7–16 year olds

Description
This scale consists of 30 trait-descriptive adjectives which the subject checks as characteristic of himself on a three-point rating scale of 'nearly always', 'about half the time', 'just now and then'. The subject then checks each adjective on the same three-point scale as how he would like to be. Of the 30 adjectives, 10 each are drawn from the evaluative, potency and activity dimensions of the semantic differential. For each group of 10, 6 are positive and 4 are negative. The scale is in essence a modification of Lipsitt's adaptation of Bills' Index of Adjustment and Values.

Test–retest reliability (2-week interval) ranged from 0.66 to 0.81 for the ages 8–14. Correlations with anxiety scales run consistently negative, ranging from −0.30 to −0.46. For boys, correlations are positive with intelligence and achievement (CAT), 0.43 (fourth-grade total battery, $N = 65$); 0.39 (sixth grade, $N = 76$). Correlation with California Test of Personality Self Adjustment Scale, 0.39 ($N = 56$ fifth-grade pupils), 0.38 with California Test of Personality Total Score. Bledsoe reports that factor analysis indicates the scale is homogeneous with a single factor present.

The instrument is largely self-administering, but Bledsoe suggests that reading the directions and the scale contents to the group is more effective at the pre-adolescent level. Above this level, a reading of the instructions is usually sufficient. The scale has been used with reasonable success with 7–16 year olds. The scale is scored by assigning a weight of '3' to the column marked 'Nearly

Always', '2' to the column marked 'About ½ the Time', and '1' to
the column marked 'Just now and Then'. The only exceptions to
this rule are the negative traits, e.g. Mean, Lazy, Selfish, where the
scoring is reversed and thus column '3' is marked '1' and '1' is
marked as if it were '3'.

While the scale has merits in its brevity and ease of completion,
the limited verbal skills required and control for acquiescence there
are several aspects which need further research. Reliability is only
moderate as to validity. The discovery of a single factor is not
consistent with the initial assumption that the adjectives reflect
three dimensions. Bledsoe (1973) reports a sex bias in the scale
with 'evaluative' adjectives demonstrating significantly higher
means for girls, perhaps reflecting a cultural factor. 'Activity' and
'potency' adjectives tended not to produce such differences. So not
only does the scale seem to index sex role description rather than
self esteem, but the existence of a single factor no longer seems
plausible if the dimensions function differentially for the two sexes.
The full scale is reproduced on p. 118 by kind permission of the
author.

17. Canadian self-esteem inventory

Source: Battle (1976; 1977a; 1977b)
Type of measure: Rating scale
Age range: 8–11 year olds and adult (two versions)

Description
The original form for 8–11 year olds was a 60-item scale,
containing a lie scale measuring defensiveness (10 items). The
other 50 items measure an individual's perception in four areas:
self, peers, parents and school. The items in the inventory were
selected from Gough and Heilbron's (1965) Adjective Check List,
Coopersmith's (1967) Self Esteem Scale, plus others developed by
the author of the scale. The subject is requested to check 'yes' or
'no' to each statement, half of which reflect high self esteem, the
other half reflecting low self esteem placed in random order. The
self-esteem score is the total number of statements checked 'yes'
which indicate high self esteem. This scale is presented in full with
instructions in Battle (1976). Test–retest correlations over a 2-day
period for boys in year groups ranged from 0.72 to 0.93; for girls
from 0.74 to 0.90; for the total sample from 0.81 to 0.89. Thus the
instrument possesses acceptable temporal reliability. A short form
of the scale has been developed containing only 30 of the original
items (Battle, 1977a). Again a lie scale (five items) and the four
areas of self, peers, parents and school are measured. A 48-hour
test–retest produced similar coefficients to those of the longer form
with reliabilities for the total sample of 110 pupils ranging from

Bledsoe Self-concept Scale

There is a need for each of us to know more about what we are like. This is to help you describe yourself and to describe how you would like to be. There are no *right* or *wrong* answers; each person may have different ideas. Answer these according to your feelings. It is important for you to give your own honest answers.

Think carefully and check the answer that tells if you are like the word says Nearly Always, About ½ the Time, or Just Now and Then. In the second column check the answer if you would like to be like the word says Nearly Always, About ½ the Time, or Just Now and Then.

THIS IS THE WAY I AM

Nearly Always	About ½ the Time	Just Now and Then

THIS IS THE WAY I'D LIKE TO BE.

Nearly Always	About ½ the Time	Just Now and Then

Nearly Always	About ½ the Time	Just Now and Then		Nearly Always	About ½ the Time	Just Now and Then
_____	_____	_____	Friendly	_____	_____	_____
_____	_____	_____	Cold	_____	_____	_____
_____	_____	_____	Brave	_____	_____	_____
_____	_____	_____	Small	_____	_____	_____
_____	_____	_____	Helpful	_____	_____	_____
_____	_____	_____	Honest	_____	_____	_____
_____	_____	_____	Cheerful	_____	_____	_____
_____	_____	_____	Active	_____	_____	_____
_____	_____	_____	Jealous	_____	_____	_____
_____	_____	_____	Quiet	_____	_____	_____
_____	_____	_____	Strong	_____	_____	_____
_____	_____	_____	A good sport	_____	_____	_____
_____	_____	_____	Mean	_____	_____	_____
_____	_____	_____	Lazy	_____	_____	_____
_____	_____	_____	Poor	_____	_____	_____
_____	_____	_____	Smart	_____	_____	_____
_____	_____	_____	Popular	_____	_____	_____
_____	_____	_____	Useful	_____	_____	_____
_____	_____	_____	Clean	_____	_____	_____
_____	_____	_____	Kind	_____	_____	_____
_____	_____	_____	Selfish	_____	_____	_____
_____	_____	_____	Dull	_____	_____	_____
_____	_____	_____	Healthy	_____	_____	_____
_____	_____	_____	Timid	_____	_____	_____
_____	_____	_____	Slow	_____	_____	_____
_____	_____	_____	Faithful	_____	_____	_____
_____	_____	_____	Lonely	_____	_____	_____
_____	_____	_____	Polite	_____	_____	_____
_____	_____	_____	Talkative	_____	_____	_____
_____	_____	_____	Happy	_____	_____	_____

0.79 to 0.92; the average value for boys was 0.80 and for girls 0.87.

An adult version of the inventory is being developed (Battle, 1977b). A 4-week test–retest reliability for 127 students is reported as 0.81, with males and females producing coefficients of 0.79 and 0.82 respectively. While reliability seems sound, no evidence of validity has been reported for any of the versions, nor has any analysis of subscores derived from the five item areas. This inventory needs to be used with care and appears to be very suitable for more research and development. The short form of the children's version is printed in full on p. 120 by permission of the author.

18. Self-image questionnaire

Source: Offer (1974)
Type of measure: Rating scale
Age range: Adolescence

Description
This scale was constructed specifically for a research project investigating the self image, identity, social relationships and general psychological world of normal (*sic*!) US adolescents. The results of the survey are reported in Offer (1974) in which Appendix 1 details the items in, and the construction of, the scale; 130 item statements for the pilot study were culled from numerous other scales and from clinical experience. The scale comprises 10 subscales which condense on factor analysis into three major factors, viz:

Factor I –	Feeling State
Scales	Emotional tune Body and self image Social relationships psychopathology
Factor II –	Mastery
Scales	Vocational–educational Superior adjustment Mastery of external environment
Factor III –	Interpersonal Relations
Scales	Morals Impulse control Family relationships

Acceptable internal consistency reliability was obtained for each of the scales ranging from 0.57 to 0.80. Eight of the scales revealed

The Canadian Self-esteem Inventory for Children – Form B

by

James Battle, Ph.D

Directions: Please mark each statement in the following way. If the statement describes how you usually feel make a check mark (√) under the 'yes' column. If the statement does not describe how you usually feel make a check mark (√) under the 'no' column. Please check only one column (either 'yes' or 'no') for each of the 30 statements. This is *not* a test and there are no 'right' or 'wrong' answers.

	YES	NO
1. I wish I were younger		
2. Boys and girls like to play with me		
3. I usually quit when my school work is too hard		
4. I have lots of fun with my parents		
5. My parents never get angry at me		
6. I am happy, most of the time		
7. I have only a few friends		
8. I like being a boy/girl		
9. I am a failure at school		
10. I usually fail when I try to do important things		
11. My parents make me feel that I am not good enough		
12. I have never taken anything that didn't belong to me		
13. I often feel ashamed of myself		
14. Most boys and girls play games better than I do		
15. I often feel that I am no good at all		
16. Most boys and girls are smarter than I am		
17. My parents dislike me because I am not good enough		
18. I like everyone I know		
19. Most boys and girls are better than I am		
20. I like to play with children younger than I am		
21. I often feel like quitting school		
22. I would change many things about myself if I could		
23. There are many times when I would like to run away from home		
24. I never worry about anything		
25. I am as happy as most boys and girls		
26. I can do things as well as other boys and girls		
27. My teacher feels that I am not good enough		
28. My parents think I am a failure		
29. I always tell the truth		
30. I worry a lot		

significant differences between small groups of 'normal' and 'disturbed' adolescents undergoing psychiatric treatment. As a result of this two scales were significantly altered.

The final scale contains 120 items, half written positively and half written in a negative direction to be rated on a six-point scale ranging from 'describes me very well', to 'does not describe me at all'. The number of items per scale is as follows:

Impulse control	– 10 statements
Emotional tune	– 10 statements
Body and self image	– 10 statements
Social Relationships	– 10 statements
Morals	– 10 statements
Family relationships	– 20 statements
Mastery of external world	– 10 statements
Vocational and Educational Goals	– 10 statements
Psychopathology	– 15 statements
Superior adjustment	– 15 statements

Negative items are scored in reverse and each subscale provides a score from the sum of its positive and negative items rated on the 1–6 scale. This questionnaire is worthy of more attention since it covers a wide variety of areas in which self conceptualisation is important. However, more data on reliability and validity are necessary before the scale is capable of application by others.

19. Young children's self-concept instrument

Source: Wattenberg and Clifford (1964)
Type of measure: Analysis of child verbalisation – projective
Age range: 5–7 year olds

Description
In a study investigating the relationship between self concept and reading achievement the authors constructed a general self-concept measure for use with the 185 7-year-old children taking part in the study. Tape recordings were made of the remarks of the children while they drew a picture of the members of their family and while responding to an incomplete sentences test devised for the purpose. Typescripts were made from the tapes which were then segmented into thought units by two independent raters. These thought units were classified as to whether or not they constituted self references. Any self references were further classified into two areas according to their content, i.e. competence; personal worth. Each self reference was again rated as to whether it was positive, negative or neutral. In each area the ratio of positive to total self reference was computed. These the authors termed the Quantified Self Concept (Competence) and the Quantified Self Concept (Good–Bad). The inter-rater correlation for the competence ratio was 0.89, and for the good–bad 0.75.

Using these ratios Wattenberg and Clifford demonstrated significant relationships between self concept and reading level –

the latter measured $2\frac{1}{2}$ years later. As a predictive measure the self concept was revealed as far superior to IQ for later success at reading.

B. Acceptance of self scales

Two scales have been designed to measure attitudes to self and attitudes to others. In other words the scales are each composed of two subscales whose items are placed at random. Since there is strong theoretical interest in the relationship between attitudes to self and others as well as the practical implications (see Ch. 8, section B), these two scales are of particular interest.

1. Self–others questionnaire

Source: Phillips (1951)
Type of measure: Rating scale
Age range: Students and adults

Description
This scale was developed for research purposes only. It consists of 50 statements, 25 to measure attitudes to self and 25 to measure attitudes to others. No indication is given concerning how the items were chosen or whether any item analysis was applied. A Likert five-point scale response mode is used. Subjects are requested to respond to each item by entering the letter A for 'rarely or almost never true for me', the letter B for 'sometimes but infrequently true for me', C for 'occasionally true for me', D for 'very often true for me' and E for 'true for me all or most of the time'.

Each item response is given a weight, ranging from 1 for an A response to 5 for an E response. The attitude-towards-self score is obtained by summing the weighted score for each item on the self scale. Similarly, the attitude-towards-others score is the sum of the item scores for the others scale. Since there are 25 items on each scale, each score has a theoretical range from 25 to 125. A high score indicates an unfavourable attitude toward self or others. Self items and other items are randomised through the scale, but all the statements are worded in the same direction allowing for the infiltration of the acquiescence response set.

The samples used in evaluating reliability and validity were drawn from college and high school populations. One sample consisted of 48 students in general psychology courses in the 1949 summer session at George Washington University. These were mostly older, part-time students. Another sample consisted of 77 students, most of whom were in their first year. Two samples were drawn from a high school in a middle-class, suburban area in

Washington, DC. One consisted of 45 students and the other of 41. Test–retest reliability, after a 5-day interval, was 0.84 for the self scale and 0.82 for others scale ($N = 45$ college students). No direct evidence of validity was reported. However, substantial correlations were reported between self scores and others scores (0.74 for 48 college students, 0.54 for 77 regular college students, 0.67 for the 45 high school second-year students and 0.51 for the 41 high school final-year students).

Since supporting evidence for the technical merit of this scale is meagre, further studies of its reliability and validity using larger and more varied samples are required. The full scale can be consulted in Shaw and Wright (1968).

2. Acceptance of self and others scale

Source: Berger (1952)
Type of measure: Rating scale
Age range: Students and adults

Description
Again, while a single test, this instrument has two subscales. Based on a Likert five-point rating system the self-acceptance scale is composed of 36 items and the acceptances-of-others scale of 28 items. These items were selected from an initial pool of 47 statements on self acceptance and 40 statements on acceptance of others on the basis of an item analysis. The top and bottom 25 per cent of a sample of 200 were selected and the difference between the mean scores of these criterion groups was used as an index of the discriminating power of the item. The standard error of the difference between means did not exceed 0.30 for any item, and all items in the final scales had critical ratios of 3.0 or more, except three which had critical ratios close to 2.0.

The subjects used in selecting items for these scales were 200 first-year sociology or psychology students. They differed widely in age, socioeconomic backgrounds and vocational interests. For reliability and validation studies, samples were drawn from day- and evening-session college students, prisoners, stutterers, speech-problem cases, adult classes at the YMCA and counselees.

The response mode is a Likert type. The subject responds to each item by entering a 1 for 'not at all true of myself', a 2 for 'slightly true of myself', a 3 for 'about half-way true of myself', a 4 for 'mostly true of myself' and a 5 for 'true of myself'.

The score for any item ranges from 1 to 5. For items expressing a favourable attitude towards self or others, a score of 5 is assigned to a response of 'true of myself', a score of 4 for 'mostly true of myself', a score of 3 for 'about half-way true of myself', a score of 2 for 'slightly true of myself' and a score of 1 for 'not at all true of myself'. The direction of the scoring is reversed for negatively worded items, the acceptance-of-self score and the acceptance-of-others score are obtained by summing item scores for each scale respectively. A high score indicates a favourable attitude towards self or others.

Split-half reliabilities were obtained for five groups ranging in size from 18 to 183. These were reported to be 0.894 or better for the self-acceptance scale for all but one group, which was 0.746. Similar reliabilities for the acceptance-of-others scale ranged from 0.776 to 0.884.

Several estimates of validity were obtained for these scales. First, one group ($N = 20$) was asked to write freely about their attitude towards themselves, and another group ($N = 20$) was asked to write about their attitudes towards others. These 'essays' were then rated by four judges and the mean ratings correlated with the corresponding scale scores. The correlation was 0.897 for self acceptance and 0.727 for acceptance of others.

Second, a group of stutterers ($N = 38$) were compared with a group of non-stutterers, matched for age and sex. The stutterers had lower mean scores than non-stutterers ($p<0.06$) on the self-acceptance scale. For the acceptance-of-others scale, a group of prisoners was compared with a group of college students, matched for age, sex and race. As expected, prisoners scored lower on the acceptance-of-others scale than the students (p about 0.02). The prisoners also scored lower on the self-acceptance scale ($p<0.01$).

Since it contains both positive and negative statements at random the acquiescence response set is somewhat obviated. This scale appears to be one of the few carefully developed instruments in the field of self-concept measurement. Evidence of its technical qualities is more extensively provided by its author than many other authors provide for their scales. It has been used in England by Burns (1975) in a study relating self-concept levels to attitudes to other individuals and ethnic groups. The full scale can be found in Shaw and Wright (1968).

The instructions and first five items are illustrated below by permission of the author.

Acceptance of Self and Others

This is a study of some of your attitudes. Of course, there is no right answer for any statement. The best answer is what you feel is true of yourself.

You are to respond to each question on the answer sheet according to the following scheme:

1	2	3	4	5
Not at all true of myself	Slightly true of myself	About halfway true of myself	Mostly true of myself	True of myself

Remember, the best answer is the one which applies to you.

Scale
+S 1   I'd like it if I could find someone who would tell me how to solve my personal problems.

S 2 I don't question my worth as a person, even if I think others do.

O 3 I can be comfortable with all varieties of people - from the highest
to the lowest.

O 4 I can become so absorbed in the work I'm doing that it doesn't bother me not
to have any intimate friends.

+O 5 I don't approve of spending time and energy in doing things for other people.
I believe in looking to my family and myself more and letting others
shift for themselves.

+ = reversed scoring items, i.e. negative items.

(From Shaw and Wright: *Scales for the Measurement of Attitudes*, 1967.
By permission of the McGraw-Hill Book Company)

C. General Techniques

These are flexible techniques without a set body of items. This
means that each technique can be adapted to suit the type of
sample and the aim of the study, with each investigator creating
particular variants relevant to his study. Some of these methods
actually allow the subject to generate his own items so that a
phenomenological perspective is adopted.

1. Q technique

Source: Stevenson (1953); Bennett (1964); Butler and Haigh
(1954)
Type of measure: Card sorting
Age range: 11 years to adult (various forms)

Description
The general Q technique has already been described. The most
well-known set of Q statements is the universe of a self-referent
statement developed by Butler and Haigh (1954). It consists of a
set of 100 statements which were claimed to be taken at random
from therapy protocols. The test–retest reliability over 6 months is
0.86. Actually the Butler and Haigh items are accidental rather
than random since potential items were restricted to those
verbalised by clients undergoing client-centred therapy. It is quite
possible that these statements constitute a sample biased in favour
of client-centred counselling, hence generalisation to other
self-evaluative situations or traits is rather a doubtful exercise.
Most of the items appear in Rogers and Dymond (1954, pp. 78,
275 and 276). They are mainly general assertions rather than being
situationally specific, e.g. 'I am a submissive person', 'I am a hard
worker', 'I am likeable'. Prior to the commencement of
counselling, each subject was requested to sort the statements in
two ways according to the following instructions:

Self-sort: Sort these cards to describe yourself as you see yourself
today from those that are least like you to those that are most
like you.

Ideal-sort: Now sort these cards to describe your ideal person – the person you would most like within yourself to be.

The average correlation for the therapy group between self and ideal was zero, but a control group who had not sought therapy produced a correlation of 0.58 which shows that a non-treatment group is much more satisfied with itself than a treatment group. After completion of therapy the clients took the self and ideal sorts again and this time the correlation was 0.34; the control group didn't change on their second Q sorts. Another control group that had sought therapy but who had not been given any therapy showed no change in their self-ideal correlations over that time period. The technique appears to have concurrent validity. But other workers, e.g. Wiener et al. (1959) show that there is limited consistency between psychologists as to which items index adjustment and maladjustment. In their study 28 psychologists sorted the Butler and Haigh items to describe how they thought 'a well-adjusted person would sort these cards'. Mean adjustment values were obtained for each item. Then the 37 items most like the 'well-adjusted' person and the 37 items least like the 'well-adjusted' person were determined. Only 33 of the 37 'most-adjusted' items and 29 out of the 37 'least-adjusted' items were common to the lists compiled by Dymond and by Wiener et al. (1959). Of the 26 items found by Dymond to be irrelevant to adjustment, 12 were judged in Wiener's study to be reliably assigned to the adjsted or maladjusted side of the continuum. Thus, content validity is low. Test–retest reliability over a 6-month period has been reported as 0.74 by Stimson (1968).

The Q sort has been used as a research tool in the exploration of self concept with various groups. These have included delinquents (Balester, 1956); hospital patients (Chase, 1957); student group counselling (Caplan, 1957). The method has been used extensively by Rogers and his associates in studying the self concept in its relationship to psychotherapy (Rogers and Dymond, 1954). Bennett (1964) has developed a self-concept Q sort for use with children. The statements were obtained from the Butler and Haigh (1954) set and Hilden's (1954) manual on Q sorts. Adaptations were made to ensure that the reading level required was not higher than 8 years; 108 self-referent statements served as a basis for two 54-item alternative forms of the sort. All the statements were evaluated by requesting judges to distribute the statements into three piles, representing high self concept, low self concept and questionable, unclear or in appropriate statements. The final set of statements numbered 52 and these were constituted into two 26-item parallel forms. The statements are presented to children on cards which are placed in a series of five pockets labelled 'most like me', to 'most unlike me'. Examples of statements included are 'I don't try as hard as I should', and 'I make a good leader'. The correlation between the two forms is 0.86. The correlation between IQ and self concept, and need-achievement and self concept are respectively 0.25 and 0.24 ($N = -98$). The test can be administered in group form taking 30 minutes for the sorting. Bennett reports that her subjects (11 year olds) found the task interesting and non-threatening.

2. Semantic differential

Source: Osgood, Suci and Tannenbaum, (1957); Warr and
    Knapper (1968).
Type of measure: Rating scale
Age range: 8 years and above

Description
This is an extremely flexible technique rather than a particular scale. It was originally developed to measure the meaning systems of individuals, essentially connotative meaning. It has become a very economic method of assessing attitudes to n objects within the ambit of one instrument. Basically the method involves sets of polar adjectives, e.g. good–bad, happy–sad, reliable–unreliable, listed down every page. Each page is headed with a stimulus word or phrase. The pairs of adjectives are listed as endpoints of a continuum divided into an uneven number, usually 5 or 7, of response gradations. Subjects are requested to consider the stimulus in terms of each of the scales, and place a check-mark in one of the divisions on the continuum to indicate the relative applicability of the polar terms. Warr and Knapper (1968) provide a comprehensive review of this technique in person perception. Factor analysis has generally revealed three distinct orthogonal factors, viz. evaluation, potency and activity, of which the evaluative is the dominant one. This led Osgood to believe that the attitudinal variable in human thinking is primary. Consequently, Osgood claimed that the semantic differential could be employed as an attitude-measuring device provided only scales loaded on the evaluative dimension were used. Since it has been argued strongly in earlier chapters that the self concept is a set of attitudes to the self, this instrument appears a most appropriate vehicle with which to measure the self concept, the ideal self, the other self, etc. The reliability and validity of the semantic differential is well documented, (e.g. Warr and Knapper, 1968). Scales which are loaded on the evaluative dimension are, for instance: good–bad, successful–unsuccessful, beautiful–ugly, cruel–kind, clean–dirty, wise–foolish, honest–dishonest, happy–sad, nice–awful.

However, Burns (1976a) reviews various investigations which reveal that scales weighted heavily on the evaluative dimension for one concept may not be strongly evaluative when applied to another concept. It would seem necessary for a factor analysis to be undertaken to discern which presumed evaluative scales actually index the evaluative dimension when used to rate the cognised, other and ideal selves. The inclusion of the 'marker' scale good–bad which generally has been shown to be strongly evaluative in judging a wide variety of concepts would aid identification of scales weighted on the evaluative dimension. Clarity and relevance of bipolar scales are seen as important advantages in this technique, but must not override the criterion of validity for indexing the evaluative factor. Potential users are advised to carry out a factor analysis to ensure that their scales do best represent the evaluative dimension for the particular self-referent concepts they are attempting to measure.

A typical layout and instructions for an evaluation of self perception by the semantic differential techniques is as follows:

The purpose of this study is to measure the *meanings* which certain concepts have for you. This is done by having you judge them against a set of descriptive scales which consist of adjectives and their opposites. You are asked to make your judgements on the basis of what these things mean *to you*. On each page of this booklet, you will find a different concept to be judged and beneath it a set of scales. You are asked to rate the concept on each of the scales in order.

Here is how you are to use the scales:

If you feel that the concept at the top of the page is *very closely related* to one end of the scale, you should place your check-mark as follows:

fair : __X__ : ____ : ____ : ____ : ____ : ____ : ____ : unfair

OR

fair : ____ : ____ : ____ : ____ : ____ : ____ : __X__ : unfair

If you feel that the concept is *quite closely related* to one or the other end of the scale (but not extremely), you should place your check-mark as follows:

weak : ____ : __X__ : ____ : ____ : ____ : ____ : ____ : strong

OR

weak : ____ : ____ : ____ : ____ : ____ : __X__ : ____ : strong

If the concept seems only *slightly related* to one side as opposed to the other (but is not really neutral), then you should place your check-mark thus:

active : ____ : ____ : __X__ : ____ : ____ : ____ : ____ : passive

OR

active : ____ : ____ : ____ : ____ : __X__ : ____ : ____ : passive

The direction towards which you check, of course, depends upon which of the two ends of the scale seems most characteristic of the concept you're judging.

If you consider the concept to be *neutral* on the scale, both sides of the scale equally associated with the concept, of if the scale is completely irrelevant, unrelated to the concept, then you should place your check-mark in the middle space, thus:

safe :____:____:____:____:____: X :____:____:____:____: dangerous

IMPORTANT:

1. Place your check-marks in the middle of the spaces not at the boundaries.
2. Be sure you check every scale for every concept, *do not omit any*.
3. Never put more than one check-mark on a single scale.
4. Do not look back and forth through the items. Do not try to remember how you checked similar items earlier in the test. *Make each item a separate and independent judgement.*
5. Work fairly quickly through the items.
6. Do not worry or puzzle over individual items. It is your first impressions, the immediate 'feelings' about the items that is wanted. On the other hand, do not be careless, for it is your true impression that is wanted.

Concept – Myself

good :____:____:____:____: X :____:____:____:____: bad

rigid :____:____:____:____:____:____: X :____:____: flexible

independent :____: X :____:____:____:____:____:____:____: submissive

democratic : X :____:____:____:____:____:____:____:____: authoritarian

disorganised :____:____:____:____:____:____:____: X :____: organised

cooperative :____:____:____: X :____:____:____:____:____: uncooperative

non-conforming :____:____:____:____:____: X :____:____: conforming

etc.

The particular scales included are those the investigator wishes to include – usually on the grounds of relevance to the concepts and hypotheses under investigation – though, as has been already argued, factorial validity for the evaluative dimension is the ultimate criterion. In using the semantic differential in self-concept study the following concepts are particularly useful to employ:

Myself As I Am.
Myself As I Would Like To Be.
Myself As Others See Me.
Myself As A Student (or Husband, Father, etc.).

To prevent the acquiescence response set scale polarity is reversed for pairs in random order, and for these the scoring on the 1–7 range is reversed. For individuals a total score reflecting level of self evaluation can be obtained on the dubious assumption – as with most other instruments – that all items are equal in salience. With groups such totals would be averaged or a weighted average response could be computed for each scale. The semantic differential technique appears appropriately for use with children of 12 years of age and upwards.

Hardstaffe (1973) used five-point semantic differential scales with 205 secondary pupils and reported that first-year secondary modern pupils perceived no differences between themselves and first-year grammar school pupils on objective attributes such as clever, successful, lazy, but considered themselves superior on personal qualities for instance, good-looking, kind and friendly. This finding suggests compensation for 11+ failure.

Burns (1975) employed the semantic differential in a study relating self concept to ethnic attitudes and acceptance of others. Analysis revealed that the way 'Myself As I Am' was perceived related significantly to ethnocentric attitudes in that there was a strong relationship between high levels of self concept and low levels of ethnocentrism.

Oles (1973) found that 8 year olds could cope with a semantic differential with only five points on the continuum, each point described verbally, viz. very : sort of : neither : sort of : very. Internal reliability attained 0.92 and test–retest reliability over half a year reached 0.44 with these children. For a more detailed account of the semantic differential technique and its application readers are advised to consult Osgood, Suci and Tannerbaum (1957) and Warr and Knapper (1968).

3. Role construct repertory technique or rep test

Source: Kelly (1955); Bannister and Mair (1968)
Type of measure: Construct generation
Age range: 10 years plus

Description

Kelly adopts a phenomenological approach which permits the subject to generate his own set of descriptions or constructs rather than respond to a fixed set of scales/traits imposed by the experimenter. Kelly devised this test, of which there are eight varieties including a group form, as a means of operationalising construct measurement (see Ch. 2, Role Construct Theory). The aim is to elicit a person's constructs so that the way he sees the world including his self in all its manifestations can be examined and interrelationships between constructs established. The popular form of the test is the Grid version. In this the subject is requested to provide a list of persons relevant to his everyday life, maybe including himself, his ideal self, his self as others see him, etc. These form the elements which are listed along the top of the grid as in Fig. 5.1. These persons or roles are each written on a separate card. The examiner selects three cards at a time (triadic elicitation), e.g. myself, best friend, mother, and asks the subject to suggest an important way in which two of these people are alike but different from the third. Elicited constructs are entered in the side column. When the subject has made the differentiation, the examiner places ticks in the appropriate cells for the two roles seen as similar as in the example below for hardworking – lazy. The subject is then asked to look at all the other people named on the cards and say which he would also call hardworking, rather than lazy. Further ticks are placed in appropriate cells. This same process is repeated for perhaps a further 15–20 times, until the examiner has before him the major constructs by which the subject construes and structures his interpersonal environment – a pattern which can be subjected to factor or cluster analysis, as can the relationships between role figures.

Role figures

Myself	Myself as I would like to be	Father	Mother	Boss	Best friend	Constructs
○	✓		⊘	✓	⊘	hardworking – lazy
⊘	⊘	○	✓		✓	kind – cruel
○	✓	⊘		⊘		dominant – submissive
✓	○		⊘		⊘	emotional – unemotional
✓			⊘	○	⊘	anxious – calm
						etc.

The circles indicate the three roles involved in each elicitation. Ticks indicate which of the role figures are seen as possessing the first pole of the construct.

Other commonly used varieties of the grid method are:

1. The full context form in which the subject is faced with all the role cards at once and asked to group them so that all people who are alike in some way are together. Constructs are identified by questioning the subject after each grouping.
2. The sequential form in which one role card of the triad is removed and replaced by another until every possible combination has been exhausted.
3. The self-identification form where the subject is asked to provide constructs he uses to identify himself in contrast to

others by presenting him with two cards representing other people and a third which also represents himself. He can then be asked supplementary questions such as, if you were with those two people what would you be talking about, how would you be feeling, etc.? This version would seem particularly appropriate for identifying components of the self concept. All the forms of the Rep Test have common features:

(a) a concern with eliciting the construct pattern for a person;
(b) a lack of fixed form or content; it is a technique not a test; form and content selection is related to each particular subject or problem;
(c) all forms are devised so that statistical test of significance can be applied to the data.

The original focus of personal construct theory (Ch. 2) was the therapeutic process, with the specific function of revealing the individual patient's personal way of construing himself and elements of his environment. For example Fransella and Adams (1965) used a Rep Grid investigation to discover the self concept of an arsonist, and thereby uncover the reasons for his fire-raising. He did not construe his fire-raising in an expected way, e.g. as a crime, as a distorted sexual activity or as an illness. It was found he construed himself as totally moral and righteous with the implication that his fire-raising was his means of punishing wrongdoers. Salmon (1963) assessed the self concept of a woman who wanted to change sex. Rep Grid analysis of her construing of men revealed a highly organised way of construing them, but her construing of females indicated such an unstructured concept that it was apparent that feminine identity was a meaningless idea to her.

Concepts of reliability and validity have little meaning in this idiographic phenomenological approach. As Kelly comments, reliability measures insensitivity to change. If a person acts in accordance with his subjective constructs then for him they are valid. One major problem with the technique is ensuring that the sample of person-role elements is representative of the person elements in the subject's environment. For example if we were investigating the self-concept constructs of an adolescent female and only included male role persons the evidence would only be partial. Kelly also stresses a further problem in that some constructs may not be able to be given verbal labels, and even when verbal labels are generated other persons may not use those labels with exactly the same meaning. A final problem is that of comparing grids when free selection of role elements and constructs are permitted. One use of the grid with groups has been to abstract the constructs used and form them into a more conventional attitude measure, i.e. find a yardstick from particular population or sample on which the research interest is focused. No satisfactory solution has yet been found as to how to summarise data from a number of grids. A useful refinement of the approach has been proposed by Kilpatrick and Cantril (1965) who integrated it into a self-anchoring scale technique. In this modification the subject is provided with a set of pictorial scales each depicting a 10-rung ladder. Each ladder describes a specific construct already elicited by the triadic technique which might refer to an element of his self image. The top rung of the ladders is rated 10 and indicates the very highest standing on the particular construct, whereas the bottom rung, rated 0, applies to the lowest self evaluation on the construct under consideration. The subject is requested to place a cross in the spaces on each ladder which most faithfully represent his current self estimate on those constructs which are generated by him, important to him and by which he orders his world. This 'ladder' rating is particularly suitable for younger children as the analogy presented pictorially is well understood, though fewer rungs may well be more appropriate for them.

4. Adjective generation technique

Source: Allen and Potkay (1973)
Type of measure: Adjective generation
Age range: 8 years plus

Description
This technique allows the subject to produce his own self-descriptive traits and in this provides a phenomenological perspective, with the subject imposing his structure on to the situation. The subject is simply asked to offer five adjectives that best describe him. These five adjectives are then compared with a set of 555 adjectives previously judged in terms of their favourability on a seven-point scale (Anderson, 1968). Allen and Potkay (1973) provide another list of 1,700 adjectives. The ratings of these adjectives act as weights for the adjectives generated by the subject. A mean score is calculated which provides a measure of the favourability of the subject's self description. Allen and Potkay report test–retest reliabilities of 0.41 over a 2-week interval and 0.74 over a longer period. In terms of construct validity a correlation of 0.40 was produced with the Self Regard subscale of Shostrum's (1966) Personal Orientation Inventory.

5. 'Who Am I?' test

Source: Kuhn and McPartland (1954)
Type of measure: Sentence completion
Age range: 10 years upwards

Description
This measure requests subjects to respond to the simple direction
question 'who am I?' 20 times. As a result it has often been
termed the Twenty Statements Test. The 'Who Am I?' test was
developed out of Bugental and Zelen's (1948) 'Who Are You?'
test. The 20 responses to the question are written in the order that
they occur to the subject who is requested not to bother about
order, spelling or logic. The value of the test is that it allows noun
forms (categories) as well as adjectives (attributes). From the data,
the authors discerned a set of consensual items that reflected social
structural anchorages so that Kuhn (1960) has been prompted to
list the following categories for coding subjects' responses:

1. Social groups and classifications, e.g. sex, age, race, religion,
   occupation.
2. Ideological beliefs, e.g. philosophic, religious, political or
   moral statements.
3. Interests.
4. Ambitions.
5. Self evaluations.

These consensual statements (i.e. those pertaining to categories
whose limits and membership are matters of common knowledge,
e.g. student, brother, Anglican, tend to be made before the subject
passes on to utter subconsensual statements (i.e. those applying to
attributes and classes which necessitate interpretation by the
respondent himself in order to place him relative to others, e.g.
bored, too fat). Bugental and Zelen (1950) found that the most
frequent categories used were name, sex, age and occupation, with
evaluative responses becoming more frequent with increasing age.
In Kuhn's study it was noted that children's answers to the
question tended to scatter over a wide range and to focus on
particular, individualistic or idiosyncratic aspects of their lives.
With increasing age, the conceptions of personal identity funneled
into the kinds of broad social categories that are also employed to
describe the social structure. Adults identified themselves more
often by occupation, class, marital status, sex, age, race, religion
and other similar criteria. Thus, when a very young child who has
lost his parents in a crowd is asked who he is, he may be able to
supply only his first name and a variety of irrelevant information
that does not give much help to those who are trying to return him
to his parents.

Two examples from Kuhn's study underline the point. A
fourth-grade girl replying to the question, 'who am I?', wrote a
series of negative statements about her behaviour, obviously
reflecting parental discipline and admonition: 'I boss too much. I
get mad at my sisters. I am a show off. I interrupt too much. I

waste time. Sometimes I am a bad sport. I fiddle around. I am careless at times. I forget.'

In contrast, the response of a university student included the following items among others: 'I am of the female sex. My age is 20. I am from (city and state). I have two parents. My home is happy. I am happy. I am of the middle class. I am a (sorority name). I am in the Waves Officer School. I am an adjusted person. I am a (department major). I attend church.' It is apparent that the latter series tells us much about the person's position in society, whereas the former series tells us about almost nothing except the parental discipline imposed upon a fourth-grade child.

The unstructured format is seen as an advantage in that it provides the subject with full scope to express his self concept. But Spitzer et al. (1966) report that subjects actually dislike this freedom and prefer more structured instruments which require less introspection. The interpretation of the order in which responses are generated has been proposed by Gordon (1968) as a function of the salience or importance of the response with salience inversely related to ordinal position, i.e. later responses are regarded as less salient. Of course psychoanalytic theory would hypothesise the opposite relationship! Gordon's (1968) and McPhail's (1972) investigations among others suggest that any relationship between salience and order is questionable.

There is an inconsistency between Kuhn's phenomenological rationale to the test and the content analysis form of scoring where the experimenter imposes his own categories. There are many problems in handling the scoring of such an open-ended instrument. One problem is that subjects provide different numbers of responses despite the request to generate a set number. Percentages are not appropriate when some subjects provide different numbers of responses despite the request to generate a set number. Percentages are not appropriate when some subjects provide only four responses. Another problem is how to code statements of varying length which may contain several distinct responses in a compound sentence. Gordon (1968) recommends coding each measuring element to avoid loss of information. Thus, while this test appears superficially of great merit, the empirical yield will have to be substantial, as Wylie (1974) points out, to warrant the extra time and effort on complex content analyses as opposed to the usual scoring of instruments.

D. Academic self-concept measures

The effect of self attitudes on academic performance is one of the major areas of self-concept investigation. As a result quite a number of academic self-concept measures have been designed.

1. Position in class scale

Source: Willig (1973)
Type of measure: Self rating
Age range: 10–12 year olds

Description
This is suggested as a very easy and rapid technique for estimating
a 10–12-year-old child's self image of academic ability. The pupil is
provided with a list of numbers from 1 to 30 in sequence. He is
asked to underline the class position he thinks he would probably
reach in a general test of school work. Willig obtained a test–retest
reliability of 0.91 with 210 boys and 356 girls in the 10–12-year
age range. He also found that his scale was significantly related to
the children's actual academic ability, teachers' ratings of the
children's task orientation, the children's academic sociometric
status and the children's academic self constructs. However, in an
unpublished study (Reid, 1976) the scale related only at a low
level with the Baker Lunn (1970) and Brookover, Thomas and
Patterson (1964) scales.

2. Self-appraisal scale

Source: Davidson and Greenberg (1967)
Type of measure: Rating scale
Age range: 10–16 years

Description
This instrument is described in detail in *School Achievers from a
Deprived Background* (1967) for which it was specifically created.
    The SAS consists of 24 items each of which has been pretested
to make certain that it was easily understood by 10-year-old
children. Split-half reliability of the test is 0.77. In giving the test,
the directions are read by the examiner while the children read
silently. The examiner continues to read each word while allowing
time for each child to rate himself. The scale appears suitable for
upper primary and secondary pupils. Positive words and phrases
(numbers 1, 2, 3, 6, 8, 9, 10, 11, 12, 15, 17, 19, 21, 23, 24) are
given a score of '2' if the cross appears in the column 'About Half
the time', and '1' if the cross appears in the column 'Hardly ever'.
The reverse scoring is used for the negative items (numbers 4, 5, 7,
13, 16, 18, 20, 22). The scale is reproduced in full on p. 137 by
kind permission of the authors.
    Cohen (1974) used this scale in a study of alienation from
school among 244 older secondary pupils in a Sheffield
comprehensive school. A significant relationship (+0.27) was
reported between low self esteem and alienation.

Self-appraisal Scale

Helen Davidson and Judith Greenberg

The City University of New York

Directions: The words on this page are used by children to describe themselves. Read the words next to each number. Put a cross (X) in *one* box on each line to show whether you think you are that way *most of the time* or *about half the time* or *hardly ever.* Remember there are no right or wrong answers.

I think I am:	Most of the time	About half the time	Hardly ever
1. neat			
2. a big help at home			
3. smart in school			
4. shy			
5. a pest			
6. very good in art			
7. scared to take chances			
8. full of fun			
9. a hard worker			
10. polite			
11. trying my best			
12. nice looking			
13. lazy			
14. full of questions about new things			
15. going to do well			
16. sad			
17. good in sports			
18. careless			
19. honest			
20. nervous			
21. good at making things			
22. bad			
23. liked by other children			
24. as lucky as others			

3. Adjective checklist

Source: Davidson and Lang (1960)
Type of measure: Checklist
Age range: 9–16 years

Description
The check list consists of 35 behavioural traits that measure the child's perceptions of his teacher's attitude towards him. It also serves as a measure of self perception. The words in the scale were selected on the basis of established trait lists, appropriate difficulty

level and an equal distribution of negative and positive connotations. Examples of the 35 words that have either a favourable (F) or unfavourable (U) rating are as follows : fair (F), a nuisance (U), afraid (U), a hard worker (F), bad (U), a good sport (F). Children are instructed to rate each trait name on a three-point scale in terms of how the teacher feels toward them. For this purpose the children select from three response categories: most of the time, half of the time, seldom or almost never. On favourable items the respective scores for these responses are 3, 2 and 1. On unfavourable items the scoring procedure is reversed.

The total score of Index of Favourability has a possible range from 1.00 to 3.00, and is obtained by adding the scores of all the words and dividing by the number of words checked. Higher scores mean the child perceives the teacher as feeling positively towards him. Self perception can also be assessed by asking the child to rate the traits in terms of how he sees himself.

On the basis of the three criteria described above for selecting items, 135 trait names were originally rated by 35 teachers and 50 junior high pupils as favourable, unfavourable or neutral. The final list contained only those words that had been rated as favourable or unfavourable by more than 80 per cent of the members in each scale. These results, then, would provide some evidence that the scale has content validity. A rank-difference correlation coefficient of 0.85 ($p<0.001$) was obtained for 105 junior high school children, based on two administrations of the checklist 4–6 weeks apart. Furthermore, a rank correlation coefficient of 0.51 ($p<0.001$) was obtained between a teacher approval score derived from a Guess Who Sociometric Technique in three elementary classes ($N=93$) and the Index of Favourability on the checklist. The authors regard this correlation as a measure of empirical and concurrent validity (Davidson and Lang, 1960).

4. Self concept of academic ability

Source: Brookover, Erikson and Joiner (1967)
Type of measure: Rating scale
Age range: 8 years to end of adolescence

Description
This scale focuses specifically upon the self concept in the context of education. The general version attempts to measure the evaluation one makes of oneself in respect to the ability to achieve in academic tasks in general as compared to others. This inventory consists of eight items each coded from 5 to 1. The specific form measures the evaluation one makes of oneself in respect to a given subject-matter area. The items for these scales are directly parallel to items in the general instrument. The four subject areas are mathematics, social studies, English and science.

In the general form, the higher the self concept the higher the numerical value on each item, with 40 being the maximum score. Scoring is essentially the same in the specific form except that each question involves four subject areas, thus giving four, eight-item tests which are scored like the general form. The instruments are self administered and designed for group administration.

Approximately 1,500 white students in an urban school setting grades 4–10 were tested in the course of the two USOE Cooperative Research Projects. The instruments have been used in other research, sometimes in a revised form. The eight-item general form produced test–retest coefficients of 0.75 for males ($n=466$) and 0.77 for females ($n=50$) after a year's interval. Internal consistency coefficients ranged from 0.82 to 0.92 for males and 0.77 to 0.84 for females, with large samples of students in grades 7–10. The general form has the characteristics of a Guttman scale with high coefficients of reproducibility. The specific form showed test–retest correlations from 0.63 to 0.80 and internal consistency coefficients in ranges similar to the general form.

The general self concept of ability scale was correlated with a variety of variables (e.g. evaluations of teacher, friends, parents; grade point average; scores on specific self concept of ability). This instrument showed consistently high correlations with the other variables.

Brookover, Erikson and Joiner (1967), using a longitudinal approach with 307 girls and 255 boys for 6 years between the age of 12 and 17, found a significant relationship between self concept of academic ability, and academic achievement at each age level. More importantly, changes in self concept of ability were reflected in changes in academic achievement. Self concept of ability showed higher correlations with achievement than other general measurements of the self concept.

A short version of the scale consists of six multiple-choice items, each scored on a five-point scale with high values reflecting more positive academic self concepts. The child is required by each item to compare himself with his peers on various elements of academic performance. This short version has no validity or scaleability reported. Cohen and Cohen (1974) have used the short form of the Brookover scale with 801 children in the north-east of England. High self concept of ability was shown to be strongly related to the pupils' liking of various school subject areas. These instruments are unusual in that they focus on specific subject areas of academic performance.

5. Academic self-concept scale

Source: Payne and Farquhar (1962)
Type of measure: Word rating list
Age range: Student and adult

Description
This instrument consists of 48 one-, two- or three-word concepts or
phrases, e.g. purposeful, below average, easily distracted. It was
developed as one of a battery of tests designed to measure
motivation for academic achievement. Each subject is requested to
rate each of these concepts or words on a four-point scale, viz.
never, sometimes, usually, always, as they believed their teachers
would rate the traits in describing him. Reliability indices range
from 0.88 to 0.93 for various samples of males and females. Payne
and Farquhar (1962) provide strong evidence of concurrent and
predictive validity.

6. Academic self-image scale

Source: Barker Lunn (1970)
Type of measure: Rating scale
Age range: 9–12 year olds

Description
This scale was specifically devised as part of a battery in an NFER
research study investigating streaming in primary schools. The scale
attempts to depict the older primary school child's view of himself
in terms of his academic performance. The subject is asked to rate
nine statements on a three-point scale. Scores range from 18, a
very positive academic self image, to 0, a very poor academic self
image.

The scale was constructed from the responses of 400 pupils
randomly selected from a large representative sample of around
2,300 fourth-year boys and girls from 28 primary schools. An
internal consistency index (alpha coefficient) of 0.88 is reported.
Barker Lunn found that boys and bright children possess more
positive self images than girls and duller children. She also showed
that children of average and below-average ability developed
poorer academic self images when taught in streamed classes than
when taught in unstreamed classes, but above-average children
demonstrated more positive academic self images in streamed than
in unstreamed classrooms.

7. Self concept as learner scale

Source: Waetjen (1963)
Type of measure: Rating scale
Age range: 11–16 year olds

Description
This 50-item scale was developed by factor analysing 400 self-
referential statements gleaned from a range of other self-report

instruments. Waetjen obtained four major factors each constituting a dimension of one's self concept as a learner. Items within each of the four factor components are judged in terms of the way an adequate learner would respond. The four components or subsections are described below, together with one item as an example (quoted by permission of the author).

Motivation subsection   These test items are measures of the subject's perception of his motivation with respect to tasks he faces in a classroom situation. The items focus on learning tasks and not procedural matters. Essentially the test items measure the learner's view of the avidity for the unusual or dissonant aspect of the classroom, e.g. I get my work done, but I don't do extra work.

Task orientation subsection.   This category of test items enable the learner to describe himself in terms of those skills and behaviours that keep the individual focused on the learning task. Thus the subject describes himself in terms of thinking, listening, timeliness of action and following directions – all as applied to classroom learning tasks, e.g. I am able to get my work done on time.

Problem-solving subsection.   These test items give insight into the learner's perceptions of his intellectual ability. In the main the items deal with perception of thinking skills, differentiation capabilities, understanding and decisiveness of action, e.g. I solve problems quite easily.

Class membership subsection.   These items concern themselves with the subjects' view of themselves of members of a group whose major reason for being is to learn. Since peers are significant others in the life of students, the degree to which one sees oneself as belonging to the learning group of peers is, therefore, a factor in learning, e.g. I take an active part in group projects and activities.

Five scores are obtainable, one from each of the four factors, and a composite score by employing the Likert technique. The measure consists of 50 statements worded either positively or negatively to which the subject responds with one of five possible answers. He places a 5 in a blank space beside the statement if he feels it is completely true, 4 if the statement is mostly true, 3 if the statement is partly true and partly false, 2 if the statement is mostly false and 1 if the statement is completely false. The score received for each positive statement is equivalent to the number he places in the blank space. The negative statements are scored by reversing the scoring procedures of the positive statements.

Reliability of SCAL is 0.90 for the test as a whole. Reliability coefficients are available for each of the four subtests. Currently the instrument is in wide use in the United States by school systems as well as researchers and universities. Permission to use the instrument must be obtained from Dr Walter B. Waetjen, President, The Cleveland State University, Cleveland, Ohio 44115.

8. Scale for inferring the self concept

Source: Combs and Soper (1963)
Type of measure: Rating scale
Age range: Student

Description
This scale was devised to help teachers to infer how each of his students perceives (*a*) himself, (*b*) his relationships with others and (*c*) others. The teacher simply rates the student on five-point scales. By adding the number under each rating, an inferred self-concept score is obtained in each of the three areas plus a total score. It must be noted that there are no reported reliability or validity indices for this scale. Any scores from this instrument must be regarded as a guide and quite tentative in its present condition. It should be only used by research workers competent to generate the required validity and reliability indices.

E. Miscellaneous instruments

1. Body cathexis scale

Source: Secord and Jourard (1953)
Type of measure: Rating scale
Age range: 12 years to adult

Description
Body cathexis is the degree of satisfaction or dissatisfaction with various parts or processes of the body. This test requires the subject to indicate on a scale the strength and direction of feeling which he holds about various parts or functions of his body. The subject is presented with a list of 46 body parts and functions, e.g. weight, teeth, energy level. Each is rated on a five-point scale as follows:

1. Have strong feelings and wish change could be made somehow.
2. Don't like but can put up with.
3. Have no particular feelings either way.
4. Am satisfied.
5. Consider myself fortunate.

Organs relating to sexual and excretory functions were deliberately omitted. The body cathexis score can either be obtained by

summing the ratings or by averaging. Secord and Jourard
(1953) report split-half reliabilities for 45 males and 45 females of
0.78 and 0.83 respectively. A correlation of 0.58 for women and
0.66 for men was obtained between body cathexis and a global
self-concept measure based on a wide-ranging list of characteristics
rated against the same rating scale as the body cathexis test. These
figures suggest that the body cathexis test has a measure of
construct validity in that individuals feel about their body in a
similar fashion to the way they feel about many other aspects of
themselves. Females were found to cathect their body irrespective
of direction more highly than men, assigning far fewer middle
categories. An attempt to show a relationship between levels of
body cathexis and anxiety was demonstrated with women (-0.41)
but not with men. This may be because body shape can provide
more anxiety for women because of the social importance and
societal evaluation of certain elements of the female form. The
scale is very much at the mercy of social desirability influences. An
internal factor analysis would be useful to discern any common
factor. Since body image is an important element of self esteem,
further refinement and development of this scale seems
worthwhile.

2. Self concept of ability as a worker scale

Source: Burke and Sellin (1972)
Type of measure: Self rating + questionnaire
Age range: Adolescent

Description
This scale is to be used as an aid in teaching and counselling the
educable retarded adolescent. It is an aid to a teacher or counsellor
to indicate:

(*a*) the kind of classroom activities which should be devised to
support the pupil as he prepares himself to enter the world of
work;
(*b*) the kind of job that should be selected specifically as it relates
to the perceived ability of the youngster; and
(*c*) how much supervision a youngster will need when he is placed
on a job.

The scale employs an interview technique and is organised into six
sections. The first is a general introduction partially to gain
rapport; section two deals with relationships with significant others;
section three concerns the subject's self concept of ability as a
worker in general; sections four to six inclusive allow the subject to
assess his self concept as a worker from the perspective of his
parents, his best friend and his teacher respectively. The authors
provide a rationale and statistical verification of the instrument.

3. Incomplete sentences blank

Source: Rotter and Willerman (1947); Rotter, Rafferty and
  Schachtitz (1949)
Type of measure: Projective
Age range: Student to adult

Description
This scale has been used mainly to assess mental disturbance and
seems to combine a projective approach with objective scoring.
The subject is able to express his own feelings and hence taps self
conception from a phenomenological view of particular value in
providing background material prior to counselling. Most subjects
complete the scale in 20 minutes and group administration is
possible. Subjects are urged to express their real feelings and
attempt every item. Examples of sentences provided are:

I like ....
My greatest worry is ....

Responses are scored by dividing them into three categories, viz.
conflict and unhealthy, positive and healthy, neutral. A seven-point
scale is obtained by producing a continuum with three levels of
conflict responses, three levels of positive responses, and the
neutral category at the centre. Extreme positive scores 0, while
extreme conflict scores 6. Rotter, Rafferty and Schachtitz (1949)
provide examples of many responses with their scoring categories.
The same authors report interscorer reliability of 0.91 for 50 male
protocols and 0.96 for 50 female protocols. A split-half reliability
corrected by the Spearman–Brown formula based on 124 male
subjects is reported as 0.84. Criterion concurrent validity
coefficients obtained between ratings of adjusted or maladjusted
and test score were 0.64 for females and 0.77 for males. Thus, this
scale appears very suitable for screening students for counselling.

4. Somatic apperception test

Source: Adams and Caldwell (1963)
Type of measure: Projective
Age range: 7–14 year olds

Description
This test consists of 10 wooden figures with removable head, legs
and arms, the complete figures ranging from $11\frac{1}{2}$ to 16 inches tall
and differing from the next larger or smaller figure by $\frac{1}{2}$ inch.
There is additionally a set of 10 heads of the same graduated sizes
as the 10 figures, and 10 sets of each of the 4 limbs, also
graduated in size as with the original figures. The child picks out

the one of the 10 figures that he feels is most like him, and also his ideal, the figure he would most like to be. He then constructs his ideal from the extra parts. Several scores are obtained: the ratio between the child's actual measurements and his self-drawing; the ratio between actual measurements and choice of body parts; and the difference between perceived and desired body image. Some norms are given for white males aged 7–14, 35 normals, 13 moderately disturbed and 10 retarded (Adams and Caldwell, 1963), but no validity or reliability levels are reported. This test would seem suitable for more research as it provides an interesting motivating and novel approach in self-concept study.

5. Children's self-conception test

Source: Creelman (1955)
Type of measure: Non-verbal – pictorial
Age range: 6–11 years

Description
This test can be administered on a group or individual basis to children aged 6–11. It is a non-verbal test consisting of 24 sets of pictures with 8 pictures in each set. Four pictures show a boy engaged in an activity common to our culture and an equal number of pictures describe an identical activity for girls. One sequence of pictures, for example, shows a child playing with his father, helping his parents dry dishes, playing independently and doing the dishes by himself.

The test is administered separately but consecutively for three different purposes. Firstly, on each set, the children are asked to select the picture they like the best and to choose the one they dislike most. Secondly, they are asked to choose the good and bad pictures within each set. Finally, they are requested to select the pictures most like them and most unlike them. In scoring, each criterion has positive and negative choices. Specific procedures for scoring responses are provided for four types of scores: self-acceptance score, self-rejection score, acceptance of social values and rejection of social values. The separate scores or combinations of scores provide a measure of self acceptance or self rejection, positive or negative self evaluation, and acceptance and rejection of moral or social standards as the child perceives them. The scoring is objective and the author provides detailed instructions on scoring and administration. The author suggests a time period from 2 to 2½ hours for testing groups of 20–25 young children to allow for frequent rest periods.

The author provides no data on either test–retest or scorer reliability, but emphasises that the latter should be 'perfect' in view of the completely objective nature of the scoring! Creelman claims only face validity for the test. She also contends, however, that the results are consistent enough with theories of self concept and other theories of child development so that the CSC may provide a useful and valid method of investigating the self conceptions of children and their relationships to adjustment and maladjustment.

Despite the lack of reliability and validity indices, this test has been included as it uses a relatively infrequent method of assessment, and one that could be developed by more rigorous research into a test most suitable for young children for whom verbal tests are inappropriate. A microfilm copy of the test is available from the University of Michigan Microfilms, Ann Arbor, Michigan for $3.58.

Further reading

Wylie, R. *The Self Concept*, Vol. 1. *A Review of Methodological Considerations and Measuring Instruments*, Lincoln: University of Nebraska Press, 1974. In this updated version of Wylie's classic 1961 book, Ch. 4 and 5 provide extremely detailed, highly technical and critical accounts of a range of instruments purporting to measure the self concept.

Developmental issues

Chapter 6

Sources and content of the self concept and adolescence

Each human is unique; each conception evolves into an entirely new creation; each birth presents a fresh organism devoid of self awareness but ready to learn about itself. The self concept is not innate but develops out of the myriad of differentiated and accumulating 'I', 'me' and 'mine' experiences. Sherif and Cantril (1947) have cited many instances in early psychological writings which outline the gradual development of self conception in children. All the early writers concluded from their observations of children that at first the young child is not clear as to what constitutes 'Self' and what is 'not Self'. For a long time the infant's sense of self includes too much, since it also encompasses those close to him in a literal sense. To be separated from his mother is to lose a part of himself as much as to be separated from a hand or foot. But gradually by a process of interaction with persons and objects in the environment the self concept becomes more clearly defined. Piaget (1954) has indicated that initially the infant floats about (psychologically speaking) in an 'undifferentiated absolute' in which there are no boundaries between his body and other objects, between reality and phantasy; but gradually he makes distinctions between what is himself and what is not and so comes to separate himself from the external world. This is the most significant learning of the sensori-motor stage. It is impossible to assess directly the nature and development of the self concept in early childhood. The processes by which the child becomes aware of himself must be assessed by inference. From the baby's behaviour we can be reasonably sure that birth brings with it a plethora of stimulation impinging on all the sense organs. This flood of sensations, or what James termed 'a blooming buzzing confusion' swamps the child who only gradually begins to make sense of it all. Some sensations come from within his own body, e.g. hunger; others from the periphery of the body, e.g. contact with mother's body during feeding or bathing; yet other sensations come via the ears, eyes, nose and tongue. Much early self exploration proceeds accidentally – touching, sucking, pulling, seeing, hearing. All these sensations come to play an important role in defining the boundaries of the body, creating one of the first components of the self concept, the body image. Some infants

initially treat bodily parts as though they were not parts of
themselves, biting fingers and wondering why they feel pain.
In essence they often deal with their bodily parts exactly as
they do with other aspects of their environments. They examine,
manipulate, twist, bite and suck in ways that suggest unawareness
that bodily parts are themselves. But this learning leads to a
rudimentary discrimination between body and not-body. A whole
wealth of sensations from the body progressively enables the infant
to define more clearly the boundaries, locations and positioning of
his body. But as Murphy, Murphy and Newcomb (1937) describe,
this discrimination has not been made clearly even at 6 months.

> He does not even know the boundaries of his own body. Each hand
> wandering over the bedspread for things which can be brought into the
> mouth discovers the other hand and each triumphantly lifts the other into
> his mouth; he draws his thumb from his mouth to wave it at a stranger,
> then cries because the thumb has gone away. He pulls at his toes until
> they hurt and does not know what is wrong. (p. 207)

Self awareness emerges slowly as the infant uses and acts on his
environment. In his explorations from which he makes eventual
sense of the world, the child notices and manipulates things that
are not him. At first he seems almost to proceed by accident, but
later he does so by design. At first when objects are placed in his
hand he is able to grasp them but not able, at will, to release them
or throw or move them about. Soon, however, he is able to grasp
and to release, to reach for things and place them in a certain spot.
When he uses this ability he probably has a dim awareness of
himself as one who can produce effects by his own actions. For
instance, when he knocks a suspended mobile hanging over his cot
to make it tinkle repeatedly. This discovery of self through motor
activity links with the equally important means of discovering self
through the sense organs. These sensations and motor activities,
however simple, play an important role in defining the boundaries
of the body, a vital stage in differentiating self from the rest of the
environment.

    The development of the self concept does not occur in an
all-or-none fashion which permits us to say that up to one point in
time the child does not possess a self concept, but then suddenly,
eureka-like, he has. As was argued earlier (Ch. 3) each person
possesses multiple self conceptions and it is reasonable to infer that
the child (and equally, too, the adult) perceives different elements
or self conceptions with varying degrees of clarity at different
times. Moreover, the process of self-concept development never
really ends; it is actively proceeding from birth to death as the
individual continually discovers new potentials in the process of
'becoming'. In summary, to have a self concept, the child must
come to view himself as a distinct object and be able to see himself

as both subject and object, distinguishing himself from other objects. He must then become aware of other perspectives, for only in that way can he be aware of the evaluations of others about him.

Of the various sources of self conception, five appear vitally important, though their relative importance differs at different periods in the life span. These five sources are:

1. Body image – an evaluation of the physical self as a distinct object.
2. Language – the ability to conceptualise and verbalise about self and others.
3. Interpreted feedback from the environment about how significant others view the person and about how the person stands relative to various societal norms and values.
4. Identification with the appropriate sex role model and stereotype.
5. Child-rearing practices.

Naturally these sources do not function independently. They are closely interwoven in the fabric of social living. For instance various types of feedback and communication are involved in most learning about self situations with parents and peer group supplying the majority of the feedback subjectively interpreted by the subject. The separation of these sources is artificial and solely for the purpose of discussing their detailed operation. The first three of those sources will be considered in this chapter.

A. Sources of the self concept

1. The physical self and body image

Learning about what is and is not self through direct experience, and perception of the physical world without any social mediation is the child's first step in his life's journey. The terms 'body image' and 'body schema' are used to convey the concept of the physical body which each individual possesses. The original sense of body schema was that of the basic identity of the body, involving an awareness of its locations, positions and boundaries derived from sense perception fed to the sensory and motor areas of the cerebral cortex. It is a diagram or map of the body and its constituent parts. Hence the body schema is fundamental to the development of the body image which is the image a person has of himself as a physical being. The body image also involves an estimation and evaluation of the physical apparatus in terms of social norms and feedback from others. Thus, it is possible to distinguish these two terms with (*a*) the body schema being the knowledge derived from sensations of the body and the positions of its parts, and (*b*) the body image being the evaluated picture of the physical self. The former is in the realm of neuro-physiology; the latter belongs to the realm of developmental psychology. As we shall see, the person's concept of himself as a physical person becomes difficult to separate early in childhood from his concept of himself as a total person. In early childhood and again at adolescence, emphasis on the physical qualities of the individual are strongly marked and at these periods physical attributes and deficiences (both real and imagined) can have considerable effects on the development of a person's overall self concept. A person perceives and evaluates his body and its parts in the same way he perceives and evaluates any other object.

The self concept is initially a body image, an evaluated picture of the physical self. It is conceivable that the first distinction an infant makes between self and non-self is based on his awareness of his own tactile, muscular and kinaesthetic sensations as he touches, bites, throws, falls, bumps, etc. Body build, appearance and size is of vital importance in developing understanding of the evolution of a person's self concept. Bodily feelings and body image become the core of the self concept in the first few years of life. As bodily controls become more efficient the child learns to master his physical world, and these successes lead to an extension of the boundaries of activity. This in turn leads the child to deal with an increasing number of significant persons in his life so his self concept becomes more differentiated as a separate entity and helps to guide this interpersonal behaviour.

During these first few years of life it is likely that the self concept is not well integrated, with the child possessing many contradictory perceptions of himself. After initial sex typing by parents at birth, body size and shape is the most conspicuous physical attribute during childhood. Most cultures favour bigness in body size, with the tall person looked up to both literally and figuratively. In adolescent society greater body size offers avenues of prestige and power for the male, some socially sanctioned, e.g. sport, and some completely antisocial, e.g. gang fights. But extreme height can be detrimental as witness the 'bean-pole' girl or boy. What is apparent is that the norm is above the mean on height and strength for males, and on bust size for females and below the mean on height and weight for females. It is quite disruptive on personality to view one's body as dimensionally too different from the desired norm. Jourard and Secord (1955a) demonstrated that males had most satisfaction with their bodies when they were big; females were more satisfied with the body if they were less tall than normal. A girl's vital statistics are one of the most valuable credentials she can have. Even when irrelevant to the issue, such identifying indices are attached, as when a young lady succeeds in some male preserve, e.g. blonde bombshell (37–24–36) graduates as engineer. Each of us can be the 'recipient' or even initiator of such statements as 'he is all skin and bones – must worry a lot' or 'he's a fat child – must be lazy.'

An individual who receives such statements describing himself in physical and often additionally in personality terms based on another's perception of his body is more than likely to incorporate these perceptions into his own concept of his body, his body image, which forms a considerable and significant part of his total self concept.

A person's height, weight, complexion, eyesight, body proportions so become closely associated with his attitudes to himself and feelings of personal adequacy and acceptability. Like all other elements of self conception, the body image is subjective, but no other element is more open to private and public evaluation. The body is the most visible and sensed part of a person. We see, feel and hear a lot of ourselves; the body is a central feature in much of our self perception.

The study of physical and psychological factors and their relationships to personality variables has interested man from the time of Hippocrates and his speculative humours. The relationships between body build and personality is at best tenuous despite the attempts of Kretschmer (1925) and Sheldon and Stevens (1942). Much of the aetiology of the relationship may lie within the realm of social learning, of stereotypes, and of expectation effects. Individuals tend to behave in line with the expectations of others. If these expectations are consistent over time and individuals, one can expect emitted behaviour consistent with the expectations. This provides a self-validating prophecy. The cultural stereotypes of the tall, thin, parsimonious Scrooge, the obese, jovial Mr Pickwick and the active, strong, athletic Tarzan each establish specific expectations of behaviour for the possessor and for the others with whom he interacts. Research does provide quite convincing evidence that different body builds evoke different reactions from others in a consistent way. A powerful, muscular boy must experience a completely different world from his puny counterpart.

How do you react to a short fat person, a tall thin person or a muscular athlete when you meet them for the first time? Think about it! Don't different body images create different feelings, attitudes and expectations about them in you? Brodsky (1954) was able to show such differentiated reactions to various body builds in an experimental situation. Using both white and negro male students as subjects, he asked them which attributes characterised any five 15-inch male silhouettes representing five body builds, viz.: (1) endomorph (obese); (2) endomesomorph (stocky, heavy and muscular); (3) mesomorph (muscular and athletic); (4) ectomesomorph (tall, thin and muscular) and (5) ectomorph (tall and thin). Irrespective of ethnic group, all subjects responded in much the same way, giving credence to the concept of a 'cultural stereotype' or characteristic reactions to each body build. The image created by endomorphy appeared consistently negative for such a short, obese person was regarded as the one who

would make the worst soldier, the poorest athlete, would be the poorest professor of philosophy, can endure pain the least well, would make the least successful military leader, would be the least likely to be chosen leader, would make the poorest university president, would be the least aggressive, would drink the most, be least preferred as a personal friend (but, ironically, would have many friends), would make the poorest doctor, and would probably put his own interests before those of others. (Brodsky, 1954, p. 15.)

The muscular, athletic mesomorph in contrast was regularly ascribed very positive characteristics. Respondents saw him as making

the best athlete, the most successful military leader, and the best soldier. They chose him as the man who would assume leadership, as well as the man who would be elected as leader. He was judged to be nonsmoker, and to be self-sufficient, in the sense of needing friends the least. However, he was most preferred as a friend, and was judged to have many friends. Respondents also said that he would be the most aggressive, would endure pain the best, would be least likely to have a nervous breakdown, and would probably drink the least. (Brodsky, 1954, p. 18.)

The tall, thin ectomorph tended to hold a position intermediate to the other two above with stereotyped characteristics less favourable than the mesomorph but not as disparaging as the endomorph's. The ectomorph was regarded as

most likely to have a nervous breakdown before the age of thirty, to eat the least and the least often, to be a heavy smoker, to be least self-sufficient, in the sense of needing friends the most (but, unfortunately, was judged to have the fewest friends), to hold his liquor the worst, to make a poor father, and, as a military leader, to be likely to sacrifice his men with the greatest emotional distress. (Brodsky, 1954, p. 21.)

Staffieri (1957) demonstrated with boys as young as 6 years old that stereotypes of behaviour are associated with body types. These boys described those with endomorphic build (obese, heavy) as socially offensive and delinquent; those with mesomorphic build (athletic, muscular) as aggressive, outgoing, active and having leadership skills; and those with ectomorphic builds (tall, thin) as retiring, nervous, shy and introverted. In addition, it was also found that ectomorphs and mesomorphs were more apt to be chosen as the most popular, the endomorphic children were not only inclined to be less popular, but more often they were among these who had negative, rejecting feelings about their corpulent body image.

The mesomorphic build was regarded as most favourable by these youngsters and was regarded as the ideal male physique. The subjects also showed a clear preference to look like a mesomorph, and could with reasonable accuracy indicate their own body type of 7 years of age. It is probably from this age, then, that dissatisfaction with one's body can arise.

Using pre-school children, Walker (1962) demonstrated similar findings to Brodsky and Staffieri. Even among these youngsters, mesomorphic children obtained more favourable ratings from teachers, with physical factors very important for boys in predicting behaviour. Expectations and stereotypes concerning physique do appear to be more firmly established for males despite the popularity of female form. The muscular, athletic build showed the strongest association with behavioural ratings. Walker noted that mesomorphs of both sexes are characterised by

dominative assertiveness (leader in play, competitive, self-assertive, easily angered, attacks others, etc.), high energy output, openness of expression, and fearlessness. The girls combine this assertiveness with socialness, cheerfulness, and warmth, the boys' items give more suggestion of hostility (quarrelsome, revengeful, inconsiderate) and of an impulsive, headlong quality to their activity (daring, noisy, quick, accident-prone, self-confident, etc.). (Walker, 1962, p. 78.)

Aloofness tended to characterise the ectomorph of both sexes, producing a cautious, quiet, hesitant, unfriendly and tense child.

Since the broad-shouldered, muscular boy and the well-proportioned young lady are more likely to gain social approval on the basis of their body build than others, then their self concepts are more likely to be highly positive. It is the feedback from others plus the knowledge that one's body build is strongly culturally approved that provides the positive gain. Mead (1934) indicates that adults frequently draw the attention of children to size, other physical attributes and sex role, while Smith (1962) suggested that people learn a cultural ideal of what a body should be like and this results in varying degrees of satisfaction with the self via a body image. This is particularly potent during adolescence.

A child's self concept is not caused by this or that body type, but it is possible to say that a child's physical appearance plays an important part as far as the feedback content he gets is concerned. Much feedback is given on the basis of purely physical appearance, at all age levels. But of course it is most potent in its effect in childhood as the self concept is forming. Children employ nicknames for each other which mostly reflect bodily appearance. Consider the problems of the endomorphic child who is the target of such barbs as 'Tubby', 'Fatso' or 'Billy Bunter', and the ectomorphic child who can be tagged with 'Skinny' or 'Big Ears'. Children are past masters at picking on, rather cruelly, those physical characteristics that stand out, then exaggerating them to the level of defamatory caricatures. When these nicknames emanate from significant others, such descriptions serve not only as physical descriptions but generalise to define the total person. The primary school-age child is extremely receptive to both peer and adult input concerning his person and performance, more ready to believe and incorporate into his personality and behaviour those things he hears about himself. Even simple and superficially harmless statements can be converted in the child's mind to vital self conceptions which are lived up to and by as if moral precepts. For instance, when John catches the table leg with his shoes Mother might say, 'It's those big, clumsy feet of yours.' He may continue to regard himself as clumsy and big-footed through all his life, tripping up, catching furniture, showing poor coordination for jumping or climbing, etc. He behaves consistently with his conception of himself. This effect is of great importance in the classroom situation in creating levels of expected performance, as will be shown in Chapter 9.

Do you remember your nickname at school? Do you recall the nicknames you attached to others, such as members of your peer group, your teachers, etc.? How did the nickname affect your feelings about yourself? Did your friends live up to the behavioural connotations of their nicknames? It is not difficult for you to realise that carrying around a descriptive name like 'Fatty', 'Specs', 'Weed' or 'Spotty' is not conducive to the development of a positive self concept. 'Oh that this too, too solid flesh would melt . . .' bewails the unhappy possessor of a physical body that fails to measure up to either its owner's or others' evaluation of the ideal body image. The proud bearer of such names as 'Killer' or 'Knocker' will have little difficulty in developing a positive self image. Names primarily employed to describe physical appearance so easily come to define the whole person. In this and other ways the body image comes to determine in considerable measure general self-esteem level. Even real names can have an effect. For a boy who answers to a peculiar or feminine Christian or surname may well have feelings in growing up that are quite unknown to a John or a William, a Smith or a Brown. Many people have changed their names legally when adults in attempts to lose associated ridicule, jokes, derogation and feelings of self hate. A new name becomes a rebirth, a revitalisation of potential with a possibility of a different life style, of different reactions from others and of a changed self concept.

Jourard and Secord (1954; 1955a; 1955b) in a series of studies found that the feelings an individual had about his physical body were similar to those he held about himself generally. When they asked their student subjects to rate their feelings of satisfaction with various dimensions of their bodies, Jourard and Secord showed that the general level of satisfaction was commensurate with their overall level of self acceptance. High self esteem thus correlated strongly with acceptance of one's physical body.

In a statistically elaborate study, Mahoney and Finch (1976), using a sample of 98 male and 129 female students attempted to determine the relative contribution of selected aspects of the body in determining the self concept. Bergschied, Walster and Borhnstedt's (1973) study which concluded that for both sexes 'face makes the difference' (p. 126) in self esteem was criticised by Mahoney and Finch as methodologically unsound. They decided instead to use a multiple stepwise regression technique that would isolate and show the contributions of various combinations of body items to total self esteem. They found a clear tendency for facial features and major body elements to contribute most to self esteem. For males, voice, chest and facial features explained most of the variance of self esteem; for females, overall physical attractiveness accounted for most of the variance, with small contributions from voice, hips, calves and height. In general these data further confirm the established link between body cathexis and self concept. The absence of body aspects found important in other studies, e.g. bust for females and height for males, may be a reflection of the student sample in this study. Just as there exists for each of us an ideal self concept, i.e. what we would like to be, so too it is possible to hypothesise an ideal body image, i.e. what we would like to look like. This ideal physical image is based on learned cultural norms and stereotypes. The closer the match between the existing body image and the ideal held by the individual then the more likely will that person manifest high self esteem generally as well as feel positive about his appearance. These ideal body images change from time to time and between cultures. There is a considerable difference between the ideal flat-chested society girl of the 1920s and the contemporary ideal 'girlie' magazine centre fold pin-up. In their final study Jourard and Secord (1955b) obtained the ideal body proportions which women students preferred. These girls increasingly disliked their own dimensions the more they deviated from the ideal. Earlier Jourard and Secord (1954) demonstrated that male acceptance of their physiques was related to large size, with men wanting to be bigger but women wanting to be slightly smaller. Calden, Lundy and Schlafer (1959) provide further evidence that males wish to be heavier and bigger, while females would like to be lighter and smaller. All their female subjects who were dissatisfied with their weight wished to weigh less, but they were more satisfied with their height than the male subjects, even though half of them wanted to be shorter. In general, men were dissatisfied from the waist up, whereas females desired changes mainly from the waist down. Both sexes judged the endomorph as the least attractive body type. As we have already noted, this dislike of the endomorphic physique is found even in young children, and Lerner, Karabenick and Meisels (1975) produced results which showed that children from 4 to 8 years disliked most the endomorphic form as measured by social distance. The mesomorph was the most acceptable build. Thus, one effect of an endomorphic body type on others' social reactions towards a person-stimulus may be the promotion of withdrawal responses, while approach reactions seem to be evoked by mesomorphy. This differential reaction to different physiques becomes more pronounced with age.

The physical self was accepted as a vital element of the self concept by William James as early as 1890, though he placed it as the least important of his four components. Irrespective of any objective facts available, a person can subjectively and erroneously misinterpret his physical appearance. Some girls diet to an excessive degree because they believe they are fat, even though other observers would argue not so and use measurement to prove it. Even the possession of freckles or the wearing of glasses can become magnified as gross defects, but the possession of physical disability can perhaps be regarded as the ultimate in conditions leading to dissatisfaction and rejection of the physical self. Richardson, Hastorf and Dornsbusch (1964) obtained self descriptions from handicapped and non-physically handicapped children in order to examine the effects of physical disability on a disabled child's conception of himself. Taped interviews were analysed into various categories. The picture produced from the self descriptions of handicapped children as compared with those of non-handicapped children emphasised the physical functional restrictions imposed by the handicap, its psychological impact, the deprivation of social experience and the limitations on involvement in the social world. Lack of social involvement and experience led to an impoverishment of the child's category usages pertaining to interpersonal relations. It appears that for these children, aged 10 and 11, direct experience in social interaction is a prerequisite for the full development of perceptual categories dealing with human relationships.

The handicapped children were very realistic in their self descriptions. Although they shared in the peer values, they were aware that they couldn't live up to the expectations that stem from the high value placed on physical activities. Physical disability does not have the same consequences for boys and for girls. For example, handicapped girls may turn to non-physical recreation, where they are not disadvantaged, but this alternative is perhaps less acceptable to the boys because among them physical activity is more highly valued. Possibly because of this, they expressed more difficulties in interpersonal relations and made more use of humour to gain some measures of acceptance. Handicapped boys also expressed more concern about aggression than did handicapped girls, possibly as a consequence of being more often targets of physical aggression, which is used less by the girls. Both handicapped boys and girls showed greater concern with the past than did non-handicapped boys and girls, possibly because of the greater uncertainty and threat in the present. They both reflect more physical restriction and less social experience within and without the family.

In summary, physical appearance is a very potent agent for attracting particular social responses. This feedback creates to a considerable degree the way a person feels about himself. The person learns through cultural stereotyping, expectations and nicknames that it is not a good thing for either sex to be, for instance, short and fat; it is far better to be a broad-shouldered Mr Atlas or a curvaceous and pretty girl. The implications are clear. Do not judge others on the basis of physical appearance, because they please or offend your eyes. Try to forget the stereotypes of personality and behaviour that Western society attaches to physical appearance in transactions with others in order to reduce the deleterious effects of learning an unwelcome self image.

2. Language and self-concept development

Obviously the development of language aids the development of the self concept, for the use of 'me', 'he' and 'them' serve to distinguish self and others. Language symbols also form the basis of conceptions and evaluations about the self, e.g. being sad, feeling happy. Feedback from others is often verbal in nature. In other words the self concept is conceived in terms of language and its development is facilitated by language. Most children commence using such pronouns as 'me', 'yours', 'mine', etc if sometimes inaccurately, from around 2 years of age, but up to that point in age, language development is slow (Gesell and Ilg, 1949). Sherif and Cantril (1947) claim emphatically that the use of such pronouns serve as conceptualisations of self and others. Many a young child has a particularly difficult time learning to use personal pronouns correctly. His initial use of 'I', 'me', 'mine', and 'you' is confused and inaccurate. He hears his mother use the word 'you' towards himself and will address himself as 'you' instead of 'I'. He may speak of himself in the third instead of the first person, for example, 'David is hungry'. He can be first, second and third person simultaneously. Cooley (1912) has suggested that young children misuse pronouns because they cannot directly imitate them. Ordinary words, such as 'apple' or 'doll', can be easily imitated, whereas words like 'you' or 'I' have to be reinterpreted by the child rather than copied directly. However, he has his chief difficulties with relationship terms such as 'brother', 'father', 'I' and 'you', since in his early egocentric years he is unaware of perspectives other than his own.

His increasing accuracy in the use of pronouns shows the child's maturing conception of his own existence and individuality. This is reflected also by the acquisition of new pronouns. Before the age of 5, first-person pronouns in the plural ('we', 'us', 'ours') appear very infrequently in the youngster's vocabulary. They increase as the child grows older and becomes more conscious of his participation in groups.

Increasing use and accuracy of pronouns reflects the child's increasing ability to conceive of himself as an individual with feelings, needs and attributes. But the pronouns are only one indicator of evidence that a differentiation has been made between self and others. Their absence, however, must not be taken as implying that the differentiation has not been established. Cooley (1912), for example, noted that although his oldest son was slow in using pronouns he engaged in acts which displayed a differentiation of self from other.

Mead (1934) notes that among the most significant adult vocalisations, from the standpoint of the child, are those that have to do with himself. These are picked up, imitated and gradually incorporated in the evolving system of signals or cues which the child uses to stimulate himself. He hears his name repeated over and over by others who accompany it with appropriate gestures, actions and words which come to indicate their feelings for and beliefs about him. By association and conditioning processes such indications tagged to his name and being become as much an identifying and categorising mark of him as is his name. He begins to think of himself along lines similar to the conceptions others have of him. Thus the genesis of true self conception may come for many infants at the point in time when they grasp the fact that they have a name. This suggests a naming or labelling hypothesis for self development. The child's knowledge of self is contingent on a separation of self from others. Central to the creation of self as social object is an identification of that object which will be called self, and this identification involves naming. But once an object is named and identified, a line of action can be taken towards it. The most important linguistic aid becomes the name. While the appearance of pronouns in the child's vocabulary indicates that a sense of self is developing, the use of personal names (or other familiar referents – e.g. mummy, daddy, etc.) suggests a growing awareness of self-as-a-distinct-object. Thus, the child may differentiate self first, and others second. Allport (1961) supports this conclusion. Although he presented no data, he suggested, by hearing his name repeatedly, the child gradually sees himself as a distinct and recurrent point of reference. The name acquires significance usually in the second year of life. With it comes awareness of independent status in the social group. For some 3 year olds, names must be printed and 'tagged-on' clothes and pegs before they (name and self) exist. Uncertainty over one's personal name is also revealed in a desire to have the name publicly announced. Such announcements ensure that the child will be acted on in at least one consistent fashion across encounters (e.g. by the name). Wolfenstein's (1968) discussions of name-games in early childhood amplify this conclusion over identity-uncertainty for 3 year olds. Wolfenstein studied such games as name-switching, name-reversals, name-calling and name-loss. She notes that frequently a child who has a name taken away or who is called by a different name becomes disturbed. Such children, it would be predicted, have yet to be committed fully to their own personal identity. Loss of name makes the child a non-person, his essential self as a distinct person has been denied.

Thus, self awareness becomes increasingly apparent when he correctly distinguishes between I, you, mine and yours, and knows his name designates him and him alone. The ability to acknowledge verbally feelings as one's own is also a sound criterion of the child possessing a rudimentary self concept, for instance, as when the child says 'I'm happy today' or 'I'm in a bad mood'. Parents can help children to define themselves by using language simply and precisely, and encouraging verbalisation.

Body language or non-verbal communication also conveys information to others about self and reflects what others think of one. A study of body language, e.g. Argyle (1967) reveals that there are codes and signs which speak louder than words. We may speak with our mouths, but as Abercrombie (1968) cogently notes we communicate with the whole body. For example, a frown, a nod, a smile, a wipe of the forehead, an aggressive movement of the arm are all examples of non-verbal communication which convey as powerfully as language one's feelings and attitudes to oneself and to others. Some might say non-verbal body language is more potent since while it is relatively easy to lie verbally (even for tactful purposes) it is almost impossible to distort the non-verbal communications emitted. These latter messages are conveyed with stark reality and truthfulness; feelings and attitudes to self and others cannot be distorted in this form of communication which we use all the time, often without realising it.

3. Feedback from significant others

Another major source of self conception, besides body image and linguistic skill, is feedback from significant others. Cooley and Mead elaborated on this source of self esteem in the early days of self-concept theory (Ch. 1). Cooley introduced the concept of the 'looking-glass' self to describe the self as perceived through the reflections in the eyes of others. The term 'significant others' means those persons who are important or who have significance to the child by reason of his sensing their ability to reduce insecurity or to intensify it, to increase or to decrease his helplessness, to promote or to diminish his sense of worth. Significant others play a confirming role in self definition. Parents are presumed to be the most significant others in a child's environment. The role of child-rearing practices and parental behaviour will be considered in the next chapter.

The neonate has no self awareness, since all his behaviour is dominated by the need to satisfy bodily needs and not by any reference to a self. Therefore the earliest feedback to the infant about how people feel about him lies in the reduction of physiological needs. As the infant is being fed, changed, bathed, he also receives a message that he is valued and accepted. Fondling, caressing, smiles and 'baby talk' dispensed by mother (and even father!) are communications indicating that the infant is esteemed. Through this a person learns to seek out the feeling of being valued by others, since it is associated in the past with the reduction of physiological discomfort.

All humans need love, acceptance and security – most of all young children. The receipt of love and acceptance is very satisfying, but to know whether he is receiving any the child must observe the face, gestures, the verbalisations and other signs of significant others, usually parents. Each experience of love or rejection, each experience of approval or disapproval from others cause him to view himself and his behaviour in the same way. During early childhood the child anchors his perception of himself very much in his own direct experience of physical self and of the reactions of significant others to him, particularly parents.

Most personality theorists and research workers agree on the role of significant others, particularly parents, being an influential source of information about oneself. Since for the young child few things are more relevant than how people react to him, it is not really surprising that the reflections of himself in the eyes of significant others ('the looking-glass self') play a crucial role in the concepts the child acquires about himself. Parents have the greatest impact in the developing conception of self as they are the fount of authority and the most likely source of trust. Murphy (1947) says therefore, that it is vitally important to save the child from acquiring an unlovely view of himself. This self portrait is gradually modified and rebuilt according to the experiences the child has had and the adjectives he hears used to describe him. But it shows diminishing returns as the picture becomes well established. Thus the child becomes less and less a perceptual object and more and more a conceptual trait system.

Snygg and Combs (1949) have also emphasised the vital effects of constructing how significant others evaluate one.

As he is loved or rejected, praised or punished, fails or is able to compete, he comes gradually to regard himself as important or unimportant, adequate or inadequate, handsome or ugly, honest or dishonest . . . or even to describe himself in the terms of those who surround him. . . . He is likely therefore to be affected by the labels which are applied to him by other people. (p. 83)

The process of identification with parents gives way in the later primary school years to a self picture that is one's own. Proneness to a particular behaviour is recognised as one's own and becomes a part of the self concept. At puberty, the awareness of body image which had been displaced by awareness of status surges back. The adolescent has to adjust to a new physical self. But even this does not in most cases disturb a well-established self concept which is not subject to wild fluctuations and changes (Engel, 1959; Thompson, 1974). Only as a result of extreme conditions does the self concept alter drastically, e.g. after survival training (Clifford and Clifford, 1967).

It has been conventionally accepted that parents are the founts of the young child's self concept through their position as significant others emitting salient feedback. However, from the phenomenal point of view it seems necessary to look from the child's perspective. Are parents the prime esteem source they are theoretically assumed to be? Kirchner and Vondraek (1975) produced results which contradicted the traditional view of the importance of parents. This descriptive study was designed as an initial effort towards understanding the sources of esteem perceived by young children. The identity, number and relative salience of esteem sources were examined via the responses of 282 day-care children aged 3–5 who were asked to identify persons who liked them. A mean of 4.3 esteem sources were mentioned. Peers and siblings were cited as esteem sources by higher percentages of children than were mothers and fathers. While age comparisons were non-significant, sex comparisons indicated that females reported significantly more esteem sources and mentioned mother, father and siblings significantly more often than males.

The potency of peers and siblings and their precedence over parents as sources of self esteem is unexpected and challenges the universal tenet of self-esteem theorists who only consider peers as of influence in later childhood. These results of Kirchner and Vondraek are consonant with earlier views of Bronfenbrenner (1971) and Borke (1972). The present results suggest that, in fact, young children have strong, positive affective responses to age-mates and support Borke's contention that traditional thinking about young children's interpersonal perceptions should be reassessed.

The fact that mother was mentioned as an esteem source by a substantially higher percentage of subjects than was father (Kirchner and Vondraek, 1975) is congruent with studies indicating that both male and female children regard fathers as more punitive, more threatening and less friendly than mothers (Kagan and Lemkin, 1960). That the young females report more esteem sources especially within the immediate family more frequently than young males is claimed to be due to one or both of the following reasons (*a*) more favourable treatment of females than males by significant others, and (*b*) greater adherence to social desirability factors in females than males. This study emphasises the need to pay increased attention to the child's phenomenal field. But a young person's relations with his own peers become increasingly even more important as he enters into his adolescent years. Peer-group influence hits a peak around middle adolescence, but begins to decline after that, when young people go their separate ways, marry and begin setting up standards for their own nuclear families.

The crucial arena for arriving at a clearer and realistic picture of one's assets and liabilities does seem to be that of peer interaction. Peers approximate in size and age, whereas at home there exists an age hierarchy with even brothers and sisters being older or younger. So at home differences in competence are expected, but in the peer group the child need only show he is at least equal with others. At home he must be love-worthy, within the peer group he must be respect-worthy, competitive and competent. The penalties of failure are self-concept components of humiliation, rejection and derogation from self and others. These different expectations between home and peer group are due to the former placing a high premium on behaviour, while the latter place it on performance. In fact, behaviour unacceptable by parents may well be ignored in the peer group, or even acceptable if the child is (say) a competent footballer.

In the upper primary school years the child's self concept continues to modify as it is influenced by his expanding social environment. The new levels of self expression derived from more advanced schoolwork, new levels of attainment and competency, extracurricular activities and complex group activities generally raises self esteem, and most pre-adolescents see themselves as capable of accomplishing all the tasks set them. Abilities and talents are usually evaluated in terms of school standing, peer acceptance, athletic pursuits and popularity. Each prefers activities which test their prowess. Thus, at this stage of life the self concept is based on an expanded frame of social relationships and comparative performances. The child has an increased sensitivity to the approval and disapproval of significant others, especially peers and teachers. The development and encouragement of some special interests, e.g. art, craft, music, sport, assists socialisation and maturation. Therefore, school allows the development of new skills, providing the individual with more evaluative contexts in which to compare himself with others and perceive the others' evaluation of him. In- and out-group categories become available, encouraging the labelling and categorising of others and self. School then continues and augments the processes that are involved in developing a self picture as Staines (1958) has shown so well in his study of the subtle influences of teachers through their verbal and non-verbal communications to pupils. Teachers' ordinary run-of-the-day comments are fraught with status, evaluational and emotional content for children. School provides new role models in the peer group replete with new demands and new expectations. These models provide standards against which the child can evaluate himself. He finds that some of his peer group do better or worse than him in academic, sporting, artistic and many other fields. Comparison cannot be avoided.

Standards set by parents or teachers are vitally important for the development of self esteem, since standards provide a means of measuring self progress, validate competence and show that others have interest in the individual. A lack of any requirement to meet standards suggests that parents and teachers have no concern for the child and is not worth bothering about (Coopersmith, 1967).

The fairly direct feedback that parents, children, adolescents and students commonly convey to each other has been shown in several studies to affect the individual's self concept, e.g. Videbeck (1960). An instance of this is described by Guthrie (1938). A group of male students played what was intended as a joke on a dull, unattractive female student. They treated her for a time as though she was tremendously popular and attractive. The shocked students found that within a year she developed an easy manner, confidence and popularity. Such a manner increased the eliciting of positive and reinforcing reactions from others. Similar feedback cycles lie behind many of the self concepts and behaviour patterns of all of us.

Wooster and Harris (1973) predicted that the high mobility of children of armed service personnel would impair the development of the self concept, since some major sources of the self image, viz. comparison with significant others, learning from others' reaction, and role playing, are more restricted than in 'static' children. Frequent changes of teachers, peer groups, neighbours would prevent the development of stable reference groups. The researchers found a low level of conviction in the views the 'mobile' pupils hold about themselves, the pupils were unsure of their parents' affection, saw themselves as of little value as friends, and doubted their success outside school. In general his changing sources of self information leaves the mobile child bewildered and unable to cope with the tasks of making judgements about himself.

There is little question but that the peer group has an enormous impact on the final embellishments that are moulded on to the core self attitudes in adolescence. The peer group is important at this stage because it replaces the family as a major source of feedback; it also provides self esteem, mutual support, standards, opportunity for practice in, and rehearsal of, tasks preparatory for adulthood. The peer group provides a milieu within which an identity may be secured, since the growing child must become less like his parents and more like his peers. Surprisingly, external standards and societal norms do not exert anywhere near the influence of interpersonal relationships with relatives and friends (Coopersmith, 1967; Rosenberg, 1965). One way to effect some, even if perhaps slight, improvement in self conception might be to alter the interpersonal environment so that the person will have more opportunity to associate with people who can become significant others and whose interests, abilities and backgrounds are more similar to his. This may necessitate the development of new interests and a deliberate willingness to make friends with those whose skills and background are similar.

B. The content of the self concept

As a growing child's environment expands, the contents of his self concept also expand, coming to include such things as possessions, friends, values and, most particularly, loved people through identification. Many types of categories and classes have been inferred from the self-report data of children. The most usual are physical, material, in-group, role, values, interests, wants, goals, etc. (Gesell and Ilg, 1949; Jersild, 1952; Staines, 1958).

Jersild's (1952) evidence concerning self conception was provided by analysing nearly 3,000 compositions written by children and young people in primary and secondary schools and colleges on the topics 'What I like about myself' and 'What I dislike about myself'. This was supplemented by personal interviews and group discussions with students. The analysis revealed that the responses made by the children appeared to fall into clearly defined categories. The most important of these, set out in what the author describes as an ascending order of psychological maturity, are:

1. Physical characteristics, including general appearance, size and weight; build and shape, and details of head and limbs.
2. Clothing, grooming and make-up.

3. Health and physical condition.
4. Material possessions and ownership.
5. Animals and pets and attitudes towards them.
6. Home and family relationships.
7. Sports, games and hobbies – participation in and ability at.
8. School and school work – ability at and attitude towards.
9. Intellectual status. Intelligence.
10. Special talents and abilities or interests.
11. Personality traits, including temperament, disposition, character traits, emotional tendencies, etc.
12. Social attitudes and relationships.
13. Religious ideas, interests, beliefs and practices.
14. Management of practical affairs; independence and self help.

Thus it was found that the younger children stressed mainly external criteria such as physical characteristics and grooming, while the older ones described themselves in terms of inner resources and the quality of relationships with other people. But, generally speaking, categories of self description prominent at one age were prominent at other age levels also. The actual detail of self description displayed some change with age, but the categories tended to remain the same. However, in a more recent British study categories did change in emphasis with age.

Livesley and Bromley (1973), as part of a major British investigation into person perception in children, asked their 320 7–14-year-old subjects to write a description of 'Myself'. These descriptions were analysed into 30 categories. The effect of between-subject variables of age, sex and intelligence on the proportions of statements in these content categories were analysed. Chronological age had a statistically significant effect on 16 out of the 30 categories. Categories manifesting a decrease in the proportion of statements with increasing age were:

1. Appearance.
2. General Information and Identity.
3. Friendships and Playmates.
4. Family and Kinship.
5. Possessions.

Categories showing an increase in the frequency of statements with increasing age were:

1. General Personality Attributes.
2. Specific Behavioural Consistencies.
3. Orientation.
4. Interests and Hobbies.
5. Beliefs, Attitudes and Values.
6. Attitudes towards Self.
7. Relations with the Opposite Sex.

8. Comparisons with Others.
9. Collateral Facts and Ideas.

The categories showing the decrease with age are those which generally relate to objective information about the person. These categories accounted for 39 per cent of the statements made by 7 year olds, but only 6 per cent in the case of 14 year olds. Only the 'Appearance' category showed a sudden increase at age 15, probably an indication of the importance to adolescents of their body image and attractiveness to members of the opposite sex.

Increased age was associated with greater use of categories referring to personal attributes, basic philosophy and attitudes towards self and others. General personality attributes and behavioural consistency accounted for 4 per cent of the statements in 7 year olds, but 35 per cent in 14 year olds. The increase in interest in self and others suggest that social relations and personal identity are important to adolescents, but the increase was not as great as might have been expected from the writings of many psychologists, e.g. Erikson. Older subjects became more detached and dispassionate in their statements describing attitudes to self, whereas younger pupils had demonstrated unashamedly egotistical remarks. The most frequently used category at all ages was 'Preferences and Aversions'.

Only three categories manifested significant effects due to the sex of the subject. Girls made less frequent references to 'Hobbies and Interests' than boys but were more concerned with 'Relations with the Opposite Sex' and with 'Family and Kinship.' Livesley and Bromley suggest that these differences may be due to the different rates of maturation between boys and girls. When intelligence was considered, children with lower intelligence tended to stress 'Friendships and Playmates', 'Relations with the Opposite Sex', 'Appearance and Identity', whereas the more intelligent subjects used 'Personal Attributes' and 'Expressive Behaviour' categories more. The tendency was for less intelligent subjects to be more concrete and superficial in their statements about themselves as compared with subjects of higher intelligence, i.e. their lower level of conceptual functioning was apparent in self description as in all other aspects of their behaviour.

Similar developmental trends to those discerned in the description of self were noted in the descriptions of others by the same pupils. However, the self descriptions were on average a third longer with most 7 year olds providing this disparity. On the other hand, the self descriptions of 15 year olds tended to be shorter than their descriptions of others. Livesley and Bromley suggest that the short descriptions of others emanating from the younger children are due to constraints of cognitive level, egocentrism and inability to decentre. These constraints also restrict these younger children in defining self by reference to the behaviour of others so that their self descriptions are highly concrete, based on general information, identity, appearance and possessions, e.g. age, hair colour, games and hobbies pursued, food preferences. In this younger age group, too, affective statements were more common in describing self than in conceptualising others. Emphasis on hobbies and abilities by these junior school children points towards competence and excellence being held as important values at this stage, allowing for implicit comparisons with others as the child tries to define his self concept in the context of schooling. There were strong similarities in content between self descriptions and descriptions of liked children which suggests that the understanding of others takes place more quickly when the other is similar to self.

By the end of the junior school the descriptions became increasingly abstract and sophisticated, with psychological qualities frequently mentioned. But despite the child's better understanding of his own personality, motivation and arousal, the descriptions still tend to be listed without organisation as a series of discrete elements, with positive and negative features juxtaposed. Livesley and Bromley indicate that the contents of adolescents' self descriptions are somewhat different from their descriptions of other stimulus persons since many of the psychological processes that the individual is aware of in his experience of himself are difficult to infer in others, e.g. motivation. The increased frequency of statements about beliefs and values made by the adolescents suggests their attempt to form a stable self concept incorporating a set of basic values. The information on the self was better organised, consistent and coherent. They appear to be very socially aware; concerned with how others evaluate them and with their effect on the behaviour of others. The adolescents were concerned in their descriptions with being different from other people. But an ambivalence between being 'modern', 'with it' and 'one of the crowd', and wishing to maintain an individual identity was evident. To be an individual and at the same time a member of a group is obviously a source of conflict for these adolescents. More details of the content analysis of these descriptions can be found in Livesley and Bromley (1973).

The direction and extent of age-related differences in self definition were also studied by Dixon and Street (1975) in 120 students from age 6 to 16 years who were asked to identify 42 items as self or not-self. Total number of self responses increased with age, and girls responded to slightly more items as self than boys. Body parts, identifying personal characteristics, and psychological processes were identified as self more frequently at all ages than significant others, self-related objects and possessions. Discrimination at all ages was made with little hesitancy. The general direction of change in this age group appears to be one of self extension after the self–other differentiation of infancy and early childhood. The data suggest that the 6 year olds are still more concerned with discriminating differences than perceiving similarities. The areas of greatest self extension – namely identification with related others, one's possessions and related objects – is reminiscent of William James' conception of the 'material me'. The age-related change appears to involve a reconceptualisation of self and not-self relations and is likely related to the child's increasing conceptual ability, as well as his extending network of relationships. In addition to this increasing self extension with age, there is a greater increase of self extension in girls than boys. This may be because girls are generally more mature than boys in cognitive skills, interests and social orientation. In fact the percentage of items identified by boys as part of self is similar to those of girls 2 years younger.

Using the 'Who Are You?' Test, Musgrove (1966) studied the self concepts of grammar school first-year and sixth-form pupils, male and female. Male first-formers tended to define themselves in terms of group status and group membership, family relationship and appearance, whereas male sixth-formers characterised themselves significantly less in those aspects but specified themselves more in sociopolitical terms. A similar pattern differentiated female first-formers from female sixth-formers. Negative self references for first-formers referred more frequently than in the sixth form to personal appearance and performance in academic subjects, but generally the sixth-formers revealed mainly negative self attitudes, whereas a positive self concept was apparent among the first-formers. The negative sixth-form self concept appears to be characterised by a rejection of others and self in the lack of reference to membership groups. Musgrove (1966) suggests that the negative attitudes of the academic sixth-formers develops due to the restrictive nature of the school for mature intelligent persons bordering on adulthood. Their more developed critical powers also contribute to their unfavourable view of themselves. Negative self attitudes may be the price required to pay for high academic attainment under highly competitive conditions. In another 'Who Are You?' study, Mulford and Salisbury (1964) were able to examine the categories used in self conceptualisation by 1,213 adults chosen by sampling procedures to represent Iowa. Only four areas of self definition had relatively high rates of mention. These were:

Religious identity	25% of all respondents
Marital role and status	34% of all respondents
Family role and status	60% of all respondents
Occupation	68% of all respondents

Such categories as sex, age and other non-family group memberships were mentioned by 17 per cent or less. Virtually none defined themselves in terms of education, race and social class. Some differences between category usage by men and women were quite noticeable. Women seemed more concerned than men with family-oriented self definitions and with anchoring themselves in non-family groups. They also more often conceived of themselves as being religious. Men placed their sex and ethnic identity as more prominent in their self concepts than women. The greater frequency of mention of most of the categories by women probably reflects the greater number of statements made by them. The mean number of responses for women was 4.7 as compared to 4.1 for the men. In effect, about half of the women made an extra statement as compared to the men, and it most frequently referred to family, religion, friends or a club, in that order. This difference in number of responses raises a question about the meaning of the statistical comparison of sex rates. However, the authors assume that the fact that men did not feel compelled to make any more statements when they had the same opportunity to do so as women, reflects their lesser concern with those particular identities in question.

Older persons (over 70) and younger persons (below 30) tended to mention age as one of their self-defining attributes more frequently than other groups. This likely reflects the importance of age connotations for the younger adult in a youth-oriented culture and the lack of other anchorages for self definition in retired persons whose family roles have also diminished. Women more frequently than men defined themselves in terms of family status and roles. The status of mother for women appears far more crucial than the status of father for men in terms of defining important self attributes. However, for both sexes family status statements decrease rapidly for older adults, particularly after 20 years of married life. Most of the total sample defined themselves in part through occupational status or work role.

The study of the self concepts of adults in old age is hardly touched save by Back (1971). He employed a semantic differential and a 'Who Are You?' test in a study of self-concept changes brought on by old age. Women as in the Mulford and Salisbury (1964) study answered in terms of personal background, such as family relations and demographic characteristics, but this emphasis Back noted declines after the 50s so that in the 60s there is no difference between the sexes in this regard. Correspondingly, personally achieved positions and characteristics, as well as personal values, became more important for women with age. This development remains constant even if controlled for varying experiences, such as retirement and child separation during ageing. Thus, neither retirement nor separation from children affects the content of the self image as much as the ageing process alone. However, the discrepancy between the self concept as known and the self concept as seen by others is influenced by these factors. Both crises of retirement and separation are important; but separation from children only affects women, while retirement or non-working affects both sexes. In general, men have the greater problem with the discrepancy between who they feel they are and what they imagine other people think about them. This is also true with non-working members of both sexes.

During the ageing process, women tend to shift their self image from their relationship to others, the social characteristics, to their own abilities and feelings; the separation from children can be viewed in this way. Freed from family obligations, they may feel that they can now much more easily be accepted for what they are, rather than for an imposed role. Men, on the other hand, are more personally involved in the work role, and difficulties with this role through ageing may make life even more difficult for them. Separation from children may, therefore, aggravate this discrepancy, making them more dependent on the work role in which they have difficulty in presenting the right image. Hence the increase in self-image discrepancy (i.e. cognised self–other self) in working men separated from children in Back's study, while for women the discrepancy decreases with age and separation from children.

When older children and adults are asked to describe themselves, most of them are able to make a distinction between what they think they are and what they would like to be or think they ought to be. A person's view of what he aspires to be or believes he ought to be is referred to as the 'ideal self'. In most persons there is some discrepancy between self-as-is or cognised self concept, and the ideal self concept. Such a discrepancy occurs, for example, when a child says he never works hard at school but should always work hard at school, or when he says he often loses his temper but he ought never to lose his temper. In some persons, the difference between what they say they are and what they should be is very marked.

When a child's view of what he is corresponds quite closely to what he believes he ideally ought to be, he expresses what seems to be a rather comfortable view of himself. When there is a marked difference between the self picture and the ideal picture, it appears that the child, in his own eyes, is failing to live up to the mark and he is, in that sense, a self-rejecting person. This is the classical Rogerian view that increasing discrepancy implies increasing maladjustment, but it may only imply for older children increasing cognitive ability. In any case, the discrepancy index is highly unsound statistically, as has been argued in an earlier chapter.

The theory behind the self-ideal self discrepancy is the assumption that the closer a person comes to be like his ideal the better he will be able to satisfy his secondary needs. Implicit in the ideals of having many friends, being good-looking, becoming a success, etc. are the feelings that one's affectional, security, competence, acceptance and status needs would be satisfied if the ideals were achieved. Any sizeable shortfall of the ideals suggests that the needs are blocked and various maladjustments are likely to manifest themselves, e.g. withdrawal, anxiety, guilt, etc.

The ideal self should presumably become important once the child has internalised the values of his identification models. Jorgensen and Howell (1969) noted that the discrepancy between self and ideal self increased between 8 and 13 years as the child becomes more aware of parental and societal standards. Havighurst, Robinson and Dorr (1946) charted the developmental trends in the ideal self as follows. It commences in childhood as an identification with a parental figure, moves during middle childhood and early adolescence through a stage of romanticism and glamour, and culminates in late adolescence as a composite of desirable characteristics which may be symbolised by an attractive, visible young adult, or may be simply an imaginary figure.

Parents or members of the parental generation play a declining role in the ideal self as it is described by children after the age of 8 or 10. 'Glamorous' adults have their day in the child's ego-ideal between the ages of 10 and 15. Anyone older than 15 who reports a 'glamorous' person as his ego-ideal is probably immature, by standards of development as found in most young people.

The environment of the child has a great effect on his ideal self. Children and young people from families of lower socioeconomic status as a group lag behind those of middle socioeconomic status in progressing through the stage of selection of a glamorous adult as the ideal. Individuals in the child's environment influence his ideal self, especially if they are young adults. Thus, an especially attractive teacher or youth group leader may symbolize the ego-ideal during the age period usually dominated by the glamorous person. Furthermore, the teaching of the school, especially if it is aimed at inculcating ideals through teaching about the lives of great people, certainly influences the child's report concerning his ideal self.

There is a great deal of evidence that the ideal self is deeply influenced by association with people who are in positions of prestige because they are older, more powerful and better able to get the desirable things of life than the child or adolescent who observes them. A boy or girl combines qualities of parents with qualities of attractive, successful young adults into a composite ego-ideal. The inference is clear that schools, churches and youth-serving agencies influence the ideals of youth as much or

more through the presence and behaviour of teachers, clergy and
youth group leaders as through their verbal teachings.

In a parallel study of New Zealand children Havighurst and
MacDonald (1955) found the same developmental trends as in the
USA. Again, with Olasehinde's (1972) investigation of the ideal
self in Nigerian children, a similar trend is shown with younger
children identifying first with persons in the home. Thereafter
there was a diminution in the role of the parents with older
children selecting ideal self from real people who personified
power, love and affection.

C. Adolescence and the self concept

Reference has already been made in Chapter 1 to Erikson's
developmental theory. The core of his approach is a concern with
identity, especially a concern with the way in which the adolescent
perceives himself. The task of adolescence is seen as one of
securing a firm identity and avoiding identity diffusion. Erikson
(1968) ignores empirical studies of the self image in adolescence
and bases his theory mainly on clinical cases he had cause to treat.
He admits his ignorance as to whether his clinical evidence is
capable of generalisation to the rest of the adolescent population.
'Whether, and in what way, disturbances such as are outlined here
also characterise those more completely placed somewhere near
the middle of the socio-economic ladder, remains, at this time, an
open question.' (p. 25) Despite this Erikson has had a considerable
effect on how adolescence is viewed, and on the implications that
period of life has presumably for each and every teenager,
particularly with his emotive application of such phrases as
'identity crisis' and 'the psychopathology of everyday adolescence'.
He argues that some form of disturbance is a normal expectation
in adolescence, with the crisis points more likely occurring towards
the end of that period. Thus, Erikson lends considerable weight to
the conventional but erroneous view of the *Sturm und Drang*
adolescent turmoil.

From this traditional perspective, adolescence is accepted as the
time when each person needs to re-examine and re-evaluate
himself physically, socially and emotionally in relation to those
close to him and to society in general. A rather thorough revision
of the self concept is seemingly implied. As Erikson (1968)
contends:

young people, beset with physiological revolution of their genital
maturation and the uncertainty of the adult roles ahead, seem much
concerned with faddish attempts at establishing an adolescent subculture
with what looks like a final rather than a transitory, or, in fact, initial
identity formation. They are sometimes morbidly, often curiously,

preoccupied with what they appear to be in the eyes of others as compared with what they feel they are, and with the question of how to connect the roles and tasks cultivated earlier with the ideal prototype of the day. In their search for a new sense of continuity and sameness, which must now include sexual maturity, some adolescents have to come to grips again with crises of earlier years before they can install lasting idols and ideals as guardians of a final identity.

This self examination is aimed implicitly and explicitly to discover and express each his own individuality. The young person with his newly found ability to think critically about his own thinking (Piagetian formal operational stage) with new feelings, desires and aspirations, labours to discover the various facets of his self concept and then be himself, since former ways of defining self seem no longer appropriate.

Adolescence is seen as a 'psychosocial moratorium' when choices have to be made, often on the basis of inadequate knowledge and experience, choices of career, of values, of life style, of personal relationships. Such choices are undertaken in the face of conflicting evidence and values within a restless and uncertain society, and aid identity exploration. Within this confusion of values adolescents appear to help each other through the discomforts and disturbances of identity crises by mutual support in cliques with endless coffee-bar chats and by stereotyping themselves as teddy boys, hell's angels, students, etc. and likewise stereotyping their opponents, parents, teachers, police, etc.

In primitive societies adolescents are perhaps spared these doubts and indecisions. Through initiation rites, often seemingly cruel in character, young people are tested out (and test themselves out) and are then welcomed into a socially recognised age category in which rights and duties and mode of living are clearly defined. In our society there are few rituals or ceremonies that mark the change in status from childhood to youth. For those who have religious affiliations, confirmation, joining the Church, may serve this purpose in part, since the young people are thereby admitted, in this one segment of their lives at least, to the company of adults. Such ceremonies serve, in addition, to reaffirm to youth that the universe is trustworthy and stable and that a way of life is clearly laid out.

What rules of law and custom exist are too diverse to be of much help. For example, legal regulations governing age of 'consent', age at which marriage is permitted, age for leaving school, for driving a car, for joining (or being required to join) the Army or Navy mark no logical progressions in rights and duties. As to custom, there is so much variation in what even families who live next door to each other expect or permit that adolescents, eager to be on their way, are practically forced into standardising themselves in their search for status. In this they are ably abetted by advertisers and entertainers who seek their patronage, as well as by well-meaning magazine writers who describe in great detail the means by which uniformity can be achieved.

The danger of this developmental period, as Erikson sees it, is self diffusion. As Biff puts it in the *Death of a Salesman*, 'I just can't take hold, Mom. I can't take hold of some kind of a life.' A boy or girl can scarcely help feeling somewhat diffuse when the body changes in size and shape so rapidly, when genital maturity floods body and imagination with forbidden desires, when adult life lies ahead with such a diversity of conflicting possibilities and choices.

Whether this feeling of self diffusion is fairly easily mastered or whether, in extreme, it leads to delinquency, neurosis or outright psychosis, depends to a considerable extent on what has gone before. If the course of personality development has been a healthy one, a feeling of self esteem has accrued from the numerous experiences of succeeding in a task and sensing its cultural meaning. Along with this, the child has come to the conviction that he is moving towards an understandable future in which he will have a definite role to play. Adolescence may upset this assurance for a time or to a degree, but fairly soon a new integration is achieved, and the child sees again (and with clearer vision) that he belongs and that he is on his way.

The course is not so easy for adolescents who have not had so fortunate a past or for those whose earlier security is broken by a sudden awareness that as members of minority groups their way of life sets them apart. The former, already unsure of themselves, find their earlier doubt and mistrust reactivated by the physiological and social changes that adolescence brings. The latter, once secure, may feel that they must disavow their past and try to develop 'majority-group' personality.

Erikson regards it as important that children can identify with adults, since for him psychosocial identity develops out of a gradual integration of all the identifications a child is able to make. However, if there is a conflict between the identity models a child is exposed to, problems can arise as with a black child in a white society, or a child taught Christian beliefs in a church school living with a father who provides a criminal model. Identity evolves from a complex of identifications, and from an awareness of one's power and weakness and of one's place in the social context. Identity involves recognising one's self and being recognised by others as being who you are.

It was comparatively simple in earlier times to form a stable self image and identity, since potential identifications were limited. But now there are bewilderingly numerous and often inconsistent possible identifications; the field is open. A kaleidoscope of identifications, and images are on offer as a daily menu from the mass media and pop culture kitchens. Garish and often inconsistent with models in the surrounding subculture, such real and unreal images can be overwhelming for some and invigorating for others in the search finally to establish the self concept. Another factor that impinges on the adolescent as he attains his identity is the insignificance and alientation of the individual within a depersonalised complex modern society with its bureacrats and computers. This technological juggernaut does not help an adolescent to gain a sense of personal identity or a feeling of competent mastery of his life. Physical maturity collides with socially sanctioned social immaturity to provide the friction that sets alight disturbances as the adolescent seeks to make life's choices in a complex society full of status ambiguities for him. All this is supposed to engender a corresponding ambiguity and confusion of self definition. Emotional changes consequent on physiological changes can also influence the self concept. The adolescent can become ill at ease, jittery, manifest nervous mannerisms giving the impression of immaturity and silliness. Unfavourable social reactions to these lead to feelings of social inadequacy and inferiority. The expression of emotions on the spot gives an impression of impulsivity and immaturity as does too frequent, too violent and apparently unjustified emotional outbursts.

Thus, a traditional conception of adolescence as a crisis period flowing from physiological change and psychological maturation within a complex society is offered. The implication from much of the literature is that this crisis is universal in Western culture and not to be missed. However, most surveys of normal youth do not support this conception.

However, this is not the place to discuss theories of adolescence but it is apropos to investigate whether self conception is affected by adolescence as Erikson would argue. Few studies exist, but Engel (1959) conducted an early study on the stability of the self concept in adolescence. She administered a Q sort to boys and girls in the eighth (13 years) and tenth (15 years) grades in the USA, and then 2 years later to the same groups who were by then in the tenth and twelfth grades. Engel found a relative stability of self concept between 13 and 15, and 15 and 17. She also found that those subjects whose self concept on first testing was negative were significantly less stable in their self concept than were those whose initial self concept was positive. Furthermore, those who persisted in a negative self-concept showed significantly more maladjustment on the MMPI than those who persisted in a positive self concept. Unfortunately, no evidence is given regarding sex differences.

Carlson (1965) carried out further investigation of the self image during adolescence. Unfortunately, Carlson's research involved only a very small sample (33 girls and 16 boys), but one which was followed up longitudinally over a 6-year period. The children were first tested at 12 years of age, and then again at 18, by means of a self-descriptive questionnaire which provided indices of social orientation, personal orientation and self esteem. Results showed that median self-esteem scores remained identical for both boys and girls over the 6-year period.

However, another study (Katz and Zigler, 1967) produced results opposed to those of the previous two researches. Katz and Zigler (1967) used 60 boys and 60 girls in the fifth (10 years), eighth (13 years) and eleventh (16 years) grades, whose real and ideal self image was assessed both by questionnaire and on an adjective checklist. Self-image disparity was defined as the degree of difference between real and ideal self image, and results showed that self-image disparity increased in a linear fashion with age, with the greatest change occurring between the 10- and 13-year levels. Based on these findings the researchers suggest that the disparity is an adaptive and to be expected feature in adolescent personality, arising out of increasing cognitive ability inevitably leading to greater capacities for self derogation, for hypothesising what one might be (cf. Piaget's formal operational stage). The discrepancy is seen as reflecting cognitive maturation and not personality disturbance. So even this investigation cannot be taken as an indisputable support for the conventional view of adolescence.

Piers and Harris (1964) compared the stability of self concept over a 4-month period among 8, 10 and 15 year olds, and found no age differences. Like Engel's, the correlations obtained by Piers and Harris at all three age levels were in excess of 0.70. Coopersmith (1967) at the end of his 3-year study of self conception was prompted to state that 'It appears relatively resistant to change. Once established it apparently provides a sense of personal continuity over space and time, and is defended against alteration, diminution, and insult.' (p. 21) Simmons, Rosenberg and Rosenberg (1973) also conducted a study to discern when, if at all, the adolescent self-image disturbance occurs. Several dimensions of the self image were measured among 1,917 urban school children aged 8–17. Compared to children in the 8–11 age group, the early adolescents, particularly those between 12 and 13, were shown to exhibit heightened self consciousness, greater instability of the self image, slightly lower self esteem and a less favourable view of the opinions held of them by significant others. Evidence was presented suggesting that the child's environment may have a stronger effect than his age in producing such changes. Children who had entered junior high school appeared more disturbed along these lines than their age peers still in elementary school. Thus, while disturbance appears, it lies in early adolescence and not as Erikson hypothesised in late adolescence, and is related to the movement into secondary school at puberty, a highly significant event for many a child, a move from a protected small school context to a larger more impersonal school where he has lost his former status as biggest and oldest and where he is constantly changing rooms and teachers. This makes the self concept more vulnerable. Age peers who remained in the elementary school did not show the disturbance in self image. In a study of the effects of transfer to comprehensive secondary school from primary school at 11 years of age (Alban Metcalfe, 1978), the self-concepts of children were tested during the final term at primary school, and retested one year later at secondary school, using the Piers–Harris Self Concept Scale. No overall differences in measured self concept were detected for boys or girls. However, when the first and second testings for children with high or low self-concept scores at primary school (top and bottom 25 per cent) were compared, it was found that the scores for the children with high self concepts decreased significantly ($p<0.01$ for both boys and girls), but that there were no significant differences for low scorers. This suggests that it is the young adolescent with a high self concept who has most to lose on changing school environment. The low-self-concept child is likely to be vulnerable, too, but it would be difficult for him to sink much lower. Perhaps more thought ought to be given to providing more support and preparation for the transfer to secondary school by teachers in both types of school.

In a more recent large-scale study by Coleman (1974) results are reported which again support the view that the self concept is relatively stable throughout adolescence. In his cross-sectional approach Coleman (1974) found that the proportions of disturbed youngsters remained constant at each age, with no differences between the two sexes at each age level either. Thus, in contrast to Erikson's contentions, there is one stage at which there is greater disturbance in self image than at any other, though it is apparent that a similar proportion of adolescents at each age level do experience negative self attitudes, and express negative themes about personal qualities on sentence-completion tasks set by Coleman. In this Coleman has evidence which does point to some teenagers struggling with identity problems, but certainly not all teenagers. Hazarding a shot in the dark, it may be that those teenagers who suffer identity crises are those who have always had problems of self-image definition, perhaps due to a diet of inconsistent and often negative feedback from significant others ever since birth.

Offer (1974) on the basis of his longitudinal study of adolescent boys from ages 14 to 18, again suggests that for most boys these years are not characterised by stress or turmoil. Other investigators (e.g. Douvan and Adelson, 1966; Weiner, 1970) also question the assumption of adolescent crisis. These studies, however, often do not deal with early adolescence; nor do they systematically measure differences in the self image longitudinally over age. Monge (1973) also produces evidence derived from factor analyses of semantic differential data of 1,035 boys and 1,027 girls from 11 to 17 years old that self-concept structure remains essentially constant throughout adolescence. There was no evidence to suggest a restructuring of the self concept around and after puberty. The self concepts of students also appear to remain relatively stable over a 9-year period in a cross-sectional study by Vidoni (1976), despite many academics' perceptions that students have become more radical. It would seem that change in self concept in adolescence for most children is dependent on experiences being subjectively interpreted as traumatic, such as violent change of environment/role/status as with school change or survival training where the youngster in being pushed to his limit develops more self confidence, feelings of competence and worth, e.g. Clifford and Clifford 1967; Payne, Drummond and Lunghi 1970. Thus, we are in a position where there is little evidence to support the idea of an identity crisis in older adolescence, or that changes automatically involve increasing self derogation and identity diffusion. There are, of course, children at all ages who manifest negative self concepts and identity problems. Those adolescents who suffer disturbance are likely those who have always borne throughout childhood such self-identity and esteem problems, for a small minority of all age levels seem to struggle with the issue. Coleman (1974) provides a suggestion that might resolve the argument. He distinguishes two forms of identity, present and future; each adolescent is seen to hold two conceptions of himself: what he is and what he will be. From an analysis of projective responses to pictures Coleman found that it was future identity conflicts that increased with age and not present self conception. Thus, with a normal population it appears that there is an increasing concern and confusion over 'what shall I be?', a finding which with future research may help to refine and amplify Erikson's picture of the ego task identity v. identity diffusion based on his atypical and disturbed adolescent patients.

D. Physical development in adolescence

It has already been argued and shown earlier in this chapter that physical attributes and their evaluation are a vital and central feature of self conception. At adolescence, rate of maturation or rate of physical development becomes significant. Physical growth can be a source of great anxiety, whether it be too slow or too fast, too little or too much. The rate of an adolescent's physical development in comparison to others in the peer group considerably affects how each youngster feels about himself, and as we noted earlier the peer group is the most important set of significant others for older children. This emphasis on physical development may seem quite theoretical, so think about these questions. Do you recall your adolescence? Did you worry about your height, or weight, or some other aspect of your appearance? Did your feelings about any physical attributes affect your general attitudes to yourself and your behaviour? Did you ever want to change any aspect of your physical self? Were you an early or late entrant into puberty? Did the physical changes of puberty have any effect on your feelings about yourself, on your interpersonal relationships, or your behaviour? Most adolescents at some time or other do think about these aspects, for contemporary television, films, advertising and magazines coupled with hero worship of sports stars, beauty queens and film stars, contribute to the expectation that certain body builds are most desirable while others are disparaged. Anxiety and concern can be fostered if the adolescent's body doesn't match up to the expected norm. The inception of heterosexual interests forces more attention on the body image at this stage, too.

From the responses of 580 15 year olds, Frazier and Lisonbee (1950) found that two-thirds of the sample wanted to change their body image, especially height, weight and complexion, with boys wanting to be taller, girls lighter and less tall, and both wanting a clear complexion. Congruence with ideal cultural norms for physical development appears very important for adolescents. It would seem that this central concern needs to be reduced through less emphasis by mass media advertising, etc. on ideal physical attributes so that the bulk of adolescents who can never achieve this ideal need feel no self defeat or self derogation.

Clothing appears to be used as a measure of self expression, attention seeking and gaining self esteem by those with low self esteem. Humphrey (1971) investigated the use of clothing by adolescents varying in self esteem, with over 500 boys and girls from 13 to 19 years old. For the boys, self esteem was positively related to the aesthetic and attention uses of clothing, while for the girls it was associated with aesthetic, attention, interest and management uses. The findings indicate that the boys and girls to whom these uses were important tended to have higher levels of self esteem or more positive feelings about self. Insecure individuals of both sexes were more interested in buying clothing and taking care of their clothes than were the more stable. Insecure boys also showed considerable concern about the appearance of their clothing.

The Institute of Human Development at the University of California has focused some of its studies of human growth on the behavioural effects of early and late puberty in both adolescent boys and girls on personality and self conception. The effects on boys seems to be different from that on girls.

Out of a group of 90 boys studied for over 4 years, Jones and Bayley (1950) studied the 16 most late-maturing and the 16 most early-maturing boys. Numerous significant differences were shown between the two groups. The slower-maturing boys were rated by adults as less mature in heterosexual social situations, as less physically attractive, less masculine, more tense and more affected. When judged by their peers these late maturers were rated as less likely to be leaders, less confident and less popular. On the other hand the early-maturing boys were evaluated as more mature by both peers and adults, and demonstrated less need to strive for status.

In a subsequent investigation conducted by Mussen and Jones (1957) a comparison was made between the self concepts, motivation and interpersonal attitudes of early- and late-maturing boys by means of a projective test (TAT). The evidence indicated that early maturers were self confident and detached, whereas the slow developers manifested insecurity and dependence on adults, often reflected in attention-getting behaviours. The same investigators (Mussen and Jones, 1957) in a further study discerned that the late maturer showed a greater motivation towards social acceptance and aggression than his more physically mature contemporary. This drive may stem from feelings of insecurity and dependence in order to attain recognition to compensate for inadequacy. The late maturer was less likely to have satisfactorily resolved the conflicts associated with the transition from childhood to adulthood with the ability to achieve independence, adequacy and satisfaction. Tryon (1939) obtained similar results, with late maturers depicted by their peers as more attention-seeking, more bossy and more restless than their more physically accelerated peers. The results of a longitudinal study by Jones (1957) revealed that most physical differences of adolescence tended to disappear in adulthood as late developers caught up, but the personality and self-conception differences related to early or late maturity still tended to characterise post-adolescent life. As adults, the early maturers tended to produce higher test scores on characteristics such as 'socialisation' 'responsibility' and 'dominance'. The slow maturers still maintained their adolescent characteristics of 'seeking help from others' lacking confidence, less social poise and showing more tenseness. The handicaps and advantages of late and early puberty carried over to adulthood to a greater extent in psychological than in physical characteristics.

The results of this series of studies on males add up to a consistent picture. A large, strong stature is a central aspect of the ideal masculine model. Thus, it can be assumed that the early attainment of the physical attributes associated with maturity serves as a social stimulus which evokes from both peers and adults a reaction of respect, acceptance and the expectation that the individual concerned will be capable of relatively mature social behaviour. Such a reaction from others serves to support and reinforce adaptive, 'grown-up' actions and contributes to feelings of confidence and security in the early-maturing boys. On the other hand, the late maturer must cope with the developmental demands of the secondary school period with the liability of a relatively small, immature-appearing physical stature. His appearance is likely to evoke from others at least mild reactions of derogation and the expectation that he is capable of only ineffectual, immature behaviour. Such reactions create a kind of social environment which is conducive to feelings of inadequacy, insecurity and defensive, 'small-boy' behaviour. Such behaviour once initiated may well be self-perpetuating, since it is likely only to intensify the negative environmental reactions which gave rise to it in the first place. This interpretation implies that the late-maturing boy is likely to be involved in a circular psychosocial process in which reactions of others and his own reactions interact with unhappy consequences for his personal and social adjustment.

In contrast to the dramatic effects bodily change has on the male self concept in adolescence, physical change, whether early or late, is much less a potent influence on the self concepts of adolescent girls. This difference in effects may be due to the male cultural norm of tall, brawny masculinity, whereas early maturing for girls contains no prestigious advantage. In fact early maturation can be a calamity: the girl will stoop to hide her tallness, or wear sloppy jumpers to disguise her developing busts. Early-maturing girls are perceived as listless, submissive and lacking poise (Tryon, 1939) and are judged to have little popularity or prestige among their peers (Jones, 1958). This picture contrasts very much with that painted of early-maturing males. The early-maturing girl is, of course, 3–4 years ahead developmentally of the average boy, and has to seek social outlets with much older males. Thus the slower-maturing girl is likely to enjoy more social advantages. In a similar study to the one conducted on males, Jones and Mussen (1958) compared early- and late-maturing girls in terms of their self conceptions, motivation and interpersonal attitudes. They found that early-maturing girls had more favourable self concepts and less dependency needs, but the relationships were far less clearcut than for males, for whom physical strength and athleticism are so important. The feminine sex role stereotype hasn't such a high premium placed on total physical make-up, though specific physical elements are important, e.g. attractive face, well-endowed bosom, etc. A girl need only possess one of these qualities to elicit favourable responses; a deficit in one aspect can be more than compensated for in another. Girls are expected to make themselves attractive and are judged on how they look, whereas boys are expected to perform feats with their bodies, with others responding to their total physical make-up not to specific aspects. On the existing evidence it is possible to make a tentative speculation that physical maturation in adolescence has a less dramatic effect on girls than boys because the former have greater flexibility for altering or changing their looks through a sensible use of cosmetics, padding, etc. but the latter can do little to alter their performance. But despite the camouflage such artificial remedies in the cosmetics field offer, the psychological damage caused already may never be eliminated completely.

Summary

The self concept appears to develop from a number of interrelated sources:

(a) body awareness and body image, furnished initially through sense perception, is the basic core round which self reference and identity is moulded;

(b) language comes to aid the slow process of differentiation of self and others as well as facilitating the understanding of much feedback from

(c) significant others in which the peer group appears more important than the parents, once early childhood is passed. The child whose body image closely matches societal ideals is one whose self esteem glows through reflected appraisals.

All this enables the child to define more clearly and progressively just who and what he is. This developmental emergence is organised in terms of personal constructs about reality that are generated by the particular social and non-social contents of repeated daily experience. This picture of development is consistent with the phenomenological approach through the individual's frame of reference. Adolescence does not appear to cause most adolescents to make drastic changes to their self concepts, though rate of maturation can be an influence on some teenagers' conceptions of themselves, especially males. The content of the self concepts tends to be dominated by objective general information, e.g. sex, age, kinship relationships and possessions in young children, whereas adolescents stress personal attributes, self evaluation and social relationships.

In essence, if a person is accepted, approved and liked for what he is and he is aware of this, then a positive self concept should be his. If others, parents, peers, teachers, ridicule him, belittle him, reject him, criticise him, for his behavioural or physical attributes, then little self respect or self worth is likely to accrue. As a person is judged by others so he comes to judge himself.

Further reading

Douvan, E. and **Adelson, J.** *The Adolescent Experience,* New York: Wiley, 1966.
Erikson, E. *Childhood & Society,* New York: Norton, 1963.
Livesley, W. J. and **Bromley, D. B.** *Person Perception in Childhood & Adolescence,* London: Wiley, 1973.
Offer, D. *The Psychological World of the Teenager,* New York: Basic Books, 1973.

Chapter 7

Sex roles, identification and child-rearing practices

The preceding chapter considered three sources of self conception which help mould the self concept throughout life. Two other sources also crucial to the development of a healthy self concept are the concern of this chapter. These two sources, both very much concerned with parental behaviour, are:

(a) the effects of parent–child interaction on the development of an appropriate sex role self concept; and
(b) the effects of different child-rearing practices.

A. Identification and sex role identity

The first reference usually made about a new-born child is a question of its biological identity directed at the officiating midwife by the euphoric mother – 'what is it?' The infallible response follows: 'it's a boy' or 'it's a girl'. This definition initiates a lifelong series of events based on biological sexual identity. But it is not being male or female that is important by itself, rather whether one is a masculine male or a feminine female. Masculinity and femininity refer to that constellation of characteristics and behaviours deemed appropriate and relevant in a society at a particular time to males and females respectively. There is no god-given law that the psychosocial attributes should match the biological ones. The relationship is learned; it is not innate and of course it is culture bound.

A keystone of the self concept is this concept of being a masculine or feminine person. A substantial number of functions outside the basic sexual one are rooted in these concepts. For example Mussen (1961) shows that successful sex role identification is related to effective personal–social functioning and even to school performance in various subjects. Whatever attributes the individual infers he possesses, the global self concept rarely appears in the neuter gender; rather each quality is attached to a given sex by the possessor, e.g. the self concept is of being an attractive lady, a handsome man.

Identification is a necessary process for self conception. Identification originally derived from psychoanalytic ideas about how personality evolves and develops over time. Essentially, identification is a largely unconscious process that influences a growing child to think, feel and behave in ways similar to the significant people in his life. More specifically, it is a process whereby a growing child takes on the behaviour and self concepts of another individual and behaves as if he were that person. Indeed, a child's emerging self concept is built on the foundation of his earliest and most primary identifications with people (or a person) most significant to him.

Identification is preceded by sex-typing, which is more on the order of modelling or imitative behaviour. Whereas identification is mainly an unconscious process of incorporation of an entire personality, sex typing is a more conscious process of copying specific behaviours. From these two processes of sex typing and identification a major element of the self concept emerges – that of sex role identity. The individual's conceptualisation of his own degree of masculinity or femininity, i.e. how far the individual fits the publicly shared beliefs about the appropriate characteristics for males and females, is termed 'sex role identity'. This sex role identity is a basic component of the self concept, and although only one aspect of the self concept, it is a mandatory and universal component.

Four major theories of sex role identification have been promoted: the psychoanalytic, the social learning, the cognitive and the sex role standard models.

1. The psychoanalytic theory of identification

The Freudian psychoanalytic model distinguishes two types of identification – anaclitic identification and identification with the aggressor (alternatively called defensive identification). Anaclitic identification is founded on the infant's excessive dependency on its mother. In Freud's view identification in girls is based mainly on this love–dependency relation, while for boys this anaclitic identification with the mother is supplanted later by identification with the aggressor around the age of 4–6 years. Identification with the aggressor demands that the boys must have strong but ambivalent feelings for his father. In the Oedipal conflict the son's love for the father is interwoven with strands of hostility for possessing the mother. Such hostile feelings produce anxiety as the boy fears punishment for his guilty thoughts in the form of castration carried out by the father. To defend against such anxiety the male child resolves the Oedipal dilemma by repressing his desires, identifying strongly with the adult male agressor and therefore enjoying the mother vicariously. The boy continually tries to become more like the father, thus acquiring masculine traits and values.

In the case of female identification, Freudian theory is more complicated. The young girl's original love object is also the mother, but this does not of course pose any threat to the father. Nor can any punitive castration be inflicted to direct identification. Freud tries to get out of the awkwardness of this scenario by manipulating the male case to that of the female situation. He argues that the girl notices her lack of a penis and regards herself as already castrated. This results in penis envy, in which all other persons are reacted to and evaluated in terms of whether they possess the valued bodily part. Mother becomes devalued since she also lacks the prized organ, and the girl turns to the father who is 'complete'. This establishes the basis for later heterosexual attraction, with marriage and the birth of a son giving symbolic fulfilment of the desire for a penis. However, in order to return to the mother as an identification figure, Freud claims the girl realises the futility of having her father as a love object at the same time as realising the possibility of the consequent loss of the mother's affection on whom she is still dependent. She then takes her mother as her identification figure, but this identification is not as strong or as complete as the male form, since believing she has been castrated she has no fear of this punishment in the future.

This psychoanalytic theory attempts to explain the development of an extensive area of social behaviour by one process. Identification was thus presumed to account for sex role socialisation, conscience, self control and adult behaviour patterns. However, studies which have attempted to discern consistency across these various components have revealed only moderate relationships, e.g. Sears, Maccoby and Levin (1965). The findings suggest that sex role learning can be rather specific, with a boy for example interested in playing with toy soldiers but equally interested in art. Hence, despite the fact that sex role stereotypes are widely shared within a culture, individuals will vary on the degree to which they adopt its specific components. Minuchin (1964) reports that girls, in particular from homes and schools that stress individual development, departed more from conventional sex role standards than did those from more traditional backgrounds.

Of course, for Freud the delineation of a specific sex role self concept is unnecessary. Sexuality is an integral part of the psychic being, and cannot be separated off. Sex role behaviour, feelings and attitudes arise out of the unconscious whirlpool of childhood conflicts and fears, not out of social reality.

In Freud's theorising, it is possible to envisage (though not to prove!) how characteristic conventional and stereotyped elements of masculine and feminine self concepts arise. But the nature of the theory does not lend itself to experimental verification and demands acceptance of basic Freudian tenets such as the role of the unconscious, libidinal drives, symbolism, etc. All this strains the credibility of the theory.

Whiting (1960) expanded on Freud's concept of defensive identification. He felt that competition was not solely in the sexual context of the Oedipal situation but also in the more broadly involved competition for other social and material resources the parent has at his command. The child's identification is motivated by the desire to have access to and control those envied resources. The theory is based on status envy.

2. The social learning theory of identification

The social learning model of identification emerges out of the behaviourist approach with an emphasis on reinforcement contingencies augmenting the vital core process of imitation of the model. Imitation is the copying of specific items of behaviour, but it is not indiscriminate. Within the compass of sex role identification, imitation is seen in terms of the child's relationship with an actual or symbolic model and that model's behavioural characteristics. Reinforcement can be involved in the equation at various points in that:

(a) the learner can be rewarded directly by the model: the matching behaviour paradigm;
(b) the learner himself feels intrinsic rewards for being able to copy desired behaviour – secondary reinforcement paradigm;
(c) the learner feels rewarded by seeing the model rewarded for the latter's behaviour – vicarious reinforcement paradigm.

The social learning theorists themselves realised the inadequacy of conditioning in socialisation. If all learning depended on the selective reinforcement of randomly emitted responses the child's repertoire would be restricted drastically. Imitation was therefore introduced into the process of learning. Studies by Bandura, Ross and Ross (1961; 1963a; 1963b) demonstrate vividly how effective nurturant and powerful models are in inducing imitative responses. Parents of course possess these qualities, and are usually consistently available. The essential basis of the social learning model is that the child learns sex role appropriate discrete responses through reinforcement and by the observation of live models and symbolic ones (e.g. in the media). The child so learns which behaviours will result in reward and which in punishment.

The work of Bandura and his colleagues demonstrate the conditions under which imitation occurs. The 1961 study (Bandura, Ross and Ross, 1961) showed that mere observation of aggression by the model would evoke imitative aggression in children, and that these responses are produced in a new milieu without any direct reinforcement of either the model or the child. In a later paper (Bandura, Ross and Ross, 1963a) they reported that children tended to copy the behaviour of adults who were rewarded or who were seen to be powerful. However, it was noted that children would equally copy the distinctive behaviour of the punished model if they (the children) were rewarded. Performance, as distinct from learning, is related to rewarding the observer. Bandura, Ross and Ross (1963b) showed evidence for cognitive mediating factors. Three groups of children watched a film and then were requested to reproduce the model's behaviour. One group watched quietly, the second group counted while they watched, while the third group described the actions as they watched. It was the last group who reproduced most fully the actions of the model, since the verbalisations appeared to facilitate their observations. So a rather complicated set of relationships between reward and imitation is suggested which are related to the specific behaviour, the source and type of reinforcement, the appropriateness of the behaviour and the cognitive development of the child. This social learning position is a rather restricted one since it tends to ignore affective and cognitive bases which seem so necessary to explain the strength and tenacity with which sex role identity is held. Feelings, motives and knowledge must be involved, and while reinforcement procedures are important one is left wondering whether environmental input in the form of reinforcement is adequate on its own.

Maccoby and Jacklin (1974) in a review of over 2,000 articles on sex role research found that the evidence, particularly in early childhood, for the social learning model is rather unimpressive.

3. The cognitive–developmental theory of identification

Kohlberg (1966) has produced a cognitive–developmental theory which argues that early in life each child makes an unalterable categorisation of himself/herself as a boy/girl, and on this judgement is subsequently based all future development of sex identity and sex role behaviour. The gender label then becomes a major organiser and determinant of the child's behaviour, feelings and traits, providing cognitive consistency. Kohlberg claims that gender is the basic fixed classification into which the child sorts itself and others, and around which most of its social perceptions and actions are organised. In this theory the sex role stereotype is not a result of reinforcement or identification but derives from universal perceived sex differences. This means that children slowly develop concepts of masculinity and femininity, i.e. when they have understood what their own sex is, they attempt to match their own behaviour to their conception of others like themselves.

The gender categorisation commences around 4 years of age, but isn't completed until around 6/7 years of age according to Kohlberg. The basis for giving these ages lies in their relationship to Piaget's stages of cognitive development which control the child's understanding. Kohlberg argues that children comprehend sex roles initially in terms of body size, shape and physical attributes. But until a child is capable of the early stages of conservation a full understanding of the permanence of gender is impossible. So up to around 7 years it is possible for a boy to think that if he changed appearance he might become a girl.

Once the judgement of gender is stable then the child is led to judge the same-sexed behaviours and objects positively. Performing 'boy' or 'girl' behaviours or manifesting appropriate traits becomes rewarding in itself, as it is in agreement with the cognitive judgement of self. This provides a positive self concept, and the child will seek out situations and models that will ensure the continuation of such self evaluation. In this way the child becomes attached to the same-sexed parent. For Kohlberg, modelling precedes attachment, but in the social learning model attachment precedes modeling.

Evidence for Kohlberg's theory is limited. With observational work, he has shown that at 7 the child can make sex-typed choices and display strong gender identity. Critical to the theory would be evidence to support the sequence of gender role concept, followed by positive self evaluation and finally identification with the same-sexed parent. Kohlberg studied only young males who do appear to demonstrate this sequence, and with boys who are interested in size and strength and believe 'strong and big is the best' the sequence from gender role concept to positive self evaluation as a male is not too hard to accept. But how do girls react in view of their likely knowledge of boys' negative evaluation of them? It may not be all that important if girls do not regard physical strength and size as important.

Despite the current shortage of evidence to support Kohlberg's theory, and the male-based orientation of it, the cognitive perspective provides a central base to which all the child's perceptions, beliefs and feelings can be attached.

This cognitive base provides a wider foundation for learning sex identity and behaviour than the hit-or-miss character of reinforcement, shaping and imitation in narrowly defined behaviours as proposed by the social learning model, though this is not to deny that such learning processes do not play a significant role in specific behavioural contexts and for particular behaviours.

4. The sex role standard theory of identification

Kagan's (1964) exposition of sex role development appears to combine the psychoanalytic, social learning and cognitive formulations. The central concept for Kagan is the sex role standard or the learned psychosocial behaviour and characteristics of each sex. These sex role standards are culturally approved for male and female and are internalised by individuals to guide and evaluate their behaviour.

The child learns to differentiate between the male and the female role standard assisted by society's concern with this dichotomy as transmitted by parents and other agents of socialisation. In addition to social learning, Kagan claims that the child identifies with the same-sexed parent because of the power and resources held by the model which the child thinks he will also acquire through demonstrating sex role appropriate behaviour. The child can then behave on the basis of what Kagan posits as a fundamental human motive – that of the need to bring one's behaviour into conformity with a previously learned sex role standard. Behaving consistently with this standard is self reinforcing, while the standard itself is strengthened by the reinforcing consequences of acting in accordance with it. All this inculcates sex-typed self-concept traits, behaviours and feelings more strongly. Thus, Kagan adds an effective dimension to the social learning model as well as a cognitive schema of a guiding standard. Congruence with the sex role standard brings positive self evaluation of one's masculinity or femininity.

Four different models of sex role identification have been outlined. None of them is sufficient on its own to explain the development of sex role identification. It would appear that imitation, reinforcement, cognitive development and appropriate models are all required in varying degrees, depending on context and behaviour. All the theories are beset by either methodological problems or incomplete articulation or inadequate evidence. However, there is general agreement that the major sources of sex role identity for the young child are the identification with the same-sexed parent and the degree to which this identification is congruent with wider culture's definition of sex roles. Thus, while the parents are the original prototypes of masculinity and feminity for the child, the gradual extension of the child's environment with school and peer group provides direct confrontation with the stereotypes of the broader community which compel the child to accommodate his original definitions to such stereotypes of maleness or femaleness. There will be considerable communality between these two sources of sex role identity, but some slight mismatches may also be apparent due to subcultural values and particular family milieux. All children need to have a sex self-concept label that is congruent with their biological sex label.

For sex role identification to be optimal the child must perceive the model as warm and nurturant, as being in control of the child's needs (e.g. love, power) and as possessing some objective bases of similarity in external traits. Those children who make only a partial identification or who have a parental model which is only partially meeting the societal standards will likely perceive the discrepancy between themselves and that societal expectation, and may well become a target of verbal or even physical abuse. Self esteem is lowered, coupled with feelings of inadequacy and anxiety, since the basic component of self conception, sex identity, is inadequately developed or inappropriate.

There exist numerous experimental studies which suggest that a nurturant relationship between father and son is vitally important in the formation of a firm and adequate masculine identity. For instance Payne and Mussen (1956) had adolescent pupils and their parents fill out the California Psychological Inventory. The 20 boys with the highest father-identification scores, defined in terms of similarity of father–son answers on the Inventory, were compared with 20 low father-identified boys. The 40 boys were then given an incomplete-stories test to assess perception of the father–son relation. The boys with a strong identification with father produced more frequent evidence of warm father–son relations and a perception of the father as nurturant than did the low-identified subjects. Moreover, the boys who were identified with the father possessed more sex-typed masculine behaviour and attitudes than the boys with minimal identification with their fathers.

In a further study (Mussen and Distler, 1959) kindergarden boys were given a test to assess degree of adoption of sex-typed masculine interests. The 10 most and least masculine boys were then tested in a doll-play situation. The doll-play themes of the masculine boys contained more evidence of a perception of the father as nurturant and powerful than the themes of the non-masculine boys. These results support the notion that identification is facilitated when the model is seen as nurturant to the child.

Experiences with other people in ways that are congruent with sex role identity, reinforces that identity. So a girl who behaves in an affectionate way and hears others praise her affectionate manner is moulded more firmly in her conviction that she is basically and emphatically feminine; similarly with a boy who displays dominance and to whom others, perceiving his dominance, react appropriately feeding back information that he is what he wants to be and believes himself to be, positive self feelings are generated. But experience with others disconfirming the individual's beliefs about his sex identity destroys a basic faith in the person as to what he or she is. The culturally approved sex role identity stereotype functions as the ideal to which individuals aspire. The closer the individual perceives his attributes are to this ideal the more positive the self attitudes to his sex role identity.

Luckily most parents want their offspring to develop appropriate sex role identities, and consequently various subtle pressures are applied such as reinforcement of the 'right' behaviour and selective presentation of toys, clothing, hobbies and the like. Additionally, young children want to be accepted by parents, siblings and peers, a need which equally directs behaviour along relevant avenues. For instance, a little boy will use his toy hammer and pretend to mend things just as he sees his father do; a little girl will use her toy vacuum cleaner to clean out her doll's house just as she has seen her mother do in their home. Little direct teaching is required for either sex typing or identification. But many subtle pressures are applied to guide the child into behaving in ways culturally relevant to his or her biological sex. Even from birth many parents dress infant males in blue and infant females in pink. At Christmas and birthdays boys are given what are conventionally regarded as boy's toys, e.g. trains, guns. Little girls become the happy recipients of dolls and sewing sets. So by the end of the pre-school years most children are well aware of what sex they are and what is expected of them in that particular definition. Much of the play activity of children can be viewed as a rehearsal for adult roles. Parents and other significant persons frequently make verbal comments to reinforce appropriate behaviour such as 'you are a big boy now not crying when you fall' or 'stop that Mary, little girls do not climb trees'. Though as was indicated earlier such specific reinforcements do not and cannot provide the complete repertoire of sex role identity without functioning in conjunction with other processes such as imitation, cognitive stage, etc. Kagan (1964) reports that as early as 3 years old, boys are aware of some of the activities and objects that our culture regards as masculine. Among girls, however, preferences are more variable up to puberty. Many girls between 3 and 10 years of age show a strong preference for masculine games, activities and objects; whereas it is not usual to find many boys who prefer feminine activities during this period. This difference in game preferences is matched by a relatively greater frequency of girls stating a desire to be a boy or wanting to be daddy rather than a mummy when they grow up (Brown, 1957).

Rosenberg and Sutton-Smith (1960) tested children aged 9–11 for game preferences. The results suggest that in the year 1960 girls were more masculine in their game choices than they had been 30 years earlier. There are social class differences in the game choices of children. Rabban (1950) asked children (age 3–8) in middle and working-class homes to select the boys they liked the best. The choices of lower-class boys and girls conformed more closely to traditional sex-typed standards than the choice of middle-class children, suggesting that the differentiation of sex role is sharper in lower-class families. Lower-class mothers encourage sex typing more consistently than middle-class mothers. Moreover, the difference in sex typing between the classes is greatest for girls.

Apparently the middle-class girl, unlike the middle-class boy, is much freer to express an interest in toys and activities of the opposite sex. This finding agrees with the fact that, among girls, there is a positive correlation between the educational level of the family and involvement in masculine activities (Kagan and Moss, 1962).

Since physical attributes such as height, weight, shape are essential elements of sex role identity, early puberty with its development of secondary sex characteristics will lead to an earlier congruence of sex role identity and bodily shape. This will facilitate positive self conception and is another aspect of the effect of rate of physical maturation on self conception which has been considered in the previous chapter. As we have seen, early physical maturation should encourage more confidence and popularity.

In Western society, males should possess aggressive, dominating and instrumental attributes while women should perceive themselves in terms of passive, dependent, conformist and expressive qualities. Affiliative and nurturant behaviours are also regarded as more appropriate for females than males. These behavioural expectations and self-rated characteristics form a sex role standard to be met by those who wish to be regarded as possessing congruent psychosocial and biological sex roles.

Since our culture assigns greater freedom, power and value to the male role, it is understandable that the girl might wish for the more attractive male role. This devaluation of the female role is probably one reason why the typical woman regards herself as less adequate and more fearful than most men (Bennett and Cohen, 1959).

The dichotomy of masculine and feminine characteristics into instrumental versus expressive (Parsons, 1955) may appear traditionally a bit 'old hat', but even contemporary research confirms that the characteristics of sex role identity are unchanged. (Burns, 1977; Broverman *et al.*, 1972). The old stereotypes still reign supreme despite formal legislation on equality and informal 'women's lib' pressure groups. Bakan (1966) proposes 'agency' and 'communion' as the two fundamental principles differentiating the aggregate of masculine attributes from the feminine ones, but these terms appear to be no more than the renaming of the Parsonian dichotomy. Agentic characteristics, e.g. activity dominance, aggressiveness, mastery, self assertion are employed by males in numerous studies requesting self descriptions (Block, 1973; Burns, 1977; Moffet, 1975). Similarly, self-perceived female self concepts are revealed in these studies as relating to communion, e.g. tenderness, dependence, cooperativeness, sensitivity, subjectivity, intuition and affiliation.

Characteristics related to traditional sex role conceptions show greatest resistance to change (Kagan and Moss, 1962) with characteristics conceived as feminine (e.g. passivity, dependency) showing a high degree of stability from childhood to adulthood in females but not in males. Similarly, aggression is highly stable in males, not in females. Boys and girls who are equally dependent in childhood diverge at about adolescence in response to differential social pressures. The boy perceives sex-specific pressure to become independent and manly; the girl, on the other hand, can (and likely will) continue to be passive–dependent because of traditional concepts of femininity. These sex role stereotypic characteristics are usually uncritically accepted and incorporated into the self concepts of males and females. One reason why most studies of adolescents' self concepts find boys holding more positive self concepts than girls lies in the fact that, in general, masculine attributes are more highly valued in Western society than are feminine ones (e.g. Sheriffs and McKee, 1957). Broverman et al., (1972) in a thorough survey show that women tend to incorporate aspects of femininity negatively evaluated by the rest of society (e.g. passivity, incompetence) alongside more positive ones (e.g. warmth, expressiveness) as indicated by female subjects' self descriptions. Adult males parallel the male child in possessing higher self concepts than their female counterparts. The concepts of the ideal male and ideal female are fairly congruent with accepted sex role stereotypes. Hence, it is not surprising that female self concepts tend in general to be less positive than those of the male, as the female stereotype contains socially judged less positive items. A female has a built-in disadvantage, even in attaining the ideal. They are trapped if they don't fit the stereotype, derogation from others can occur, but if they do achieve the ideal for a Western woman they then possess self concepts containing some less than positive traits. However, Tolor, Kelly and Stebbins (1976) has shown that women who reject their sex role stereotype display greater assertiveness and more positive self concepts. In other words unusual psychological strength in a woman is associated with high self esteem which allows the woman to free herself from stereotypic restrictions on her self perception.

Sex differences in self esteem seem to occur from late primary school age onwards as the young girl tunes into the fact that the stereotypic characteristics of the female self image are less valued than those of the male. Until then the self esteem of girls, as well as that of boys, derives largely from the mastery of age-appropriate skills. However, beginning in prepuberty and increasing through adolescence, the girls shift their source of self esteem from achievement to heterosexual affiliation. Girls who identify with both the stereotypical feminine model and the achievement model will experience role conflict and, hence, have lower self esteem than boys. This does seem to occur, as witness the study by Fein et al. (1975), for example. Smith (1975) applied Sears' Self Concept

Inventory to 171 upper primary school pupils. Generally the children possessed favourable self concepts, confirming previous investigations (Coopersmith, 1967; Connell *et al.*, 1975). However, a sex difference appeared in most aspects of the self concept measured. Boys consistently rated themselves more favourably than girls on seven out of nine subscales (physical ability, appearance, convergent mental ability, divergent mental ability, social relations, social virtues, school performance). On the remaining two scales (work habits, happy qualities) the boys were slightly but not significantly ahead. It indicates that as early as middle childhood girls were beginning to evaluate themselves less favourably than boys.

So by adolescence, most studies (e.g. Connell *et al.*, 1975; Smith, 1975) reveal that boys possess more positive self concepts than girls. This difference appears to stem from the different sources of the male and female self concept in that the central facets of masculinity and femininity bear traits which are differentially evaluated by society, and these young people are already well aware of this. Successful identification for a girl will present her with a wardrobe of less socially desirable personality garments; the boys' kit-bag holds a most socially acceptable set of behavioural clothing. Douvan and Gold (1966) make a general distinction between the centrality of personal achievement to self concept in boys and the importance of personal attractiveness and popularity to girls.

Most girls derive a sense of esteem through social interpersonal adequacy. Boys can establish their sense of self esteem in varied ways – by direct sexual expression, by independence and autonomy, by asserting competence to achieve in various competitive areas (athletics, intellectual activity, leadership in school affairs, responsibility in a job). Girls' greater dependence on specific social validation of their femininity means that dating, acceptance and popularity are more critical to them than to boys (Douvan and Adelson, 1966; Kagan, 1964). Popularity validates feminine self worth, a guarantee of future marriage ability.

Analysis of mobility aspirations among adolescents bear on the relationship between competence and self esteem in the boy. Boys who aspire to upward mobility – who appear from all available evidence to be a highly competent group – also show a strong sense of self esteem. They are rated by interviewers as poised and self confident. Downwardly mobile boys are less competent and less achievement-orientated and more often wish for changes in the self that are so extensive or so central that they indicate self rejection. Interviewers rate these boys much lower on poise and self confidence (Douvan and Adelson, 1966). In data for girls, there are no clear simple links between achievement–competence in the work sphere and self esteem. But interpersonal skill and a developing concept of feminine adulthood relate closely to measures of self esteem (Douvan and Adelson, 1966).

Lower self-concept scores may also accrue to girls because girls appear to be more willing than boys to disclose their weaknesses. Bogo, Winget and Gleser (1970) noted for example that boys obtained higher scores on 'lie' and 'defensiveness' scales than girls, such scales reflecting the extent to which the individual disguises his 'true' feelings and presents a more favourable picture of himself than he ought. A more extensive and detailed survey of research on self-concept differences between boys and girls may be found in Maccoby and Jacklin (1974).

Wilson and Wilson (1976) were also able to show that males and females have different sources for their self esteem. Male self esteem derives from success experiences in vocations, positions of power and competition. Female self esteem was derived from the achievement of personal goals, body, image, existential concerns and family relationships. The clustering of these sex differences by source of self esteem appears to characterise sex-related socialisation patterns. They also found that these sex-linked sources contribute in different weights for different individuals. This raises the serious question of the utility of a global measure of self esteem. Additionally, the male and female differences in measured self-concept scores may be an artifact of the measurement technique. That is, the adjectives or statements included in any self-concept scale are bound to affect mean sex, social class or any other variable score if those scale items are more favourable to one component of the variable than the others. Hence, a rating scale containing items more favourable to girls than boys cannot but help generate higher self esteem for girls and of course, vice versa. This is posited as an explanation for Bledsoe's (1964, 1973) results which are two of the very few studies that have revealed higher self esteem for girls than boys just prior to adolescence. Bledsoe (1964) originally suggested that the earlier maturation of girls plus their frequent contact with women teachers and mothers enables them to develop a more satisfying self image, with the first stages of schooling also presenting and stressing qualities of neatness, docility and conformity – a woman's world to which boys are less successful in measuring up to. In his subsequent study, as a result of analysing responses to individual items, Bledsoe (1973) discerned that the rating differences favourable to girls were those connoting 'goodness', e.g. polite, clean, kind, sincere, cooperative, friendly, unselfish, etc. These qualities, Bledsoe suggests, are usually associated with feminine rather than male stereotypes. So the content of an assessment instrument may well be determining the results to a large extent rather than revealing real differences between groups or individuals. This again points to the necessity of interpreting results with caution.

Numerous studies indicate the importance of an adequate sex identity for better adjustment to the demands of daily life. Mussen (1961) found that high masculinity among adolescent boys is related to other indices of psychological health such as self esteem and to positive rewarding relationships with fathers. In Douvan and Adelson's (1966) national study of adolescents, a similar measure of traditional feminine interests among girls related strongly to other areas. Girls who scored low on feminine orientation were much less developed socially, less poised and graceful in interacting with adults, had a lower level of social energy and a more restricted time perspective than the highly feminine girls. Heilbrun (1965) found that male college students who identified with their fathers were better adjusted and had a stronger sexual identity (more certain about their 'maleness') than males who were not so identified with their fathers. Similarly, Helper (1955) found that the degree of 'likeness' or 'identification with' the father was related to the popularity of high school boys. That is, popular, likeable boys were more identified with their fathers. Just as the father plays an increasingly important role in the boy's life as he grows older, there is also evidence (Bayley and Schaefer, 1960) to show that the mother assumes a more prominent role in the girl's life as she grows older. Hence, boys thrive in a more patriarchal context and girls in a more matriarchal one.

Conscious concern about sex role resolutions is clearly frequent among girls at least by college age (Komarovsky, 1946). This great concern with feminine goals reflects the fact that identity for the girls is tied closely to the identity of the man she marries, but it also results from the fact that by college age girls are aware of the conflict between other more individual goals and the culture's definition of femininity. Add to all of this the fact that validation of femininity is not a matter of individual choice or action; it depends on the girl being chosen – and one wonders only that girls do not have greater anxiety about it. For boys, the case is somewhat different. Identity for them has at least two foci – the self-as-worker and the self-as-male. The boy is allowed to settle both issues independently; society does not define them as conflicting goals.

The centrality of personal achievement to self concept in boys, and the importance of personal attractiveness and popularity to girls appear repeatedly in the findings of Douvan and Adelson (1966). When asked what makes them feel 'important and useful', for example, the boys refer to work and achievement; girls more often to acceptance, popularity and praise from others. Similarly, the achievement theme appears in the worries boys report, while girls more commonly worry about peer acceptance and popularity. When the chance to be a big success is pitted against security, most boys choose the opportunity to achieve. The achievement issue is not simply less important for girls, it is different. Girls are not without their ideals, but these dreams are not of personal achievement or success; their personal goals are to attract and to retain love.

Occasionally, some children fail to identify themselves with an appropriate sex-linked role. When a boy relates excessively to his mother and other females, various aspects of his behaviour begin to reflect female characteristics. Such an effeminate boy is usually rejected by other boys, and fixation of a feminine style of life becomes a possibility, as does homosexuality. During the pre-adolescent years and at the time of pubertal changes, some girls strive to be masculine, but these efforts usually lessen as adolescence advances. Masculine traits frequently characterise a girl who has only brothers and naturally is forced to compete with them. It is advantageous for girls to have understanding mothers and for boys to have fathers who show interest and encouragement. This enhances proper sex role identification – a basic necessity for the healthy development of the child's personality. But a mature sex model of the opposite sex is a necessary requirement for a child also in order to fashion his or her later relationships to members of the opposite sex. A too close and too deep association with members of the same sex is infrequently encountered, but can occur especially when cross-parent relationships are poor. If the cross-parent relationship is missing because of death, divorce or separation the child is deprived of a model from which he or she can gain understanding of the qualities and traits of the sex role as it pertains to members of the opposite sex.

Components of sex role self concepts are less consistent and depart from conventional expectations in girls brought up in families with more modern ideas and values, who espouse radical child-rearing and family-relationship philosophies. This was the conclusion of Minuchin (1964) who compared sex role self concepts in children from traditional homes and schools stressing socialisation to general standards with those of children from 'modern' homes. Unequivocal commitment to own sex role, aggressive expression in boys and family orientation in girls were more consistently characteristic of children from traditional backgrounds. Thus, family socialisation techniques are vital in their impact on the sex role self concepts developed.

Identification for girls seems a little more complicated than for boys. Some cross-sex identification of girls with their fathers does not seem harmful (McCandless, 1967). There is in fact less pressure on girls to be ladylike, but boys must be manly. A girl can wear jeans, shirts, even a tie, but what boy would be caught dead in a dress! Girls can associate with boys in play activities without ridicule, but a boy playing with a group of girls at their activities is frowned on and derided.

The conclusion seems to be that a boy learns to be masculine through identifying with a warm, firm but accepting father whom he values and feels close to. Girls need a warm, accepting mother to maximise their feminine identification, but can also profit from some identification with father as this may facilitate understanding of a future husband and male offspring. A person has incorporated his sex role into his self concept when appropriate sex role behaviour becomes automatic and no longer deliberate or conscious.

The peer group, both at school and play, also provides heavily sex-typed values and activities, often accentuated to a considerable degree. Until well into adolescence such groups are single sexed and regard with disdain members of the opposite-sexed peer group. Since peer approval is a major source of self esteem (Ch. 6) children generally conform and want to behave in ways approved by the peer group. The school environment too, supplements the home in influencing sex role identity and behaviour. Teachers can directly inculcate sex role expectancies by stating their views on particular behaviours. In addition, the assignment of tasks in the classroom and the teaching materials used may transmit messages about appropriate sex role behaviour. Reading books often teaches sex role behaviour along with reading skills, for example. Curricula offered to boys and to girls are often different, including appropriate, and excluding what are deemed to be inappropriate subjects for each sex.

B. Child-rearing practices

Although it can take various forms throughout the world the family is the universal and primary agent of socialisation. The family group provides all the initial indications to the child as to whether he is loved or not loved, accepted or not accepted, a success or a failure, worthy or unworthy, because until schooldays the family is virtually his sole learning context. The first 5 years of life are accepted by most psychologists as the ones in which the basic framework of the personality and self conception are laid down. This is because the young child is so vulnerable, with a high degree of physical, social and emotional dependence on the family group, members of which become so important to him. He knows few others, and all his needs are supplied within this group. Thus, parents and siblings become highly significant others, with whom the child participates in intimate and intense day-to-day interactions. These first human relationships act as prototypes enabling the child to consider what can be expected later in life in his dealings with others. As the parents handle their infant, satisfying or failing to satisfy its needs for food, love, comfort and security, they have an unremitting influence on it. The child begins to feel the world is either benign and to be trusted, or hostile and not to be to be trusted. If a child's first interpersonal relationships gives him the wrong view of life at the outset what hope is there for the future? The parents' loving care helps the child to develop a basic sense of security and trust, especially during the first year. The period between 2 and 5 seems crucial for working out a satisfactory balance between dependence and autonomy.

Psychologists have attempted to categorise various child-rearing practices and the consequent personalities developed in children subject to these differing practices. But such classifications are more akin to half truths born of a tidy mind. In reality it is difficult to fit 'parenting' into neat categories, especially when the evidence is derived frequently from subjective recollections of parents and children and affected by the usual forms of distortion. However, certain trends are quite apparent, especially with respect to the effects of authoritarian, permissive, rejecting and warmly accepting homes. Parents tend to adopt child-rearing attitudes and practices which are similar to those formerly espoused by their parents. This copying is likely due to identification (Symonds, 1939; Radke, 1946).

The pattern of child rearing facilitating positive self concepts was first discerned by Stott (1939) who after studying 1,800 adolescents noted that children coming from homes where there was acceptance, mutual confidence and compatibility between parents and children, were better adjusted, more independent and thought more positively about themselves. Those children from homes where family discord reigned were in general less well adjusted. Behrens (1954) also demonstrated that a parent's personality style can influence a child's self concept for better or worse.

Coopersmith (1967) made a monumental study of the antecedents of self esteem among 1,700 10–12 year olds. He employed three indices of self esteem: self evaluation, teacher evaluation and projective test material. After dividing the group into three levels of self esteem – high, moderate and low – three sources of data were drawn on to discover associations with the levels of esteem. This data was sought from:

(a) laboratory tests of subject's memory, level of aspiration, response to stress, etc.;
(b) clinical tests and interviews investigating ability, personality, attitudes, styles of response; and
(c) interviews with parents to tease out child-rearing factors.

From this information pen-portraits of the formative influences and personal characteristics of each self-esteem level were constructed.

Pupils with a high degree of self esteem showed themselves to be active and successful, both socially and academically. They were eager to express opinions in discussion and not merely content to listen. They were not particularly sensitive to criticism nor did anxiety or psychosomatic problems cause them much trouble. They were not self conscious or preoccupied with personal difficulties but trusted their own perceptions, and their approach to other persons demonstrated the expectation that they would be well received. They considered themselves as valuable, important and worthy of respect, and able to exert an influence on others. New and challenging tasks were sought and enjoyed, in an optimistic manner, expecting success.

Those boys characterised by a medium level of self esteem were similar to the high-esteem subjects in many respects for they too tended to be optimistic, expressive and able to take criticism. But they also tended to be dependent on social acceptance to remove any uncertainty they felt in their personal worth. This insecurity of worth made them far more active than the higher self-esteem group in seeking out social experiences that would enhance self evaluation.

A discouragingly depressive picture is painted by those registering low self esteem. This group generally felt isolated, unlovable, incapable of expressing or defending themselves and too weak to overcome their deficiencies. Passive, socially non-participating, self conscious, sensitive to criticism, they dwelt on their own inner problems. They shrank from those social interactions that might give further confirmation of their supposed incompetencies. A considerable amount of psychosomatic illness was noted in this group. They had a general lack of faith in their abilities and ideas, and stuck to known and safe situations. They were pessimists feeling controlled by external events rather than feeling in personal control.

Surprisingly, Coopersmith found no relationship between self esteem and physical attractiveness, size of family, height, social class or income level. The boys in Coopersmith's study appear to have evaluated themselves, their achievements and treatments within the bounds of their own interpersonal environment and had not taken more general and abstract norms of society into account. Day-to-day personal relationships provided the major sources of self evaluation rather than external standards. This, too, was the conclusion noted in Chapter 6 in the discussion of environmental feedback.

Coopersmith found that these differences between persons varying in self esteem were strongly associated with parental attitudes and child-rearing practices, especially parental warmth and the sort of rules and disciplines imposed by the parents on the children.

The parents of high-self-esteem boys manifested warm interest in the child's welfare, and gave other signs that they regarded him as a significant person. Such parents also tended to be less permissive, demanding high standards of behaviour and enforcing rules consistently. They used reward rather than punishment and the child felt he was dealt with firmly but fairly. Thus, definite and consistently imposed limits on behaviour were associated with high self esteem. Such clear limits meant that less drastic forms of punishment were needed and that children knew where they stood, able to make decisions about their own behaviour within clear limits. Those parents who were cold, withdrawn, inconsistent or rejecting reared a child characterised by withdrawal, displaced hostility, dependence and passivity. Such a child interprets the inconsistent parental restrictions as indications of rejection, hostility and lack of acceptance. Only if a child is loved, accepted and is aware of this will he interpret discipline as an expression of parental care. The existence of limits provide the child with a social world in which he can be successful when the chosen limits are suitable. Without limits or with inconsistent limits the child never really knows what is expected, or what is right. This situation is anxiety provoking and prevents successful achievement of known and expected tasks. Self esteem thus appears to grow out of parental warmth and acceptance, and success in required demands that lie within the child's capabilities. Basking in favourable appraisal the child comes to evaluate himself in a similar favourable light.

Parents of low-self-esteem boys tended to be extremely permissive, but inflicted harsh punishment when they felt it was required. The boys considered their parents unfair and regarded the relative lack of rules and limits as a criterion of the parental lack of interest. High-self-esteem boys, on the other hand, functioned within a well-defined constitution of behaviour and expectations which was established through mutual consent and discussion. The parents were benevolent despots providing guidance, non-punitive treatment and respect for children's views.

High-self-esteem boys had higher aspirations than low-self-esteem boys – a difference which reflected the greater value parents of the former placed on the achievement of standards of excellence. These parents set up definite standards of performance, provided feedback on level of success and offered guidance on what would be required to obtain success. In other words the high-self-esteem child was presented with challenges to his capacities and led to learn and appreciate his strengths and weaknesses. Thus, high-self-esteem boys had higher goals and were more successful in attaining those goals. Low aspirations were characteristic of those who had low self esteem. Parental expectations (or lack of them) set up a self-fulfilling prophecy (often so noticeable in the school situation).

Coopersmith also found that the degree to which parents wanted children to be self confident was related to self-concept development. Those parents who preferred to keep their offspring submissive and dependent lowered self esteem and kept children tied to parents' apron strings. But such children are psychologically crippled, distrustful of the outside world, lacking self worth. It would seem that the influence of parents on children's self concepts is incredible. Child-rearing practices emphasising respect, warmth and acceptance associated with firm, consistent discipline and high standards of expected performance facilitate high levels of self esteem.

Coopersmith showed, too, that style of drawing and other creative work differed between boys varying in self esteem. Boys with high self esteem were more original and creative in their drawings than those with lower levels of self confidence, with their drawings characterised by sensitivity and humour. The drawings of boys of medium self esteem were more restrained and static, less complex and less vigorous. The boys with low self esteem draw small, constrained, distorted figures indicative of their lack of confidence. The figures drawn by the three categories of boys suggested distinct differences in their perceptions of themselves and other people.

The parents of the children in Coopersmith's study were also interviewed. On the basis of these data mothers of children with high self esteem were rated as higher in self esteem and emotional stability than were the mothers of children with medium and low self esteem. Indirect evidence on the fathers of the children indicate that fathers of children with high self esteem are more likely to be attentive and concerned with their sons, and the sons in turn are more likely to confide in their fathers. Also, the interaction between husband and wife in families of children with high self esteem is described as more compatible and marked by greater ease of exchange. It was also found that there were more previous marriages in the families of low-self-esteem children than in the families of medium- or high-self-esteem children.

With regard to early history and experiences, self esteem was higher among first and only children than in children born later. Mothers who were uncertain about methods of feeding and who shifted from breast to bottle early were morelikely to have children with low self esteem. Coopersmith concluded that children with high self esteem tend to have more positive social experiences during the early years. Other results based on questionnaire responses of the parents showed that close relationships existed between boys of high self esteem and their parents, with parental love expressed in the interest they showed in the boys' welfare. They were concerned about the boys' friends and knew who they were; they were available to discuss problems and participated in joint activities with their offspring.

In summary, Coopersmith observes that there is no golden rule to create high self esteem, no common pattern of parenting but combinations of at least two of the following: acceptance, limit definitions, respect and parental self-esteem, are necessary with a corollary of a minimum of rejection, disrespect and ambiguity. The findings from Coopersmith's studies suggest that positive self concepts are more likely to emerge if children are treated with respect, provided with well-defined standards and provided with reasonable expectations of success. The development of the ability to respond constructively to challenge seems essential to becoming a person who evaluates himself as of some worth. On the other hand, the freedom to explore the environment in an unrestricted and unguided way coupled with consistent permissiveness appears to engender anxiety, doubts about self worth, low expectations of success and an inability to develop sound social relationships based on mutual respect.

However, it is possible to argue that high self esteem in Coopersmith's study is due to reinforcement in a frequent and consistent manner rather than a mere interpretation by the child that his parents are interested in him. The high probability of reinforcement for behaviour consistent with the norms of the majority culture leads to higher self evaluations, to a more stable view of the social environment and to more stable behaviour. The child has a clearly depicted model and is consistently reinforced for behaviour congruent with the model's behaviours. Father's presence, attention, concern, coupled with a stable marriage, presents a firm model with which to identify and a valid pattern of the norms of the culture. Low self esteem then emerges from a vague inconsistent programme of social reinforcement with poorly delineated or even conflicting models for behaviour.

On a learning theory basis the general conclusion would seem to be that the knowledge of and adherence to the norms of the majority culture derived from stable and nurturant parental attachments lead to a greater probability of social reinforcement from parents, teachers and peers, resulting in high self evaluation.

The pattern of rearing of high-self-esteem boys in Coopersmith's study is a recurrent theme in psychological literature. Such a climate of acceptance coupled with positive non-contingent reinforcement reappears in many situations, for instance in Rogerian client-centred therapy, and in handling youngsters in school. Other studies report similar findings to Coopersmith. For example, Medinnus and Curtis (1963) noted that mothers with high self esteem have children who also possess high self esteem. Similarly, low-self-esteem children tend to come from families with low-self-esteem mothers. It would seem that high-self-esteem parents convey confidence, trust, love and acceptance of their offspring which feeds the latter's self concept through parental feedback and through identification with the attributes of liked parents. Bayley and Schaefer (1960) have also indicated that mothers who were punitive, irritable and hostile had daughters who were rated unhappy, sulky, gloomy and hostile, whereas daughters rated popular, outgoing and adjusted had mothers who possessed similar characteristics. There is far less empirical work on fathers, but Coopersmith (1967) discerned that fathers of high-self-esteem children take a more supportive and active role in rearing their children than fathers with low-self-esteem children.

Rosenberg (1965) investigated the conditions associated with high and low esteem in over 5,000 adolescents. He discerned that it was the amount of parental attention and concern that was strongly associated with levels of self esteem and not the broader social context as indexed by such variables as social class and ethnic group membership. He showed that adolescents who have closer relationships with their fathers are higher in self esteem than are those with more distant, impersonal relationships. In turning from the more complex and global variables of society such as social class, and ethnicity to the specific relationships in the effective interpersonal environment that affect self esteem, both Coopersmith and Rosenberg have given an indication of those intimate features of home environment that the child equates with success and self worth.

Two further important findings relate self esteem to religion and to order of birth. In the case of religion, Rosenberg shows that social prestige in the community at large has little influence on self esteem. Jews, who are lower in the hierarchy of general social prestige, are more apt to be high in self esteem than are either Catholics or Protestants. This apparent anomaly appears to stem from the great amount of interest and attention that Jewish children, especially boys, receive from their parents. Within the family itself, only children and particularly only male children are higher in self esteem. These results provide us with a more concise knowledge of the conditions that lead children to interpret experiences as successes. By showing that broader social forces have little impact (at least until adolescence), such results narrow our focus to the specific parental attitudes and behaviours that can and do influence self esteem.

In a study of the antecedents of self esteem in Australian university students Watkins (1976) found that there were significant relationships between self esteem and father's educational status and between low self esteem and conflict between parents. These results confirm earlier findings of Rosenberg (1965) and Coopersmith (1967). But unlike those previous workers, no association was found between self esteem and disciplinary techniques employed by parents.

In a cross-cultural study, Ziller *et al.* (1968), investigated differences in family relationships between Asian, Indian and

American children which were presumed to be related to self esteem. The latter was measured by the topological Self Social Construct Test (see Ch. 5). The extended family environment of the Indian child is presumed to have implications for his self concept. In this form of social setting the child will have many parent surrogates. The child may be nearly as close to his aunts as to his mother and, indeed, all females of the joint family may be thought of by the child as having essentially similar or even identical functions. In this way, the child is not disciplined by or responsible to a single individual. There is a warmth, acceptance and closeness extended to all Asian children who make life meaningful for the parents. The Indian child is more highly valued by the extended family, is more enmeshed in the family matrix which largely determines the child's social universe, is inseparable from parents and parent surrogates, is less separated from parents in terms of status barriers, and tends to be the focal point of the family, the family's reason for being.

Thus Ziller *et al.* (1968), proposed that in contrast to the American child, the Indian child possesses higher self esteem, higher social interest, higher identification with parents but a lower range of identification with others. The Indians had higher self esteem and closer identification with parents and teacher than the American sample. Ziller *et al.*, argue that this difference is a result of Indian self identity and family identity being intertwined in a close network, whereas high self esteem is in jeopardy in the USA under more open family situations. The Indian students also showed higher self acceptance.

Coopersmith's work is unfortunately limited by being restricted to male middle-class pre-pubertal subjects. From the work of Davie, Butler and Goldstein (1972) it is noticeable that both working-class boys and girls show a range of personality characteristics associated with low self esteem, such as depression, withdrawal and aggression to a far greater extent than middle-class children. Davie also reports that in certain areas of academic competence working-class children perform more poorly than middle-class children. Thus working-class children appear handicapped in their search for self esteem by lack of achievement, less clearly defined standards and less competent parents.

All humans commence life completely dependent on other humans, and in a complex world no one ever attains complete independence of others. But we want children to develop a relative measure of independence so that they learn to cope, take the initiative, solve their own problems and eventually stand on their own feet as the next generation, rather than seeking help and attention all the time. Dependency in children seems to stem from maternal over-concern and over-protectiveness (e.g. Coopersmith, 1967). Most independent boys in a study by Mueller (1966) perceived their fathers as strong but not interfering, leaving the boy to develop yet sure help was on hand if it might be needed. Restriction of freedom and contact with others also hampers the development of independence. Contact with others is necessary for the child to test his powers outside the protective shield of his parents' influence. A restricted child who is indulged and constrained is like a house plant surviving in an artificial environment but lacking psychological strengths to cope with the demands of a more rigorous existence. The need for continual reassurance seen in such dependent children suggest a self concept lacking feelings of competence, worthiness and fulfilment.

Agression in childhood is pretty nigh universal. Most young children produce frequent angry outbursts and tantrums, since understanding of cause and effect is poor and frustration is frequent. Agressive behaviour usually decreases with age as more understanding and socialisation enable tolerance of frustration to increase. But those children who continue to display high levels of aggression tend to be unhappy possessors of low self esteem (Rosenbaum and Stammers, 1961). Coopersmith noted, too, that low-self-esteem children were more likely to displace hostility against inanimate objects. Aggression in post-infancy appears to be learned by the child from adult models (e.g. Bandura, 1965). Punitive acts by a parent can be interpreted as the norm for the way in which adults behave. If adults behave this way how can it be wrong for others to copy them? In addition to providing a wrong model, the counter-attack of the parent generates more hostility, resentment and aggression in the child which is likely to be redirected or displaced on to a 'scapegoat' which cannot retaliate, e.g. a younger child, a toy, etc. Many bullies may be children who themselves are physically abused by parents. Recognition and acceptance that each of us can be made angry and possess aggressive feelings is essential for a healthy self concept. This recognition allows constructive action to occur in order to solve the problem without resorting to aggression.

The work of Frenkel-Brunswik (1948), Gough (1950), Kutner (1958) and many others have shown that authoritarian parents like things clear-cut and unambiguous. Thus, any punishment or discipline is not diluted with tenderness, acceptance and reasoning. They may actually perceive the child at certain times as 'all bad'. This parental behaviour creates for the child a self concept which emphasises for the child that he is poorly accepted, bad and disapproved of. The responses of the child of authoritarian parents are more intense than those of the child of non-authoritarian parents, since frustration from his developing, confused and generally oriented negative self concept is added to the ordinary drive level. In addition, such a child develops widely generalised expectancies of punishment in new or unclear situations with the corollary of anxiety and discomfort. Hence the child becomes persistently anxious in a wide range of what are to him ambiguous situations.

Authoritarian parents permit their own needs to take precedence over those of the child. They often assume a stance of infallibility. On no account can they be wrong or thwarted. But, in contrast, permissive parents seem to avoid confrontation with children, leaving the latter without guidelines.

Hence, both authoritarian and permissive parents tend to inhibit a growing child's opportunities to engage in vigorous interaction with others. Unrealistically high standards that cannot be met plus severe punishment, or, on the other hand, expecting little or anything, prevents a healthy self concept emerging. Parental restrictiveness, rigidity or lack of interest makes the child feel he isn't loved or accepted. Punishment from a cold, disinterested or even punitive parent can be interpreted as, 'I am being punished because they don't love me.' However, the child punished by a warm, caring parent is likely to argue, 'I am being punished because what I did was wrong.' The authoritarian parent generates a vicious circle of hostility and counter-hostility in the parent–child relationship. The child's self concept is replete with resentment and anger which can be displaced so easily on to scapegoats. Social withdrawal and shyness can also mark such a child, a child who fears to do for fear of failure, criticism and punishment. Thus, a child is such authoritarian surroundings becomes prejudiced against himself, feeling inferior, weak, dependent. These self feelings are likely to be displaced on to others so that low levels of self esteem are positively associated with low levels of esteem for others, a point taken to more depth in Chapter 8. An authoritarian family structure can provide a child with a feeling of insecurity, inferiority and worthlessness, since irrational authority is the rule, independence and spontaneity are snuffed out, and respect for the child's feelings is lacking. These feelings of weakness and worthlessness have a debilitating effect on the self concept.

Mussen and Kagan (1958) conclude that severe parents have more conflicts with their children. Hence the children have more experiences with their parents in which yielding or conforming reduces anxiety. Consequently, through generalisation, these children adopt yielding as a way of life and such conformists manifest marked distrust of other people which Mussen and Kagan (1958) speculate, 'may be generalised responses stemming from original fear and distrust of parents' (p. 60).

Despite the problems of the definition of, and methodological approaches to, maternal deprivation, studies in that area highlight in a stark and extreme form the effects of very adverse human relationships in childhood militating against the development of positive self attitudes. Such distortions in attachment are learning situations which teach the unfortunate offspring to interpret himself as rejected, neglected, unloved, unacceptable or incompetent or any combination of such debilitating attributes.

Some tension does occur from time to time between most adolescents and their parents as the former try to grow up and employ their new-found competencies. Parents generally do want their adolescents to display maturity, common sense and independence, but usually within more restricted limits than the offspring would wish. Someone once wisely noted that adulthood occurs about 2 years earlier than any parent cares to admit, but 2 years later than the adolescent may claim. Most parents do not easily let go of their emerging adolescent who must work harder and cope with harder challenges to prove to their parents and themselves that they really can make it on their own and that their self concepts are sufficiently firm to operate within the responsibilities and setbacks accompanying independence. But parents who hold on too tightly can cause a young person seeking his freedom to either feel guilty ('my parents must need me') or inadequate ('they don't trust me on my own'). As Douvan and Adelson (1966) note there is a curvilinear relation between parental involvement with a young person and the young person's developing sense of personal autonomy. This implies that both too much or too little involvement can inhibit the adolescent's achievement of independence. Security necessary for self control is underdeveloped in the latter condition; but too much involvement may generate over-dependency which interferes with the growth of a sturdy self concept.

The impact that parents can have on an adolescent's self concept is affected by the sex of both the adolescent and the parent. For example a boy's self concept depends to some extent on the level of affection existing in his relationships with his father. Mussen *et al.* (1963) in a cross-cultural study showed that boys whose fathers showed insufficient paternal affection were less secure, less confident and less well socially adjusted than those boys whose fathers manifested sufficient affection. Bronfenbrenner (1961) revealed that three parental behaviours, viz. rejection, neglect and affiliative companionship were related to the development of responsibility.

Children's self concepts do seem to be similar to the view they believe parents have of them, and their level of self esteem is associated with the parents' level of regard for them (Jourard and Remy, 1955; Helper, 1955). For instance adolescents judged to be less responsible tend to report that their parents criticise and ridicule them, providing unfavourable comparisons of them with other children. The development of leadership qualities appears to be associated with the degree of parental protectiveness. Over-protection undermines the child's confidence and ability to assert himself. With a self concept containing little confidence or perceived competence the adolescent becomes 'backward in coming forward'. Bronfenbrenner 1961 notes a sex difference in the effects of parental treatment leading to independence, responsibility and leadership in adolescents: 'affiliative companionship, nurturance, principled discipline, affection and affective reward appear to foster the emergence of leadership in sons but discourage it in daughters' (p. 236).

An explanation may be that these characteristics of responsibility and leadership are rewarded highly in males but not strongly expected in females, who are not likely therefore to receive much reinforcement for displaying them. As we have already argued earlier in this chapter, the expectations and characteristics of femininity and masculinity are different in our culture so that the same parental treatments may have different effects on boys from girls. Different practices are also required to develop the required (if stereotyped) sex role self concepts. For instance, love-oriented child caring is more effective in developing healthy self conception in girls (Sears, Maccoby and Levin, 1957). On the other hand with boys, parents are likely to invoke more physical punishment, be more permissive of aggression and stress independence and achievement. Parents seem to direct boys towards control of the environment; for girls their aim is to protect them from the environment. This may help to explain why girls manifest more cooperation, obedience and social adjustment than boys. Although love and warmth is necessary for boys developing self esteem, a different balance of discipline and firmness against affection is necessary from that offered to girls. As Coopersmith showed, boys need consistent parental discipline in concert with love-oriented strategies. Just as assertiveness in girls is less valued by others, so too is dependence and lack of self assertion in boys.

In general, research suggests that a healthy self image is a result of a balance between affection and control, a balance that is different for boys and girls. Problems are likely for both sexes where low levels or inconsistent levels of emotional support are provided, but such difficulties augment for boys if parents also fail to provide firm authority.

Alienated youth who leave home, reject parental and societal values and behaviour, to create their own subcultural groups have probably been alienated for many years through parental treatment. Its manifestation only became apparent when the individual was physically able to leave the nest. Their independence and professed free thinking probably hide a somewhat negative self concept. The adherence to the new subculture provides a means of positive evaluation against standards and values of their own choosing. They repudiate normal society and with it their own inadequacy. Negative identity is preferable to remaining a nonentity, and reflects a desperate attempt to regain some mastery in a situation in which available positive identity elements are regarded as an imposition by society.

Sears (1970) in a study of 11 year olds found that high self concepts were associated with small family size, early ordinal position and high parental warmth. For both boys and girls femininity characteristics were associated with low self concepts. The femininity characteristics were those of occupational and recreational choice, timidity and social conformity. It would seem that by the age of 11 children feel that women's work, activities and anxiety are not valuable possessions compared to male ones. Thus high-self-concept males are very masculine in outlook, while for women to have high self concepts means denying some basic elements of femininity since to be feminine is to be inferior. Sears' results pertaining to the requirement of parental warmth supports the previous work of Coopersmith (1967) though the warmth had been measured 7 years previously. The evidence on family size and birth order in Sears' study is consistent with the view that the first-born and small families are conducive to the development of high self esteem. The realities of family life are that parents only have a finite amount of time and energy to devote to their offspring. Hence, more children means more competition for the sort of attention that induces high self esteem. Again the more siblings there are, the more competition there is for status which brings more opportunity for derogation. However, the battle is unequal with the first-born enjoying a period with no competitors, while later children not only have competition from the beginning but have the everlasting handicap of being smaller, younger, less effective than their older competitors, and at any one time may have less talent for making themselves seem worthy of admiration within the family frame of reference. Thus, it is to be expected that only the oldest children would have better self concepts than the middle and youngest ones, and that the larger the family the poorer would be self concepts, regardless of ordinal position.

These predictions are fairly well supported by Sears' obtained data. The larger the family, the poorer was a child's self concept. In terms of birth positions the singleton and oldest children had more positive self concepts. Academic competence, too, was clearly related to the children's self concepts. Parents also learn the role of being a parent on the first-born; he is in effect a guinea pig, receiving large doses of parental anxiety and over-protection as parents try to do their best, often in a rather uncertain way. Parents seem to require higher standards of the first-born who establishes standards for the later born. But these later born unable to compete tend to have lower aspirations. Rosenberg (1965) and Coopersmith (1967) also demonstrated that birth order has a significant effect on the self concept. However, other studies, e.g. Nystul (1974) and Stotland and Dunn (1962), could not produce evidence relating to this association. In view of such inconsistent results it would be that a clearer understanding of birth-order effects would emerge if other family structure variables such as sex of siblings, number of siblings and closeness in age of siblings were taken into account. Many researchers simply evaluate first-born against the rest as later born, e.g. Nystul (1976).

Another universal element of everyone's self concept (apart from the self concept of a psychopath) is the moral aspect. The moral arm of the self concept is very important since it reflects acceptance of society's values. There are several signs that a healthy conscience development has occurred. Firstly, if a child can resist temptation even when he won't be found out; secondly, if a child attempts to instil moral values in others so acting the parental role; and thirdly if a child has the capacity to admit guilt and apologise, so recovering self esteem again.

Conscience development is a function of identification, with the child incorporating his parents' moral standards and values. Sears, Maccoby and Levin (1957) noted that love-oriented child-rearing techniques using praise and withdrawal of love produce children with strong consciences compared to physically oriented techniques using rewards and punishments. The moral self presumably develops only because of the need to obtain approval and avoid disapproval. Parents as the purveyors of culture have the task of defining what is good and what is bad so that the child will feel he is good when his behaviour is congruent with socially accepted behaviour and bad when it isn't. Since parental approval is related to 'good' so is parental love. Bad becomes associated with being unworthy. The child has now become his own evaluator.

How can a parent tell whether a child has generally a positive or negative self concept? Well, the answers to the following questions may improve the parent's awareness of the level of the child's self esteem.

1. Does the child generally seem self confident? Verbal cues can help to indicate how a child feels about himself, e.g. 'I can manage that all right'; 'I'm no good at this'.
2. Does the child boast or make up tales to boost himself among the peer group or family? This is usually an attempt to compensate for perceived deficiencies.
3. How does the child cope with failure? In our competitive society failure is a feature of everyone's life at some time, especially for children in the school milieu. Lack of feelings of competence and self worth lead the child to avoid situations which might confirm his self expectations, e.g. psychosomatic illnesses; unofficial school absenteeism; avoidance of play and social situations with peers.

4. Is the child afraid of new experiences? Such a hesitant child also fears failure and withdraws.
5. Does the child seek constant reassurance? A need for positive and continual feedback is indicative of a lack of confidence.
6. Does the child enjoy and seek independence? The willingness to take responsibility and be positively motivated indicates confidence in ability and own worth.
7. How does the child feel about his physical appearance? His avoidance of social situations and verbal behaviour may suggest a negative attitude, e.g. 'I'm too fat'; 'I've got a spotty face', 'the others don't play with me because I'm too small'.

Summary

No one theory seems adequate to offer a complete explanation of sex role identification. Differential identification with parents and parent surrogate models, acquisition of sex-typed skills and sex role congruent experiences are each influential in determining the degree to which an individual labels himself as masculine or feminine. Appropriate sex role identity demands a same-sex parent whose behaviour is relevant, who is nurturant and rewarding, and an opposite-sexed parent who also supports and rewards the correct identification.

Child-rearing practices are seen as crucial in self-concept development because:

(a) the self-concept is learned;
(b) much of this learning comes from feedback from significant others, particularly parents;
(c) parents are present most consistently in the important early years; and,
(d) the child has a physical, emotional and social dependence on them so that they are in a unique position to influence the child's learning about himself.

Three family conditions seem strongly conducive to the development of high self esteem:

(a) warm acceptance by parents of the children;
(b) establishment and enforcement by the parents of clearly defined limits of behaviour for the children;
(c) respect by parents for individual initiative taken by children within those limits.

There quality of the relationship is far more important to self-esteem generation than the quantity. Hence, neither affluence nor socioeconomic level are closely related to high self esteem.

Further reading

Borgatta, Edgar F., and **Lambert, W. W.** (eds). *Handbook of Personality Theory and Research in Child Development,* Skokie, Ill.: Rand McNally, 1968, Chs. 4, 5.

Bowlby, J. *Child Care and Growth of Love,* London: Penguin Books, 1966. A leading researcher reviews the effects of early environment on the child's ability to love and be loved.

Coopersmith, S. *The Antecedents of Self-Esteem,* San Francisco: W. H. Freeman, 1967. An investigation of the conditions and behaviours which affect the developing self concept in pre-pubertal males.

Douveen E. and **Adelson J.** *The Adolescent Experience.* New York: Wiley, 1966.

Ginott, H. G. *Between Parent and Child.* New York: Macmillan, 1965. A handbook of practical suggestions for dealing with daily problems in child-rearing.

Medinnus, G. R. (ed.). *Readings in the Psychology of Parent–Child Relations,* New York: Wiley, 1966.

Rosenberg M. *Society and the Adolescent Self Image,* Princeton: Princeton Univ. Press, 1965.

Young, Leontine. *Life Among the Giants,* New York: McGraw-Hill, 1965. The author explains what it is like to be a child and teaches her adult readers how to be children again by helping them understand the world from a child's point of view.

Further reading

...

The self concept
in everyday life

Chapter 8

The self concept and behaviour

This chapter attempts to provide an overview of the role of self conception in a number of important areas of interest to social scientists. Obviously it is quite feasible to relate levels of self concept to all sorts of other named variables, hence a choice of a few areas has been made to demonstrate the role of the self concept in mediating a wide variety of behaviour. Some of these areas contain but a few pieces of research. Hopefully this survey, with experimental results, implications and clues it provides about self conception and behaviour, will stimulate others to replicate, modify, refine and extend previous work or even venture into uncharted waters to study other behavioural correlates of the self concept.

A. The self concept and client-centred therapy

As the writings of the phenomenologists have made us aware, the individual organises his perceptions within a meaningful system. New experience is interpreted in terms of meanings already held. Part of this perception is self perception; part of this meaning is self meaning. This creates a 'snowballing' process. The individual conceiving of himself as a particular sort of person, and conceiving the world as having particular characteristics, has an orientation or set which prejudices subsequent perceptions. In fact one's conceptual system gives meaning to one's experience, especially experience of oneself. In this light, the tenacity with which an individual holds on to even what is apparently an erroneous image and set of behaviours as judged by an outside observer, becomes understandable, for the image·provides a frame of reference without which the individual is lost, unable to understand anything related to himself. To the behaver, though, these perceptions and responses make his kind of sense. Utilising this core of a private system of 'logic' the individual strives to maintain his integrity as the sort of person he conceives himself being. Evidence imcompatible with the self concept is threatening. Such evidence is thus ignored, denied or distorted. For instance if a person conceives of himself as a failure, any success will be attributed to luck, or seen as some form of deceit perpetrated on him by others trying to give encouragement when in his opinion his performance does not merit it.

A healthy self conception with its feelings of worth, competence, adequacy and confidence is an acquired set of attitudes. An unhealthy self conceptualisation replete with feelings of inferiority, inadequacy, failure, worthlessness and insecurity is likewise learned and hence can be replaced, or unlearned, with learned healthy modes substituted. Much of this learning and change in self conception occurs in the natural transactions of daily events. However, when the change needed is fairly radical and severe, individual therapy and intensive group experience seem to be necessary and major forces in the metamorphosis. One advantage in favour of any person seeking change is that most people really do want to advance towards psychological good health and evolve more positive self concepts with constructive behaviours for social living. Maslow (1962) has argued that just as Freud saw the past existing in the present in each person, so now psychologists must equally emphasise the existence of the future within the present individual in terms of his hopes, potentials, goals and ideals.

Those suffering from low self esteem and lack of worth often display characteristic behaviours which help identify such persons. Firstly, they can be very sensitive to criticism, since criticism is regarded as further validation of their inferiority. Secondly, a hypercritical attitude is employed to defend the shaky self image and redirect attention on to the shortcomings of others rather than those of oneself. Thirdly, there is a persecution complex in which failure is placed on the ulterior designs of others and blame is projected on to others; in this way personal weakness and failure is denied. Fourthly, there is often an over-response to flattery; any praise is better than none and security is increased by grabbing at this straw. Finally, the person with negative feelings of worth is likely to manifest seclusiveness, timidity and a lack of interest in competition. This withdrawal and refusal to participate is an attempt to prevent supposed inferiority being demonstrated publicly too often, thus confirming what the person believes about himself.

The diagnostic signs of a healthy positive self image are, for example, an ability to modify strongly held values and principles in the light of new experience, a lack of worry over the past and the future, a confidence to cope with problems even in the face of the occasional failure, acceptance of self as a person of equal worth with others despite differences in specific talents and attributes, and a sensitivity to the needs of others.

Most theoretical approaches to psychotherapy include among their goals either one or both of the following aspects of adjustment: (1) that the individual undergoing therapy revises his concept of himself in relation to the world in which he lives, and (2) that he alter his behaviour so as to conform more closely to the expectations of society. It is also recognised that these two areas of adjustment are not unrelated. The self concept, within the ambit of psychotherapy, is indissolubly linked to the Rogerian client-centred approach. It is the basic concept in Rogers' theory (Ch. 2) and possesses in his terms four basic characteristics:

1. It strives for consistency.
2. It causes the person to behave in ways consistent with it.
3. It denies or distorts experiences which are perceived as threats.
4. It can change as a result of learning.

Rogers (1951) indicated that what transpires in the process of client-centred therapy seems best explained by reference to the self concept and to changes in individuals' self concepts. He noted that most of the verbal interchange in therapy had to do with self conception. The client felt that he was not being his 'true' self and felt dissatisfied with his self concept as he viewed it. A more positive and accepting view of self was a general trend which progressively developed as therapy proceeded. Rogers' approach in therapy is non-doctrinaire, aimed at using the client's own awareness of himself in the present then developing this awareness so that feelings about self and experience of self become congruent. The task of the therapist is (*a*) to create a warm, unconditional, accepting non-critical milieu, and (*b*) to help to clarify the awareness and experiences of the client by reflecting the latter's verbalisations back to him. No interpretation is imposed. This examination of self and experience in this sort of non-threatening ethos permits and encourages changes in the self concept enabling the assimilation into awareness of previously denied feelings. As self perception changes then so does behaviour.

The self concept becomes a continuing, organismic valuing process, no longer static but able to readjust and develop as new experiences are integrated. The self concept then becomes based in genuine experience, open and sensitive to inner feelings, to the feelings of others and to the realities of the environment. The whole aim is to release the person's potential so that psychological maturity is a state in which significant experience is fed into a developing and ongoing self concept capable of enhancement and actualisation. The characteristics usually exhibited by a person becoming a more fully functioning individual according to Rogers are those such as:

a move towards being himself;
a move towards meeting his own expectations rather than those of others;
a move towards greater acceptance of others;
a move towards greater acceptance of self;

a move towards guiding his own life;
a move towards more openness in self experience.

Rogers has maintained extensive files of verbatim transcripts of therapy sessions. In 1954 he presented a full analysis of a single case, that of a Mrs Oak. This case illustrates the centrality of the self concept to personal problems and the changes that occur in self conception as therapy proceeds and which facilitate self acceptance and self insight. At the outset Mrs Oak spent most of the sessions talking about specific problems with her husband and daughter. But eventually there was a move from these reality problems to descriptions of her feelings, e.g.

Mrs Oak: And, secondly, the realization that last time I was here I experienced a–an emotion I had never felt before – which surprised me and sort of shocked me a bit. And yet I thought, I think it has sort of a . . . the only word I can find to describe it, the only verbalization is a kind of cleansing. I–I really felt terribly sorry for something, a kind of grief. (Rogers, 1954, p. 311.)

The therapist provided a supportive climate allowing Mrs Oak to become aware of feelings she had previously denied, e.g.

Mrs Oak: And then of course, I've come to . . . to see and to feel that over this . . . see, I've covered it up. (Weeps.) But . . . and . . . I've covered it up with so much bitterness, which in turn I had to cover up. (Weeps.) That's what I want to get rid of! I almost don't care if I hurt.
Therapist: (gently): You feel that here at the basis of it, as you experienced it, is a feeling of real tears for yourself. But that you can't show, mustn't show, so that's been covered by bitterness that you don't like, that you'd like to be rid of. You almost feel you'd rather absorb the hurt than to . . . than to feel the bitterness. (Pause.) And what you seem to be saying quite strongly is, I do hurt, and I've tried to cover it up.
Mrs Oak: I didn't know it.
Therapist: M-hm. Like a new discovery really.
Mrs Oak: (speaking at the same time): I never really did know.
Mrs Oak (cont.): But it's . . . you know, it's almost a physical thing. It's sort of as though I–I–I were looking within myself at all kinds of . . . nerve endings and-and bits of–of . . . things that have been sort of mashed. (Weeping.) (Rogers, 1954, p. 326.)

This increased awareness and experiencing led to even greater personality disorganisation at first. However, she soon became able to recognise her feelings and accept them, and see herself as a worthwhile person. She felt free to be herself, lacking self doubt, experiencing little threat from others, and capable of making independent decisions. These changes noted in therapy, were also paralleled in projective test reports and in Q sorts. From the latter it was revealed that correlations between self concept and ideal self concept pre- and post-therapy moved from 0.21 to 0.79; self-concept post-therapy was similar to ideal self-concept self pre-therapy ($r = 0.70$). In other words as therapy proceeded her concept of herself in the present became progressively more like how she would like to be.

Another client of Rogers', a Miss Vib, produced the following perceptions of herself at the commencement of therapy:

I feel disorganized, muddled: I've lost all direction; my personal life has disintegrated.

I feel nothing matters; I don't have any emotional response to situations; I'm worried about myself.

I haven't been acting like myself; It doesn't seem like me; I'm a different person altogether from what I used to be in the past. I don't understand myself; I haven't known what was happening to me I have withdrawn from everything, and feel all right when I'm all alone and no one can expect me to do things.

I don't care about my personal appearance.

I don't know anything anymore.

I feel guilty about the things I have left undone.

I don't think I could ever assume responsibility for anything. (Rogers, 1947, p. 360.)

By the ninth session 38 days later her perception of self and behaviour have altered. Some examples of her statements at this point were:

I'm feeling much better; I'm taking more interest in myself. I do have some individuality, some interests. I seem to be getting a newer understanding of myself. I can look at myself a little better. I can accept the fact that I'm not always right. I feel more motivation, have more of a desire to go ahead. I still occasionally regret the past, though I feel less unhappy about it; I still have a long way to go; I don't know whether I can keep the picture of myself I'm beginning to evolve. I do feel more like a normal person now; I feel more I can handle my life myself; I think I'm at the point where I can go along on my own. (Rogers 1947, p. 361.)

She began to have a more realistic perception of herself, viewing without distress her limitations as well as her assets, and knew she could now control her behaviour, which became more forward-looking and effective.

Six weeks after the cessation of therapy, Miss Vib wrote: 'I am getting more happiness in being myself. I approve of myself more, and I have so much less anxiety.' (Rogers, 1947, p. 362.)

These two examples illustrate the basic trend that the crucial change lies in the way the client has come to perceive himself in terms of positive and negative feelings and attitudes towards the self which are expressed as being currently held. The result of the therapy would appear to be 'a greater congruence between self and ideal. The self and the values it holds are no longer so disparate' (Rogers, 1951, p. 141). The self is seen as worthwhile, something the individual could live with. Realistic in perception the person accepts himself as he is.

The whole rationale of such a therapeutic approach is that given certain psychological conditions, i.e. warm, unconditional acceptance, the individual has the capacity to reorganise his perceptions of himself and the environment which as a corollary produces appropriate changes in his behaviour. The self concept becomes its own architect, producing new designs for living.

B. Self concept and acceptance of others

The doctrine that love for oneself is identical with selfishness, and is the alternative to love for others, has pervaded theology, philosophy and psychology. The Protestant Ethic places much stress on a selfish striving for self achievement. In his theory of narcissism, Freud says, in short, that man has a fixed quantity of libido, which in the infant has as its objective the child's own person, primary narcissism. Later the libido is directed from one's person towards other objects. If a person is blocked in this, the libido is redirected to one's own person, secondary narcissism. Freud is here implying a basic inverse relationship between ego-love and object love. The more love I express towards the outside world, the less I have available for myself and vice versa.

The basic contradiction between love for oneself and love for others has been seriously questioned by Fromm (1939). At a philosophic level, without any experimentally derived evidence, Fromm claims that the notion that love for others and love for self are contradictory and is completely untenable. If it is a virtue to love one's neighbour as a human being, why can't one love oneself as well? A principle that claims love for mankind but which taboos love for self exempts the self from the category of human beings. Fromm's thesis is that since we ourselves are an object of feelings and attitudes in the same way as others, then attitudes towards others and towards ourselves must run parallel and are far from contradictory. Love for others and love for ourselves are not alternatives. Neither are hate for others and hate for ourselves. On the contrary, an attitude of love for themselves will be found in those who are capable of loving others. Hatred against others is inseparable from hatred against oneself. In other words, love and hatred are indivisible as far as the difference between 'objects' and self is concerned. Even the biblical thought, 'love thy neighbour as thyself' (St Matthew 17:17) implies that respect of one's own integrity, love for and understanding of one's own self, cannot be divorced from respect, love and understanding of other individuals.

Fromm hypothesises that selfishness is the basis of this lack of concern and love for others. The selfish person is concerned with himself all the time, never satisfied, always afraid of missing something, of being deprived, envious of those who might have more. This selfishness is, however, rooted in a lack of fondness for oneself. Fromm's claim is that this person, who does not approve of himself, is in a constant anxiety concerning his own self. He has no inner security, as this can exist only on the basis of fondness and self acceptance. He has to be concerned about himself, greedy to get everything since he lacks security and satisfaction. Thus, while it would seem that these persons cannot direct love outwards to others because on the surface they appear to love themselves inordinately, they are actually not fond of themselves and their narcissism and selfishness is no more than an overcompensation. Freud's view of the narcississtic person is only true in the sense that he has withdrawn his love for others; but he doesn't turn it towards himself. He loves neither himself nor others. Fromm suggests that the neurotic is selfish as he is over-anxious about himself and blocked in his relationship to others. What he needs to develop is self love, since it is only from this acceptance and satisfaction that love for others can spring.

Adler (1927) was another who made observations on this relationship when he contended that the tendency to disparage arose out of feelings of inferiority as an overcompensation. His claim is that one technique for resolving inferiority feelings is to develop a life style based on various defence mechanisms which gain one a feeling of superiority, e.g. day-dreaming, rationalisation. This drive to superiority in those who feel inferior and lacking in personal worth, demands that failings should not be one's own fault but attributed to the fault of someone else, thus endangering attitudes to others. Ansbacher and Ansbacher (1956) quote Adler: 'The life plan of the neurotic demands categorically that if it fails it should be through someone else's fault and that he should be freed from personal responsibility.' (p. 270)

Sullivan (1953) accepts Mead's (1934) interpretation of the social origins of personality and describes personality development in terms of the individual's interpersonal relationships with his significant others. He believed that the awareness of other people is a continuing factor of life and has a large evaluative component. The individual is constantly guarding himself against loss of self esteem since it is this loss that produces the feelings of distress that are termed 'anxiety'. Anxiety is an interpersonal phenomenon that occurs when an individual expects to be, or is indeed, rejected or demeaned by himself and others. Those of low esteem, Sullivan suggests, have received or are anticipating some form of rejection, and try to thwart such rejection by minimising contacts and/or attacking others. Horney (1937), too, stated that the person who

does not believe himself lovable is unable to love others, and out
of her later work (Horney, 1950) was able to discern that, 'the
more anxiety is released by psycho-analysis, the more the patient
becomes capable of affection and genuine tolerance for himself and
others'. (p. 129)

In a similar vien, Fromm-Reichmann (1949) has remarked,
based on therapy observations that, 'one can respect others only to
the extent that one can respect oneself' (p. 167). And again:
'Where there is low self-esteem there is . . . low esteem of others
and fear of low appreciation by other people.' (p. 168)

Allen (1942) also pointed intuitively to this observation in his
discussions of therapy with children:

Many of our casual, everyday observations of people have led us to
suspect that the individuals who are prone to express negative attitudes
towards others, to be constant fault-finders, also harbour negative self
attitudes. Conversely those who seem to like and respect themselves are
inclined to be positive, at least in their attitudes towards others and to be
generally less critical of those around them. (p. 15)

It would appear then that quite a number of therapists have
expressed similar points based on their observations, but all of a
qualitative nature. Further observations of the suggested
relationship have emanated from the work of Rogers and his
colleagues who have studied the verbalisations of their client
receiving therapy. They have attempted to qualify this relationship
from judges' ratings of the negative and positive 'self' and 'other'
references as expressed by clients during recorded interviews. Their
work, too, supports the positive relationship between attitudes to
self and to others. For them the basic change in the client lies in
the way he comes to perceive himself and as a corollary to
perceive others. As the number and proportion of positively toned
self references increase, so too do the number and proportion of
positively toned references to others (Rogers, 1951). Using a small
sample of 14 therapy cases Raimy (1948) was able to conclude
that 'what a person believes about himself is a factor in the social
comprehension of others' (p. 154). These parallel changes
occurring during client-centred therapy have been empirically
tested. Using statements made by 10 clients during recorded
sessions Sheerer (1949) found 'a definite and substantial
correlation (+0.51) between attitudes of acceptance of and respect
for self and attitudes of acceptance of and respect for others'
(p. 175). Stock (1949), in a similar study, confirmed Sheerer's
results with a correlation of +0.38, but of Stock's 10 counselling
cases, 7 had also been used by Sheerer.

Only a few studies have been conducted to discover whether this
relationship also holds for longer and non-clinical groups. Phillips
(1951) using his own questionnaire, demonstrated a correlation of

+0.74 between attitudes to self and others in a university class. Berger (1952), with his own scale, produced a correlation of +0.65 between acceptance of self and acceptance of others for 33 evening class students, and one of +0.36 for 183 day students. However, the scale used by Phillips was dogged by the acquiescence response set. Berger did attempt to obviate this problem by randomising positive and negative items in his scale.

The evidence points with reasonable clarity towards a positive relationship between acceptance of self and acceptance of others. However, the 'other' has tended to be in the form of a generalised other. It would seem appropriate to consider whether the relationship also holds towards certain defined others, e.g. ethnic, political, religious groups, etc. If the relationship is of general application then those persons who score high on scales measuring ethnocentrism should be found among those least accepting of self. Theoretically other groups or out-groups should be perceived as a threat because of real or imagined differences between them and the particular in-group with whom the individual, possessing the negative self concept, identifies.

From the small number of researches conducted in this relationship between self attitudes and ethnocentrism, no consistent pattern has emerged. For example, Brodbeck and Perlmutter (1954) reported that subjects with high dislike of self scores (on a specially devised and unpublished scale!) tend to prefer the European over the American way of life. That is they dislike their own group! However, as all the items in the instrument were reported as negative phrased, there is the question of the influence of a response set. Perlmutter (1954) showed also that subjects reporting low self esteem showed significantly more desire to travel abroad than did subjects displaying high self esteem. However, since three out of five of the comparisons involved preferences to live in England (the subjects were American), the question of role of language similarity cannot be ruled out. Rokeach and Fruchter (1956) found low, but statistically significant correlations, between self-rejection scores and scores from both F and E scales. However, the self-rejection scores were based on only five items, and since all the scales are worded in the same direction, this result, supporting the theoretical relationship in the right direction, cannot be unreservedly accepted. Finally, in an exploration of the hypothesis that psychotherapy will increase one's acceptance of, and respect for others, Gordon and Cartwright (1954) constructed an Other Attitude Scale based on items from the California E, F and PEC scales. Pre- and post-therapy measurements showed no statistically significant differences in attitude change. These four studies produced no conclusive picture. But pervading the research all the time were deficiencies in design and methodology to confound any reliable and valid conclusion.

A few studies have been conducted using specific others. For example, Zuckerman, Baer and Monashkin (1956) found significant correlations between self acceptance and acceptance of father with a group of in-patients, but this was measured in terms of self-ideal discrepancies which have serious statistical limitations. Bossom and Maslow (1957) found that the 22 most secure judges rated standard photos as 'warm' more often than did the least secure judges. Security was inferred from the Maslow S-I Test. Zelen (1954) obtained completely negative results. Self acceptance was indexed by the California Test of Personality, but it failed to produce the expected positive relationships with acceptance of others as measured by sociometric techniques. Zelen's subjects were children and he is unclear as to why this result occurred. Zimmer (1956) also produced puzzling findings. He asked airmen to rate the self, a harmonious peer and an annoying peer, on eight evaluative trait scales. For all traits the correlations between self and others were low and not significant.

Previous work on the relationship then appears to have been characterised by speculative theory and experimental work, often dubious in design, mainly in a clinical setting. Using non-clinical subjects Burns (1975, 1978) has demonstrated quite convincingly with trainee teachers in Britain that the relationship between self concept and attitudes to others is strong. The 'others' involved a wide range of others such as specific persons (e.g. father) measured on a semantic differential; group others (e.g. West Indians) measured by ethnocentrism and social distance scales; and the generalised other (measured by an acceptance of other scale). The first study (Burns, 1975) revealed an array of statistically significant positive correlations between attitudes to self and attitudes to the three categories of others designated above. Trent (1957) demonstrated this relationship with negro children. He found that negro children who manifested a high level of self acceptance expressed significantly more positive attitudes to others, irrespective of whether the other was black or white, than children who were least self accepting.

There would appear to be evidence from one study (Tolor, Kelly and Stebbins, 1976) that the relationship between self attitudes and acceptance of others is stronger for women than for men. In this study acceptance of others was measured by non-verbal topological index of psychological distance and the self concept by the Tennessee scale (Fitts, 1965). Tolor speculates that the sex difference is related to the social differentiation of sex roles in Western culture. Men take a more instrumental role, since they are relatively exempt from biological functions. Thus, they seek active mastery and achievement of objective tasks, especially in the area of occupational responsibility. Women, because of their identification with child care functions, tend to be more expressive, which results in a stressing of human relationships. It is quite possible, therefore, that the different values assigned to interpersonal relationships by the sexes reflects itself both in the closer spacing of responses by women in comparison to men and in their exhibiting a stronger relationship between self-concept adequacy, on the one hand, and interpersonal propinquity on the other hand.

Since some of the 'others' to whom attitudes have been assessed belong to out-groups and ethnic minorities, it is very apparent that self attitudes are positively related to ethnic attitudes, and to degrees of tolerance and prejudice. In fact, the strongest relationships between self attitudes and attitudes to others do occur in respect of specific 'coloured' stimuli on the Semantic Differential (Burns, 1975). Although the various correlations of self attitude with the several kinds of others overlap, there is a tendency for the size of the correlations to increase as the relationship moves from that between self with the generalised other, through to that with the 'white' in-group, and finally to the highest levels of all with the 'coloured' out-group members. Where specific 'coloured' stimuli are involved, those student teachers with low self concepts apparently stick rigidly to conventional attitudes, whereas those who have more positive feelings about themselves feel free to divorce themselves from stereotyped convention, strike out on their own and refuse to evaluate others in a negative way solely because of some ethnic attribute. The lower correlations for the generalised other and for the 'white' stimuli may occur because conventional attitudes and relations to these categories are more fluid, with judgements having less concrete criteria, such as colour, on which to anchor.

While those with high positive self attitudes possessed more positive attitudes to particular others, especially coloured others, than those with less positive self appraisal, a significant rank-order correlation ($+0.87$) between the ranks for the means of high and low acceptance of self subgroups indicated that, irrespective of the level of self attitudes, the student teacher subjects maintained a very similar ordering of concepts. The lowest rated concepts for both groups were the four coloured stimuli, hence even those who rate themselves and others more positively still differentiate between different types of others, and record less favourable attitudes to those stimuli bearing an attribute of colour.

In a study of social distance expressed towards 24 stimulus persons who represented every possible combination of six levels of ethnic groups, two levels of religion and two levels of social class, Burns (1978) showed that subjects with low levels of self acceptance placed significantly far more weight on ethnicity in assigning social distance than did subjects with high levels of self acceptance. In this respect the significant differences in the weightings the low acceptance of self and high acceptance of self criterion subgroups gave to ethnicity and occupation in their respective evaluations of others are understandable and expected findings bearing on the suggested positive relationship between acceptance of self and acceptance of others. A person who is secure and confident because of his positive self appraisal, appears able to accept and have more positive attitudes towards others, and lay less stress on ethnic characteristics in evaluative procedures, than those with a lower level of self acceptance who are unsure of their own merit.

Putting social distance between self and others appears to be a means of protecting an inadequate self concept and thereby preserving psychological security in ways congruent with cultural norms by creating an out-group at one and the same time alien and of low social class. Such colour and class differences seem to provide a source of real threat to the insecure, but also a target at which hostility can be directed. Perceived characteristics, especially ethnic ones, are emphasised and used as the basis of judgement in a rationalisation that different equals strange equals threat. Fear of losing status and security of group membership results in a powerful attempt to identify as one with the group, directing hostility and rejection at out-groups seen in various combinations as coloured, of an inferior social class, as strangers, in visible and obvious ways different from self and from known and secure ways of behaving. In all their different cloaks of many hues, members of other ethnic groups are threatening and strange. Many psychologists (e.g. Rosenberg 1965) have evidence of the relationship between insecurity, the feeling of threat from others, anxiety and low feelings of personal worth. Any person who evaluates himself largely in negative terms is a threatened individual. So a substantial body of experimental work proves that self acceptance is related to acceptance of others, but how is acceptance by others related to self acceptance?

Fey (1954) made a study of this and his research helps answer that question. Using a group of 58 third-year medical students, he obtained: measures of self-acceptance; acceptance of others; each subject's judgement of how well he was accepted by others; and an estimate of actual acceptability or popularity. Among other things, he found that the high self-accepting (positive-self-concept) men were more accepting of others, estimated their own popularity higher than did the less self-accepting men, but were not actually any more popular. Fey then divided his subjects into two groups, (*a*) those who markedly overestimated their popularity (strong self-enhancing tendencies), and (*b*) those who grossly underestimated their popularity (strong self-derogatory tendencies). Paradoxically, he found the self-derogatory group to be significantly more popular than the self-enhancing group. Fey speculated that individuals who are very self-accepting but who reject others are likely to have 'defensively organized' attitudes of superiority, are insensitive to their actual group social status, tend to depreciate others and are consequently rejected because they threaten the security of other people. On the other hand, it was found that men who have low acceptance of themselves along with high acceptance of others, are seen as non-threatening and therefore more well-liked. Fey went on to speculate that the prototypic well-adjusted person (i.e., the one with high self–other acceptance) may not appear to 'need' friendships or to repay it. His very psychological robustness is resented, or perhaps it is perceived and rejected as a façade. There is a striking similarity between Fey's research findings and Maslow's clinical speculations about why it is that some of us are inclined to lose our aplomb and self-possession, even grow uneasy, anxious, and feel a bit inferior in the company of persons we regard as superior in one way or other.

In sum, self acceptance, which we could say is a lack of cynicism about the self, appears to be associated with accepting other people. This indicates that the self-accepting person views the world as a more congenial place than the self rejector and is less defensive towards others and about himself because of it.

If self esteem and esteem for others are indeed correlated, as the evidence suggests, why is this so? Fromm has suggested that both attitudes to self and to others are based on the same set of childhood learning experiences. When children have been treated hostiley and their freedom has been wilfully curtailed, they develop a 'character conditioned hatred' towards both self and others. Unfortunately, Fromm does not specify exactly why this disposition should include both self and others. The relationship between self esteem and acceptance of others is explained by Rogers (1959) in a slightly different way. For Rogers the regard received from others may be of two types: conditional or unconditional. Conditional regard depends on meeting the other person's criteria of evaluation in order to be accepted. In contrast, unconditional regard is not dependent on the other's criteria of the evaluation. The person is prized not for what he does but for his intrinsic value as a human being. Rogers notes that when regard is conditional, the person begins to evaluate himself conditionally – acceptable only if he meets certain criteria. When self evaluation is conditional, the person defends against seeing himself in certain ways. By generalisation he learns to evaluate others conditionally too. The most significant others who become threatening through their evaluations are of course parents. The seeds of derogation both of self and others are sown early in life. So the general contention is that the relationship between attitudes of self and attitudes to others exist because the processes leading to the development of both, are the same, viz. child-rearing practices. The antecedents of self esteem, maternal deprivation and ethnocentrism have been well documented respectively by Coopersmith (1967), Rutter (1972) and Adorno *et al.* (1950), and it is those vacillating, cold, unaffectionate interactions with parents, where there is little praise or positive evaluation, that lead to the child also learning a concept of himself that is replete with feelings of lack of self worth and insecurity. Burns (1975) analysed the scores of the High Acceptance and Low Acceptance of Self groups to the Semantic Differential scales on the two 'parent' concepts, and several important relevant mean differences manifested themselves in a statistically significant manner. The High Self Acceptance criterion group saw both parents as more good, tolerant, fair, kind, friendly and valuable than the Low Self Acceptance group. Parental performance which is interpreted as tolerant, fair, kind and good by the child is likely to produce children who are also able to value themselves highly.

As Chapter 7 suggests, the experiences and learnings involved in the various child-rearing practices not only form the bricks out of which the rising edifice of self evaluation is constructed, but also many of the attitudes a person has towards others come partly by generalisation from the attitudes he has to his parents as well as from identification with parental attitudes and behaviour. The attitudes a person has for his parents could well be a function of how much they manifest love and acceptance of him. If they do manifest love for him he learns to regard himself highly and need not be preoccupied with the possibility of receiving such negative reinforcements as rejection and isolation. He is less apt to behave defensively, and in turn less likely to receive negatively reinforcing behaviour from others which would lower his regard for them. One could further postulate that stimulus generalisation occurs between learned information about, and attitudes to, oneself, and learned information about, and attitudes to, others. In these suppositions there lies the basis that attitudes towards self are antecedent to attitudes towards others. Subjects with high levels of self acceptance fortified by the parental vote of confidence are willing to approach social encounters and expect success. Those with low self esteem, through previous interpreted life experiences, anticipate failure and rejection. This saps motivation to interact with others. Culturally induced prejudices and stereotypes, often strongly emphasised in a home where parents are not warm and nurturant, act as a rationalisation and in concert with the displacement of frustration at feeling inadequate ensure in general a lack of positive responses to others. Child-rearing practices would thus appear to be antecedent to both self and other attitudes. Thus the pattern of research findings on the relationship between self concept and attitudes to others suggests that the relationship holds in many contexts with a wide range of subjects and 'others'. There is support for those psychoanalysts, who for some time have claimed, without empirical justification, that the tendency to disparage arises out of feelings of inferiority, and that a person who believes himself unlovable is unable to love others, since self love and love for others walk hand in hand (Adler, 1927; Horney, 1937; Fromm, 1939). Affective relationships with others appear to require adjusted personalities so that the psychic economy isn't diverted and drained off merely to deal with intrapersonal tensions. The results are consistent, too, with the empirical work performed by the client-centred therapists on therapy cases, and this consistency across 'normal' and 'non-normal' groups suggests that the relationship is probably present throughout the whole spectrum of the population. The present results also promote Rogers' eighteenth proposition, which states the relationship in terms of client-centred therapy, from the level of intuitive hypothesis to the realms of proven fact, and support his speculation that self rejection could be a major factor in individual hostility, in industrial frictions, intergroup relations and even international clashes.

Rogers (1951) was even prompted to speculate: 'What if it turns out that industrial friction, attitudes towards minority groups, hostilities towards foreign peoples, are based largely on the attitudes one holds towards oneself?' (p. 150)

These statistically significant relationships between self attitudes and many different kinds of others, ranging from specific ethnic minority members to the generalised other, supply psychology with a principle which is of great utility in attempting to understand and explain the problems of social conflict and hostility which are so detrimental to human relationships. The importance of such a finding is without question. As Rosenberg (1965) concludes, 'The cement of social life does not consist of grand passions or cosmic philosophies. It consists of casual conversations and relationships, small talk, the easy interchange of ideas, and the sharing of minor enthusiasms.' (p. 168) The individual's self concept would appear to play a significant role in all this. What a person thinks of himself does not form a closed system, imprisoned and encapsulated, having no relevance beyond the boundary of his own being; on the contrary, it reaches out to manipulate his relationships with others. The self concept apparently brings to bear a unique perspective for viewing one's relationship with one's social environment.

In that attitudes to self are antecedent (however briefly) to attitudes to others, might well mean that changes in attitudes to others can only come about through changes in attitudes to self. Increased acceptance of foreigners, minority groups, neighbours, colleagues, spouses and the like, might best be achieved through some form of group-therapy experience, in which possibilities of altering the individual's acceptance of and respect for himself exist when carried out in an ethos of understanding and acceptance. In situations of industrial tension or professional friction the most effective means of approach might be through dealing with the attitudes of the person towards himself rather than searching for solutions solely via external factors.

The great value of the experimental validation of the basic relationship between attitudes to self and attitudes to others is that the atmosphere of understanding and acceptance which leads to improved relationships with others is the very ethos likely to create a therapeutic experience in itself and consequent self acceptance for those who are exposed to it. There may be in this relationship – if organised in the correct way in family, group therapy, classroom, church, work contexts, etc – a dynamic psychological chain reaction with tremendous potential for the solution of many of the interpersonal, intergroup and international relationship problems that have plagued mankind in both past and present, and which prognosticate immense social upheaval for the future if little is done to generate more acceptance of others. Psychologists and educators need to devise practical programmes for creating this therapeutic climate in which any members of society can learn to accept themselves and develop more positive self conceptions. For instance, the recent development of 'encounter groups', with their climate of trust and healing capacity (Rogers, 1967), is a major positive approach designed to allow an individual to understand himself and others (Bayne, 1972).

Both child-rearing practices and teaching methods must be based on a policy of the acceptance and nurturance, providing children with encouragement and success in terms of their individual capabilities. Intensive group-experience techniques have an appropriate role to play in modifying adult attitudes to self and others, but are limited not only in economic viability but also in terms of numbers of persons that can be catered for. Although many of the group techniques were originally devised for those requiring therapy, this general approach with its atmosphere of acceptance and respect is widely applicable in fact to everyone. What non-clinical group experiences could be provided? Well, there has been a proliferation of various group approaches applying a variety of theoretical orientations during the last two decades. The next section provides a survey of some of the research on the effects of such group experiences on the self concept.

C. The self concept and non-clinical intensive group experience

Intensive group experience is perhaps the best overall term to cover a wide variety of other labels. It is a general approach to human relations training, encompassing what are sometimes also termed 'encounter groups', 'sensitivity groups' and 'T-groups', which all have considerable areas of communality. Whatever the favoured name, the group sessions provide participants with the opportunity to learn more about themselves, learn about their functioning in interpersonal situations and generally improve their insight and evaluations of self and others. The group in every case is small with stress on the feeling level rather than on the intellectual level of communication. The sequence of events is not structured; group members as individuals decide what they will talk about, and what problems they wish considered. The rationale behind the intensive group experience, whatever its specific approach and theoretical orientation, is that the freedom and lack of structure enable the individual to feel safe enough to lower, little by little, his defences and façades. This facilitates a more direct relationship on a feeling basis with other group members, leading to more understanding and acceptance of self and of others, coupled with more positive attitudes to self and to others. There is a veritable flood of evidence to support the claims that intensive group experience induces change in self attitudes and in attitudes to others in a positive direction.

Even anecdotal data suggest that intensive group experience can lead to some sort of change. For example, partipants voluntarily express such statements as, 'It was pretty rugged in spots but I really had a good hard look at myself honestly for the first time', or 'It certainly helped me to understand myself better and has changed the way I relate to people'. This viewpoint is summarised by Gibb (1970) when he states, 'Changes do occur in sensitivity, ability to manage feelings, directionality of motivation, attitudes towards the self, attitudes towards others, and interdependence.' (p. 2114)

Rogers (1970) takes each of the terms Gibb uses in this summary statement and spells out their implications more fully. 'Sensitivity' is seen as implying greater awareness of one's own feelings and the feelings and perceptions of others, as well as involving openness, authenticity and spontaneity; 'managing feelings' is interpreted as referring to the ownership of one's feelings and the congruence between feelings and behaviour; 'directionality of motivation' implies concepts such as self actualisation, self determination, commitment and inner-directedness; while 'attitudes towards the self' are seen as including self acceptance, self esteem, congruence of perceived and ideal self, and confidence. Concluding his review of the literature, Rogers (1970) states; 'I believe it is clear that research studies, even though they need to be greatly extended and improved, have demolished some of the prevalent myths about encounter groups, and have established the fact that they do bring about much in the way of behaviour change.' (p. 134) Campbell and Dunnette (1968), wrote in their review of the effectiveness of T-group training that 'the evidence, though limited, is reasonably convincing that T-group training does induce behavioural change' (p. 98) in certain settings.

Gibb (1970) in his review of human relationships training has produced a categorisation of nine different types of intensive group experience. These are:

1. Creativity–growth groups in which the purpose is to induce experiences to expand human awareness.
2. Marathon groups which focus on uninterrupted interpersonal intimacy.
3. Emergent groups which are non-programmed and have no leader.
4. Authenticity groups which focus on openness and consonance.
5. Sensitivity groups which are concerned with here-and-now experiences.
6. Programmed groups in which experiences are directed by absent leaders.
7. Microexperience groups which are limited in time and focus on interpersonal skills.
8. Inquiry groups which are concerned with data gathering and formal learning.
9. Embedded groups in which the groups are an ongoing constant experience within an organisation.

Though such categories are useful, they obviously do not take into consideration the wide variety of specific treatment techniques which further increase the diversity of treatment variables, nor are they mutually exclusive. Gibb also listed six major categories of outcome areas on which different groups focus. They included:

1. Sensitivity of self and others.
2. Managing feelings.
3. Managing motivation.
4. Functional attitudes towards self.
5. Functional attitudes towards others.
6. Independent behaviour, i.e. self perception, insight and attitudes towards self and others.

(a) The effects of group experience on the self concept

Gibb (1970) summarised studies of groups which dealt with self perception and self evaluation and concluded that persons show an increase in their self evaluation as a result of participation in groups. Kaye (1973) also shows positive changes in the self concept as a result of T-group interaction, and Stanton (1975) demonstrated that one intensive weekend could produce significant improvements in self awareness for an experimental group over a control group which had no group sessions and which manifested no change in self awareness as measured by Gross' (1947) Self Insight scale.

Campbell and Dunnette (1968) reviewed 44 articles related to evaluating the outcomes of T-groups. They concluded that the evidence 'is reasonably convincing' that T-group training induces behavioural change in terms of self insight, self acceptance, self attitudes and attitude to others. McIntire (1973) was able to show that not only did T-group participation contribute to increased self actualisation but that the changes were still maintained one year later. Eiben and Clack (1973) compared two different methods of conducting T-groups. A 'participating' group involving discussion and practical exercises showed greater gains in more areas of self actualisation than a 'didactic' group who had listened to a lecture on the theoretical aspects of group sensitivity training and had read a specific textbook in private. It would seem that participation in an active positive way is vital for lasting and effective change.

Rubin (1967a) discerned significant increases in self acceptance and decreases in ethnic prejudice as a result of a T-group experience, two changes which were strongly correlated. This finding adds weight to the earlier suggestion that intensive group experience would facilitate interpersonal relations and reduce ethnic friction. In a second study, Rubin (1967b) found increases in T-group participants' self acceptance and acceptance of others, both inside and outside of the group. McIntire (1969) administered the Personal Orientation Inventory (a measure of self actualisation to students before, after, and 1 year after a 6-week course which included an intensified period of sensitivity training. He found an increase in self acceptance between the pre-test and the first post-test, with no change between the first post-test and the second, indicating that self-acceptance increase is stable. In a study by Hewitt and Kraft (1973) participants in an encounter-group experience produced significant improvements in self concept but, equally important, believed that they had improved their ability to relate to others compared to a control group. Thus there exists considerable support for the contention that participants in group sessions show significant changes on measures of self actualisation as a result of various therapeutic group experiences.

Intentionally directed input in the form of recording insights in a log gained during a group experience was shown by Snadowsky and Belkin (1974) to increase significantly the relationship between an individual's self concept and the way he believed others perceived him. This increased accuracy was seen to be directly attributable to intentionally forcing cognitising insights and group experiences, since a control group failed to demonstrate such increased congruity. Representative comments from experimental group members expressed the value of writing comments and thoughts, reliving the experiential moments and making them think more deeply. The value of this finding lies not only in the increasing knowledge it provides about increasing the effectiveness of training groups but also it may lead to a reduction to the overcommitment of many therapists to a solely experiential and anti-intellectual approach to personal growth. Cognitive input, if incorporated in a defined way, can clearly enhance feelings, and act as a catalyst for realistic self appraisal.

Even the taking of a psychology course has been shown by Costin (1959) to increase self insight significantly, whereas students who did not take psychology failed to reveal any change. Gross' self-insight scale was administered to 179 undergraduates before and after an introductory course in psychology, which was part of a 2-year general education programme. The group as a whole showed a small but significant increase in its self-insight score. Both men and women whose scholastic achievement in the course was in the upper half of their class increased their self-insight scores, significantly and to the same extent. In the lower half, men also increased self insight significantly, but women did not change. Costin concluded that changes in self insight were positively related to information acquired from the course as measured by objective examinations, although course learnings not evaluated by the examinations also probably played a part in effecting change. As a control measure, Gross' scale was given to 97 students before and after a verbal communication course, also a part of the general education programme. No significant change in self-insight score occurred in this control group. This finding lends some validity to the reason many students give for taking psychology courses, that of increasing self knowledge.

(b) The effects of marathon and spaced group sessions

In a study of the differential effects of length of time spent in encounter groups and the degree to which self-concept changes are maintained, Watkins, Noll and Breed (1975) established three groups with 12 subjects in each. The number of hours each group met varied and was determined by setting the length of the first group to approximate to a marathon, viz. 20 contact hours out of a period of 28 hours. Since the length of the second group was intended to be brief, 4 hours was selected. The third group's length was arbitrarily set at 12 hours, which is midway between the other two groups. Subjects were assigned to groups randomly. Shostrum's (1966) POI scale was applied to evaluate any changes. Although all three groups showed positive changes in self actualisation as a result of their group experiences, the changes at post-test were significant only for the 12-hour group and for the 20-hour group. However, the changes measured 1 month later were very significant for all three groups. The magnitude of these changes is the same as has been observed by Culbert, Clark and Bobele (1968) and by Foulds (1970). Other analyses showed that treatments were not significantly different from each other, either at post-test or at follow-up. In terms of the specific goals of this study, it at first appears that changes in self actualisation were a direct function of time spent in encounter groups and that the marathon group was the one which produced highly significant changes which were detectable in the week immediately following treatment. However, since all of the groups demonstrated change in a positive direction and analyses of covariance indicated that none was significantly better than another, the advantage of extended exposure to group experiences has not been clearly demonstrated. The measurements taken at the 1-month follow-up revealed that the 20-hour group had maintained its gain and that the 12-hour and 4-hour groups had both shown further gains which in both cases were significantly different from their initial scores. The authors were frankly surprised in that they had been somewhat swayed by the common assumption that while encounter groups may produce striking changes, these changes are transient and quickly extinguished in the real world. The present results suggest that growth groups may be potent means for producing changes towards self actualisation, although the limitations of a self-report questionnaire and follow-up measures taken only 1 month later require caution when generalising about the lasting effects produced by groups.

King, Payne and McIntire (1973) also studied the impact of organisational forms of sensitivity training on the self concept. They found that a 'marathon' session of 24 hours' duration increased self acceptance significantly more than 'spaced' sessions of 3–4 hours once a week over a term. This difference seemed to occur because a marathon session provides a prolonged intense experience if the descriptions provided by the participants are to be relied on. Spaced sessions are not so described. In a marathon group, because of the accepting group atmosphere which is maintained throughout and because of fatigue, an individual member usually finds his psychological defences are weakened and remain weakened throughout the marathon. In a spaced session group, individuals have time between each session to re-establish defences. It follows that immediately following a marathon we would expect more self-attitude change than at the end of any spaced session including the final one.

In a second experiment (Watkins, Noll and Breed, 1975) established another set of three experimental groups, each consisting of 12 hours of group encounter. The first group (one session, 12 hours) lasted from 8.00 a.m. until 10.30 p.m. with two

75-minute breaks for lunch and dinner. The second group (two sessions, 6 hours each) met from 6.00 p.m. until midnight on two consecutive Friday evenings. The third group (six sessions, 2 hours each) met from 8.00 p.m. until 10.00 p.m. on six occasions spanning 1 week. Each group contained 11 subjects, and again Shostrum's POI scale was employed. Analysis of the results suggests that the massed and partially massed sessions produced significant gains in positive self evaluation, whereas the distributed sessions generated non-significant improvements, though other forms of analyses (covariance) indicated all three methods did not produce significantly different gains. The trend does suggest that an extended group session is more efficient than the time-honoured short frequent sessions so characteristic of individual and group psychotherapy.

In a follow-up study, Reddy (1973) reported self-concept changes as still demonstrable at 1 year later. Some participants in Reddy's study showed gains in self concept by the close of the experimental sessions, whereas others made major gains after returning home. As common sense suggests, individuals change at different rates and at different times.

It seems worth while to inquire as to what it is that occurs in the group process that significantly affects the self concept of participants. To date, there are few experimental results which relate to this important question. However, it appears that there are at least two factors which are meaningful to many sensitivity group participants and may relate to the process question. First, most individuals perceive more negative self traits than do outside observers. As group members openly explore aspects of themselves, many begin to realise that their inadequancies, both real and imagined, are not unique and that even persons they may admire share many of their 'hang-ups'. Secondly, members learn that even when their shortcomings become common knowledge to the group, they can still be accepted by the group. Such feedback comes in abundance.

The fact that the process of learning in sensitivity training groups is viewed as centring around feedback is hardly surprising. Since the turn of the century, learning theorists have postulated the central role of feedback in learning. Feedback is viewed as fulfilling a variety of needs – e.g. reducing tension, providing positive or negative reinforcement and evidence of success or failure, indicating the degree of similarity to a social model, degree of completion of tasks and so on. Thus, in one form or another, feedback is generally considered essential to the learning process.

(c) An example of a group exercise

Hazell (1975) describes a structured group encounter exercise which, while offering depth and power, also provides protective devices so that emotional conflict is at a minimum and does not require the presence of an experienced facilitator (leader). The exercise, named 'Query', is action oriented rather than analysis oriented. Designed to provide group members with insights for future action rather than explanations of why their troubles exist, it is also insight oriented in that it helps each member see needed action from his own perspective rather than from the perspective of others about what he should do. The exercise applies these concepts in that customary climate of loving acceptance of whatever comes up, while the structure specifically excludes conflict between members in the forms of advice-giving behaviour and defensive behaviour. The insights for action which may be produced can be considered as the voluntary outcome of mutual experience drawing on the resources of the group, rather than as therapy drawing on the expertise of a leader. The facilitator purely operates to maintain helpful processes.

The 'Query' exercise involves asking the 'focus' or subject a series of questions about what changes he needs to make, what alternatives exist, how such changes could be effected, etc. The focus responds, for example, by offering instances of disturbing situations, of what possibilities and alternatives are possible and how he could effect change, etc. The questioning rotates round the group with the 'focus' person changing when questioning of him seems fruitful no longer. Hazell (1975) provides more detail for those interested in this basic exercise. Of course, supplementary encounter exercises can be introduced when subjects are more at ease and trust each other. For example the familiar 'trust' games where a person relaxes while others physically support him, or 'feedback' in which group members describe their perceptions of how the 'focus' appeared to be thinking and feeling, or 'doubling' whereby another group member role plays the 'focus' attempting to express what he feels are the 'focus'' true feelings and answers. Finally, some role playing by 'focus' allows him to act out his proposed action/solution. The whole basis of 'Query' is to prevent resentment, defences and anxiety with the victim pushed into an emotional corner without any loophole for escape. In many respects it resembles brainstorming and appears very appropriate for normal groups who do not require deep emotional catharsis to solve everyday problems or develop more self understanding.

Lacking your own private therapist and receiving no invitations to join in an intensive group experience how can you as an individual increase the positive valence of your self concept, sharpen your awareness of your self and make yourself more open to experience? The best way is the sharing of experience with people you can trust, whom you can allow to get close to you. As in a therapy group, by their interaction, comment, reflection and sharing, they facilitate awareness of many self perspectives previously hidden or distorted. There are also ways of exploring self alone, though there is a danger of becoming obsessively introspective. Here are a few individual exercises you might wish to attempt.

1. Who am I? Do you recall the 'Who Are You?' Test in Chapter 5. Write at least a dozen separate answers to the question, 'Who am I?', each on a separate piece of paper. These self definitions should include such areas as role, profession, feelings, image, personality, social relations, etc. Number each answer from one onwards in order of importance. Then, with them all turned face down turn over the least important and concentrate on it. Ask yourself what it really means to you, what you would be like if it were not part of you. Repeat this procedure with each answer in turn. This may enable you to become aware of other aspects of yourself.

2. Experiencing. This exercise is to facilitate your being aware of what you feel and want rather than what you think are your feelings and wants. Focus your entire attention on your present experiencing, becoming totally absorbed in an unselfconscious way, i.e. don't think about it, just experience your sensations and emotions. Try this exercise only for a few minutes at a time at first, lengthen the period later. This exercise should enable you to admit into full awareness your true feelings on a wide range of matters rather than the feelings you believed you ought to experience.

3. Relaxation and awareness. This exercise aims to improve awareness of self as an organism. Lie down on a bed, and relax as much as you can by breathing deeply and slowly with eyes closed. Focus on parts of the body in turn, e.g. left leg, right leg, each arm, pelvis, chest, face muscles, etc, firstly tensing them for 3 or 4 seconds then relaxing them. Then try to clear your mind of all thoughts, and become aware of different parts of the body and the sensations in each of these parts in turn. Over several days, you will gradually become more able to relax and aware of sensations in the body you normally ignore.

4. Self concept. Write brief sketches of yourself, and your ideal self. Compare them and isolate discrepant aspects. What would be required to reconcile these? It is possible to reconcile them? Why do you value specific aspects of your ideal self?

5. Images. In this exercise the aim is to express self in images rather than words. Just experience the images, don't try to explain them until afterwards when you might care to recall and examine them for what they may reveal about your feelings.

D. The self concept and social comparison feedback and appraisal

Festinger (1954) in establishing a theory of social comparison processes claims there is a drive or basic motivation to evaluate one's self. This drive for self evaluation has implications not only for the behaviour of persons in groups but also for the processes of formation of groups and changing membership of groups. To the extent that self evaluation can only be accomplished by means of comparison with other persons and with societal standards the drive for self evaluation is a force acting on persons to belong to groups, to associate with others – an important factor in making the human being gregarious. It has been emphasised that the notion of self evaluation being shaped significantly by feedback received from others has a long history in psychology (e.g. Mead, Cooley).

(a) Two opposing theories: self esteem versus self consistency

There are two theories which have been posited as explanations of how an individual reacts to failure and success experiences and evaluations from others: these are the self-consistency and self-esteem theories. The rationale of self-consistency theorists is that an individual's actions, attitudes and his receptivity to information from other people are strongly affected by a tendency to create and maintain a consistent cognitive state with respect to his evaluations of himself. This argues that individuals with a high self concept find positive evaluations from others consistent and negative evaluation inconsistent. Individuals with low self evaluation would, on self-consistency theory, find negative evaluations consistent, but positive evaluations inconsistent.

In contrast, self-esteem theory implies that everyone needs to bear favourable attitudes towards himself, and that the more this need is frustrated the more strongly the individual will wish to have it satisfied. Since low-self-esteem individuals would be more hungry for and yet more frustrated in their needs for positive self evaluations, they should respond more favourably to positive evaluations from others and respond in a more dejected and hostile way to failure than should individuals high in self esteem. In a review of studies of these two theories Jones (1973) found that self-esteem theory was more appropriate to explain behaviour, with the unhappy self derogator glowing when praised and unhappy when derided. Self-consistency theory was rarely supported in the numerous studies he reviewed.

Shrauger and Lund (1975) also evaluated these two opposing theories, but found in contrast to Jones (1973) support for the consistency theory. In their study the most important way that high- and low-self-esteem individuals differed in their response to evaluative feedback was in the credibility they ascribed to their assessor. For high-self-esteem subjects, the assessments of an evaluator's competence in terms of both his knowledge of the subject, his general capability and lack from bias was substantially dependent on the favourability of the evaluator's judgements. By contrast, low-self-esteem subjects showed no significant difference in their ratings of the competence of the evaluator, whether he gave them favourable or unfavourable feedback. Their results showed little if any support for self-esteem theory. In no respect did low-self-esteem subjects indicate relatively more favourable reactions to the high-awareness evaluator or less favourable reactions to the low-awareness evaluator then did high-self-esteem subjects.

The fact that high-self-esteem subjects found the low-awareness evaluator less credible than did low-self-esteem subjects is more in line with consistency theory. People who hold generally positive views about themselves respond more negatively to the source of a negative evaluation on a specific attribute than do those who hold generally negative self perceptions. High-self-esteem individuals, when faced with negative assessments of themselves, were more likely to question the evaluator's competence as a judge of their ability. This may be one means by which they were able to fend off the recognition or acceptance of information which was threatening to the favourability of their self image. There is as yet little resolution of the self esteem versus self consistency controversy – some results favour one theory while other results support its rival. But one recent study provides a hint that, depending on the operation of certain variables, each theory has its range of application. Walster (1965) initially produces conflicting results. He notes firstly that high-self-esteem people expect more acceptance while low-self-esteem people expect more rejection, i.e. a consistency-theory approach. However, he later confuses the issue by claiming that low-self-esteem people have a greater need for approval than do those with high self esteem, i.e. a self-esteem theory. The resolution between such conflicting approaches seems to reside in the context of the evaluation by the other, whether it is public or private, mutual or non-reciprocal. Interpersonal evaluations occurring in public which are mutual, suggest self-esteem theory is relevant with low-self-esteem subjects seeking to elicit favourable public evaluations from others in response to their positive evaluation of the other. When evaluation is not public, low-self-esteem persons attribute less favourable evaluation to others in order to defend themselves and devalue the source of likely low evaluations of themselves consistent with their own self evaluations. However, a study by Baron (1974) showed that low-self-esteem subjects consistently evaluated unknown others in both public and private conditions in an unfavourable way. This confirms the tendency for low self acceptance and low acceptance of others to go hand in hand.

Self-esteem theory does provide an explanation for the fact that the way in which we perceive others' reactions to us also influences our attitudes to them. There is considerable evidence to support the proposition that we tend to be attracted to those who evaluate us positively and dislike those who provide negative feedback. In a study by Jones, Gergen and Davis (1962) undergraduate males were interviewed by advanced graduate students. Following the interview, half of the subjects learned that the graduate interviewer had a very positive opinion of them, while the other half learned that he disapproved of many of their personal characteristics. Subjects then evaluated the interviewer on an array of dimensions. Clear-cut results emerged; those receiving positive appraisals were overwhelmingly more positive in their evaluations of the interviewer. This self-esteem hypothesis is based on the notion that low self esteem represents a kind of approval deficit, and since approval is generally desired by people, the low-self-esteem subjects should desire it more. One problem in testing this or other models involving self esteem is in correctly identifying people of low and high self esteem. While there are few ambiguities surrounding low-self-esteem responses on a questionnaire, there are problems with high-self-esteem responses.

(b) Two forms of high self esteem

Some high-self-esteem persons (in terms of test score) may in fact be offering a defensive response rather than indicating 'true' high self esteem, by denying and suppressing threatening experience (Block and Thomas, 1955). Stotland *et al.* (1957) predicted that if high-self-esteem individuals protect themselves from negative evaluations, then they would de-emphasise objective failure and would emphasise an objective success. It was found that level of self esteem affected evaluation of one's performance in failure, but not in success. Individuals with high self esteem rated their failure performance significantly better than did individuals with low self esteem. Seemingly then, subjects with high self esteem are less accepting of failure or threatening experiences. Thus, two kinds of high self esteem seem to occur. On the one hand there is a defensive style where failure is guarded against and made seem unimportant when it occurs. On the other hand, genuine high self esteem requires less concern to avoid or repudiate failure, since failure is not particularly threatening. People with genuinely high self esteem may be better able to accept failure, or they may be more likely to try to improve areas of relative failure rather than repudiating evaluations in those areas. Schneider and Turkat (1975) provide support for these two types of high self esteem. Assessing defensiveness by the Marlowe Crowne SD scale, defensive high-self-esteem individuals presented themselves more positively than genuine high-self-esteem individuals in reaction to negative information, while there were no differences in reaction to positive information. To the extent that positive self presentations indicate a need for approval, it appears that defensive high-self-esteem individuals may be differentiated from genuine high-self-esteem individuals by their stronger need for approval in the fact of negative information. In a failure situation, defensive high-self-esteem individuals will be strongly affected by and more dependent upon the evaluations of others for their feelings of self worth. Thus, they would be more concerned with the presentation of a socially desirable appearance than individuals with genuine high self esteem. The reaction to challenging or threatening information is to compensate with a positive self presentation. The genuine high-self-esteem individual seems to be less dependent upon the evaluations of others for his feelings of worth.

(c) Differential effect of feedback on high and low self esteem

Self-esteem differences also reflect differences in 'defensive style', with the high-self-esteem person blocking out, distorting or in some manner invalidating unfavourable self-referent input. Thus, while high- and low-self-esteem groups seem equally receptive to positive feedback, the high-self-esteem person defends himself more against negative feedback. Other studies have shown that the high-, as compared to the low-, self-esteem person tends to forget more readily information related to a failure experience, to evaluate objectively similar performance as more favourable and to indicate less attraction toward people whom he sees as not liking him. It appears that discrediting the source is sufficiently effective to reduce whatever threat a high-self-esteem person may find in a negative evaluation. If he can do this he may not need to modify sharply his affective reactions to the evaluator or his interpretations of the evaluator's reaction to him.

Since people with high self esteem protect themselves from negative self evaluation and are less vulnerable to the impact of outside events, they are less affected by the communication of failure experiences and more responsive to success experiences than are persons of low self esteem. Furthermore, they are responsive to the expectations for their performance communicated to them by their social group. Different levels of self esteem induce different patterns of protective reactions to failure experiences. People of high self esteem seem to be less willing to permit their self image to be vulnerable to influences from others. Such differences related to varying levels of self esteem appear to be based on different defence mechanisms employed by high- and low-self-esteem persons (Cohen, 1954). Many high-self-esteem persons appear to use avoidance defences, e.g. reaction formation, to block and ignore expression of unacceptable influences. Low self esteem is associated with a preferential use of expressive defences, e.g. projection and regression to play out impulses dependent on situations and events.

Another difference between 'highs' and 'lows' in self esteem would appear to be that the latter are more subject to social influence than persons high in self esteem (Hovland and Janis, 1959). The underlying reason for this differential susceptibility may be that 'lows' are less certain in their beliefs, especially beliefs about themselves. When presented with new tasks, low-self-concept persons estimate their likely performance in line with information derived from others about their expected level of performance. This expectation then determines their performance level. High-self-esteem persons are not guided totally by expectations of others, but take into account their own motivations, goals and abilities which they value more highly than do the 'lows' (Stotland and Cottrell, 1961).

Cohen (1959) in a seminal article surveys research on the relationship between self concept and persuasibility, and has pointed to the general importance of self esteem as a determinant of the person's responsiveness to influences for mass media and social interaction. The evidence suggests that people of high and low self esteem differ in their responsiveness to persuasive communications: those with low self esteem are more easily swayed than those of high self esteem, who are better able to resist influence in mass-communication situations. Individuals of different degrees of self esteem tend to differ in their reactions to the threatening exercise of power over them. Those with high self esteem appear to repudiate the power situation with greater ease and are more self protective and self enhancing, whereas those with low self esteem seem to be more dependent upon the situation and more vulnerable to its pressures. This is consistent with findings to be reported later in this chapter where low self esteem bears some relationship to focus of control, the degree to which a person feels in control of what happens to him.

Since an individual's experience in a variety of contexts contributes to his overall level of self esteem, persons of low self esteem suffer characteristic failure experiences, whereas those with high self esteem are generally more successful in meeting their aspirations. This implies that persons with low self esteem differ from those who are high in self esteem in their reactions to an immediate experience relevant to their need satisfaction. Individuals with high self esteem react to new situations with expectations of success, since characteristically they have been successful in the past in meeting the challenge. Those with low self esteem, expecting failure, are more vulnerable to the effects of failure experiences, thereby reinforcing the discrepancy between self and ideal self. Persons of low self esteem allow their attitudes about themselves and others to be more affected by what other persons communicate to them concerning their performance and responsibilities. (Cohen, 1959). This suggests that in school situations where teacher expectancy effects can be devastating, the influence will be greatest on those who are least able to bear the cross. Since persons of high self esteem appear to be less susceptible to events in mass communications and power situations, they are in general, less susceptible to interpersonal influence in social interaction; persons with high self esteem are also less susceptible to influence from those of low self esteem than vice versa (Thomas and Burdick, 1954). Persons of high self esteem may exert more influence attempts than persons of low self esteem when they interact.

(d) Level of self esteem and interpersonal perception

The frequency with which a person uses certain dimensions to describe others is related to how relevant he sees those dimensions as being to his own self evaluation, according to a study by Shrauger and Patterson (1974). This finding was not merely due to differences in the frequency with which various dimensions were used by people in general, since the association was still very strong when this factor was removed. Also, the fact that the self ratings and the stimulus person descriptions were obtained 1 month apart suggests that the relationship was not simply a function of temporal contiguity of their measurement but reflected some more stable relationship. The fact that similar dimensions of judgement are used in the evaluation of both oneself and other people would seem to enhance the potential importance of social comparison processes in interpersonal judgements. It suggests also that an important consideration in finding relevant dimensions for interpersonal perception studies would be how significant the dimensions are for the subject's evaluation of himself. Shrauger and Patterson (1974) also studied the relationship between how satisfied a person was with himself on a dimension and how frequently he used that dimension in judging others.
High-satisfaction dimensions were clearly used more frequently than low-satisfaction dimensions, and tended to be attributed more frequently to liked others. This is the basis of liking others who are more similar to ourselves. A final discovery was that high-self-esteem subjects employed satisfying dimensions for self and other descriptions more than did low-self-esteem persons. Thus, in the process of evaluating others, both high- and low-self-esteem persons may through comparative appraisal be reinforcing and maintaining their customary level of self regard. Low-self-esteem subjects also indicated less satisfaction on more

important dimensions and more satisfaction on less important dimensions than did high-self-esteem subjects. Thus the two self-esteem groups differ in the importance they ascribe to an area of behaviour in terms of how competent they feel in it.

The self concept is far more resistant to change when others are perceived to define one's self concept congruently with one's own beliefs (Backman, Secord and Pierce, 1963). This stability permits consistency in the behaviour of both subject and others, enabling social relationships to develop and continue. The subject appears active in this search for congruence of self attitudes with others' perceptions of self by showing preference for interaction with those who treat him in a manner congruent with self concept while avoiding those who do not. He also misperceives the feedback from others so that he believes they see him as he sees himself and finally he can and does emit behaviour designed to elicit from others reactions that validate his self definitions. So in these ways individuals manipulate their self concepts in order to enter into social relationships. There appears to be immense pressure to change self definitions which are not congruent with the feedback from others. (Backman, Secord and Pierce, 1963; Maehr, Mensing and Nafzger, 1962). We come to view and value ourselves as others have taught us to view and value ourselves. This is particularly apparent in childhood (Ch. 6).

In a study of self-concept change outside the usual clinical setting, Kipnis (1961) investigated the effects of the perceived similarity and dissimilarity of friends on the self concept. It was found that individuals perceive their friends to be more like themselves than others whom they like less well. Individuals who changed their self evaluations over a 6-week period, did so in the direction of making their self evaluations closer to that of their best friends, irrespective of whether their friend had a more positive or a more negative set of perceived attributes. It is certainly a case of birds of a feather flocking together. This sort of change has implications for the therapy situation in that a client must perceive his therapist as possessing positive traits and also be aware of differences between himself and the therapist for changes to occur in a positive direction. Also of importance is the fact that in this comparison process lies the source of many of those undesirable behaviours and attributes which children more especially, but also adults, may adopt and internalise when identifying with and joining anti-social and delinquent groups. A wrong choice of friend or model can change self perception and behaviour to a socially disapproved form.

Using a face-to-face interview technique Leonard (1975) also investigated the role of the self concept on attraction for similar and dissimilar others. He confirmed that persons with favourable self concepts were more attracted to others with similar attitudes than to those with dissimilar attitudes. Persons with negative self concepts did not show any particular preference. Any sort of interpersonal relationship was avoided as it might tend to confirm what was already painfully believed.

(e) Self concept through feedback from appraisal by others

More convincing, though, than simple correlational studies of self attitudes and other attitudes are experimental studies which demonstrate measurable change in a subject's self conception as a function of the systematic alteration of another person's overt communication of his opinion of the subject. Benjamins (1950), in an early study was able to reveal alterations in students' self conceptualisations relating to false reports of their performance on a test. Re-rankings of their self estimate of performance after this false information showed changes paralleled by changes in test score on an alternate form of the original test. Strong and Gray (1972) showed that in small groups if one student was given results which were either higher or lower than the rest of the group, self ratings altered from pre- to post-test in the same direction. Social comparison caused the changes in self evaluation. Subjects receiving the low marks viewed their lower performance as a further example of inability to achieve.

When a person fails and this failure is observed by an 'expert', self evaluation lowers. This decrease is far more if the person was strongly motivated to keep his evaluation high. In other words, observed failure in areas important for the individual is disastrous for self evaluation on those aspects (Stotland and Zander, 1958). A person who fails tends to become sensitive to the opinions of others, but his feelings are affected by the validity he attributes to the judgements of others. A classic direct attack of this phenomenon was initiated by Videbeck's (1960) study of speech students who read aloud before an 'expert' in oral communication. Half the subjects chosen randomly were given a positive evaluation from the expert on certain elements of oral communication; the other half received criticism on these same points. Before and after the experimental session subjects rated themselves on these evaluated aspects, on other elements not specifically mentioned by the expert, and thirdly on diverse unrelated abilities. The results were fairly clear-cut. The subjects who received negative appraisals lowered their self estimates in a downward direction, whereas those who had been given positive feedback raised their self estimates. These effects generalised to the other related and unrelated abilities though the changes were not as great. This demonstration by Videbeck illustrating the role of appraisals of others led to further studies, especially attempts to determine the conditions under which such appraisal is most effective.

Maehr, Mensing and Nafzger (1962) continued the experimental manipulation approach by replicating Videbeck's (1960) findings in another context, that of physical education. They had high school students perform simple physical tasks which were then praised or criticised. Changes in self ratings were manifested in predicted directions as a result of approval and disapproval. But additionally and perhaps more significantly there was a spread of effect to areas of self conception not directly praised or criticised.

In a further study (Haas and Maehr, 1965) such induced changes in self conception were not only measurable but also still persisted 6 weeks later with the greater and longer-lasting changes reflecting greater amounts of approval or disapproval treatment. They used various physical tasks of motor skills and body coordination on male adolescents who received feedback from a physical education expert. As with the earlier studies the changes in self conception also spread though with less potency to related and unrelated areas of performance. Such changes then are real and stable.

Gergen (1971) suggests six characteristics of the appraiser and appraisal which influence the degree of the feedback effects.

1. Credibility of the appraiser appears intuitively important. When the appraiser is an expert or knowledgeable he becomes credible and hence his impact will be greater. For a young child, parents are 'experts' and are therefore quite influential in the effects of their communications on him. Peers and teachers later come to have the same function.

2. Personal communication or what Gergen calls 'personalism' also seem vital (Gergen, 1965). Personalism exists where the communicator appears sincere, attentive and interested in the subject. Impersonalistic communication is ignored as it appears insincere, impersonal and may be motivated by ulterior reasons. Dickoff, Altrocchi and Parsons' (1961) study exemplifies this. In an interview set up using women students, the interviewer agreed with the self evaluations of one group while giving evaluations more positive than their self evaluations to a second group. Half the subjects in each group were told that the interviewer was as honest as possible in appraising them; the other half were informed that the interviewer wished them to volunteer for another experiment, i.e. suspect motives. The results showed that where the suspect motives were employed subjects rejected the views of the communicator about them, with this effect increasing with the increasing flattery.

3. The number of confirmations received by the subject will emphasise the appraisal and confirm it by the very consistency of feedback. 'With long term exposure to a particular appraisal, the person's relevant view of self may be determined for life strongly resistant to change if not immutable.' (Gergen, 1971, pp. 47–8.) Parents are likely to have a profound effect because

of the continuous exposure of their offspring to their specific communications.

4. Discrepancies between self concept and the opinion of others affects the significance of the feedback for the individual. Marked discrepancies can have two opposing effects. Pressure can increase to alter the self concept if the discrepancy is large. We feel we have misjudged ourselves and look for confirmation of the other's views. But it can happen that such a discordance of judgements suggests that the other person's view is inaccurate and worthless. No revision of the self concept is likely to be effected. In no way will my evaluation of myself as a competent car driver be lowered by criticism from a person who has never been my passenger or even seen me drive. The credibility of the evaluator involved is invoked. Bergin (1962) showed that the amount of change in self evaluation effected by discrepant opinion was a function of the credibility of the source of the discrepancy.

5. Positive evaluations appear to be more rapidly learned and more quickly forgotten than negative appraisals.

6. Consistency of the tone of the communication influences the acceptance and effect of the communication. The rare criticism has little effect, especially if the context or performance area is one which renders the recipient less sensitive to criticism, i.e. of little importance. The brilliant student linguist is not going to lose much sleep if on a vacation job, packing articles into containers, the boss tells him he is inefficient and useless at the task.

The strength of the appraisal of others to effect change in the recipient's self concept in a positive direction would be most potent when the evaluator is personalistic in approach, is credible, is consistent in his evaluation, provides evaluation frequently and indicates positive points.

However, this analysis only offers an image of man as a passive reflection of the opinions of others. A more active technique available is that of social comparison in which our evaluated image is constructed by comparing ourselves to others, frequently peers, since they possess the attributes important to us. Festinger (1954) suggests that validity of self assessment is tested by comparison with the beliefs and attitudes of others. Applying James' formula of self esteem equals success divided by pretensions, the assessment of success is central, and this is where subjective interpretation of standards and comparison with objective standards come in. For example subjective interpretation is involved where an adolescent girl finds herself uninvited to a dance all her friends have been dated for. Is this a reflection of her beauty, dancing ability, sociability or what? She is likely to feel below par on all these compared to her friends. Objective standards exist in school, sporting activities, job performance, etc. It is painfully obvious for many how they compare to set standards of attainment in diverse areas.

Finally, in interpersonal transactions the focusing in on one subject while ignoring the others involved provides an inaccurate analysis, suggesting a one-way flow of self-referent information. Human life involves others; transactions influence all parties. The self concepts of all participants in social relationships are subject to modification. Each perceives the other as well as perceiving the other perceiving him, producing an idea of what the other thinks of him. A cyclic and complicated network of interpreted feedback is operating in all relationships. Laing, Phillipson and Lee (1966) have produced a detailed analysis of this process involving meta and meta-meta perspectives. Changing one's perceptual set or the meanings we attach to people and events is one major way of improving perception of others. Don't treat individuals on the basis of stereotypes or prearranged categories. A hippy is not necessarily grubby; a bald man is not necessarily old; an effeminate man is not necessarily a homosexual; a coloured person is not necessarily unintelligent. In other words treat each person as an individual and not as a category. Another vital element in improving social relationships is to try and understand the perceptions of others and the idiosyncratic meaning they apply to experience. Reduce your egocentricity as much as possible. Exposure to and understanding of the perspectives of others may enable self perceptions to modify too.

E. The self-concept: cultural disadvantage and minority ethnic group membership

There is a classical and entrenched view, particularly in the USA, that the self esteem of disadvantaged coloured persons is lower than that of whites. The former are presumed on both common-sense and experimental grounds (e.g. Clark and Clark, 1958) to receive many negative evaluations from significant others, and to face societal barriers. Disadvantaged children (usually coloured) are regarded as likely victims of low self concepts because of discrimination, poverty, majority group expectations and unstimulating environmental conditions. These conditions are supposed to lead to a denigration of self worth (e.g. Witty, 1967; Tannenbaum, 1967). Coopersmith (in Verma and Bagley, 1975) chides his fellow psychologists for their impressionistic and intuitive writings about black self esteem before the 1960s.

In a very real sense much of what has been written about black self-esteem is based on inferences made by white psychologists concerned with suffering and human dignity and willing to accept those inferences without direct investigation. Viewed in historical perspective the direct examination of black self-esteem is a very recent event and almost all of the studies before 1960 were descriptive and impressionistic in nature. (p. 154)

The pen portraits produced were of coloured persons overwhelmed by powerlessness, rejection, isolation and discrimination with corollaries of identity confusions, low self esteem, feelings of incompetence, etc, all drawn with considerable poetic licence. However, most recent experimental studies reveal that disadvantaged children not only possess positive self concepts but sometimes higher self concepts than advantaged groups (e.g. Trowbridge, 1970; Soares and Soares, 1969). The latter workers suggest that this occurs because most disadvantaged children are exposed only to other disadvantaged people and neighbourhoods. According to the expectations of such a subculture, they function satisfactorily. In contrast, advantaged children have higher expectations to live up to. Carter's (1968) study of Mexican-Americans who possessed positive self concepts showed that they related themselves to their own cultural group and not 'Anglo' society. Merely because the white advantaged groups look on the coloured disadvantaged groups in a negative fashion, there is no reason to assume the latter look at themselves in the same way. Their significant others are part and parcel of their own environment. Rosenberg (1965) noted that 'negroes, who are exposed to the most intense humiliating and crippling forms of discrimination in virtually every institutional area do not have particularly low self esteem' (pp. 56–7).

Soares and Soares (1971) found that the change from neighbourhood schools to high schools, with its greater competitiveness on societal rather than subcultural standards, and its lesser security contributed to the lowering of self esteem of disadvantaged and advantaged pupils alike.

In an evaluation of other data on the issue of black self esteem Rosenberg (1973) reveals another dozen studies which also find minimal or no differences between the self esteem of black and white children. The available evidence suggests that either the self esteem of the negro has increased markedly in the last decade or that the inferences gained from observations of the black experience are discordant with and unsupported by more direct evaluation.

All this led Heiss and Owens (1972) to recast the traditional premise and suggested several alternative hypotheses by taking account of

(*a*) social class variables;
(*b*) specific areas of self evaluation rather than a global evaluation; and
(*c*) the negro reference group.

Essentially they contended that it is wrong to assume that all coloured persons use whites as significant others; the evaluations of other coloured persons are more relevant, paralleling the situation where whites evaluate themselves against other whites. The criteria of worth may well be achievable subcultural norms, rather than those of the dominant white society. Additionally, blacks can blame 'the system' in order to insulate themselves further against low self esteem. When social class is introduced into this argument it can be seen that the argument has greater applicability to lower-class blacks than middle-class ones. The middle-class coloured person is less able to use the face-saving devices noted above, as his reference group is more likely to be the white community with 'white' criteria of worth being applied. Hence it is possible to hypothesise that lower-class coloured people will manifest higher self esteem than lower-class white people, while middle-class coloured people will manifest lower self esteem than middle-class whites.

Some traits to which blacks apply self evaluation are of little concern for whites or for wider society, e.g. performance as parent, as spouse, as conversationalist, attractiveness to opposite sex and athletic ability. Other traits such as those operating in the world of work and education are subject to society's norms, i.e. white norms. With low evaluations in terms of the white measuring rod, all blacks irrespective of social class should be affected, producing low self esteem in these latter areas. Heiss and Owens (1972) tested these ideas with a sample of over 4,000 coloured persons and over 4,200 whites.

For four traits, viz: evaluation of self as an offspring, parent, spouse and conversationalist, expectations are borne out. There are essentially no differences in the total sample. The slight differences in the lower social class all favour the black respondents. In the higher social class groups the racial differences are again negligible. In sum, the data for these variables are consistent with expectations. On attractiveness there is no racial difference in the low social class, but middle-class negroes rate themselves higher in attractiveness than do middle-class whites. Thus, coloured persons do not consider themselves unattractive as might have been thought. But when work and educational related traits are involved whites do rate themselves higher in both social groups than black persons rate themselves. This supports the accepted beliefs since many of the relevant evaluations come from the majority community. In summary, findings indicate that the relationship between the self evaluations of blacks and whites varies depending upon the traits involved. For characteristics such as performance of family roles there is no difference in the higher social class and a difference favouring blacks in the lower-status group. For other traits, such as willingness to work hard, there is a tendency for whites to rate themselves higher. The differences in the trends relate to variations in the nature of the significant others, variations in the likelihood of using dominant society standards, and differences in the availability of a system-blame explanation. The general trend of the data seems to permit a tentative acceptance of these factors. One important finding is the small size of the differences. There was a general similarity of the white and black subjects. What difference does exist in Heiss and Owens' study is to be found in the proportions who rate themselves above average. On most traits, very few in both groups rate themselves below average. There is no evidence here that blacks are 'crippled' by low self evaluations. All in all, it would seem that the traditional view distorts the situation beyond recognition. Of course, this use of a reference group to maintain a coloured person's level of self esteem is facilitated by such a person seeing around him in contemporary society a growing body of evidence such as coloured persons in influential positions, as successful business and professional people. So the rejection of a negative stereotype and its replacement by a positive form is nurtured, especially by the activities of coloured organisations.

A study by Bruch, Kunce and Eggeman (1972) also points to the problem of interpreting self-concept scores in isolation without considering other factors. In their study, coloured disadvantaged students had higher self-esteem scores than advantaged white students. In a more detailed analysis of the data they found that older students showed less esteem for father than younger ones. But the disadvantaged's high self esteem appeared to be a form of bluffing or overestimation of attributes which also led to a devaluation of others, producing greater discrepancies between attitudes to self and attitudes to parents. This discrepancy is claimed to occur because the disadvantaged youths are more predisposed to parental devaluation as a preparation for independence shortly to impose itself on them. Advantaged students may have had better preparation for the future and need not devalue parents as a defence mechanism to enhance their own self concept to cover up worries about capabilities of handling the future. As a result white students' self esteem was on average not as high as the black disadvantaged ones.

Even in South Africa, Momberg and Page (1977) using Coopersmith's scale could discern no significant difference between English, Afrikaner and Coloured self esteem among school and university students, save between Afrikaner and Coloured 12-year-old pupils. Their conclusion was that being Coloured or Afrikaner did not affect self esteem. Studies in Britain, too, on the self concepts of various immigrant groups reveal a similar pattern in that scarcely any differences can be noted between the self concepts of various immigrant groups and white persons, though admittedly the research has only involved samples of children. For example Louden (1977) was unable to discern any significant differences in self esteem between Asian, West Indian and English adolescents. Verma (Verma and Bagley, 1975) reports using Coopersmith's Self Esteem Inventory to collect data on Asian, West Indian and white children attending British multiracial secondary schools. There were no statistically significant differences between any of the groups, though the West Indians tended to manifest slightly lower self esteem than the other two groups. Perhaps this is because even in Britain most coloured people reside in predominantly coloured neighbourhoods; they live with others who partake of their culture and who share their social experience. Significant others are highly likely to support and purvey standards, attitudes and perceptions consonant with those held by the individual. They do not see the immigrant condition from the perspective of educated and sympathetic white people.

Ziller *et al.* (1968) discerned results opposite to conventional expectations when Indians in the lowest castes produced significantly higher self-esteem scores than members of higher castes. It was suggested by the investigators that these low-caste children were comparing themselves with children of their own caste and within such a limited frame of reference they could register high self esteem. Again, as with the negroes in Heiss and Owens' (1972) study, self esteem is determined by the population defined as the significant other. The Indian pupils even had a higher mean self esteem than American pupils. This was ascribed to the fact that since school attendance is a privilege in India, these pupils felt rather select.

Degree of assimilation of the host or majority culture also influences self esteem. In a study of degree of acculturalisation of Red Indian reservation children Lefley (1974) showed that self esteem was significantly lower in Seminole children who had assimilated white culture than in Miccosickee children whose tribe had maintained their own culture. It suggests again that exposure to the dominant culture and evaluation against the norms of that culture imparts a message of inferiority. In both Indian groups the older children manifested lower self esteem than the younger ones, which may reflect greater exposure to majority culture with age. Many of the pieces of research noted above suggest implicitly that minority groups which attempt to maintain cultural solidarity and integrity are better able to maintain self esteem. Otherwise standards, values and significant others are increasingly likely to be those of the majority culture.

F. The self concept: locus of control and field independence

(a) Locus of control

An interesting variable that would appear on armchair analysis to have some bearing on how a person perceives himself, on how he reacts to others and on how he feels others affect him, is the concept of locus on control. Some people perceive their behaviour and environment as under external control, e.g. by luck, chance, unknown but powerful others, authority, etc; other people believe that they have more control over their own destinies, so that internal control via skill, ability, experience and inherent potential is used to control behaviour and influence events. Theoretically, the attitudes a person holds about himself should bear some relation to this locus of control dichotomy. A person who feels insecure, lacking in self worth and low in feelings of personal adequacy, should be oriented towards external control rather than internal control. The high-self-esteem person, with his positive sense of adequacy should feel more in control of what he does and what happens to him rather than under control from outside forces. Externals may not only perceive a lack of own control but actively seek external control, because of their feelings of personal inadequacy.

In a verbal memory task during which subjects were required to self evaluate their performance on the first test then self evaluate and self reinforce on the second, Bellak (1975) found that externals produced lower self evaluation. Such externals seemed to believe that their behaviour was not effective in securing results and was dependent on external reinforcement for evaluation of behaviour.

Externals are also depicted as having difficulty with interpersonal relations (McDonald, 1971), with low self evaluation (Hersch and Schiebe, 1969), and with poor personal adjustment (Warehime and Foulds, 1971). Externals also manifest large discrepancies between self and ideal and perceive internal control as their ideal (Lombardo, Saverio and Solheim, 1975). The latter researchers also found externals manifesting less self acceptance than internals. Dua (1970), using a behaviourally oriented psychotherapy programme with externals, found that as a significant reduction in externality occurred so too were self attitudes and attitudes to others improved. Chandler (1976) also noted a significant relationship between feeling controlled by external events and low self concepts.

(b) Field dependence/independence

Field dependence/independence also shows an association with self conception. Witkin (1949; 1965) identified a mode of perceiving in which the perceiver focuses on the stimulus object and can ignore and resist the influence of the background in which it is set. This is the mode of the field-independent person. The field-dependent person is markedly affected by variation in background, slower in perceiving the stimulus object. Witkin discerned that field-dependent persons were inclined to be passive, submissive and low in self esteem. They were very dependent on external supports, and felt influenced by externalities. Field-independent persons tended to be independent, less anxious, high in self esteem, felt adequate and competent and in control of events. There is thus a set of parallels between field dependence, independence, external–internal locus of control and low–high self esteem. The undermining factor for this set of relationships appears to be child-rearing practices. Witkin found that field dependents tended to come from homes which were restrictive, required conformity and discouraged curiosity. Field-independent children were encouraged to be responsible and independent within a secure environment. These 'home' characteristics are similar to those which respectively debilitate or enhance the self concept. (Ch. 7).

G. The self concept and anxiety

The relationships between levels of anxiety and self conception are clouded by social desirability. Research generally tends to reveal a negative relationship, i.e. high levels of self esteem are concomitant with low levels of anxiety. For example, with college females Mitchell (1959) concluded that the better the self concept the less anxiety manifested. In a study involving a comparison between high- and low-self-esteem subjects, Lamp (1968) observed that the low-self-esteem subjects were higher in anxiety than the high-self-esteem subjects. Similarly, studies by Wittrock and Husek (1962), Coopersmith (1967), and Ausubel and Robinson (1969) have provided evidence that a negative relationship between level of anxiety and favourableness of self concept or self esteem appears to exist.

Lipsitt (1958) applying his own rating scale and the Children's Manifest Anxiety scale 300 9–11 year olds was able to report highly significant negative relationships, with the self-disparaging child admitting more to the possession of symptoms held to reflect anxiety. Similar work and results are reported by Many and Many (1975) and Furlong and LaForge (1975). The investigation of Many and Many (1975) utilised a sample of over 4,000 children who sat Coopersmith's measure of self esteem and two measures of anxiety. All the correlations between self esteem and anxiety were negative, confirming many previous findings. Similarly, Feldhusen and Thurston (1964) produced evidence of better integration of self concept in less anxious children, integration referring to realistic, organised and accepting psychological responses to self and to self in relation to others. The anxious child may be less free to examine his own behaviour and self conceptions which may preclude his acquiring of a realistic self conception.

Rosenberg (1965), too, was able to discern anxiety as a corollary of low self esteem in adolescents. His low-self-esteem subjects were more likely to report experiencing various physiological indicators of anxiety such as hand trembling, sick headaches, heart pounding, etc. Rosenberg argues that anxiety tends to generate low self esteem, as Horney postulated with her concept of basic anxiety, but he subscribes also to the view that for some subjects low self esteem produces anxiety through the operation of four conditions:

(a) Unstable and fluctuating self images of low-self-esteem persons creates anxiety.

(b) Low-self-esteem persons frequently have to present a false front to the world. This is a strain, creates tension and results in anxiety.

(c) Low self esteem makes a person sensitive to evidence that confirms his inadequacy. This vulnerability is anxiety provoking.

(d) Worthlessness and inadequacy creates isolation, both physical and emotional from others. As we have seen previously, a low-self-esteem person cannot share himself with others. Life has to be faced alone, but this is a source of anxiety.

The relationship between low self concepts and anxiety can also have its origins in the learning of negative attributes. For instance, if a child is told he is fat and this verbal stimulus is accompanied by other children or even parents taunting him unkindly, the latter acts may generate responses of anxiety/insecurity. By a classical conditioning paradigm it is quite a simple step to show that the thought stimulus 'I am fat' will elicit the same response of anxiety. So the learning situation involving negative connotations also usually involves negative anxiety responses.

However, a major problem which may be masking the true relationship is that of social desirability. Anxiety scales are highly correlated with social desirability (Edwards, 1957). Highly anxious subjects have a strong tendency to choose socially undesirable traits when providing self descriptions in what appears to be an attempt to show how much they seek help and counselling. Other subjects will produce culturally good accounts on both. Another related problem is that similar statements are presented in both types of scale, thus spuriously raising correlations, i.e. in measuring self conception and anxiety the same response can be an index of both. For instance if a subject reports on a self-concept scale that he is 'a worrier' or 'a failure' or 'indecisive', he notches up a point towards low self esteem, but similarly on an anxiety scale those qualities equally increase anxiety scores. The relationship may thus be an artifact of social desirability and similarity of test content. Cowen *et al.* (1957) revealed something of this contamination when they conducted a lie scale analysis of self-concept data.

Subjects with high lie scores produced better self-concept scores
than subjects with low lie scores. When anxiety was held constant
by comparing high and low 'liers' in a low anxiety group, high lie
subjects continued to have better 'adjusted' self-concept scores.
Furlong and LaForge (1975) with an adult sample showed in an
analysis of items that anxiety is related to self description,
particularly on tension, worry and steadiness areas, but tends not
to show any relationship to self-descriptive items for which social
desirability is not clear-cut, or for intellectual efficiency and
physical attractiveness.

H. The self concept and occupational choice

A major approach to vocational guidance and occupational choice
has been to view individuals in a given vocation as sharing a
common personality and common needs. The dominant theory
along these lines is that of Super *et al.* (1963) who identify the self
concept as the determinant of job choice, so that an individual's
occupation and the picture of the kind of person he is will be
compatible. Super's theory of vocational development views each
person as moving through a series of life stages each of which is
characterised by a different vocational developmental task with the
final selection of a vocation reflecting the thoroughness with which
he has implemented his self concept into the world of work.
Vocational development becomes synonymous with the
development of the self concept. Vocational adjustment depends
on the implementation of this self concept. Super's five life stages
are outlined in the following sequence.

1. Growth stage (birth—14)
The self concept develops through identification with key figures in
family and in school; needs and fantasy are dominant early in this
stage; interest and capacity become more important in this stage
with increasing social participation and reality-testing. Substages of
the growth stage are:

Fantasy (4—10).   Needs are dominant; role-playing in fantasy is
   important.

Interests (11—12).   Likes are the major determinant of aspirations
   and activities.

Capacity (13—14).   Abilities are given more weight, and job
   requirements (including training) are considered.

2. Exploration stage (age 15—24)
Self-examination, role tryouts and occupational exploration take

place in school, leisure activities, and part-time work.
Substages of the exploration stage are:

Tentative (15—17).   Needs, interests, capacities, values and
   opportunities are all considered. Tentative choices are made and
   tried out in fantasy, discussion, courses, work, etc.

Transition (18—21).   Reality considerations are given more weight
   as the youth enters labour market or professional training and
   attempts to implement a self concept.

Trial (22—24).   A seemingly appropriate field having been
   located, a beginning job in it is found and is tried out as a life
   work.

3. *Establishment stage (age 25—44).*
Having found an appropriate field, effort is put forth to make a
permanent place in it. There may be some trial early in this stage
with consequent shifting, but establishment may begin without
trial, especially in the professions. Substages of the establishment
stage are:

Trial (25—30).   The field of work presumed to be suitable may
   prove unsatisfactory, resulting in one or two changes before the
   life work is found or before it becomes clear that the life work
   will be a succession of unrelated jobs.

Stabilisation (31—44).   As the career pattern becomes clear, effort
   is put forth to stabilise, to make a secure place, in the world of
   work. For most persons these are the creative years.

4. *Maintenance stage (age 45—64).*
Having made a place in the world of work, the concern is now to
hold it. Little new ground is broken, but there is continuation
along established lines.

5. *Decline stage (age 65 and on).*
As physical and mental powers decline, work activity changes and
in due course ceases. New roles must be developed; first that of
selective participant and then that of observer rather than
participant.
Substages of this stage are:

Deceleration (65—70).   Sometimes at the time of official
   retirement, sometimes late in the maintenance stage, the pace of
   work slackens, duties are shifted, or the nature of the work is
   changed to suit declining capacities. Many men find part-time
   jobs to replace their full-time occupations.

Retirement (71 on).   As with all the specified age limits, there are
great variations from person to person. But complete cessation
of occupation comes for all in due course, to some easily and
pleasantly, to others with difficulty and disappointment, and to
some only with death.

The eighth, ninth and tenth propositions of Super's theory are
centrally concerned with self conception.

Eighth proposition:

The Process of Vocational Development is Essentially that of Developing
and Implementing a Self-concept: it is a Compromise Process in which the
Self-concept is a Product of the Interaction of Inherited Aptitudes, Neural
and Endocrinal Make-up, the Opportunity to play Various Roles and
Evaluations of the Extent to Which the Results of the Role Playing Meet
with the Approval of Supervisors and Fellows.

The development of one's self concept takes place through
life's experiences. It is moulded by the reactions of others. In
adolescence a person is drawn towards those activities which
facilitate the projection of the image the person would like others
to have of him. This can be stated in terms of trying to achieve an
ideal. Invariably society does not submit allowing the individual to
mould it to his will. It is the individual who must compromise and
accept something less than his ideal.

Super sees this coming to terms with the realities of life's
possibilities as the central problem of vocational choice.

Ninth proposition:

The Process of Compromise Between Individual and Social Factors,
Between Self-concept and Reality is one of role Playing Whether the Role
is Played in Fantasy in the Councelling Interviews, or in Real Life
activities such as School Classes, Clubs, Part time Work and Entry Jobs.

Opportunities for actually trying out various occupational roles
are limited. The individual must therefore try out roles in
imaginary situations in order to test them against his self concept.
He uses a variety of sources for information – home peers, friends
and acquaintances in employment, the mass media, the school,
careers officer and so on. Many of these sources fail to present a
true picture to the person and mismatching with resultant friction
takes place.

Tenth proposition:

Work Satisfaction and Life Satisfactions Depend upon the Extent to
Which the Individual Finds Adequate Outlets for his Abilities, Interests,
Personality Traits, and Values: they Depend upon his Establishment in a
Type of Work, or Work Situation, and a way of Life in Which he can Play

and Kind of Role Which his Growth and Exploratory Experiences have led him to Consider Congenial and Appropriate.

Super argues that satisfaction in an occupation depends upon the extent to which the work and the way of life which goes with it enables the individual to play the kind of role he wants to play. In this respect his conclusion has similarities to elements of Festinger's theory of cognitive dissonance and Rogers' theory of personality.

This point, however, suggests that a person may become reconciled to an occupation for which he is mismatched if he is nevertheless correctly matched in other aspects of his life. This conclusion is in keeping with Super's view that vocational development cannot be separated from life development.

In many respects what Super writes is rather banal and obvious. His stages merely repeat a truism that people know more about occupations as they get older. The search for an occupation which fits in with the self concept and the compromises which must inevitably occur is sound if rather obvious. However, his attempt to integrate the self concept into vocational guidance is welcome as a stimulus to further research in that area, for neither self image nor self esteem can be ignored in attempting to prevent 'square pegs being fitted into round holes'. A number of studies have in fact investigated self conception and career choice. Putnam and Hansen (1972) showed that their female subjects chose feminine role concepts which were consistent with self concept, though only 10 per cent of the vocational-maturity score could be accounted for by self-concept score.

Soares and Soares (1966) studied students training to be teachers of three different subjects to discern whether they possessed different self concepts. The results indicated that persons in the three subject areas could be so differentiated.

Science males – self confident, self-sufficient detachment, cautiousness, individualistic.
Science females – enthusiastic, critical, idealistic, considerate, perfectionist.
Music males – impulsive, sensitive, indecisive, worried, self sufficient.
Music females – considerate, enthusiastic, extroverted, sensitive.
PE males – very self confident, very self sufficient, tough, deliberate, socially adjusted, aggressive, individualistic.
PE females – very enthusiastic, very considerate, outgoing, sensitive, ambitious, reject female role, adventurous.

But whether (and to what degree) these characteristics are present in the individual before he chooses a major field, whether they are reinforced as he gradually becomes involved in the area, or whether interest in certain regions of concentration prompt the emergence of various personality traits for fulfilment, are all moot questions. It is probable that individuals are in related fields because they have similar personality characteristics, similar needs and manifest a similar pattern of social adjustment. However, though the goal of teaching may be a common denominator, future teachers do seem to be differentiated according to their specific teaching area.

Evidence that persons' different occupations have self images which reflect the characteristics required in those careers also comes from studies by Reich and Geller (1976a, 1976b). In their first study they found the nurses described themselves as serious, cautious, industrious and methodical with a capacity to relate to others. But whereas previous studies of nurses (e.g. Davis, 1969) also showed that nurses were submissive and timid, Reich and Geller's (1976a) nurses portrayed themselves as more aggressive, confident and assertive than the norm (Adjective Check List, Gough and Heilbron, 1965) and significantly lower than the norm on dependence on other's help. It may be that the choice of nursing as a career is in part the outcome of strongly denied dependency needs. The changes in the nurses' self image over the last decade suggests that notions of the role of nurses has changed. Obedience to rules is less important now than independence, with the opportunity to make decisions in the wards.

In their second study (Reich and Geller, 1976b) social workers completed the Adjective Check List and portrayed themselves as industrious, self confident, friendly. However, they scored significantly below the norm for affiliation, indicating some unease in situations of prolonged contact with others. It seems that determination to do well, to succeed in goal-directed pursuits motivates them more than their desire to care for others in selecting a career in social work. Again, although social work is a helping profession the subjects scored no higher than the norm on nurturance, which measures degree of benevolence and solicitous behaviour offered to others.

Watkins (1975) tested the hypothesis that self esteem influences vocational choice, in that an individual selects a career which is need-fulfilling and in which he expects to be adequate. This hypothesis was originally outlined by Korman (1966, 1969) and differs from Super's in its prediction about low-self-esteem persons. By Korman's theory a person of high self esteem (who consequently perceives himself as need-fulfilling and adequate) is likely to choose a vocation which will satisfy his needs and in which he will be adequate because such a vocation is in balance with his self perception. On the other hand, a low-self-esteem person is characterised by a sense of personal inadequacy and an inability to achieve need satisfaction in the past. Such a person, Korman argues, is likely to choose an occupation which he knows will neither satisfy his needs nor suit his abilities. Korman's (1966) results supported his hypothesis and he concluded that they provided 'negative evidence for a simple "match self to occupational stereotype" process in vocational choice' (p. 485).

Watkins' results did not support Korman's view. Rather his data seem to indicate that both the high- and the low-self-esteem student teachers have chosen an occupation that they perceive as suiting their abilities and as likely to satisfy their most important occupationl needs. These findings are in accord with Super's self-implementation theory of vocational choice which Korman considers an oversimplification. While Watkins' evidence, based solely on a sample of student teachers, cannot be considered as refuting Korman's position, it can perhaps be regarded as casting doubt on its validity. Far more support needs to be found for Korman's hypothesis than is at present the case.

I. The self concept: smoking and drug use in adolescence

Adolescents who smoke possess a self concept which contains several different elements from that of the non-smoking schoolboy (McKennell and Bynner, 1969). Attitudes to toughness, precocity and educational success are the differentiating ones. The typical smoker sees himself as tough and the non-smoker as being immature and lacking toughness. This suggests adolescents are attracted to smoking behaviour by the toughness it represents. Precocity is also seen as an attribute of the young smoker. This precocity refers in the study to specialised interest in attracting the opposite sex. While all the pupils in the study valued educational success, the smokers saw themselves as failures in that area with non-smokers seen as successes. The non-smokers rated themselves high on educational success. Smoking with its connotations of toughness and maturity provides a compensatory image to offset a less favourable academic image. All this suggests that attempts to make anti-smoking appeals will be more effective if smokers could be encouraged to alter their perceptions of the non-smoker to one where the latter is perceived as not lacking in toughness, masculinity and maturity, and if some academic success could come their way through a suitable structuring of the work with reinforcement given for improving on previous best performances.

The use of drugs and alcohol is seen as two major problems in adolescent culture. Generally studies of adolescent alcoholics show personality differences between alcoholics and non-drinkers, e.g. Braught *et al.* (1973), but there appear no discernible differences in personality between drug users and non-drug users. In studies

using self-concept measures Simon *et al.* (1974) and Peterson
(1972) found no differences in levels of self esteem between
marijuana users and non-users. While Demeritt (1970) and
Schaeffer, Schukit and Monissey (1976) found no differences
between general drug use and self-esteem, studies of heavy and
non-use of alcohol reveal that alcoholics generally possess lower
self concepts than non-drinkers, with alcoholics perceiving
themselves as aggressive, impulsive, anxious and depressed, e.g.
Brill, Crumpton and Grayson (1971); Krug and Henry (1974);
Schaeffer, Schukit and Morrissey (1976). Only one study reveals a
relationship between self conception and drugs, but this
investigation (Brehm and Back, 1968) was concerned not with
drug users but with non-users and their attitudes to drugs. Those
subjects with a low self esteem who devalued their self image and
had a great desire to change their image were more willing to
accept the use of drugs to effect this hope for change. Only fear of
bodily damage and lack of control would be seen as acting as
restraints. This research may explain why no differences are found
between drug users and non-users, since the low self concepts of
those with positive attitudes to drug taking may, on becoming drug
addicts, lose the self doubt, impotence and unhappiness that
plagued their lives previously. Thus a drug-induced increase in self
esteem is not an untenable supposition, though no actual proof yet
exists.

J. The self concept and delinquency

Sociologists tend to view delinquency simplistically, as a lower
socioeconomic or subcultural problem. This fails to explain why
not all lower-class juveniles become delinquent and why conditions
which supposedly give rise to delinquency do also produce in many
youngsters responsible productive behaviour. Some part of the task
of explaining delinquency must invoke psychological phenomena.
Reckless, Dinitz and Murray (1956) introduced the notion of the
self concept as an insulator against delinquency after finding that
pupils with a positive self concept were unlikely to become
delinquent.

  Deitz (1969) investigated the possibility that delinquency
represents internalised conflict which disturbs the delinquent's
relations with himself and with members of society. But
delinquents in his study were not found to possess lower self
concepts than non-delinquent controls as measured on a semantic
differential. This may have arisen because this instrument fails to
penetrate the delinquent defence system which may be more
impermeable than the non-delinquent one, for other workers, e.g.
David and Lawton (1961), using projective devices have discerned

lower delinquent self concepts. Deitz's delinquents did reveal significantly less self acceptance than the control group.

Thompson (1974) also notes that normal and delinquent adolescents do not vary greatly in self-concept level; however, the older delinquents saw themselves as perceived far less favourably by others than did the 'normals'. As a result the delinquents tended to be peer oriented since only their chosen friends tended not to undervalue them.

As has been noted already, lack of self acceptance strongly relates to inability to accept others, but whether this can be translated into a need for aggression towards others and symbolically towards society is conjectural. Non-delinquents displayed closer identification with parents than delinquents in Deitz's study. This suggests disturbed parent–child relationships have possible ecological relevance in the development of delinquency. It was argued in Chapter 6 that identification, especially with correct sex role, plays an important part in self-concept development. Parents should be nurturant, competent, non-competitive with one another and should manifest sexually appropriate traits. Since one's self concept is infused with sexual components, it is necessary for males in relating both to women and men in adult life to have the benefit of internalised dispositions that result from close and intimate interaction with a competent and rewarding father whose behaviour approximates the socially desired role. The mother is an equally important participant in this enterprise. Through the personification of a misinterpreted role she can debilitate the father–son attachment and undermine the son's self identity to the extent that it may result in unstable interpersonal relationships.

Paternal rejection would be one of the suspected reasons for the lack of parental identification, yet delinquents do not perceive themselves as being more rejected by their fathers than do non-delinquents. A tentative explanation is that rejection is only one of the conditions of weak parental identification. The image of competence that the father presents in this ongoing process is equally important. Thus, even in lieu of perceived paternal rejection, a lack of competence or mastery could weaken the father–son attachment. Delinquents also see themselves as inaccurately perceived by parents (Deitz, 1969; Thompson, 1974). This discrepancy between cognised and other self is a source of maladjustment. A pattern of delinquent dynamics begins to take shape. Delinquents are less self accepting, identify less with parents and feel less understood by parents than non-delinquents. The core of their problem appears to be self denigration and rejection. Self rejection and perceived rejection by others go hand in hand as usual. Changes in self concept are noted by Eitzen (1976) in delinquents who have undergone behaviour modification. This shift was strongly positive, and was concomitant with a shift in how the delinquents now perceived significant others evaluating them, and as noted earlier this perception by others provides a source of discrepancy in the self concepts of delinquents. This approval from others changed the content of the self-fulfilling prophecy.

Parental styles in delinquent homes usually display features noted by Coopersmith in the home background of low-self-esteem boys. For instance, they are erratic, unpredictable and contain little evidence of any genuine interest in children. Often the father is rejected as a model by the son because of the former's weakness, drunkenness or authoritarianism. Many delinquents find their delinquent behaviour the only way to display some measure of competence at something. Shore, Masimo and Ricks (1965) showed that by changing delinquents' feelings about their competence, generally their self esteem changed for the better, and this in turn preceded changes in the perception of authority figures.

Hurlock (1967) in a review of investigations on delinquency notes that an unrealistic self concept is likely to be associated with delinquency since it increases the probability that the child 'will try to compensate for the feelings of inadequacy that come from falling short of an unrealistic self image by behaviour that deviates from the socially accepted pattern' (p. 458).

So self perceptions and inferred perceptions of others promote delinquent behaviour as a means whereby working-class boys recoup self esteem lost through deafeat in middle-class institutions on middle-class terms. The expectancy effect is particularly strong, too, for a delinquent producing behaviour that validates the expectancy. Once in trouble it is difficult to avoid future trouble; everyone expects it. So the delinquent has stamped into him by social pressure a concept of himself as a delinquent, behaving in ways that people (peers, police, neighbours, teachers, etc) in his neighbourhood expect him to do. Many ex-gaolbirds do try to mend their ways, but society's negative attitudes to them merely confirm their self concepts, and behaviour congruent with this image is likely to occur.

Some juvenile delinquents have distorted body images stemming from sex-inappropriate builds. Their anti-social activities are regarded by many investigators (e.g. Glueck and Glueck, 1950) as an attempt to compensate for the unfavourable impression they believe they have on others. Dishonest behaviour was shown by Aronson and Mettee (1968) to be a function of self esteem. They gave subjects false feedback aimed at temporarily inducing either an increase in self esteem, a decrease in self esteem or no change in their self esteem. They were then allowed to participate in a game of cards, in the course of which they were provided with opportunities to cheat under circumstances which made it appear impossible to be detected. Significantly more people cheated in the low-self-esteem condition than in the high-self-esteem condition. The results were interpreted in terms of cognitive consistency theory in that high self esteem acts as a barrier against dishonest behaviour because such behaviour is inconsistent with the self picture. In effect, if a person is tempted to cheat it will prove easier for him to yield to this temptation if his self esteem is low; cheating is not as inconsistent a behaviour for those of low self esteem. It may be the desire for consistency rather than the lack of ethics that motivates the low-self-esteem person. He may cheat to lose; in this way he maintains his view of himself as a loser and failure. The high-self-esteem person has less need to cheat because he generally feels competent to succeed.

Roberts (1972) made a study of the self images of delinquent adolescent girls in New Zealand. Using the 'Who Am I?' technique, Roberts found an indication that the younger the girl when her life was first disrupted by home breakup the more adverse the effect on her self image. Vagrants had poorer self images than thieves, as had girls whose previous history included earlier custodial treatment. Girls with higher self images tended not to be reconvicted, whereas girls with low self images tended to be reconvicted and not outlast their parole year. More intelligent delinquents had higher self images while poor self images were associated with any kind of physical handicap. A group of controls had higher self images than the delinquents and were more certain of their identification as women.

Thus the complex aetiology of delinquency contains many elements of inadequate self conception, of self images at variance with the images others hold, of less clear sexual identification, with resulting in antisocial attempts to regain esteem. A shift in self image that leads to perceptions that others, particularly parents and teachers, view one more positively seems likely to create more socially approved behaviour.

K. Self concept and illness

Two studies by Schmale (1958) and Canter (1960) suggest that one's attitude towards life and self are factors both in the onset of illness and in the recovery therefrom. These studies serve nicely as a point of departure for a discussion of a revolution which is going on in current thinking about wellness and disease, a revolution that has profound implications for practitioners in the healing professions. Schmale's and Canter's work suggest that if we want to find psychological factors that predispose towards lowered resistance to illness, that foster reduced effectiveness in living, we should look into transactions and events in everyday life that produce a sense of hopelessness, such as a loss of the sense of identity and self esteem, loneliness-producing events or ways of life.

Events that make a person feel unimportant, worthless and low in self esteem render him vulnerable to forces of illness. Sickness, whether mental or physical, may be a way in which individuals express hopelessness against their current way of life. They are more receptive to stress and viruses because their whole being is sick, with lowered resistance to any complaint that is around. Psychosomatic illnesses are a major result of the inability of a person to cope, and adjust his self concept to experience and behaviour. They enable withdrawal to occur with quite justifiable reasons as far as the sufferer is concerned. Sickness provides a temporary respite from pitting the self concept against situations in which it cannot stand judgement. The healing powers of self re-evaluation and of behavioural change are hardly ever prescribed; faith is placed in the power of drugs. Faith in self, confidence, more positive self feelings have healing powers, especially when administered through therapies. Money spent by drug companies on temporary alleviation could in some cases be better spent.

It is generally accepted that many forms of psychiatric illness result from various modes of defence against anxiety. Guilt, shame and depression are characteristic features of many neurotics, and psychiatrically ill persons. Hill (1968) noted a debilitating lowering of self esteem in depression. Guilt is seen as inferring depreciation and disapprobation from others. The other self, so strong an element of the self concept, is drastically lowered. Obsessionals suffer from this guilt neurosis. Shame is a deeper disturbance in which the individual questions his total worth as a person, which can occur when feelings and thoughts utterly alien to the person's self concept exist at a conscious level. There is, of course, potentiality for personal development in this if the thoughts can be integrated into an expanding self concept. But the 'sick' person lacks the confidence and assurance to seize this possibility. Personal relationships become impoverished and the depressive, protesting his total worthlessness and sinfulness, imprisons himself to a sentence of crippling intro-punitive torture. Foulds and Bedford (1977) support this view and claim that 'states of anxiety and/or depression are the most common accompaniments and evasions of this deep underlying shame or potentially catastrophic lowering of self esteem' (p. 238). They argue, too, that the paranoid projects blame to defend his self concept while the manic patient denies his problems by developing excessive self esteem.

Psychiatric patients undergoing treatment where the emphasis is placed on 'reality confrontation', i.e. verbal feedback to patients about their behaviour as it appears to others, show self-concept changes. The perceptions of the patient are used as a focal point of the treatment in order to achieve greater reality consensus with members of his community (Kennard and Clemmy, 1976). Most patients saw themselves more positively on discharge, though a reversal effect occurred with a few patients possessing a highly positive self concept on admission changing to a negative one. Such patients were generally schizophrenic or paranoid, and for these the projective defences used to attribute blame are broken down as a result of the reality confrontation technique.

Compared to 'normal' controls, psychiatric patients and neurotics generally have a less favourable self concept (Marks, 1965; Luria, 1959). Another study of neurotic patients by Bond and Lader (1976) again revealed the less favourable self concepts of such persons compared with controls. They saw others as being more relaxed. Their ideal selves were similar to the normal controls' actual self concepts, possibly because they have faith in treatment as a cure for their symptoms in the future.

L. The self concept and physical attraction

An individual's self attitudes have also been cited as a key determinant of romantic love. High self esteem facilitates reciprocal admiration, respect and attraction from an affectionate other, since non-defensive self-accepting individuals are more capable of loving others and experiencing satisfying fulfilling personal relationships, as has been argued by Fromm (1939) for example. However, self-esteem theory would argue that persons low in self esteem would be more receptive to opportunities for romantic love and evaluate a romantic partner more favourably than those with high self esteem who have less need for self esteem. In a major study Dion and Dion (1975) found support for the self-esteem theory, with low-self-concept persons expressing attitudes of greater love, greater liking and more trust towards their romantic partners, evaluating their partners more favourably.

Mathes and Kahn (1975) tested the hypothesis that physical attractiveness is positively correlated with happiness, psychological health and self esteem with 211 men and women undergraduates. Physical attractiveness was measured by judges' ratings, while happiness, psychological health (neuroticism) and self esteem were measured by self-report inventories. Physical attractiveness was found to correlate positively with happiness ($r=0.37$), negatively with neuroticism ($r= -0.22$) and positively with self esteem ($r=0.24$) for women but not for men (corresponding r's$=0.09$, 0.03, and -0.04, respectively). These results were accounted for by the suggestion that physical attractiveness 'buys' more for women than for men, and the most prominent outcomes obtained by physical attractiveness – friends and dates – are of greater value to women undergraduates than men, though the correlation above for women is not strong. The superior outcomes obtained by the attractive women made them happy, psychologically healthy and proud of themselves. Our culture tends to define the successful woman as one who is able to affiliate, whereas the successful man is one who is able to achieve. But generally it would seem that physical attractiveness may help to create a happier, better-adjusted person through the receipt of large doses of positive feedback and acceptance from others. As the correlations in Mathes and Khan's study indicate, physical attractiveness doesn't necessarily imply high self esteem. When a physically attractive person receives favourable feedback but the compliments have little to do with physical attractiveness, the recipient may suspect the sincerity of the complimenter. Such favourable information can well be discounted as it is seen as an attempt to flatter. This difficulty in assessing the meaning of praise creates uncertainty in self evaluation and general worth of physically attractive persons (Sigall and Michela, 1976).

Summary

This brief excursion into some of the behavioural correlates of the self concept illustrates the ubiquity and potency of the self concept in determining the courses of a wide range of behaviours.

Psychotherapy theory and practice as devised by Rogers (1951; 1959; 1961) suggest that the self concept plays a central role in human behaviour, that changes in the self concept produce changes in behaviour, and that the greater the congruence between the self concept and reality the less the person is maladjusted and dissatisfied. Similar effects to those arising from client-centred therapy are also produced by a variety of intensive group experiences. Such therapies are seen as effecting the changes necessary for improving interpersonal relationships. Considerable evidence exists that self conception is strongly related to attitudes to a wide range of others. As therapy improves the self concept, then, as a corollary, attitudes to others improve. The basis of the change depends on conditions being provided within such groups for the participants to be faced with new frames of reference against which to view themselves and others and by which engrained and defended attitudes are induced to change.

The effects of social comparison and evaluation appear to be mediated by each person's need to obtain some measure of self esteem. Self-esteem theory tends to find more support in the experimental setting than self-consistency theory, for generally even those of low self esteem look for positive regard. Manipulation of feedback creates lasting and effective changes in specific self conceptions which can spread to many other areas of self conception, though particular characteristics of the appraiser and the appraisal may downgrade or accentuate the effects of the feedback. Ethnic minorities and adolescent subcultures are cases in point where choice of 'significant other' can mar or improve self esteem.

Further reading

Bugental, J. F. T. (ed.), *Challenges of Humanistic Psychology,* New York: McGraw-Hill, 1967.

Hamachek, Don E. (ed.), *The Self in Growth, Teaching and Learning,* Englewood Cliffs, NJ: Prentice-Hall, 1965.

Hamachek, Don E. (ed.), *Human Dynamics in Psychology and Education,* Boston: Allyn & Bacon, 1968.

Moustakes, C. E., *The Self: Explorations in Personal Growth,* New York: Harper & Row, 1956.

Rogers, C. R. (1959), A theory of therapy personality and interpersonal relations as developed in the client centred framework, in S. Kock (ed.) *Psychology: A Study of a Science,* Vol. **3,** New York: McGraw-Hill, pp. 184–256.

Chapter 9

The self concept
in the context of education

Studies on the self concept have been particularly prolific in two areas (*a*) therapy, and intensive group work (see Ch. 8), and (*b*) education, the focus of this chapter. These two areas have produced a considerable amount of experimental data on the behavioural manifestations of the self concept because of the ready availability of 'captive' subjects on whom research workers can impose themselves. Unfortunately, virtually all the research in this area, as in the rest of the self-concept field, is American. Studies on the self concept in Britain are few indeed.

Aspects of education which have been explored through self-concept studies have tended to be directed towards answering the following general questions:

(*a*) What is the relationship between the pupil's self concept and his academic performance?
(*b*) What roles do feedback, reinforcement and expectations play in modifying self conception and attainment?
(*c*) What is the effect of different forms of school organisation on pupil's self concepts.
(*d*) What is the relationship between the teacher's self concept, and his classroom style.
(*e*) Can modifications of pupil and teacher self concepts through counselling, intensive group work, etc, be made and have these any effect on pupil and teacher classroom performance?

1. The self concept and academic attainment

Although education may superficially appear to be purely a cognitive domain, academic performance is a function of a tangled skein of variables, many of a non-cognitive character, though it takes a perceptive layman to recognise this. How often parents are heard to utter such statements as, 'Mary doesn't do very well at school; she has a low IQ.' Other parents may even get as far as indicting the 'environment' in its various manifestations such as 'home background' or 'neighbourhood' or 'social class'. Until the late 1950s even educationalists had tended to restrict their investigations into the factors influencing academic performance to these variables of IQ, social class, parental interest, etc, despite the recognition that such variables provided only a partial explanation of academic performance. It became apparent that personality–motivational influences needed to be invoked too, the major one seemingly being the self concept, that dynamic and motivating set of attitudes held about oneself.

Another reason why the self concept is currently regarded as a crucial element is that we recognise that education has diverse aims. Concentration on work is now recognised as providing an ill-balanced education. The educated person is not merely a memory bank of academic facts. Physical, social and emotional development are equally within the aegis of the school. This widening of purpose injects self-concept development as a central theme in non-cognitive development, and this is also linked with the all too recent awareness that academic development and progress cannot be considered in isolation from other aspects of human development. Anyone currently concerned with education is forcibly struck by the complexities of the process. In America it was the work of Snygg, Combs and Jersild that publicised the self concept as an important variable influencing the performance of both teacher and taught. The initial impetus in Britain came with the work of Staines (1958) in his careful observation and research into classroom practice from which he was able to conclude that not only was the self concept present in all learning but was also a major outcome of all learning situations, though its presence might pass unnoticed by teachers intent on the inculcation of academic knowledge and skill.

Self concept and personal educational performance seem, even on armchair analysis, to be closely linked. For after all, educational institutions are the arenas in which all young persons are compelled to compete, and in doing so are forced to reveal personal adequacies and inadequacies in public contests, frequently on unequal terms with others in events not even of their own choosing, against externally imposed standards. Given the heavy emphasis on competition and the pressures applied by teachers and most parents on children to achieve success, it isn't surprising that children employ academic attainment as an important index of self worth. The evaluations of others become self evaluations, so that a successful student comes to feel competent and significant, a failing student comes to feel incompetent and inferior. The child's world is school, his basic tasks are school tasks; it is the most salient area of his life, and yet so public, open to inspection by significant others. It is no wonder that with the unavoidability of academic pursuits, the cultural stress on success and the ubiquity of assessment and competition life in school is a patent influence on self esteem. Children arrive at school for the first time with a predisposition towards achievement or failure already engendered by the amount of parental interest, love and acceptance offered them. Each child has formed fairly firm pictures of his self worth which provides him with an array of self expectations about how he will behave in his school work and how others will react to him as a person. Each is already invisibly tagged, some enhancingly by a diet of nourishing interest and affection, and others crippled by a steady downpour of psychic blows from significant others denting, weakening and distorting their self concepts. So children enter the school milieu with a self concept already forming, but still susceptible to modification. Teachers and peer groups begin to replace parents as a major source of self information. With their aura of expertise, authority and evaluation, teachers are 'significant others' who feed the pupils' self concepts with a menu of positive, neutral and negative reinforcement, and create an ethos in the relationship which may enhance or debase academic performance.

Schools stand for even more evaluation than the child has already contended with at home. Appraisal of academic work, of sporting ability, of social behaviour cannot be avoided. Most pupils face daily reminders of their potentials and limitations; rewards, punishments, success and failure are on offer on a massive scale. Perhaps William James (1890) was the first to show awareness of the effects of performance on self-concept level. As he wisely pointed out: 'With no attempt there can be no failure; with no failure no humiliation. So our self feeling in this world depends entirely on what we back ourselves to be and to do.' (p. 313) Unfortunately, most pupils have little choice about the areas in which they must perform, and suffer evaluation, or in which they wish to make their mark on the world.

A flood of studies convey the same message; differences in self esteem are associated with differences in academic achievement. Fink (1962) found a significant relationship between low self concept and academic under-achievement, and that this relationship appears stronger in boys than in girls. Shaw and Alves (1962) concluded that male under-achievers have more negative concepts of self than do achievers. Based on the findings of one study, Combs (1964) reported that under-achievers saw themselves as less adequate to others, perceived peers and adults as less acceptable, showed a less effective approach to problem solving, and demonstrated less freedom and adequacy of emotional expression; low achievers tend to express more negative self feelings than high achievers. For instance Walsh (1956) in a study involving 20 primary schoolboys with IQs over 120 who were 'under-achievers' and who were matched with 20 other boys who had similar IQs but who were high achievers, found that bright boys who were low achievers had more negative feelings about themselves than did high achievers. In addition, she noted that low achievers differed reliably from high achievers in

(a) feelings of being criticised, rejected or isolated;
(b) acting defensively through compliance, evasion or negativism; and
(c) being unable to express themselves appropriately in actions and feelings.

The personality characteristics and attitudes towards achievement of two groups of fourth- and fifth-grade children differentiated in reading ability were analysed by Zimmerman and Allebrand (1965). Subjects in this study consisted of 71 'poor' readers and 82 'good' readers equated as nearly as possible for age, sex, ethnic composition and intelligence. Compared to the poor reader, the good reader was found likely to describe himself as well adjusted, motivated and striving for success. This is in contrast to the picture presented by poor readers, who, according to the investigators, would willingly admit to feelings of discouragement, inadequacy and nervousness, and whose proclaimed goals are often ephemeral or immediate – especially in avoiding achievements.

Jones and Grieneeks (1970) examined the relationship between measures of self perception and academic achievement in a sample of 877 students at college level. The measures of self perception used were the Self-Expectations Inventory, the 'Who am I?' technique and the Self Concept of Ability Scale. Academic achievement was measured by grade point average and a Scholastic Aptitude Test. The purpose of the study was to establish whether self perception appeared to be the most accurate predictor of academic achievement, and which measure of self perception would be the most valid measure. The results showed a positive relationship between all the measures of self perception and academic achievement. Jones found the self concept of ability measure to be the best predictor of academic achievement, even above measures of IQ and aptitude. In a study conducted by Simon and Simon (1975) dealing with a sample of 10 year olds, the relationship between self esteem, and standardised academic achievement was examined. The Coopersmith Self-Esteem Inventory (Coopersmith, 1967) was used to measure self esteem and the SRA Achievement Series was used as a measure of academic achievement. Results indicated a significant relationship between self esteem and standardised academic achievement for both sexes.

Self conception can affect performance at quite an early age too, as Wattenberg and Clifford (1964) show. They found that an unfavourable self conception and achievement is already established in many children before they enter first grade. They studied 128 kindergarten students in two schools, one serving lower-class, the other middle-class neighbourhoods, measuring intelligence, self-concept, ego strength and reading ability of all the students when they were in kindergarten, and then again when these same students finished second grade. They found that measures of self concept and ego strength made at the beginning of kindergarten were more predictive of reading achievement 2½ years later than were measures of intelligence. In other words, the self attitudes of the kindergarten students were a more accurate indication of his potential reading skills than his intelligence test scores. Some large-scale cross-cultural studies by Smith (1969) provide strong indications of the contribution of self-concept elements to academic performance. From data collected on 37 samples comprising 5,777 9–11 year olds, Smith found that the variables which provided the highest correlations with academic performance pertained to self attitudes and personal motivation. The use of these self-concept elements enabled Smith to more than double the accuracy of prediction of performance and of 'dropping out' of school in his samples.

However Borislow (1962) was unable to detect any significant differences in general self-concept level between students who turned out to be under-achievers and those who turned out to be achievers. The crucial factor seemed to be whether the student intended to strive for success. Those who intended to strive but under-achieved did possess a more pessimistic picture of themselves as a student, both before and after academic performance.

Borislow's work suggests that the relation between self concept and academic performance is complex with motivation requiring an insert into the formula, as well as a differentiation between global self conception and self concept as a student being necessary. This specific academic self concept was further revealed in a major study by Brookover, Thomas and Paterson (1964) using over 1,000 12 year olds. Results showed that:

(a) There is a significant positive correlation between self concept and performance in the academic role; this relationship is substantial even when measured IQ is controlled.

(b) There are specific self concepts of ability related to specific areas of academic role performance which differ from the general self concept of ability. These are, in some subjects, significantly better predictors of specific subject achievement than is the general self concept of ability.

(c) Self-concept is significantly and positively correlated with the perceived evaluations that significant others hold of the student.

In the second phase of Brookover *et al.* monumental longitudinal study, self concept of ability was seen to be a significant factor in achievement at all age levels. In the third and final phase (Brookover, Erikson and Joiner, 1967) by which time the students were 17 years old the authors were able to note that:

The correlation between self-concept of ability and grade point average ranges from 0.48 to 0.63 over the six years. It falls below 0.50 only among boys in the 12th grade. . . In addition, the higher correlation between perceived evaluations and self-concepts tends to support the theory that perceived evaluations are a necessary and sufficient condition for the growth of a positive of high self-concept of ability, but a positive self-concept of ability is only a necessary, but not a sufficient condition for achievement. The latter is further supported by the analysis of the achievement of students with high and low self-concept of ability. This revealed that although a significant proportion of students with high self-concepts of ability achieved at a relatively lower level, practically none of the students with lower (less positive) self-concepts of ability achieved at a high level. (pp. 142–3)

Brookover's statement does make us realise that a positive self conception is important, but by itself positive self esteem will not guarantee success. These correlations are higher than those usually obtained because the scale was specifically designed to tap school-related self conceptions.

Stenner and Katzenmeyer (1976) investigated the relationship between self concept, ability and school achievement using two ability tests, six achievement tests and seven scales of the Self Observation Scales (SOS) with 225 11 year olds from rural areas in West Virginia. The correlation between the SOS scores and the achievement areas was found to be significantly greater than that between SOS and IQ, thus supporting the notion that self concept plays an important part in predicting academic achievement.

These studies quoted above are just a few of a plethora of investigations on the relationship. Thus, there is overwhelming evidence of the positive association between self concept and academic achievement. The numerous research studies summarised by Purkey (1970) and LaBenne and Green (1969) are more than adequate testimony to the fact that low self esteem or self concepts that do not contain the view that the child is competent or can succeed in his school-based activities, but tend to produce under-achievement and poor performance levels, and in some cases withdrawal from academic activities. What is equally certain is that children who possess positive self concepts are able to make more positive and clearer appraisals of their ability to perform in the school milieu and actually produce results in their academic studies which are superior to those turned in by pupils with more uncertain and negative feelings about themselves. In surveying

American research Purkey (1970) concluded that 'overall the research evidence clearly shows a persistent and significant relationship between the self concept and academic achievement' (p. 15).

However, several qualifications need to be made regarding the general trend of the relationship as found in the data. Firstly, the array of correlations linking self-concept level and achievement, while positive and statistically significant, tends to hover in the region of 0.30 and 0.40, a level which is not all that striking, indicating only that up to around 16 per cent of the variance in academic performance can be 'explained' in terms of self-concept level. The above statement is meant to be cautionary rather than damning, since the opening remarks of this chapter suggested that the self concept was only one of a number of variables that affect academic performance. Hence, it would be surprising to find the self concept having an overwhelming influence. But it is certainly too important to be disregarded, and must be ranged alongside those other more usual explanations of IQ, social class, parental interest, etc – all of which need to be invoked to produce an overall picture of why some children succeed while others fail. A major reason for the only moderate correlations found lies perhaps in the frequent use of general self-concept scales which are far too wide ranging, with items nosing into a broad spectrum of areas unrelated to educational endeavours. As was argued in Chapter 3 the self concept is a constellation of specific attitudes to the self. Hence, how people feel about themselves in a particular context needs to be assessed by a self-concept measure with items all related to that context. This is why Brookover, Thomas and Patterson's (1964) scale for example provides higher correlations with academic attainment (0.48–0.63) than other more general self-concept scales.

The second qualification lies in the observation that the most significant associations between attainment and self esteem occur at the negative or low end of the scale. That is, low attainment and failure is more predictably associated with low self esteem than high attainment and success is with high self esteem. Thus the debilitating consequences of low self esteem on academic performance or reciprocally of poor academic performance on self esteem have far more effect than the reciprocal facilitating consequences of high levels of self esteem and academic performance.

Thirdly, correlational studies cannot determine causality. Does a positive self concept provide a student with the attitudes and approach to his work that are likely to ensure success, or does academic success nourish and augment positive feelings a student comes to hold about himself? An armchair analysis suggests that both these causal relationships exist, each facilitating the other in a reciprocal fashion. Studies that attempt to isolate which variable is the independent one are inconsistent in their findings.

In a recent attempt to untangle the direction of the causal relationship between academic self concept and academic attainment, Caslyn and Kenny (1977) analysed data from a longitudinal study of 556 adolescents to compare the self-enhancement model with that of the skill-development approach. Self-enhancement theory suggests that self-concept variables affect level of academic performance, hence to improve achievement levels the self concepts of ability of pupils need to be made more positive through various feedback mechanisms, e.g. counselling, reinforcement. The proponents of the skill-development model claim that academic self-concept level is primarily a consequence of academic attainment. For this method of teaching, personalised instruction and curriculum structure are seen as keys to improve level of self concept of ability. Caslyn and Kenny's results were clearly supportive of the skill-development model in which academic achievement is causally predominant over self concept of ability. Perceived evaluations and feedback from others follow as a consequence rather than precede as a cause of level of self concept of ability.

Gabbler and Gibby (1967) concur, showing that failure and success affect a person's self evaluation. Their study explored two broad aspects of the effects of stress resulting from failure: (1) the effects upon self concept; and (2) the effects on intellectual productivity. The subjects had never before failed in school. An experimental and a control group were both administered three tests – an English grammar test, the Gibby Intelligence Rating Schedule and a test of word fluency. Three days later both groups were again given a test of word fluency, but just before the testing, members of the experimental group received slips of paper indicating they had failed the previous test. The scores of the experimental and control groups were then compared. The results indicated that under the stress of the failure situation even quite able children performed less effectively. Furthermore, as shown by self-referent statements, children in the experimental group tended to regard themselves less highly, tended to believe that they were not as highly regarded by significant others in their lives, and showed a decrement in intellectual productivity. The negative effect of failure was manifested in both the reported self concept and the measured cognitive function.

The influence of level of performance on self concept is clear at college level too. Entry to college brings doubts to most students as they are presented with a new variety of experiences such as looking after oneself away from home, developing new friendships and coping with higher level work. Each new student has to prove himself and maintain his self esteem. Since only a few students can be granted high grades, even successful pupils may only receive average grades. Some will then perceive in this situation that they will never see themselves as successful, regardless of how hard they work. They suffer loss of self esteem and develop feelings of academic inferiority. These feelings of inferiority may remain limited to the academic competition or they may not, but they can begin to affect the student's behaviour in other areas, especially in his relationship with his fellow students.

In the attempt to preserve self esteem, the students may rationalise their poor performance in a number of ways. They may say they don't like the course, or the teachers, or that the teachers are biased against them. Rationalisation, displacement and compensation are invoked readily. With the later defence the student is likely to substitute other behaviours as a source of self esteem, e.g. sport, pop music, bohemianism. Centi (1965) found this pattern of behaviour in students who did not achieve the high grades they had come to expect from their earlier school performance.

However, other studies support the opposite argument that self concept affects academic performance, and improvement in the latter is preceded by self-concept enhancement. For example Brookover, Patterson and Thomas (1965) attempted to discover whether enhancing the academic expectations of low-achieving adolescents would improve school attainment. The enhancement was undertaken:

(*a*) by increasing parental evaluations of the student;
(*b*) by having an 'expert' inform the student about his ability; and
(*c*) by creating a significant 'other' (a counsellor) whose high academic expectancies and evaluations might be internalised by the student.

The first approach was the most successful. As parental perception changed in a positive direction, so too did the self perceptions of the students. However, improvement was not maintained when the treatment ceased. Lawrence (1971, 1972), using several counselling approaches with retarded readers, demonstrated a significant gain in reading attainment over control groups. Again, it would seem that modification to self perception has considerable effects on academic performance.

Brookover regards self concept of ability as a threshold variable. He argues that low social class membership cannot be a sufficient cause of academic failure since not all pupils from the low social class perform poorly at school. Similarly, not all middle-class children achieve high levels of academic attainment. He suggests that if the self concept is below a threshold point then not even middle-class children of high ability will do well. This argument explains those cases which sociologists with their myopic emphasis on environmental/demographic variables find so embarrassing; such cases as children from inner city slums who achieve high standing in some profession. Brookover introduces the idea of the self concept as a threshold variable that intervenes between social class and academic attainment.

At the present state of knowledge it seems reasonable to assume that the relationship between self concept and academic attainment is reciprocal, not unidirectional. Academic success raises or maintains self esteem, while self esteem influences performance through expectations, standards, recognition of personal strengths, higher motivation and level of persistence. There is a continuous interplay between the benefits gained from self esteem increasing the likelihood of increased competencies and academic success, and the influence of academic success on increasing confidence, expectations and standards. This is obviously a beneficient cycle if both or even one of the sides of the equation is fairly positive; however, a destructive cycle is set in motion when one or both are at a low level, with low self esteem undermining confidence and setting low expectations or with poor performance levels reducing self esteem. It is a highly scrambled chicken and egg situation.

But since it is difficult in practice to separate out the reciprocal effects of level of self concept and academic performance, many workers do, however, tend to look at each variable of the self concept–performance relationship separately. This does not imply a lack of understanding about the reciprocal nature of the effects but reveals a weakness in available research techniques, and in practice workers are content at present to describe the conditions under which either factor may be the dependent variable, with the other the independent variable. For example Stains (1958) demonstrated how learning experiences affected self-concept level in the classroom, but in the same paper he went on to show how, once developed, the self becomes a factor in all subsequent learning in general and in perception, selective recall, transfer phenomena and motivation in particular. Many studies reveal a low but positive correlation between self concept and intelligence. For example Coopersmith (1967) quotes 0.28 and Simon and Simon (1975) quote 0.29. Thus intellectual factors are of low importance in determining levels of self esteem.

There appears to be a sex difference in the self concept–achievement relationship. Purkey (1970) discerned a consistent and significant relationship between the self concept and academic achievement which was stronger for boys than girls. Shaw, Edson and Bell (1960) in studying the self perception of under- and over-achievers noted that male subjects in the latter group scored significantly higher than those in the former group, on an adjective checklist. Female achievers actually scored lower than female under-achievers on 'Ambition' and 'Responsibility'.

Perhaps such sex differences are a result of the social expectations for males in Western society, especially in terms of academic progress and ambition. Female self concepts may focus on different areas from male ones. Veness (1962) noted that girls are more concerned with personal appearance and social relationships than boys, who showed more concern with academic progress.

Most general self-concept studies tend to suggest that the self concept is stable from pre-adolescence onwards. However, using scholastic self-concept scales a number of studies (e.g. Morse, 1964), reveal a sharp drop in self-esteem level at 8 years old which continues to 10 year olds. The recovery is only attained by the late teens. The reasons for this decrease are not really known, but it seems that this marks the real start of academic evaluation effects so that while society quite effectively socialised young people the process is not very effective in making them secure within themselves. From 8 years of age confidence wanes as school ceases to be a secure supporting place. A sense of personal failure is constantly communicated to many youngsters; self esteem is discouraged rather than enhanced.

Numerous studies have found a significant and positive relationship between self concept and academic achievement in disadvantaged and in ethnic minority group pupils too (e.g. Coleman, 1966; Paschal, 1968; Epps, 1969). Just as conventional wisdom claimed that coloured persons possess low self concepts, a speculation clearly rejected in Chapter 8, so too, many educationalists believed that coloured pupils would carry a burden of a negative self image which would inhibit their educational performance. While it is apparent that in general disadvantaged and coloured minority children have lower attainment records for various socioeconomic, cultural and linguistic reasons, their self concepts are not significantly different in level from those of more socially favoured groups (e.g. Gibby and Gabler, 1967; Renberger, 1969; Deblaissie and Healy, 1970; Zirkel and Moses, 1971; Verma and Bagley, 1975; Louden, 1977). Thus the supposed negative self concepts of such pupils are no more than the projection of the majority culture's stereotype of them.

As with many educational decisions made on 'political' grounds, the American desegregation decision of 1954 was based on opinion rather than empirical evidence. The supposed 'psychological damage' of inferiority and negative self esteem inflicted on coloured children through a segregated educational system does not stand up in the light of research data (e.g. Scott, 1969; Zirkel and Moses, 1971; Zirkel and Greene, 1971; Rosenberg and Simmons, 1973). In general there are non-significant differences between coloured pupils in segregated and non-segregated schools. Interestingly, other American findings indicate that when coloured inner-city children are placed in integrated schools they develop a lower self image.) The children may find it more difficult to achieve academic and social success in the midst of the more highly competitive middle-class environment (Levine, 1968). Frerichs (1971) noted that although there was no statistically significant difference between the self-esteem levels of high and low IQ coloured children, there were significant differences in self esteem when the children were redivided into high and low success groups by reading and examination marks. Even disadvantaged coloured children thrive academically and in self esteem if provided with realistic success experiences. *effects of academic group-ing.*

As long as a child remains within his own cultural environment he seems generally well able to maintain positive feelings about himself. The social forces that have created the partial segregation of minority, especially coloured groups, as a corollary provide comfortable but temporary and misleading insulation for their young people against direct assaults on their self concepts. Buoyed up by the supportive interactions with significant others of their own reference group and the accepted standards of their group, little stigma becomes attached to not doing well at school. As Rosenberg and Simmons (1973) remark:

poverty, broken family, the low prestige level of the black race, poor school performance and rejection of the Black do not turn out to have the negative consequences generally assumed. What does have an unequivocal impact on their self-esteem in these environments is what they believe their significant others think of them. The great proportion of the child's daily interpersonal interactions occur with parents, friends and teachers. If these significant others hold favourable opinions of him, respect him and like him then a firm foundation for a healthy self-esteem may be established. (p. 144) *significant others opinions are vital*

All this of course works well for the self esteem of any child who can so demean academic success. However, those who do wish to achieve in terms of majority group standards, especially at late secondary and college ages, must stand thereby to lose some self esteem. However, two problems confuse the issue. Firstly, most investigators measured global self concept on which, as we noted in chapter 8, minority group members using significant others and standards from their own subculture, come out reasonably well. If self concept of achievement were employed in which the minority group member would be measured uncomfortably against the standards and expectations of the school as a middle-class and majority-group institution, then differences might well be expected. Though it is still possible that the coloured pupils could devalue academic success to maintain self esteem.

This argument leads into the second problem. Many investigators have suggested that the similarity of majority and minority self esteem levels is due to defensive reactions and a deliberate attempt to paint a favourable self image. The devaluing of school-related criteria noted among coloured children may be an explicit example of this defensive tendency.

Perhaps the self concepts of coloured groups in America were in reality rather negative until the 1960s. Since then the changing negro image presented by the mass media, and the work of the various black activist movements, have improved ethnic pride. Roth (1970), for example, found that a group of 12-year-old negroes held extremely positive opinions on ethnic pride in a geographical area where groups were active in programmes building up black pride. However, most of the research in this area is American, and neither the pattern of race relations nor the background of the immigrant groups in Britain can be equated with those in America. While colour may be an underlying aspect of virtually all immigrant experience, its salience and significance depends very much on context. The challenge is to help disadvantaged pupils hold positive self concepts and yet function and hold expectations at a realistic level.

2. Feedback from significant others and the expectation effect

The role of feedback has been a constant theme in this book, apparent in both theory and practice. Feedback in the form of verbal and non-verbal communication provides reinforcement (both positive and negative) for behaviour and information about oneself, both of which influence self conception, and the expectations others hold of one, and which one holds about oneself. Teachers, parents and peer group are the significant others of the pupil. Research tends to have concentrated on the effects of the first two. The reciprocal influence of self concept and academic performance noted earlier in this chapter is made more complex by the interpolation of feedback and expectations into the process to form a circular effect. This is illustrated in Fig. 9.1.

The sequence of relationships in Fig. 9.1 runs like this. A child who thinks well of himself will perform reasonably adequately. The teacher will perceive him favourably. Her favourable perceptions and expectations fuel the pupil's self regard. He continues to progress in his work, and so the cycle continues. The child who has had a menu of failure comes to school thinking poorly of himself and performs in accordance with this opinion. Teacher is likely to regard him unfavourably, and this is sensed by the pupil who is pushed further into the slough of failure and low self esteem. The child may withdraw, not bother trying and maintain status with friends who also devalue teacher and education. Or, he may be ashamed, feel guilty and anxious. Both possibilities can lead to avoidance of school, deliberate absence, low motivation and even

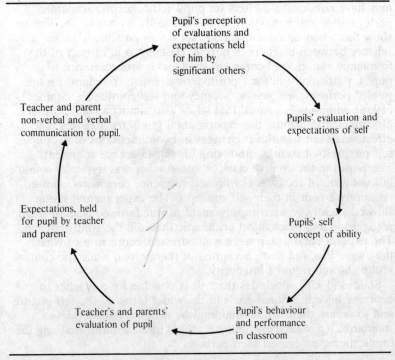

Fig. 9.1 The circular process of self concept, behaviour and feedback.

delinquency. School phobics have noticeably low self concepts (Nichols and Berg, 1970).

It is difficult to ascertain which of the variables acts as the primary instigator in the above circular process, but it is clear that they reinforce one another. As Davidson and Lang (1960) point out: 'The implication is clear. It is essential that teachers communicate positive feelings to their children and thus not only strengthen their positive self appraisals but stimulate their growth, academically as well as inter-personally.' (p. 112) The self concept brought into school by the 5 year old can theoretically be considered primary as it already contains embryonic self concept of ability components derived from parental comments on mastering or failing to master developmental and learning tasks at home. The pupil's behaviour will conceivably be largely a function of this previous experience in his early days at school, behaviour which the teacher will reinforce for good or bad and which will promote certain expectations of the child in the teacher's mind.

There is no clear statement deriving from research data as to whether teachers or parents are the crucial significant other, for findings do not consistently support one or the other. Teachers may have considerable effect on pupil self concepts, academic performance and behaviour. Staines (1958) was one of the first to show this when he demonstrated that it was possible to distinguish reliably between teachers in normal classrooms in respect of the frequency and kind of comment they make with reference to pupils, particularly in their positive or negative comments on the pupils' performance, status, potency and self confidence. Staines (1958) additionally proved that while also aiming at the 'normal' objectives of teaching, the experimental group teacher was able to effect small but significant changes in two dimensions of his pupils' self picture by carefully modifying his self-reference comments. The pupils in the control class, whose teacher was 'typically sound' but unaware of the effect of his self-reference comments, showed no improvement in their self concepts. The experimental group showed slightly greater improvement in standardised tests of word recognition and mechanical arithmetic than did the control group. The experimental group were well adjusted, more sure of what they were like and more accepting of themselves, while the control group showed signs of insecurity.

Staines (1958) concludes that: 'It is possible for a teacher to conceive his educational goals in the wider terms of the self picture and to secure these while attaining the necessary academic standards.' (p. 422) How many teachers have, without realising the implications, unleashed such barbs as:

> 'Ann, come to the front, as you are the smallest.'
> 'John, you never get it right do you?'
> 'What a silly girl you are!'

Other children frequently receive such positive remarks as:

> 'Mary, take this message to the headmaster, I can trust you to remember it', or,
> 'Good boy, look at what Peter has done everybody', or again,
> 'Frank, you're a strong boy, come and help me move this desk.'

The normal run-of-the-mill verbalisations of the teacher are fraught with evaluation and expectations of pupils. But few teachers have realised how potent it all is, as Staines so convincingly reveals.

A simple observation schedule was used by Ensor (1976) to record teacher–pupil dyadic interactions in four separate classrooms. Two groups of pupils in each classroom were identified; those with a high self concept of their ability (SCA) and those with a low SCA. Ensor found that the high-SCA children received more favourable communications from their teachers, initiated more acceptable behaviour patterns with their teachers and were more favourably evaluated by their teachers. In turn the low-SCA children received more behavioural criticisms from their teachers, initiated less acceptable behaviour patterns with their teachers and were less favourably evaluated by their teachers than their high-SCA counterparts.

Whereas Staines' work illustrates the effects of the teacher's comments to his pupils at the classroom level in the primary school, Palfrey (1973) demonstrated how the head teachers' attitudes and expectations can affect their pupils' self concepts in the secondary school. Two secondary schools serving the same catchment area were compared. The headmistress of the girls' school communicated positive expectations to her pupils, whereas the headmaster of the boys' school tended to communicate negative expectations to his students. The responses of the fourth-year boys and girls to a questionnaire were compared and it was found that the girls' responses were more positive in their self evaluations. Palfrey (1973) suggests that: 'Headteachers, through continuous communication with the pupils and staff, not only serve to enhance or diminish the child's evaluation of himself but will also import to the pupils in their charge a self image which reflects the head teacher's highly subjective evaluation of the pupils both as "clients" and also as human beings.' (p. 127) However, these findings must be interpreted with caution as the sample was small and no rigorous statistical testing was undertaken.

Among primary aged children, Davidson and Lang (1960) showed a positive relationship between children's perceptions of their teachers' feelings towards them and the children's perceptions of themselves; they further demonstrated a positive relationship between favourable perception of teachers' feelings and academic achievement, and between favourable perception of teachers' feelings and classroom behaviour judged desirable by teacher.

Nash (1973) noted significant positive correlations between the teachers' perceptions of their pupils (using a triadic elicitation procedure (based on Kelly's personal construct theory of personality) and the pupils' own estimates of their class positions. A rank order of relative ability within the class was also found, derived from the pupils' estimates of each other's positions, and this too was found to correlate positively and significantly with the teachers' perceptions of their pupils. The weight of empirical evidence, then, supports the view that the teacher is an important significant other in the academic life of the primary school pupil.

However, some pieces of research suggest that parents rather than teachers are still the major adult significant other of the school-aged child. Brookover, Patterson and Thomas' (1965) investigation into specific strategies for enhancing low-achieving students' self concept of ability is one, which we noted earlier in this chapter. The experiment attempted to enhance the academic expectations and evaluations parents held for their children. The parents were told to reinforce any positive statement of ability by the student and to avoid negative statements about his ability. The other two experiments involved counselling the students, using fully qualified counsellors, and introducing an 'expert' from the University who presented to the students directly and formally in classroom situations, information that they were academically able and ought to achieve at higher levels. The only experiment which proved successful involved working with the parents.

It may well be for many pupils, though, that the reports and actions of the teacher serve as the basis for parental judgements of their children's ability. Using adolescent white and negro students Kleinfeld (1972) found that for the former, parents were more important as significant others than teachers in helping to form their academic self concepts; for negroes the teachers were more important. The weight of evidence does seem to fall towards the teacher as being the major source of feedback influencing academic self concept and performance.

The reason why feedback from significant others is so important in modifying self concepts is that it contains others' definitions and expectations of us. We tend readily to accept their judgements and so come to behave in accordance with those definitions. This process is in effect a self-fulfilling prophecy. The unwitting influence that people have on each other, on their behaviours and on the views they hold about themselves has a considerable impact on educational performance through the mediation of self conception. As Rosenthal and Jacobson (1968) claim in their much-quoted study on the self-fulfilling prophecy in education, a self-fulfilling prophecy is concerned with how one person's expectation for another person's behaviour can quite unwittingly become a more accurate prediction simply for its having been made. This again emphasises the possible greater importance of the self concept on attainment than vice versa, though of course the attainment achieved then fuels the next set of expectations perceived as held by others about future performance levels, with consequent effects on self conception.

Rosenthal and Jacobson (1968) carried out an investigation in a Californian school which sought to demonstrate that randomly selected pupils about whom their teachers had been told would make 'intellectual spurts' in fact subsequently demonstrated significant IQ gains compared with their classmates. The study has been criticised on statistical grounds by numerous educationalists, but despite this failure of the study to convince other educationalists that the self-fulfilling prophecy can be reliably and validly demonstrated in education, it stimulated further research.

Pidgeon (1970) produced an important monograph containing a number of studies demonstrating the role of teacher and pupil expectations on performance in school. Of particular importance in determining teacher expectation was the extent to which the teacher believed innate ability played a major role in determining attainment levels. Pidgeon believes that this factor, linked with similar beliefs about selection and streaming and the operation of these systems by such teachers, is the major cause of the expectation effect. Pidgeon offered evidence of the effects on children's achievement on a variety of factors including type of school, nature of the curriculum, date of birth and stream assignment. He argues that these effects are mediated by teachers' expectations. For example, date of birth leads teachers to expect more from older members of their classes. In a study of feedback on a maths test, Callison (1974) administered to 28 8 year olds the first half of the Piers–Harris Self Concept Scale followed by a maths test. One half of the group were then told they had made high scores on the maths test; the other half were informed they had performed poorly. The second half of the self-concept scale was then completed. The children given negative feedback showed a significant decrease in self-concept score on the second half of the Piers–Harris scale compared to the first half. Pupils given positive feedback showed no significant change, possibly because their sound maths performance had been expected by them and was no surprise. This study, along with the others mentioned in Chapter 8 (e.g. Haas and Maehr 1965), demonstrates the power of even one single instance of negative feedback to exert considerable influence on the self concept.

Palfrey's (1973) study, already discussed, shows how the segregation of children into good and bad academic prospects was determined by the head teacher's subjective beliefs. Other support for the expectation effect comes from a study by Burstall (1970) concerned with the teaching of French to low-ability children of primary school age. She developed and administered a scale measuring the attitudes of teachers towards teaching the subject to such children. After 2 years she found that low-scoring children in the sample of slow learners were found to be concentrated in a small number of schools where the teachers had expressed a negative attitude towards the teaching of French to low-ability children.

Children bearing first names judged desirable by teachers tend to have more positive self concepts (Garwood, 1976). First names were also found to lead to different teacher expectations so that name stereotyping plays some role in the classroom. Other studies by Parlady (1969) and Rubovits and Maehr (1973) confirm the expectancy effect. Coopersmith's (1967) study also showed that parents who expected their children to live up to the standards they established were more likely to encourage healthy self esteem in their offspring than parents who did not have these expectations. From the work of Shaw and Dutton (1962) it would appear that parents of under-achieving children have more strongly negative attitudes towards their children than do the parents of achieving youngsters. However, the study does not reveal definitely whether these attitudes are one of the results of under-achievement, or one of its causes. From a logical point of view, it is easier to build a case for such attitudes as causal rather than resultant factors. This finding was particularly marked for boys. Thus, many under-achievers start school under a handicap and simply justify their parents' expectations. The strong grip of constant demeaning squeezes out the last drops of self confidence and worth. Expectations represent a belief in the pupils' competency and ability. When established at reasonable levels they provide a vote of confidence out of which positive self esteem can grow.

Teachers apparently tend to interact more positively and favourably with 'brighter' children, and the latter respond by being more effective pupils, thus confirming the teachers' expectations. Pupil reputations are notorious for being passed on from one teacher to another, increasingly determining the child's performance for good or bad. 'Watch him, don't turn your back on him, he's up to all sorts of tricks', to 'He's a hard worker, you'll always get good work from him', are typical of the staffroom comments heard in every school. Non-verbal communication by facial expression, tone of voice and gaze direction also communicate expectations.

A grade or mark given by a teacher is often equated by the pupil with what he believes the teacher thinks of him as a person. The occasional low mark for a pupil who has a backlog of successful experiences in school usually serves to motivate him, and prompts improvement. However, a continuous flow of failures swamp a pupil into a morass of negative self attitudes. 'Why try', the pupil says to himself, 'I'm no good at school work'. Only when assessment is seen by pupils and teachers as a means of fostering improved individual performance, of encouraging self challenge, of facilitating the exploration of areas of weakness and the strengthening of areas of competence is it aiding the self concept.

Returning to Fig. 9.1, the weakest link in the vicious circle, and therefore the point of attack, is academic performance which can be manipulated by the teacher providing realistic tasks and expectations within the capabilities of the pupil. However, success cannot simply be equated with getting work finished, attaining high scores or giving correct answers. Work which is so easy or repetitive for which little effort is required to ensure full marks can be boring and frustrating, providing no positive experience. Similarly, work that is too difficult, quite beyond the knowledge and competency of the pupil, is equally frustrating and anxiety provoking. Hence, success experiences need to be perceived phenomenologically from the point of view of the pupil. This perspective suggests that success has two components: firstly, a clearly delineated personal goal that is potentially attainable, and secondly, progress towards that goal. Of course the teacher guides the child to suitable goals and provides a milieu in which by a series of progressively moving subgoals the child is led forward academically, competing against his previous best rather than against externally imposed standards he may never be able to attain. Even the most handicapped child can obtain success experiences.

Innovations intended to foster a positive self concept and high self esteem have been introduced into schools, but many of these innovations have little theoretical or experimental support and tend to be ineffective. For example, informing children that they are successful, encouraging them to persist or flattering or rewarding them, are all unlikely to increase feelings of self esteem (Brookover, Patterson and Thomas, 1965; Weiner, 1971). Nor do educational innovations that focus on the open classroom or allow the child complete expressiveness or exploration necessarily foster a positive self concept or high self esteem. Such well-intentioned procedures often establish conditions that are likely to leave the child feeling uncertain of his skills and strengths without standards to refer to. Teachers should not offer false praise for inadequate performance. Pupils know fairly well how they have done. Any attempt to sugar the pill through a false notion of kindness is actually unkind, as the pupil must eventually test himself against the reality of his experience. The kindest approach is to be completely honest with the pupil, but this is only possible where the pupil feels secure and accepted by the teacher. In this ethos pupils can profit from the truth and utilise the knowledge of their strengths and weaknesses to plan for the future.

So the axiom, nothing succeeds like success, can be operationalised in the classroom. Reinforcement can be provided for all pupils by programming work to suit individuals, by placing demands on students which each can meet without fear of failure. Therefore the task cannot be too easy, this removes satisfaction, or too hard, this causes anxiety and failure. There must be a slight mismatch between existing performance and what will be required to succeed. Hunt's (1971) proposals about intrinsic motivation seem very relevant here. Teachers must accept individual differences rather than assume that most pupils can attain the same levels at the same time.

Considerable research indicates, too, that children will work harder at tasks and are thereby more likely to achieve a positive self concept if they believe that they, rather than chance or the teacher, are responsible for the successes they achieve (Rotter, 1966). In fact, a large-scale national survey indicated that a pupil's belief is his control over his destiny was more important to achievement than any other school factors measured, such as facilities, teachers and curriculum (Coleman, 1966). This concept of external locus of control was briefly noted in Chapter 8, section F(a).

The three conditions which facilitate the high self esteem of pupils in the classroom milieu are virtually parallels to those indicated by Coopersmith (1967) as enhancing self esteem in the home environment (Ch. 7). These three are:

1. The teacher's acceptance of the child, while at the same time recognising the child's strengths, problems and limitations. By accepting the child the teacher indicates that the child is worthy of the teacher's attention and respect. This respect enables the child to come to terms with his abilities and limitations.
2. The existence of explicit limits, clearly defined and consistently enforced, which provide standards of conduct and behavioural expectations.
3. The provision of respectful treatment which is given to pupils who observe limits and act in accordance with rules and guidelines of the classroom.

As we shall see later in this chapter, the ability of the teacher to provide these conditions depends quite markedly on the teacher himself possessing a positive self concept. This allows him to function in a competent confident way able to accept all pupils as individuals in a supportive environment providing clear and realistic expectations at an individual level. Another line of attack to improve pupil self concept is by direct counselling, which in reality provides the same sort of conditions noted above, i.e. acceptance, respect, limits in a supportive milieu, but undertaken in a more sophisticated and planned way.

3. Counselling and the pupil's self concept

Counselling can be provided for pupils to help improve their self concepts in some schools where trained counsellors exist. Of course most teachers counsel pupils at varying levels of sophistication as part and parcel of their ill-defined teaching duties. As was noted in earlier chapters, the most powerful model in counselling, utilising the self concept as its core, is Rogers' non-directive client-centred therapy. In this the school counsellor will take a stance which avoids overt evaluation or judgements; his aim is to understand the pupil's feelings and to accept him without laying down conditions for the acceptance.

The objectives are:

1. The pupil's self-discovery of his aspirations, goals and needs.
2. The strengthening of the pupil's ability to make his own decisions and set his own direction in life.
3. The pupil's building up of a positive picture of himself as a person of worth, meriting the respect of others.

This model is consonant with the aims of modern education and our ideas of the value of individuality, but young people may not possess the skills, insight and experience needed for self discovery, self awareness and the implementation of the necessary new behaviours required. A totally non-directive model may not be feasible at school level. The alternative directive approach is a behavioural learning model in which the counsellor plays a more active role, reinforcing and shaping behaviour, and planning the steps by which the pupil will attain his goal. There is the implication of imposition by the counsellor, but the programme can be designed to meet each pupil's needs. A combination of the two approaches based on the work of Carkhuff (1969) would seem to employ the best of both, with the counsellor initially providing purpose and direction until the pupil can take over.

A number of workers have made deliberate attempts to evaluate the effects of counselling on pupil self concepts and attainment. Bruce (1958) found that pupils who were subjected to a programme that enabled them to understand and develop greater insight into their own behaviour and into the behaviour of people around them showed gains in self understanding and improved self acceptance over a control group.There was still considerable discrepancies between self and ideal self in the experimental group, but they displayed lower anxiety and felt more comfortable about the discrepancies. What seems to be important is not the size of the discrepancy itself, as Rogers claimed, but the feelings a person has about it. So what to one person might seem to be a threatening discrepancy became a challenge, an indication of aspirations, a source of motivation, to members of the experimental group. Pigge (1970) reports on a study investigating the effects of group counselling on self concepts of 9–10 year olds in Texas. Three groups of 10 pupils each with a school counsellor had 18 50-minute sessions each spaced one per week. A control group not exposed to any group counselling activities was formed. Using a multi-media approach to initiate discussion, a supportive ethos was devised in which students felt free to verbalise, with little counsellor prompting or structuring. Using a semantic differential pre- and post-counselling, the self concepts of the participants altered favourably but not significantly over the control group. The area most affected positively by the counselling experience involved interpersonal relationships. Lawrence (1971, 1972) has demonstrated that an effective approach with retarded readers is to boost their self concepts through individual personal counselling. The rationale is that the retarded child has for various reasons become discouraged, and lost confidence. This produces a negative self concept and a belief that he is unable to succeed. A self-fulfilling prophecy establishes itself as a lack of effort, and withdrawal produces the expected failure. The counselling enables the child to express his emotional problems, gain support, develop confidence and improve his image of himself. As a corollary the counselled pupils recorded a rise in reading attainment.

Several experimental programmes have been introduced in some US schools in which teachers help their students to grow in self esteem through practical methods. For instance, in one California school district a Self Enhancing Education Scheme is employed. Discussions of self and individual performance are conducted in class-size groups. A counsellor also uses group counselling with teachers and parent groups. The scheme focuses not only on what a child can do but on what his potential is when freed from self doubt. The children and teachers work together in determining the organisation of the learning tasks so that each child is challenged by personal goals with likelihood of success.

In a study with college students Cooper (1974) examined the hypothesis that an intensive group encounter experience between teacher and taught could improve their relationship. Rogers (1970) had despondently bewailed the fact that education was lethargic in making use of such group methods to enhance teacher–student relationships. As a result little empirical data actually exist to support the notion that in the educational context intensive group methods aid communication and facilitate more meaningful relationships between teacher and student, leading to more effective learning. Cooper's data revealed that students attending the encounter group with their teacher showed significant increases in their perceptions of their teacher on his level of regard and congruence, and a movement in the direction of significance on his empathy. In contrast, no change was observed on any of the scales for the control students. The evidence does support the contention that improved teacher–student relationships can emanate from such group experiences and these acceptant empathic relationships should also create a better learning environment.

4. School organisation

The organisation of the school appears to have some bearing on self-concept development because certain types of expectations, teacher–pupil relationships, teaching styles and overall ethos tend to be associated with particular organisational forms.

(a) Streaming

Acland's (1973) survey of research on streaming in primary schools suggests that 'non-streamers' base their stance on the enhancing effects of non-streaming on pupil self concepts. But earlier work by Barker Lunn (1970) in an NFER comparative study of streaming and non-streaming, involving 5,500 pupils over their junior school careers in 72 schools – 36 non-streamed and 36 streamed – revealed that school organisation and teacher type only affected the self concepts of average and below-average pupils. Type 1 teachers believed in non-streaming, showed favourable attitudes to slow children, were permissive, were tolerant to noise, were not in favour of physical punishment and made less use of traditional lessons. Conversely, type 2 teachers believed in streaming, tended to stream children by seating, were less interested in slow children, were non-permissive, less tolerant to noise and talking, were favourable to physical punishment and made frequent use of traditional lessons. For children of above-average ability there was no difference in academic self image between the two types of school organisation or the different teacher types. Teacher type was a particular influence on average ability children in that those taught by a 'non-streamer' in an unstreamed school had more positive self concepts than their counterparts in streamed schools. The poorest self concepts in the average ability range were held by pupils in unstreamed schools, but taught by type 2 teachers who favoured streaming. Streaming had beneficial effects on the self concepts of boys of below-average ability, but this effect was not so evident with girls. Non-streaming seemed to provide much opportunity for the low-ability child to compare himself unfavourably with brighter and more successful classmates, and feel that teachers compared him with the latter too. This had debasing effects on his self concept. However, in a follow-up study, Ferri (1971) found that in secondary school, both boy and girl slow learners had developed more favourable self concepts. Ferri claimed that this change arose from such pupils no longer being in classes with wide ability ranges and hence being able to show competency when compared to others of similar ability. The work of Lunn and Ferri appears to indicate that grouping procedures themselves have minimal effect on self concept in that high achievers tend to report more frequently the possession of positive self concepts than do low achievers. Also, it is apparent that teacher attitude and expectancy is vitally important, in that teachers who favour streaming but teach in an unstreamed school create a context similar to that in a streamed school, replete with its evaluational and competitive overtones. As Wiseman (1973) saw, teachers are far more important in terms of their attitudes and expectations than organisational structures. Emmett (1959) and Thomas (1974) concur in this importance of the teacher–pupil relationship. In Thomas' study a similar level of self evaluation was revealed across three streams – a result of the teaching climate of the whole school which appeared to be democratic, and warmly supporting of every child *qua* child.

What streaming does is to exacerbate the expectation effect. The top streamers glow in the reflected appraisals of their teachers; the

not so fortunate pupils in the lower streams learn to function at the
level expected of them, thus validating the teacher's expectation
and judgement. Despite ruses by educationalists to name streams
after animals, famous people, planets or colours, pupils are well
aware of the rules of the game, of the quality of the group to
which they are assigned, and the expectations of the group which
they will gear themselves to meet (Luchins and Luchins, 1948).
The danger with streaming is this disturbing tendency to establish
and reinforce the child's concept of his ability and perpetuate it.
Like a disciplined army the streamed battalions move through the
educational battlefield without any individual breaking rank.

The frame of reference is important

(b) Special school/class placement

The ultimate in streaming is the allocation of educationally
subnormal (ESN) pupils into special schools or classes. For
evidence on the effects of special school placement on self concept
in Britain, only the study by Lewis (1971) is available. He found
higher mean self-concept scores for his ESN day school boys than
for a group of academically average comprehensive schoolboys. In
New Zealand, Higgins (1962) also found a significant difference
between the self concepts of slow learners in a special school and
those in a normal school in favour of the former. An explanation
of this unexpected high self-concept level is that the frame of
reference employed by these segregated ESN pupils is the
immediate interpersonal environment of the ESN school. So while
such special placement provides a much-needed sympathetic,
controlled environment in which self confidence and self esteem
can be nurtured, at the same time no realistic experiences of
personal limitations are offered. It will be remembered that
coloured and disadvantaged children were also able to maintain
positive self concepts through the same mechanism as this.

Evidence from America, however, suggests that special
placement is harmful to self esteem. Lawrence and Winschell
(1973), reviewing the evidence on school placement for the slow
learner and the severely subnormal, concluded that segregated
placement patterns are not ordinarily conducive to overall positive
concepts of self and cannot be justified on that basis. Andrews
(1966) concurs, suggesting that below-average ability children have
difficulty in gaining feelings of success and this has a debilitating
effect on self-concept development. However, so different is the
special school system in America that it is fruitless to seek
comparisons with the English system.

Of allied interest to special school placement is special class
placement. Again, little work has been done in this country in
showing links with level of self concept, though the practice of
putting pupils with learning difficulties in remedial classes is very

common. An important start has been made by Nash (1973) using the technique of participant observation. A single mixed comprehensive school was chosen together with its five feeder primary schools. Each of the latter schools were visited for 3 weeks at a time when a close observation was made of the senior class. Nash then followed them up into the comprehensive school where some of the slower learning children were placed into a remedial class setting. In seeking to elicit the criteria for placing a child into a remedial class he found that the main variable was not learning need but whether or not the primary teacher had found the child troublesome, passive or immature and lacking confidence. He concluded that a 'self-fulfilling prophecy' process had been set in motion with the attendant possibility of deepening levels of negative self esteem by the segregation of slow learners.

teacher's passing on judgements to one another as pupils move on

Clearly, both a positive self concept and realistic self awareness are required. Programmes which gradually provide for both sets of experiences are needed so that a sudden traumatic shock does not devastate the ESN pupils' mental health on leaving school and entering the outside world in a 'full-time' capacity. To this end some schools and authorities attempt a partial integration of educationally retarded children, and studies of this approach reveal improved and more realistic self concepts with increased levels of performance. For example, in Carroll's (1967) study retarded pupils showed a significant decrease in self derogation after 8 months of half-day normal class placement. A control group of retardates who were segregated and had no school contact with normal children were significantly more derogatory of themselves. In the area of reading, the retardates attending half-day normal classrooms made significant improvement over those in the segregated setting. Normal classroom experience permits the retarded child to accustom himself to living in the 'normal' environment in which they will have to cope in future and earn a living.

Over the last few years proponents of progressive schools have claimed very potent effects for that form of schooling, despite the lack of data and the variety of methods under that general nomenclature. Many supporters suggest that pupils in progressive classrooms enjoy learning more, have enhanced self concepts and increased self confidence. Ruedi and West (1973) compared self concepts of pupils in progressive schools with those in traditional schools, i.e. an individualised context versus a structured class context. However, the results did not support the claims made by the devotees of progressive education. There was no significant difference between the two approaches as far as self-concept levels were concerned. A similar study by Groobman, Forward and Peterson (1967) was also unable to detect differences in self-concept levels despite the assumed emphasis by informal schools on personal development. Obviously the successful attainment of academic standards is equally vital for self-concept development.

Cohen and Cohen (1974) in a study involving 801 final-year primary children produced data which suggested associations between high and low self concepts of ability, differing areas of the school curriculum and certain methods of classroom organisation. Compared with children with a high self concept of ability, those children with a low self concept of their ability showed greater dislike for areas of the curriculum which offered, both to the pupils and the teachers, direct opportunity for the observation and comparison of the quality of an individual's work; such curriculum activities included mathematics and doing tests. The same children with low self concept of ability preferred passive, anonymous situations such as watching TV or music, art and craft, where their self concepts were not at risk. The low-self-concept group did show a liking for maths when the teacher eschewed the practice of giving stars and recording marks.

What the evidence on school organisation points to is that it is not only the form of organisation that matters but the attitudes, values and personal philosophy of the teaching staff involved in articulating the system, the sort of expectations they hold for certain types of pupil, the teaching styles and organisation they feel most comfortable with and the attitudes they hold about themselves. It is these that matter, since it is personal encounter rather than organisational form which comprises the pupils' contact with education. So it is to the teacher that we must now turn.

5. The teacher

Because of the social origin of the self concept, the quality of the interpersonal environment within the classroom also monitors the self attitudes of many pupils. The teacher–pupil encounter is permeated on the teacher's side by his general outlook and philosophy of life. We have concentrated on pupils up to now, but of course teachers also possess self concepts which affect their own and the pupils' behaviour, their ability to build up sound relationships with the pupils, their style of teaching and their perceptions and expectations of themselves as teachers and of children as learners.

(a) Teacher self concept

Research on teaching, usually trying to answer the question what makes a good or effective or successful teacher, has had a long but to some extent an unproductive history. There exists a plethora of findings but few are solid, and replicable, or hang together in a meaningful way (The source of trouble has been the lack of a reliable, objective, universal criterion of teacher effectiveness.) The impossibility of discovering such a single criterion is inherent in the diverse nature of the teacher's role, and in the many and varied activities he performs in a wide range of contexts. Researchers have been moved to admit that the problem of teacher effectiveness is so complex that no one today knows what the competent teacher is. But from the compendious array of research into teacher effectiveness a major trend emerges: successful teaching measured in terms of either pupil performance or ratings by others requires teachers who are able to form satisfactory human relationships and create a warm, supportive, accepting classroom ethos.)

Studies by Hart (1934), Bousfield (1940) and Witty (1947) suggest that at all levels of teaching it was the teacher's personal style of communicating what he knew that affected the response of the learners to the teacher as a person and the achievement levels reached. Teachers who were aloof, overbearing and unable to interact with the learners were assessed most negatively by the latter. Similarly, other workers, e.g. Cogan (1958) and Reed (1962) have found that it was the effectiveness of the teacher in creating a warm, supportive, interpersonal milieu which facilitated student performance.

Moreover, pupil behaviour is a major outcome of teacher behaviour since the teacher is a necessary though not sufficient condition for purposeful productive pupil performance, and pupil behaviour is a response to the way the teacher provides for learning situations in which the pupils are initiates (Ryans, 1961).

For example, Ryans (1961) demonstrated that in elementary school high positive relationships exist between observed 'productive pupil behaviour', e.g. alertness, participation, confidence, responsibility and observed patterns of behaviour in the teacher which reflect understanding, empathy, warmth, friendliness. In secondary schools the same relationships were found to exist but were not so pronounced. Spaulding (1963) showed that the self concepts of pupils were apt to be more positive in classrooms in which the teacher was 'socially integrative' and 'learner supportive'.

Effective teachers then appear to be differentiated from ineffective ones by demonstrating:

(a) a willingness to be more flexible;
(b) an empathic ability, sensitive to the needs of pupils;
(c) an ability to personalise their teaching;
(d) an appreciative reinforcing attitude;
(e) an easy, informal, warm, conversational teaching manner; and
(f) emotional adjustment.

In other words, effective teachers create a different learning environment from ineffective teachers.

That teachers can be clearly differentiated in terms of personal teaching style and its effectiveness on pupil attainment and attitudes has much empirical support, but what causes these personal differences in teaching style? And if it can be identified, can those responsible for producing teachers develop it in their protégés? A substantial clue to the basis of the differences can be found in the literature. For instance, Ryans found that teachers reported to have high emotional stability frequently named self confidence as a dominant trait in themselves. They also preferred active contact with people. Those with low emotional stability scores preferred not to have contact with others, possessed less self confidence and were more authoritarian. In a review of several studies Combs (1965) was able to conclude that those rated as good teachers saw themselves as:

(a) identified with others rather than alienated and apart from others;
(b) adequate to cope with most contingencies;
(c) reliable and dependable;
(d) likeable and wanted rather than ignored and rejected; and
(e) people of consequence, dignity and worthiness, rather than feeling that they mattered little and were unworthy.

These personality characteristics which appear to discriminate effective from ineffective teachers are clearly related to the self concept. The role teachers have to play must heighten their awareness of themselves and others, for teaching is a sharing of self with others. Hence, attitudes to self and to others would seem to be of vital importance in influencing interpersonal behaviour in the classroom and as a corollary in influencing preferred teaching style also.

As we noted in Chapter 8, section B, there is the well-documented relationship between the possession of positive self attitudes and the possession of positive attitudes to others (e.g. Sheerer, 1949; Burns, 1975). Secondly, Omwake (1954) and Fey (1954), among others, also noted a strong relation between self acceptance and perceiving others as more accepting. Hence the possession of positive self attitudes facilitates the construction of warm, supportive relations with others; this acts as a therapeutic mechanism to promote the development and continuity of positive self attitudes in those others. Davidson and Lang (1960) showed that pupils were well able to evaluate their teacher's feelings towards them, and those who saw the teacher as one who presented favourable regard to them were the possessors of more positive self concepts and higher scholastic performance. Staines (1958) was able to identify teachers whose verbal material and management of the teaching situation would enhance pupils' self concepts. Combs (1965) indicated that effective teachers have a more positive attitude to themselves than do ineffective teachers.

Student teachers rated high on teaching practice tended to manifest significantly higher self concepts than those rated low on teaching practice (Garvey, 1970). Success in teaching is certainly associated with a positive view of oneself, confidence and adjustment. Crane (1974) concurs in his study with British student teachers. He found that there was a significant relationship between attitudes towards self and others and adjustment to teaching groups of students who had never considered withdrawal (i.e. who were well adjusted), those who had seriously considered withdrawal (less well adjusted) and those who withdrew voluntarily (unable to adjust) could be clearly differentiated by their self attitudes and attitudes to others. In a study of teachers' values by Rosenberg (1955) 57 per cent of 'people-oriented' individuals remained in the teaching profession during the 2-year period of the study, while only 2 per cent of 'non-people-oriented' individuals did so.

In a study of emotionally handicapped children, LaBenne (1965) found a highly significant relationship between the teacher's self concept and the pupil's perception of himself in the classroom, as did Edeburn and Landry (1974) whose self-accepting teachers tended to produce more positive self concepts in pupils than teachers low in self acceptance. Schuer (1971) found a significant gain in academic achievement level in disturbed and maladjusted pupils who saw their teachers as possessing a high degree of unconditional regard for them. Mason and Blumberg (1969) found that high-school students, who, judged by independent assessors to have learned the most, rated the perceived acceptance of themselves by their teachers significantly higher than those students judged to have learned least.

So research tells us that positive self concepts in teachers facilitates not only their own classroom performance as a confident, unanxious, respected guide to learning, but also pupil performance which flourishes in all respects when the pupil is in relationship with someone who projects trust and belief in their capacity and a warm, supportive ethos enhancing the pupil's view of himself as someone of worth. Expectancies from such teachers lead to higher pupil self esteem and performance.

(b) Teacher self concept and teaching method

The different approaches to teaching favoured by persons differing in level of self attitudes and in level of attitude to others, are those theoretically expected to be favoured, since a person low in self esteem will likely try to reduce the need for personal relationships, thereby adopting traditional methods. These place the teacher in an unambiguous position with regard to his role and status, pursuing essentially impersonal relationships in task-oriented rather than in person-oriented behaviours. The progressive approach, with its more intense personal relationships, is threatening to those with negative self and other attitudes. Conformity, rigidity and status are necessary for them. But the person who has a positive self concept has no need to defend; an unstructured, highly personal contact offers no threat. He can relate to, and accept all pupils, irrespective of their characteristics and behaviours. This is not to say that such a person condones whatever the pupil does or is, but rather he does not reject an individual out of hand because of some particular attribute.

Burns (1976b) was able to show this association quite clearly. Student teachers who preferred child-centred methods of teaching rather than impersonal traditional approaches tended to possess significantly more positive self concepts than the student teachers who preferred the more formal methods. Since teachers with low self concepts favour a more traditional approach, with its evaluation and competition, and the possession of such low self concepts engenders a relative restriction in establishing warm personal relationships, then it is likely that many pupils under their aegis would be more liable to develop less positive self attitudes in this atmosphere of competition, impersonality and inflexibility of teaching style, with consequent effects on performance.

Trowbridge (1973) conducted a study to investigate the relationship between teacher self concept and teaching style. The Tennessee Self Concept Scale (Fitts, 1965) was chosen to index the self concepts of 302 elementary teachers and 56 secondary teachers working in a range of rural and urban schools representing a diversity of income and ethnic groups of pupils. Teaching style–thinking processes was measured by verbal interaction analysis based on Guildford's (1956) classification of thinking operations as defined in his model of the Structure of the Intellect. Audio-tape samples of teachers' classroom behaviour were obtained and tallies were made according to the categories of Memory, Cognition, Convergent, Divergent and Evaluative thinking used by the teacher. It was found that teachers with lower self concepts talk more and as a corollary provide less opportunity for their charges to talk than teachers with higher self concepts. The correlation between proportion of classroom time teacher talked and teacher's self concept was -0.624. Teachers with higher self concepts tended to spend less time on routine 'non-thinking' activities than those with lower self concepts. These routine activities were such things as handing out books, collecting in work, taking the register, etc. There was also a positive and significant relationship between the self concept and the tendency to use divergent and evaluative thinking. Teachers with low self concepts were more likely to use convergent thinking and memory in their classroom teaching. As Trowbridge concludes, the evidence points to the teacher's self concept telling us much about the way he teaches. An increase in divergent and evaluative thinking in the teacher's style of teaching may be brought about by making the self concept more positive. All this supports the basic rationale that one might expect teachers with more positive self concepts to feel freer to allow pupils to develop divergent and evaluative approaches to schoolwork. Teachers who are unsure of themselves are more likely to stick to stereotyped formal lessons, involving memory, 'right answer' kind of questions and convergent thinking, as Burns (1976b) found.

Stern (1942) reviewed 34 studies (largely of college classes) comparing non-directive and directive instruction in their influence on two types of learning outcomes: (*a*) gain in cognitive knowledge and understanding, and (*b*) attitude change toward self and others. In regard to cognitive gains, he concluded that in general, it would appear that the amount of cognitive gain is largely unaffected by the autocratic or democratic tendencies of the instructor. However, when he summarised the findings related to attitude change towards the self and others, the conclusion is somewhat different for he noted that regardless of whether the investigator was concerned with attitudes towards the cultural out-group, toward other participants in the class, or towards the self, the results generally have indicated that non-directive instruction facilitates a shift in a more favourable, acceptant direction. This is what we might have expected, bearing in mind the results of client-centred counselling. But it is likely to be the teacher with positive self concepts who will be willing to try out non-directive informal classroom techniques, and hence only he who can change such self attitudes and attitudes to others in pupils in a favourable direction. It must be noted, however, that such phrases as child centred versus teacher centred, democratic versus autocratic, formal versus informal, have tended to be used as loose synonyms to reflect a crude dichotomy between differences in teaching approach and the amount of pupil involvement in the process of education, and really label extreme ends of the continuum of teaching style. Most teachers tend to be flexible, using a ratio of formal to informal teaching to suit the particular lesson. It is the low-self-concept teacher who would seem to be the most rigid and inflexible, sticking to known and safe techniques.

It may be that if governments, administrators and head teachers wish to develop educational systems based on certain teaching approaches, then it is necessary for the teachers involved to possess the level of self attitudes and attitudes to others required for their adoption of the approach in both spirit and practice. The basic educational philosophy of the teacher looks as though it resides in his attitudes to others, and by extension ultimately in the level of his attitudes to self. It might well be that, depending on the sort of educational system planned, one part of the selection procedure for potential teachers should be an index of the self concept. That is, providing instruments capable of assessing such a quantity with acceptably high levels of reliability and validity can be devised. If informal, highly personalised, unstructured teaching approaches are required then those teachers lacking doubts about self worth may ensure the functioning of the system far better than those who have low levels of self acceptance. The latter may only be effective in an approach requiring formal teacher-imposed subject matter and impersonal relationships. Obviously these dichotomies between types of teacher and types of method are crude, but the implication is certainly there. One can surmise that many innovations in the methodology of teaching and in the internal organisation of some schools have foundered on, among other things, the failure of teachers to work the innovations in the way they were meant to, because teachers have been either unwilling or unable to adapt (e.g. Barker Lunn, 1970). Low self esteem functions like a lens, limiting the perspectives from which the teacher's role is viewed. Thus constrained, the teacher with a low evaluation of himself would find it difficult to undertake another type of role. A change from formal to informal style creates a threat to the self concept as known, since the latter style is more demanding, both intellectually and emotionally, exposing personal inadequacy and insecurity. The progressive approach to teaching places more demands on the teacher, as he has to be a better type of person in a great variety of ways. The effects that 3 years in a college of education has on the personality of the students is perhaps as important as what is learned in the cognitive area.

The facilitator of learning must be above all else a secure person. Little headway can be made in understanding others or in helping others to understand themselves unless he is endeavouring to understand himself. The person with low self evaluation sees those with whom he interacts through the biases and distortions of his own needs, fears and anxieties. Only when the teacher has self awareness and sufficient self esteem can his own needs (e.g. for recognition, importance, power, etc) be reduced so that teaching is based on the needs of the children and not those of the teacher. While informal education relieves the teacher of the burden of omniscience, it adds the burden of fallibility, a situation in which the teacher must feel comfortable in admitting to children: 'I don't know much about this. Let's see if we can find out together.'

(d) Changing teachers' self concepts

In view of what we know about teachers' self concepts on their teaching behaviour and on the self concepts and performance of their pupils it would appear that strenuous and extensive efforts need to be made to prepare teachers who will be sensitive to others, and who view teaching as a human process involving human relationships and human meanings. We need to introduce and expose teachers to sensitising processes and subtle complexities of personality structure. Teaching about group processes does occur in colleges but, for the most part, in an abstract theoretical vein, unconnected to the students' real needs. It was clearly demonstrated in Chapter 8, sections A and B, that intensive group experiences and counselling processes could effect change in the self-esteem and self-acceptance levels of participants in a favourable direction. These techniques could be used in the initial training of teachers and in-service courses too. As self attitudes are learned they are therefore modifiable in a favourable direction. More importantly for teachers engaged in interpersonal relationships, the same therapeutic climate that brings changes in self concept also creates as a corollary increasing levels of acceptance of others. In this way group dynamics and other counselling processes effect a two-pronged attack on the low-self-concept person, making him more competent and secure in himself, as well as facilitating improved interpersonal relations which act as feedback to the blossoming self.

Some studies already point the way in this direction. Perkins (1958) using a Q-sort method among 9 and 11 year olds, has demonstrated that teachers' perceptions of children's self concepts are, in general, positively and significantly related to these children's expressed self concepts, i.e. teachers accurately perceive the self concepts of the children in their class. However, different groups of teachers perceived their pupils' expressed self concepts with varying degrees of accuracy. It was found that teachers who had completed 3 years of an in-service, part-time child study programme showed a greater correspondence between their perceptions of children's self concepts and these children's expressed self concepts than did teachers who had never participated in such a child study programme. He suggests that this occurred because the former teachers had greater sensitivity to, and provided for, children's needs far better than the latter group.

McClain (1970) reports on the provision of mental health courses for teachers in training. The results showed that the participants progressed towards self actualisation in terms of smaller self–self-ideal discrepancies. Many students reported in writing that they felt more comfortable in themselves after the course. Studies by Carkhuff (1969) also point to the need for special training for teachers if teachers are to become more effective in promoting satisfying interpersonal encounters with children which will facilitate self-worth development in the latter.

However, specialised courses are not essential, for as Jersild suggests the teacher can gain a deeper understanding of his self concept by posing himself questions like the following:

Do I regard myself as a crystallised finished person or one who is still learning and growing? The latter is one who can critically examine new experiences and is willing to immerse himself into the intellectual and social challenges inherent in the teacher's role. Rogers (1956) has suggested that the continuous becoming of an individual must include his willingness to be a process that is ever-changing. Some mistakes are inevitably part of the learning process, but the developing person is one who can take a disappointing situation and learn something from the experience.

Do I possess flexible self assurance? Research on effective teaching consistently demonstrated that successful teaching is related to emotional maturity and self assurance. Such teachers show more spontaneity, initiative and empathy and fewer negative attributes such as conflict with others, emotional coldness and rigidity in behaviour. If teachers can replace fears and anxieties by self assurance which enables the acceptance of both good times and bad and yet remain intact, then they are able to be flexible to meet new and ever-changing classroom challenges in a dynamic working situation of up to 6 hours per day with a group of up to 40 lively young minds.

Do I tolerate diversity of point of view? Am I comfortable when a pupil takes issue with me? Have I sufficient intellectual flexibility to avoid such dogmatic assertions as, 'the only way to teach is . . .; the only good text on this topic is . . .; there is only one way to learn this'.

Do I see myself as a person able to accept positive criticism, as part of my personal and professional development, and openly discuss my personal and professional problems? This question is relevant to suggestions that forms of group therapy might aid the development of positive self concepts. Jersild (1955) found that teachers regarded it as a useful venture to discuss their real professional problems in a shared human experience with its intimate involvement.

Some questions the teacher could profitably raise with himself in order to understand the perceptions he has of his pupils might include the following:

(a) Am I aware of my pupils' perception of the environment, especially their feelings, attitudes, beliefs and perceptions about me? Do I see myself through my pupils' eyes?

(b) Am I person oriented rather than event or thing oriented? Do I like to build personal relationships with my pupils, working alongside them, or maintain an impersonal, disinterested, distant approach? Am I more concerned with the subject than with the pupils' needs and perceptions?

(c) Do I search for the causes of pupils' difficulties rather than merely being content to consider the child incapable? Do I modify constructively the 'failing' pupil's programme of work so that he is more likely to gain some success, understanding and a sense of achievement? Do I believe in individual differences so that learning situations are created in which each is expected to perform according to his abilities and not to some arbitrary class standard?

(d) Do I foster a love for learning and an interest in my subject through my teaching behaviour?

By using these and other similar questions the teacher should gain more insight into his own teaching behaviour; he will begin to think and reflect, an essential start to discovering and understanding oneself and others. Self understanding precedes understanding of others. All those whose work places them in constant daily transactions with others have an obligation to try to understand themselves, but as Jersild (1955) points out, to gain self knowledge, one must have the courage to seek it and the humility to accept what one may find. Without self knowledge a society can only be erudite, never wise. We should not leave such a vital element of learning to sheer luck. It ought to be one of the objectives of a rounded education.

Summary

This chapter has surveyed the roles of pupil and teacher self concepts on academic attainment, teaching behaviour and interpersonal relationships in the classroom. Numerous studies indicate a direct relationship between the child's self concept and his manifest behaviour, perceptions and academic performance. Successful students are typically characterised by self confidence, self acceptance, feelings of adequacy and personal competence, and generally more stable feelings of positive self regard. On the other hand, research shows that unsuccessful students are characterised by feelings of uncertainty, low self regard, self-derogatory attitudes and strong inferiority feelings. The manner of the teacher in presenting the subject matter is of critical importance, because teaching activities have specific reference and meaning for the development of the student's self concept. Some of these activities are internalised by the student as being self-defeating, and the circular effects of these conceptions reinforce an inability to learn certain kinds of academic material. The central place of the teacher as an agent influencing the developing self concept of the student is emphasised with the teacher's own self concept strongly associated with the type of expectations about pupils he emits, with his teaching style, with his classroom ethos and with his acceptance of others. It would appear that teachers must alter their own self concepts before they can effect change for the better in those of their pupils. In accepting themselves, teachers would become more warm and accepting of others, and this supportive, encouraging atmosphere should get the best out of all pupils. In other words, it is the quality of the relationship that seems most important, and this depends to a large extent on what the teacher is like as a person. Personal encounter, not organisational form, matters.

It would seem that the self concept is a ubiquitous and integral part of any learning situation. It plays an inevitable part of both the outcomes and conditions of learning, whether the teacher is aiming for it or not. It is also clear that teaching methods can be adapted and counselling techniques employed so that definite changes of the kind sought for will occur in the self concepts of the pupils. Since academic success is associated to a moderate extent with positive self esteem, no teacher is wasting time in attempting to improve any child's conception of himself as this is more than likely to produce subsequent increases in academic performance than concentrating on academic goals alone. Self understanding and relationships with others are so crucial a part of one's life that they ought to form a major part of any educational programme, but schools have tended to ignore and evade the issue, and deliberately planned efforts to guide pupils and teachers towards a better understanding of themselves and their interpersonal relationships are rare.

Further reading

Covington, M. V. and **Beery, R. G.** *Self Worth and School Learning,* New York: Holt, 1976.
Hamachek, D. E. *The Self in Growth, Teaching and Learning,* Englewood Cliffs, NJ: Prentice-Hall, 1965.
LaBenne, W. D. and **Greene, B. I.** *Educational Implications of Self-Concept Theory,* Pacific Palisades, Calif.: Goodyear, 1969.
Purkey, William W. *The Self and Academic Achievement,* Englewood Cliffs, NJ: Prentice-Hall, 1970.
Rogers, Carl R. *Freedom to Learn,* Columbus, Ohio: Charles E. Merrill Books, 1969.
Torrance, E. Paul, and **Strom, R. D.** *Mental Health and Achievement,* New York: Wiley, 1965.

Epilogue

The contemporary emphasis by social scientists concerned with the psychological health of individuals and of the community is on developing strategies and invoking processes to build up the constructive aspects of human personality that enable a person to function effectively in all areas of his public and private life. It is no longer merely a question of treating mental and behavioural disorder when it arises, but also to search out ways to generate those human capacities that strengthen the organism psychologically so that it can deal effectively with those stresses that will inevitably impinge upon it at some time or other. This 'approach to health' orientation has its parallel in medicine whereby it is better to immunise against infection than to treat the infection later. It has been the major tenet of this book that the kinds of experiences necessary for the development of effective and competent behaviour immunising the person against feelings of insecurity, anxiety, incompetency and the like are those which give rise to a positive self concept, such as acceptance and regard from significant others, success and achievement in salient areas.

At the end of the day, with much of the research literature and theoretical views surveyed, what gleanings of advice can be offered to parents, teachers and other professionals who are daily concerned with helping others? Only one thing is certain and that is since the self concept has only been partially studied much remains to be discovered and it would be presumptious to prescribe a blueprint at this stage which would specify action to be taken in this or that situation. The processes involved in developing a positive self concept have yet to be fully detailed. There are still many blanks in the jigsaw, and while the overall picture is reasonably clear the blanks are filled currently with educated guesses. However, some basic ground rules appear consistently through a wide variety of self-concept research in various areas. These would suggest that to ensure the development of positive self concepts:

(a) Provide opportunity for success and ensure the tasks and demands placed on a person are suitable to his potential, that is there is likely to be a successful outcome and realistic acceptance of ability.

(*b*) Show interest in and unconditional acceptance of the person –
smile, greet, talk to, etc.

(*c*) Don't emphasise failings and shortcomings but concentrate on
positive facets.

(*d*) Don't be too critical or cynical but provide encouragement.

(*e*) Make any necessary criticism specific to the context rather
than it become a criticism of the whole person so that the
person fails on a particular task – he is not a failure *in toto*.
Reject the bad behaviour not the whole person.

(*f*) Prevent a fear of trying through fear of failing.

(*g*) Be pleased with a worthwhile attempt and give credit for
trying.

But the best guidance with which to leave the reader would seem
to be the following poem, which contains in a nutshell the basic
principles which determine how each and every one comes to feel
about themselves, invoking trust, respect, encouragement and
warm acceptance from all to all.

If a child lives with criticism
He learns to condemn
If a child lives with hostility
He learns to fight
If a child lives with ridicule
He learns to be shy
If a child lives with shame
He learns to feel guilty
If a child lives with tolerance
He learns to be patient
If a child lives with encouragement
He learns confidence
If a child lives with praise
He learns to appreciate
If a child lives with fairness
He learns justice
If a child lives with security
He learns to have faith
If a child lives with approval
He learns to like himself
If a child lives with acceptance and friendship
He learns to find love in the world.

Source unknown.

References

Abercombie, K. (1968) Paralanguage, *Br. J. Dis. Comm.*, **3**, 55–9.

Acland, H. (1973) Streaming in English primary schools, *Br. J. Educ. Psychol.*, **43**, 151–61.

Adams, N. M. and Caldwell, W. (1963) The children's somatic apperception test, *J. Gen. Psychol.*, **68**, 43–57.

Adler, A. (1927) *The Practice and Theory of Individual Psychology*, New York: Harcourt Brace.

Adorno, T. W., Frenkel-Brunswik, L., Levinson, D. J. and Sanford, R. N. (1950) *The Authoritarian Personality*, New York: Harper.

Alban Metcalfe, B. M. (1978) Changes in self concept on transfer from primary to secondary school, unpub. M.Sc. thesis, Bradford Univ.

Allen, B. P. and Potkay, C. R. (1973) Variability of self description on a day to day basis, *J. Pers.*, **41**, 638–47.

Allen, F. (1942) *Psycho-therapy with Children*, New York: Norton.

Allport, G. W. (1943) The ego in contemporary psychology, *Psychol. Rev.* **50**, 451–78.

Allport, G. W. (1955) *Becoming: Basic Considerations for a Psychology of Personality*, New Haven: Yale Univ. Press.

Allport, G. W. (1961) *Pattern and Growth in Personality*, New York: Holt.

Allport, G. W. and Odbert, H. (1936) Trait names: A psycholexical study, *Psychol. Monogr.*, **47** (211), 1–171.

Anderson, H. H. (1968) Likeableness ratings of 555 personality trait words, *J. Pers. Soc. Psychol.*, **9**, 272–9.

Andrews, R. J. (1966) The self concepts of pupils with learning difficulties, *The Slow Learning Child*, **13**, 47–54.

Angyal, A. (1941) *Foundations for a Science of Personality*, New York: Commonwealth Fund.

Ansbacher, H. L. and Ansbacher, R. A. (1956) *The Individual Psychology of Alfred Adler*, Allen and Unwin: London.

Argyle, M. (1967) *Psychology of Interpersonal Behaviour*, Penguin: London.

Argyle, M. and Lee, V. (1972) *Social Relationships*, Bletchley: Open Univ. Press.

Armstrong, R. G. (1958) The Leary interpersonal check list: a reliability study, *J. Clin. Psychol.*, **14**, 393–4.

Aronson, E. and Mettee, D. (1968) Dishonest behaviour as a function of differential levels of induced self esteem, *J. Pers. Soc. Psychol.*, **9**, 121–7.

Ausubel, D. P. and Robinson, F. G, (1969) *School Learning*, New York: Holt.

Babladelis, G. and Adams, S. (1967) *The Shaping of Personality*, New York: Prentice-Hall.

Back, K. W. (1971) Transition in ageing and the self image, *Int. J. Ageing and Hum. Dev.*, **2**, 144–7.

Backman, C. W., Secord, P. F. and Pierce, J. R. (1963) Resistance to change in the self concept as a function of concensus among significant others, *Sociometry*, **25**, 102–11.

Bakan, K. W. (1966) *The Duality of Human Existence*, Chicago: Rand McNally.

Balester, R. J. (1956) The self concept and juvenile delinquency, *Diss. Abstr.*, **16**, 1169–70.

314   *References*

Bandura, A. (1965) Influence of models' reinforcement contingencies on the acquisition of imitative responses, *J. Pers. Soc. Psychol.*, **1**, 589–95.

Bandura, A., Ross, D. and Ross, S. A. (1961) Transmission of aggression through imitation of aggressive models, *J. Abnorm. Soc. Psychol.*, **63**, 575–82.

Bandura, A., Ross, D. and Ross, S. A. (1963a) A comparative test of status envy, social power and secondary reinforcement theories of identification learning, *J. Abnorm. Soc. Psychol.*, **67**, 527–34.

Bandura, A., Ross, D. and Ross, S. A. (1963b) Imitation of film mediated aggressive models, *J. Abnorm. Soc. Psychol.*, **66**, 3–11.

Bannister, D. and Mair, J. M. (1968) *Evaluation of Personal Constructs.* London: Academic Press.

Barker Lunn, J. C. (1970) *Streaming in the Primary School,* Slough: NFER.

Baron, P. H. (1974) Self esteem, ingratiation and evaluation of unknown others, *J. Pers. Soc. Psychol.*, **30** (1), 104–9.

Battle, J. (1976) Test–retest reliability of the Canadian self esteem inventory for children, *Psychol. Rep.*, **38**, 1343–5.

Battle, J. (1977a) Test–retest reliability of the Canadian self esteem inventory for children, *Psychol. Rep.* **40**, 157–8.

Battle, J. (1977b) Test–retest reliability of the Canadian self esteem inventory for adults, *Percept. Motor Skills*, **44**, 1–2.

Bayley, N. and Schaefer, E. S. (1960) Maternal behaviour and personality development, *Psychiat. Res. Rep.*, **13**, 153–73.

Bayne, R. (1972) Psychology and encounter groups, *Bull. Br. Psychol. Soc.*, **25**, 285–9.

Behrens, M. L. (1954) Child rearing and the character structure of mother, *Child Dev.*, **25**, 225–38.

Bellak, A. S. (1975) Self evaluation, self reinforcement and locus of control, *J. Res. Pers.*, **9**, 158–67.

Benjamins, J. (1950) Changes in performance in relation to influences on self conceptualisation, *J. Abnorm. Psychol.*, **45**, 473–80.

Bennett, E. M. and Cohen, L. R. (1959) Men and women: personality patterns and contrasts, *Genet. Psychol. Monogr.*, **60**, 101–53.

Bennett, V. D. C. (1964) Development of a self concept Q sort for use with elementary age school children, *J. Sch. Psychol.*, **3**, 19–24.

Berger, E. M. (1952) The relation between expressed acceptance of self and expressed acceptance of others, *J. Abnorm. Soc. Psychol.*, **47** (4), 778–82.

Bergin, A. E. (1962) The effect of dissonant persuasive communication upon changes in self-referring attitudes, *J. Pers.*, **30**, 423–38.

Bergscheid, E., Walster, E. and Borhnstedt, G. (1973) The happy American body, *Psychol. Today*, **7**, 119–31.

Bertocci, P. A. (1945) The psychological self, the ego and personality, *Psychol. Rev.*, **52**, 91–9.

Bidney, D. (1953) *Theoretical Anthropology,* New York: Columbia Univ. Press.

Bills, R. E. (1953) A validation of changes in scores on the index of adjustment and values as measures of changes in emotionality, *J. Consult. Psychol.*, **17**, 135–8.

Bills, R. E. (1958) *Manual for the Index of Adjustment and Values,* Auburn: Alabama Polytechnic.

Bills, R. E., Vance, E. L. and McLean, O. S. (1951) An index of adjustment and values, *J. Consult. Psychol.*, **15**, 257–61.

Bledsoe, J. C. (1964) Self concepts of children and their intelligence, achievement interests and anxiety, *J. Indivl. Psychol.*, **20**, 55–8.

Bledsoe, J. (1967) Self concept of children and their intelligence, achievement, interests and anxiety, *Child. Educ.*, **43**, 463–8.

Bledsoe, J. C. (1973) Sex differences in self concept: fact or artifact? *Psychol. Rep.* **32**, 1253–4.

Block, J. H. (1973) Conceptions of sex role, *Amer. Psychol.*, **28**, 512–26.

Block, J. H. and **Thomas, H.** (1955) Is satisfaction with self a measure of adjustment? *J. Abnorm. Soc. Psychol.,* **51,** 254–9.

Blodgett, H. C. (1929) The effect of the introduction of reward upon maze behaviour in rats, *Univ. Calif. Publ. Psychol.,* **4,** 113–34.

Bogo, N., Winget, C. and **Gleser, G.** (1970) Ego defenses and perceptual styles, *Percept. Motor Skills,* **30,** 599–604.

Bond, A. and **Lader, M.** (1976) Self concepts in anxiety states, *Br. J. Med. Psychol.,* **49,** 275–80.

Borislow, B. (1962) Self evaluation and academic achievement, *J. Counsel. Psychol.,* **9,** 246–54.

Borke, H. (1972) Chandler and Greenspoon's ersatz egocentrism, *Dev. Psychol.,* **7,** 107–9.

Boshier, R. (1968) Self esteem and the first names of children, *Psychol. Rep.,* **22,** 762.

Bossom, J. and **Maslow, A. H.** (1957) Security of judges as a factor in the impressions of warmth in others, *J. Abnorm. Soc. Psychol.,* **55,** 147–8.

Bousfield, W. A. (1940) Student's ratings on the qualities considered desirable in college professors, *School and Society,* 24 Feb., 253–6.

Braught, G., Brakarsh, D., Follingstad, D. and **Berry, K. A.** (1973) Deviant drug use in adolescence, *Psychol. Bull.,* **79,** 92–106.

Brehm, M. H. and **Back, K. W.** (1968) Self image and attitudes towards drugs, *J. Pers.,* **36,** 299–313.

Brill, N. Q., Crumpton, E. and **Grayson, H. M.** (1971) Personality factors in marijuana use, *Archs. Gen. Psychiat.,* **24,** 163–5.

Brisset, D. (1972) Toward a clarification of self esteem, *Psychiatry,* **35,** 255–63.

Brodbeck, A. and **Perlmutter, H.** (1954) Self dislike as a determinant of marked ingroup–outgroup preference, *J. Psychol.,* **38,** 271–80.

Brodsky, C. M. (1954) *A study of Norms for Body Form-behaviour Relationships,* Washington DC: Catholic Univ. of America Press.

Bronfenbrenner, U. (1961) Some familiar antecedents of responsibility and leadership in adolescents, in J. Putrells and A. R. Bass (eds) *Leadership and Interpersonal Behaviour,* New York: Holt.

Bronfenbrenner, U. (1971) Reactions to social pressure from adults v. peers, in Chess, S. and Thomas, A. (eds) *Annual Progress in Child Psychiatry and Child Development,* New York: Bruner Mazel.

Brookover, W. B., Patterson, A. and **Thomas, S.** *Self Concept of Ability and School Achievement.* Cooperative Research Project No. 845, East Lansing, Michigan State Univ.

Brookover, W. B., Patterson, A. and **Thomas, S.** (1965) *Self Concept of Ability and School Achievement: Improving Academic Achievement Through Students' Self Concept Enhancement,* II, US Office of Education, Research Project 1636, Michigan State Univ.

Brookover, W. B., Thomas, S. and **Patterson, A.** (1964) Self concept of ability and school achievement, *Sociol. Educ.,* **37,** 271–8.

Brookover, W. B., Erikson, E. L. and **Joiner, L. M.** (1967) *Self Concept of Ability and School Achievement,* III, Cooperative Research Project No. 2831, East Lansing, Michigan State Univ.

Broverman, I. K., Vogel, S., Broverman, D. M., Clarkson, F. E. and **Rosenkrantz, P. S.** (1972) Sex role stereotypes: a current appraisal, *J. Soc. Issues,* **28,** 59–78.

Brown, D. G. (1957) Masculinity–femininity development in children, *J. Consult. Psychol.,* **21,** 197–202.

Bruce, P. (1958) Relationship of self acceptance to other variables with sixth grade children oriented in self understanding, *J. Educ. Psychol.,* **49,** 229–37.

Bruch, M., Kunce, J. T. and **Eggeman, D. F.** (1972) Parental devaluation, *J. Counsel. Psychol.,* **19,** 555–8.

Bruner, J. S. and **Goodman, C.** (1947) Value and need as organising factors in perception, *J. Abnorm. Soc. Psychol.,* **42,** 33–44.

Bugental, J. and Zelen, S. (1948) Who are you? A preliminary report on a method of studying the phenomenal self, *Amer. Psychol.*, **4**, 387.

Bugental, J. and Zelen, S. (1950) Investigation into the self concept: 1 the WAY technique, *J. Pers.*, **18**, 483–98.

Buhler, C. (1935) *From Birth to Maturity,* London: Kegan Paul.

Burke, D. A. and Sellin, D. F. (1972) Self concept of ability as a worker scale, *Excptl Child.*, Oct., 145–51.

Burns, R. B. (1975) Attitudes to self and to three categories of others in a student group, *Educ. Stud.*, **1**, 181–9.

Burns, R. B. (1976a) The concept-scale interaction problem, *Educ. Stud.*, **2**, 121–7.

Burns, R. B. (1976b) Self and teaching approaches, *Durham Res. Rev.*, No. 36, 1079–85.

Burns, R. B. (1977) Male and female perceptions of their own and the other sex, *Br. J. Soc. Clin. Psychol.*, **16**, 213–20.

Burns, R. B. (1978) The influence of various characteristics of others on social distance registered by a student group. *Irish J. Psychol.* (in press).

Burstall, C. (1970) *French in the Primary School,* Slough: NFER.

Butler, J. M. and Haigh, G. V. (1954) Changes in the relation between self concept and ideal concepts consequent upon client centred counseling, in C. R. Rogers, and R. F. Dymond (eds) *Psychotherapy and Personality Change,* Chicago: Univ. Chicago Press, pp. 55–75.

Calden, G., Lundy, R. M. and Schlafer, R. J. (1959) Sex differences in body concepts, *J. Consult. Psychol.*, **23**, 378–9.

Callison, C. P. (1974) Experimental induction of self concept, *Psychol. Rep.*, **35**, 1235–8.

Calvin, A. P., Wayne, A. and Holtzman, H. (1953) Adjustment and the discrepancy between the self concept and inferred self, *J. Consult Psychol.*, **17**, 206–13.

Campbell, J. P. and Dunnette, M. D. (1968) Effectiveness of T group experiences in managerial training and development, *Psychol. Bull.*, **70**, 73–104.

Canter, A. (1960) The efficacy of a short form of the MMPI to evaluate depression and morale loss, *J. Consult. Psychol.*, **24**, 14–17.

Caplan, S. W. (1957) The effect of group counselling on junior high school boys concepts of themselves in school, *J. Counsel. Psychol.*, **4**, 124–8.

Carkhuff, R. R. (1969) *Helping and Human Relations* (2 vols.), New York: Holt.

Carlson, R. (1965) Stability and change in the adolescent self image, *Child. Dev.*, **35**, 659–66.

Carroll, A. W. (1967) The effects of segregated and partially integrated school programmes on self concept and academic achievement of educable mental retardates, *Excptl. Child.*, **34**, 92–9.

Carter, T. P. (1968) The negative self concepts of Mexican American students, *School and Society*, **96**, 217–19.

Caslyn, R. J. and Kenny, D. A. (1977) Self concept of ability and perceived evaluation of others: cause or effect of academic achievement, *J. Educ. Psychol.*, **69**, 136–45.

Cattell, R. B. (1946) *Description and Measurement of Personality,* London: Harrap.

Cattell, R. B. (1950) *Personality. A Systematic, Theoretical and Factual Study,* New York: McGraw-Hill.

Cattell, R. B. and Child, D. (1975) *Motivation and Dynamic Structure,* London: Holt.

Centi, P. (1965) Self perception of students and motivation, *Catholic Educ. Rev.*, **63**, 307–19.

Chandler, T. A. (1976) A note on relationship of internality, externality, self acceptance and self ideal discrepancies, *J. Psychol.*, **94**, 145–6.

Chase, P. H. (1957) Self concept in adjusted and maladjusted hospital patients, *J. Consult. Psychol.*, **21**, 495–7.

Chein, I. (1944) Awareness of self and the structure of the ego, *Psychol. Rev.*, **51**, 304–14.

Chodorkoff, B. (1954) Self perception, perceptual defense, and adjustment, *J. Abnorm. Soc. Psychol.*, **49**, 508–12.

Clark, K. B. and **Clark, M. P.** (1958) Racial identification and preference in negro children, in E. P. Maccoby *et al.* (eds), *Readings in Social Psychology*, New York: Holt.

Clifford, E. and **Clifford, M.** (1967) Self concepts before and after survival training, *Br. J. Soc. Clin. Psychol.*, **6**, 241–8.

Cogan, M. L. (1958) The behaviour of teachers and the productive behaviour of their pupils. *J. Exp. Educ.*, **26**, 89–124.

Cohen, A. and **Cohen, L.** (1974) Children's attitudes towards primary school activities, *Durham Res. Rev.*, **32**, 847–56.

Cohen, A. R. (1954) Some explorations in self esteem, unpub. paper, Univ. of Michigan.

Cohen, A. R. (1959) Some implications of self esteem for social influence, in C. I. Hovland and I. L. Janis (eds), *Personality and Persuasibility*, New Haven: Yale Univ. Press.

Cohen, L. (1974) Labelling and alienation in a British secondary school, *Educ. Rev.*, **26**, 100–8.

Cohen, L. (1976) *Educational Research in Classrooms and Schools: A Manual of Materials and Methods*, London: Harper and Row.

Coleman, J. S. (1966) *Equality of Educational Opportunity*, Washington DC: US Government Printing Office.

Coleman, J. S. (1974) *Relationships in Adolescence*, New York: Routledge.

Combs, A. W. (1964) The personal approach to good teaching, *Educ. Leadership*, **21**, 369–77.

Combs, A. W. (1965) *The Professional Education of Teachers*, Boston: Allyn and Bacon.

Combs, A. W. and **Soper, D. W.** (1957) The self, its derivative terms and research, *J. Indivl Psychol.*, **13**, 134–45.

Combs, A. W. and **Soper, D. W.** (1963) The relationship of child perceptions to achievement and behaviour in the early school years, Cooperative Research Project, No. 814, Univ. of Florida.

Combs, A. W., Soper, D. W. and **Courson, C. C.** (1963) The measurement of self concept and self report, *Educ. Psychol. Meas.*, **23**, 493–500.

Connell, D. M. and **Johnson, J.** (1970) Relationships between sex role identification and self esteem in early adolescents, *Dev. Psychol.*, **3**, 268.

Connell, W. F., Stroobant, R. E., Sinclair, K. E., Connell, R. W. and **Rogers, K. W.** (1975) *Twelve to Twenty*, Sydney: Hicks Smith.

Constantinople, A. (1969) An Eriksonian measure of personality development of college students, *Dev. Psychol.*, **1**, 357–72.

Cooley, C. H. (1912) *Human Nature and the Social Order*, New York: Scribners.

Cooper, C. L. (1974) The impact of marathon encounters on teacher–student relationships, *Interpersonal Dev.*, **5**, 71–7.

Coopersmith, S. (1967) *The Antecedents of Self Esteem*, San Francisco: Freeman.

Costin, F. (1959) The effect of an introductory psychology course on self insight, *J. Educ. Psychol.*, **33**, 83–7.

Couch, J. and **Kenniston, P.** (1960) Yeasayers and naysayers, in Mednick and Mednick (eds), *Research into Personality*. New York: Holt.

Courson, C. C. (1965) The use of inference as a research tool, *Educ. Psychol. Meas.*, **25**, 1029–38.

Cowen, E. L. (1956) An investigation of the relationship between two measures of self regarding attitudes, *J. Clin. Psychol.*, **12**, 156–60.

Cowen, E. L., Heilizer, F., Axecrod, H. S. and **Alexander, S.** (1957) The correlates of manifest anxiety in perceptual reactivity, rigidity and self concept, *J. Consult. Psychol.*, **21**, 405–11.

Cowen, E. L. and **Tongas, P. N.** (1959) The social desirability of trait descriptive terms, *J. Consult. Psychol.*, **23**, 361–5.

Crane, C. (1974) Attitudes towards acceptance of self and others and adjustment to teaching, *Br. J. Educ. Psychol.*, **44**, pt. 1, 31–6.

Creelman, M. B. (1955) The C.S.C. test. *Diss. Abstr.*, **15** (10).

Crowne, D. P., Stephens, M. W. and Kelly, R. (1961) The validity and equivalence of tests of self acceptance, *J. Psychol.*, **51**, 101–12.

Culbert, S. A., Clark, J. V. and Bobele, H. K. (1968) Measures of change in self actualisation in two sensitivity training groups, *J. Counsel. Psychol.*, **15**, 53–7.

David, S. and Lawton, M. (1961) Self concept, mother concept and food aversions in emotionally disturbed and normal children, *J. Abnorm. Soc. Psychol.*, **62**, 309–16.

Davidson, H. H. and Greenberg, J. W. (1967) *School Achievers from a Deprived Background*, Project No. 2805, City College of the City Univ. of New York.

Davidson, H. H. and Lang, G. (1960) Children's perceptions of their teachers' feelings towards them related to self perception, school achievement and behaviour, *J. Exp. Educ.*, **29**, 107–18.

Davie, R., Butler, N. and Goldstein, H. (1972) *From Birth to Seven*, 2nd Report of the National Child Development Study, London: Longman.

Davis, A. J. (1969) Self concept, occupational role expectations and occupational choice in nursing and social work, *Nursing Res.*, **18**, 55–9.

Deblaissie, R. R. and Healy, G. W. (1970) *A Comparison of Spanish American, Negro and Anglo Adolescents Across Ethnic, Sex and Socio-economic Variables*, Las Cruces: Clearing House on Rural Education and Small Schools.

Demeritt, M. W. (1970) Differences in the self concept of drug abusers, non users and former users of narcotics and/or non narcotic drugs, *Diss. Abstr.*, **31** (3A), 1008.

Dietz, G. E. (1969) A comparison of delinquents with non-delinquents on self concept, self acceptance and parental identification, *J. Genet. Psychol.*, **115**, 285–95.

Dickoff, H., Altrocchi, J. and Parsons, O. A. (1961) Changes in self-ideal discrepancy in repressors and sensitizers, *J. Abnorm. Soc. Psychol.*, **61**, 67–72.

Dion, K. K. and Dion, K. L. (1975) Self esteem and romantic love, *J. Pers.*, **43**, 39–57.

Dixon, J. C. and Street, J. W. (1975) The distinction between self and not-self in children and adolescents, *J. Genet. Psychol.*, **127**, 157–62.

Dobzhansky, T. (1967) *The Biology of Ultimate Concern*, New York: New American Library.

Douvan, E. and Adelson, J. (1966) *The Adolescent Experience*, New York: Wiley.

Douvan, E. and Gold, M. (1966) Modal patterns in American adolescents, in M. Hoffman and L. Hoffman (eds), *Review of Child Development Research*, Vol. 2, New York: Russell Sage.

Dua, D. P. (1970) Comparison of effects of behaviourally oriented action and psycho therapy re-education in introversion–extraversion, emotionality and internal–external control, *J. Counsel. Psychol.*, **17**, 567–72.

Eastman, D. (1958) Self concept and marital adjustment, *J. Consult. Psychol.*, **22**, 95–9.

Edeburn, C. and Landry, R. (1974) Self concepts of students and a significant other: the teacher, *Psychol. Rep.*, Aug. pt. 2, 505–6.

Edgar, P., Powell, R. J., Watkins, D., Moore, R. J. and Zakharov, O. (1974) An analysis of the Coopersmith self esteem inventory, *Aust. Psychol.*, **9**, 52–63.

Edwards, A. L. (1957) *The Social Desirability Variable in Personality Assessment and Research*, New York: Holt.

Edwards, A. L. (1959) Social desirability and the description of others. *J. Abnorm. Soc. Psychol.*, **59**, 434–6.

Eiben, R. and Clack, R. J. (1973) Impact of participatory group experience on counsellors in training, *Small Gp Beh.*, **4**, 486–95.

Eitzen, S. (1976) The self concept of delinquents in a behaviour modification treatment program, *J. Soc. Psychol.*, **99**, 203–6.

Emmett, R. G. (1959) Psychological study of the self concept in secondary modern school pupils, M.A. thesis, Univ. of London.

Engle, M. (1959) The stability of the self concept in adolescence, *J. Abnorm. Soc. Psychol.,* **58,** 211–15.

Engel, M. and **Raine, W. J.** (1963) A method for the measurement of the self concept of children in the 3rd grade, *J. Genet. Psychol.,* **102,** 125–37.

Ensor, E. G. (1976) A comparison of dyadic interactions between high and low self concept of ability children and their teachers, unpub. M.Sc. thesis, Bradford Univ.

Epps, E. G. (1969) Correlates of academic achievement among northern and southern urban negro students, *J. Soc. Issues,* **25,** 55–70.

Epstein, S. (1955) Unconscious self evaluation in a normal and a schizophrenic group, *J. Abnorm. Soc. Psychol.,* **50,** 65–70.

Epstein, S. (1973) The self concept revisited: or a theory of a theory, *Amer. Psychol.,* May, 404–16.

Erikson, E. H. (1956) The problem of ego identity, *J. Amer. Psychoan. Assoc.,* **4,** 58–121.

Erikson, E. H. (1963) *Childhood and Society,* New York: Norton.

Erikson, E. H. (1965) Psychoanalysis and on-going history: problems of identity hatred and non violence, *Amer. J. Psychiat,* **122,** 241–50.

Erikson, E. H. (1968) *Identity, Youth and Crisis,* New York: Norton.

Fein, D., O'Neill, S., Frank, C. and **Velit, K.** (1975) Sex differences in pre-adolescent self-esteem, *J. Psychol.,* **90,** 179–84.

Feldhusen, J. F. and **Thurston, J. R.** (1964) Personality and adjustment of high and low anxious children, *J. Educ. Res.,* **57,** 265–7.

Ferri, E. (1971) *Streaming: Two Years Later,* Slough: NFER.

Festinger, L. (1954) A theory of social comparison processes, *Hum. Rel.,* **7,** 117–40.

Festinger, L. (1957) *A Theory of Cognitive Dissonance,* New York: Harper.

Fey, W. F. (1954) Acceptance of self and others and its relation to therapy readiness, *J. Clin. Psychol.,* **10,** 266–9.

Fink, M. (1962) Self concept as it relates to academic underachievement, *Calif. J. Educ. Res.,* **13,** 57–62.

Fisher, M. (1934) *Language Patterns of Pre-school Children,* New York: Columbia Univ. Press.

Fitts, W. H. (1965) *Manual Tennessee Department of Mental Health Self Concept Scale,* Nashville: Tennessee.

Foulds, G. A. and **Bedford, A.** (1977) Self esteem and psychiatric syndromes, *Br. J. Med. Psychol.,* **50,** 237–42.

Foulds, M. L. (1970) Effects of a personal growth group on a measure of self actualisation. *J. Hum. Psychol.,* **10,** 33–8.

Fransella, F. and **Adams, B.** (1965) An illustration of the use of a Rep Grid technique in a clinical setting, *Br. J. Soc. Clin. Psychol.,* **5,** 51.

Frazier, A. and **Lisonbee, L. K.** (1950) Adolescent concerns with physique, *School Rev.,* **58,** 397–405.

Fredericksen, N. and **Messick, S.** (1959) Response set as a measure of personality, *Educ. Psychol. Meas.,* **19,** 137–57.

Freeman, F. (1950) *Theory and Practice of Psychological Testing,* London: Pitman.

Frenkel-Brunswik, E. (1948) A study of prejudice in children, *Hum. Rel.,* **1,** 295–306.

Frerichs, A. H. (1971) Relationship of self esteem of the disadvantaged to school success, *J. Negro. Educ.,* **40,** 117–20.

Freud, A. (1946) *The Ego and the Mechanisms of Defence,* New York: International Univ. Press.

Freud, S. (1923) *The Ego and the Id,* London: Hogarth Press.

Friedman, I. (1955) Phenomenal, ideal, and projected conceptions of the self, *J. Abnorm. Soc. Psychol.,* **51,** 611–15.

Fromm, E. (1939) Selfishness and self-love, *Psychiatry,* **2,** 507–23.

Fromm, E. (1964) *The Heart of Man,* New York: Harper and Row.

Fromm-Reichmann, F. (1950) *Principles of Intensive Psychotherapy,* Chicago: Univ. Chicago Press.

Furlong, A. and **LaForge, H.** (1975) Manifest anxiety and the self concept, *J. Genet. Psychol.,* **127**, 237–48.

Gabbler, R. G. and **Gibby, R.** (1967) The self concept of negro and white children, *J. Clin. Psychol.,* **23**, 144–8.

Garvey, R. (1970) Self concept and success in student teaching, *J. Teach. Educ.,* **21**, 357–61.

Garwood, G. (1976) First name stereotypes as a factor in self concept and school achievement, *J. Educ. Psychol.,* **68**, 482–7.

Gergen, K. (1965) The effects of interaction goals and personalistic feedback on the presentation of self, *J. Pers. Soc. Psychol.,* **1**, 413–24.

Gergen, K. J. (1971) *The Concept of Self,* New York: Holt.

Gesell, A. and **Ilg, F.** (1949) *Child Development,* New York: Harper.

Gibb, J. R. (1970) Effects of human relations training, in A. Bergin and S. Garfield (eds), *Handbook of Psychotherapy and Behaviour Change,* New York: Wiley.

Gibby, R. G. and **Gabler, R.** (1967) The self concept of negro and white children, *J. Clin. Psychol.,* **23**, 144–8.

Glueck, S. and **Glueck, E.** (1950) *Unravelling Juvenile Delinquency,* New York: Harper.

Goffman, E. (1959) *The Presentation of Self in Everyday Life,* New York: Doubleday Anchor.

Goffman, E. (1967) *Interaction Ritual: Essays in Face-to-Face Behaviour,* Chicago: Aldine Press.

Goldstein, K. (1939) *The Organism,* New York: American Book Co.

Goodenough, F. (1938) Note on the development of self awareness, *J. Genet. Psychol.,* **52**, 333–46.

Gordon, C. (1968) Self conceptions: configurations of content, in C. Gordon and K. Gergen (eds.) *The Self in Social Interaction,* Vol. 1, New York: Wiley.

Gordon, C. and **Gergen, K. J.** (eds) (1968) *The Self in Social Interaction,* Vol. 1, New York: Wiley.

Gordon, I. (1966) *Studying the Child in School,* New York: Wiley.

Gordon, T. and **Cartwright, D.** (1954) The effect of psycho-therapy on attitudes to others, in C. Rogers and R. Dymond (eds), *Psychotherapy and Personality Change,* Chicago: Univ. Chicago Press.

Gough, H. G. (1950) Children's ethnic attitudes: relations to parental beliefs concerning child training, *Child Dev.,* **21**, 169–81.

Gough, H. G. and **Heillbron, A. B.** (1965) *Adjective Check List Manual,* Palo Alto: Consulting Psychologists Press.

Groobman, D. E., Forward, J. and **Peterson, C.** (1976) Attitudes, self-esteem and learning in formal and informal schools, *J. Educ. Psychol.,* **68**, 32–35.

Gross, L. Z. (1947) Construction and partial standardisation of a scale for measuring self insight, Ph.D. dissert. (unpub.), Univ. of Minnesota.

Guildford, J. P. (1954) *Psychometric Methods,* New York: McGraw-Hill.

Guildford, J. P. (1956) The structure of intellect, *Amer. Psychol.,* **14**, 469–79.

Guthrie, E. R. (1938) *Psychology of Human Conflict,* New York: Harper.

Guthrie, E. R. (1952) *Psychology of Learning,* New York: Harper.

Haas, H. I. and **Maehr, M. L.** (1965) Two experiments on the concept of self and the reaction of others, *J. Pers. Soc. Psychol.,* **1**, 100–5.

Hall, C. S. and **Lindzey, G.** (1957) *Theories of Personality,* New York: Wiley.

Hamid, P. (1969) Word meaning and self description, *J. Soc. Psychol.,* **79**, 51–4.

Hanlon, E., Hofstaetter, P. and **O'Connor, J.** (1954) Congruence of self and ideal self in relation to personality adjustment, *J. Consult. Psychol.,* **18** (3), 215–18.

Hardstaffe, M. (1973) Some social conceptions of secondary modern school pupils, M.Sc. dissert. (unpub.), School of Research in Education, Univ. of Bradford.

Hart, W. F. (1934) *Teachers and Teaching,* New York: Macmillan.

Hartmann, H. (1958) *Ego Psychology and the Problem of Adaptation,* New York: International Univ. Press.

Hawkins, K. (1972) West Indian boys in school, unpub. M.Sc. thesis, Univ. of Bradford.

Havighurst, R. J. and **MacDonald, D. V.** (1955) Development of the ideal self in New Zealand and American children, *J. Educ. Res.,* **49,** 263–73.

Havighurst, R. J., Robinson, M. Z. and **Dorr, M.** (1946) The development of the ideal self in childhood and adolescence, *J. Educ. Res.,* **40,** 241–57.

Hazell, W. J. (1975) Query. An action-insight exercise, *Small Gp Beh.,* **6,** 494–500.

Heider, F. (1958) *Psychology of Interpersonal Relations,* New York: Wiley.

Heilbrun, A. B. (1965) The measurement of identification, *Child. Dev.,* **36,** 111–27.

Heiss, J. and **Owens, S.** (1972) Self evaluations of Blacks and Whites, *Amer. J. Sociol.,* **78,** 360–9.

Helper, M. M. (1955) Learning theory and self concept, *J. Abnorm. Soc. Psychol.,* **51,** 184–94.

Henderson, E. H., Long, B. H. and **Ziller, R. C.** (1965) Self-social constructs of achieving and non-achieving readers, *Reading Teacher,* **19,** 114–17.

Henle, J. and **Hubble, T.** (1938) Egocentricity in adult conversation, *J. Soc. Psychol.,* **9,** 227–34.

Hensley, W. E. and **Roberts, M. K.** (1967) Dimensions of Rosenberg's self esteem scale, *Psych. Rep.,* Apr., **38,** 583–4.

Hersh, P. D. and **Schiebe, K.** (1967) Reliability and validity of internal–external control as a personality dimension, *J. Consult. Psychol.,* **31,** 609–13.

Hewitt, J. and **Kraft, M.** (1973) Effects of an encounter group experience on self perception and interpersonal relations, *J. Consult. Clin. Psychol.,* **40,** 162.

Higgins, L. C. (1962) Self concepts of mentally retarded adolescents, unpub. B.Litt., Univ. of New England.

Hilden, A. H. (1954) Manual for Q sorts, Washington Univ. (mimeo).

Hilgard, E. R. (1949) Human motives and the concept of the self, *Amer. Psychol.,* **4,** 374–82.

Hill, Sir D. (1968) Depression: disease, reaction or posture, *Amer. J. Psychiat.,* **125,** 445–57.

Horney, K. (1937) *Neurotic Personality of Our Times,* New York: Norton.

Horney, K. (1939) *New Ways in Psychoanalysis,* New York: Norton.

Horney, K. (1945) *Our Inner Conflicts,* New York: Norton.

Horney, K. (1950) *Neurosis and Human Growth,* New York: Norton.

Hovland, C. I. and **Janis, I. L.** (1959) *Personality and Persuasibility,* New Haven: Yale Univ. Press.

Hovland, C. I., Lumsdaine, A. A. and **Sheffield, F. D.** (1949) *Experiments on Mass Communication,* Princeton: Princeton Univ. Press.

Hume, D. (1928) *On Human Nature,* Oxford: Clarendon Press.

Humphrey, C. (1971) Clothing and the self concepts of adolescents, *J. Home Econ.,* **63,** 246–50.

Hunt, J. McV. (1971) Using intrinsic motivation to teach young children, *Educ. Tech.,* **2,** 78–80.

Hurlock, E. B. (1967) *Adolescent Development,* New York: McGraw-Hill.

Jackson, D. N. and **Messick, S. J.** (1957) A note on ethnocentrism and the acquiescent response set, *J. Abnorm. Soc. Psychol.,* **54,** 132–4.

James, W. (1890) *Principles of Psychology,* New York: Holt.

Jensen, J. M., Michael, J. J. and **Michael, W. B.** (1975) The concurrent validity of the primary self concept scale for a sample of third grade children, *Educ. Psychol. Meas.,* **35,** 1011–16.

Jersild, A. T. (1952) *In Search of Self,* New York: Bureau of Publications, Teachers' College, Columbia Univ.

Jersild, A. T. (1955) *When Teachers Face Themselves,* New York: Teachers College, Columbia Univ.

Jones, E. E. (1964) *Ingratiation,* New York: Appleton-Century-Crofts.

Jones, E. E., Gergen, K. J. and **Davis, K.** (1962) Some reactions to being approved or disapproved as a person, *Psychol. Monogr.*, **76**, Whole No. 521.

Jones, J. G. and **Grieneeks, L.** (1970) Measures of Self perception as predictors of scholastic achievement, *J. Educ. Res.*, **63**, 201–3.

Jones, M. C. (1957) The later career of boys who were early or late maturing, *Child Dev.*, **28**, 113–28.

Jones, M. C. (1958) A study of socialisation at the high school level. *J. Genet. Psychol.*, **93**, 87–111.

Jones, M. C. and **Bayley, N.** (1950) Physical maturing among boys as related to behaviour, *J. Educ. Psychol.*, **41**, 129–48.

Jones, M. C. and **Mussen, P. H.** (1958) Self conceptions, motivations and interpersonal attitudes of early and late naturing girls. *Child Dev.*, **29**, 491–501.

Jones, S. C. (1973) Self and interpersonal evaluations: esteem theories v. consistency theories, *Psychol. Bull.*, **79**, 185–99.

Jorgensen, E. C. and **Howell, R. J.** (1969) Changes in self, ideal self correlation from ages 8 through 18, *J. Soc. Psychol.*, **79**, 63–7.

Jourard, S. M. and **Remy, R. M.** (1955) Perceived parental attitudes, the self and security, *J. Consult. Psychol.*, **19**, 364–6.

Jourard, S. M. and **Secord, P. F.** (1954) Body size and body cathexis, *J. Consult. Psychol.*, **18**, 184.

Jourard, S. M. and **Secord, P. F.** (1955a) Body cathexis and personality, *Br. J. Psychol.*, **46**, 130–8.

Jourard, S. M. and **Secord, P. F.** (1955b) Body cathexis and the ideal female figure, *J. Abnorm. Soc. Psychol.*, **50**, 243–6.

Judd, L. and **Smith, C. B.** (1974) Discrepancy score validity in self and ideal self concept measurement, *J. Counsel. Psychol.*, **21**, 156–8.

Judson, A. and **Cofer, C.** (1956) Reasoning as an associative process, *Psychol. Rep.*, **2**, 469–76.

Jung, C. G. (1960) *Collected Works* (14 vols.), Princeton: Princeton Univ. Press.

Kagan, J. (1964) The acquisition and significance of sex typing and sex role identity, in M. Hoffman and L. Hoffman (eds), *Review of Child Development Research*, Vol. 1, New York: Russell Sage.

Kagan, J. and **Lemkin, J.** (1960) The child's differential perception of parental esteem, *J. Abnorm. Soc. Psychol.*, **61**, 440–7.

Kagan, J. and **Moss, H. A.** (1962) *Birth to Maturity,* New York: Wiley.

Kant, I. (1934) *Critique of Pure Reason,* London: Macmillan.

Katz, P. and **Zigler, E.** (1967) Self image disparity: a developmental approach, *J. Pers. Soc. Psychol.*, **5**, 186–95.

Kaye, J. D. (1973) Group interaction and interpersonal learning, *Small Gp Beh.*, **4**, 424–48.

Kelly, G. A. (1955) *The Psychology of Personal Constructs,* New York: Norton.

Kennard, D. and **Clemmy, R.** (1976) Psychiatric patients as seen by self and others, *Br. J. Med. Psychol.*, **49**, 39–53.

Kenny, D. T. (1956) The influence of social desirability on discrepancy measures between real self and ideal self, *J. Consult. Psychol.*, **20**, 315–19.

Kilpatrick, F. P. and **Cantril, H.** (1965) Self anchoring scaling. A measure of individual unique reality worlds, in R. E. Hartley and E. L. Hartley (eds), *Readings in Psychology,* New York: Crowell.

King, M., Payne, D. and **McIntire, W. G.** (1973) The impact of marathon and prolonged sensitivity training on self acceptance, *Small Gp Beh.*, **4**, 415–23.

Kipnis, D. M. (1961) Changes in self concepts in relation to perceptions of others, *J. Pers.*, **29**, 449–65.

Kirchner, P. and **Vondraek, S.** (1975) Perceived sources of esteem in early childhood, *J. Genet. Psychol.*, **126**, 169–76.

Kleinfeld, J. (1972) The relative importance of teachers and parents in the formation of negro and white students' academic self concepts, *J. Educ. Res.*, **65**, 211–12.

Kohlberg, L. (1966) A cognitive developmental analysis of children's sex role concepts and attitudes, in E. Maccoby (ed.), *The Development of Sex Differences,* Stanford: Stanford Univ. Press.

Komarovsky, M. (1946) Cultural contradictions and sex roles, *Amer. J. Sociol.,* **52,** 184–9.

Korman, A. K. (1966) The self esteem variable in vocational choice, *J. Appl. Psychol.,* **50,** 479–86.

Korman, A. K. (1969) Self esteem as a moderator in vocational choice: replications and extensions, *J. Appl. Psychol.,* **53,** 188–92.

Kretch, D., Crutchfield, R. S. and **Ballachey, E. L.** (1962) *Individual in Society,* New York: McGraw-Hill.

Kretschmer, E. (1925) *Physique and Character,* London: Routledge and Kegan Paul.

Krug, S. E. and **Henry, T. J.** (1974) Personality, motivation, and adolescent drug use patterns, *J. Counsel. Psychol.,* **21,** 440–5.

Kubo, Y. (1933) Judgements of character traits in self and others, *Jap. J. Appl. Psychol.,* **1,** 105–116.

Kuhn, M. H. (1960) Self attitudes by age, sex and professional training, *Sociol. Quart.,* **1,** 39–55.

Kuhn, M. H. and **McPartland, T. S.** (1954) An empirical investigation of self attitudes, *Amer. Sociol. Rev.,* **19,** 68–76.

Kutner, B. (1958) Patterns of mental functioning associated with prejudice in children, *Psychol. Monogr.,* **72,** 7.

LaBenne, W. D. (1965) Pupil teacher interaction in a senior ungraded school, unpub. Ph.D. thesis, Univ. of Michigan.

LaBenne, W. and **Green, B.** (1969) *Educational Implications of Self Concept Theory,* Pacific Palisades: Goodyear Pub. Co.

LaForge, R. (1963) Research use of the I.C.L., *Oregon Res. Inst. Tech. Rep.,* **3** (4).

LaForge, R. and **Suczek, R. F.** (1955) The interpersonal dimension of personality, *J. Pers.,* **24,** 94–112.

Laing, R. D., Phillipson, H. and **Lee, A. R.** (1966) *Interpersonal Perception,* London: Tavistock.

Lamp, L. M. (1968) Defensiveness, dogmatism and self esteem, *Diss. Abstr.,* **29,** 2194B.

Lawrence, D. (1971) The effects of counselling on retarded readers, *Educ. Res.,* **13,** 119–24.

Lawrence, D. (1972) Counselling of retarded readers by non-professionals, *Educ. Res.,* **15,** 48–51.

Lawrence, E. A. and **Winschell, J. F.** (1973) Self concept and the retarded: research and issues, *Excptl. Child.,* **39,** 310–19.

Lazarus, R. S. *et al.* (1952) Autonomic discrimination without awareness: a study of subception, *Psychol. Rev.,* **58,** 113–22.

Leary, T. (1957) *Interpersonal Diagnosis of Personality,* New York: Ronald Press.

Lecky, P. (1945) *Self Consistency,* New York: Island Press.

Lefley, H. P. (1974) Societal and family correlates of self-esteem among American Indian children, *Child Dev.,* **45,** 829–33.

Leonard, R. L. (1975) Self concept and attraction for similar and dissimilar others, *J. Pers. Soc. Psychol.,* **31,** 926–9.

Lerner, R. M., Karabenick, S. A. and **Meisels, M.** (1975) Effects of age and sex on the development of personal space schemata towards body build, *J. Genet. Psychol.,* **127,** 91–101.

Levine, D. U. (1968) The integration–compensatory education controversy, *Educ. Forum,* **32,** 323–32.

Lewin, K. (1936) *Principles of Topological Psychology,* New York: McGraw-Hill.

Lewis, A. R. J. (1971) Self concepts of adolescent E.S.N. boys, *Br. J. Educ. Psychol.,* **41,** 222–3.

Linton, H. and **Graham, E.** (1959) Personality Correlates of Persuasibility, in, I. Hovland and I. Janis (eds), *Personality and Persuasibility,* New Haven: Yale Univ. Press.

Lipsitt, L. P. (1958) A self concept scale for children and its relationship to the children's form of the MAS, *Child Dev., 29,* 463–9.

Livesley, W. J. and **Bromley, D. B.** (1973) *Person Perception in Childhood and Adolescence,* Wiley: London.

Locke, J. (1960) *Concerning Human Understanding,* London: Oxford Univ. Press.

Loevinger, J. and **Ossorio, A.** (1959) Evaluation of therapy by self report, *J. Abnorm. Soc. Psychol., 58,* 392–4.

Lombardo, J. P., Saverio, C. and **Solheim, G.** (1975) The relationship of internality–externality self acceptance and self ideal discrepancies, *J. Genet. Psychol., 126,* 281–8.

Long, B. H., Henderson, E. H. and **Ziller, R. C.** (1967) Developmental changes in the self concept during middle childhood, *Merrill Palmer Quart., 13,* 201–19.

Long, B. H., Ziller, R. C. and **Henderson, E. G.** (1968) Developmental changes in the self concept during adolescence, *Sch. Rev., 76,* 210–30.

Louden, D. M. (1977) Conflict and change among W. Indian parents and adolescents in Britain, *Educ. Res., 20,* 44–53.

Luchins, H. I. and **Luchins, E. H.** (1948) Children's attitudes towards homogeneous groupings, *J. Genet. Psychol., 72,* 3–9.

Luria, Z. (1959) A semantic analysis of a normal and neurotic therapy group, *J. Abnorm. Soc. Psychiat., 58,* 216–20.

McCandless, B. (1967) *Children, Behaviour and Development,* New York: Holt.

McClain, E. W. (1970) Personal growth for teachers in training through self study, *J. Teach. Educ., 21,* 372–7.

McCleary, R. and **Lazarus, R. S.** (1949) Autonomic discrimination without awareness, *J. Pers., 18,* 171–9.

McDonald, A. P. (1971) Internal–external locus of control, *J. Counsel. Psychol., 18,* 111–16.

McDougall, W. (1908) *Introduction to Social Psychology,* London: Methuen.

McIntire, W. G. (1969) Relationship of sensitivity training to degree of self actualisation, Univ. Connecticut (unpub. M.A. thesis).

McIntire, W. G. (1973) The impact of T group experience on level of self actualisation, *Small Gp Beh., 4,* 459–65.

McKennell, A. C. and **Bynner, J. M.** (1969) Self image and smoking behaviour among school boys, *Br. J. Educ. Psychol., 39,* 27–39.

McLeod, R. (1964) Phenomenology. A challenge to experimental psychology, in T. Wann (ed.), *Behaviourism and Phenomenology,* New York: Wiley, pp. 47–63.

McPhail, C. (1972) The classification and ordering of responses to the question, 'who are you?', *Sociol. Quart., 13,* 329–47.

Maccoby, E. E. and **Jacklin, C. N.** (1974) *The Psychology of Sex Differences,* Stanford: Stanford Univ. Press.

Maehr, M. L., Mensing, J. and **Nafzger, S.** (1962) Concept of self and the reaction of others, *Sociometry, 25,* 353–57.

Mahoney, E. and **Finch M.** (1976) Body cathexis and self esteem, *J. Soc. Psychol., 99,* 251–8.

Many, M. A. and **Many W. A.** (1975) The relationship between self esteem and anxiety in grades 4 through 8, *Educ. Psychol. Meas., 35,* 1017–21.

Marks, I. M. (1965) *Patterns of Meaning in Psychiatric Patients,* Maudsley Monographs, London: OUP.

Maslow, A. H. (1954) *Motivation and Personality,* New York: Harper.

Maslow, A. H. (1962) Some basic propositions of a growth and self actualisation psychology, in A. W. Combs (ed.), *Perceiving, Behaving, Becoming,* ASCD Year Book, Washington DC.: NEA.

Maslow, A. H. (1967) Neurosis as a failure of personal growth, *Humanitus, 3,* 153–70.

Mason, J. and **Blumberg, A.** (1969) Perceived educational value of the classroom and teacher–pupil interpersonal relationship, *J. Sec. Educ., 44,* 135–9.

Mathes, E. W. and **Kahn, A.** (1975) Physical attractiveness, happiness, neuroticism, and self esteem, *J. Psychol., 90,* 27–30.

Mead, G. (1934) *Mind, Self, and Society,* Chicago: Univ. of Chicago Press.
Medinnus, G. R. and **Curtis, E. J.** (1963) The relation between maternal self acceptance and child acceptance, *J. Consult. Psychol.,* **27,** 542–4.
Mednick, S. A. (1960) Body image, personality and chi square, *Contemp. Psychol.,* **5,** 316–17.
Minuchin, P. (1964) Sex role concepts and sex typing in childhood as a function of school and home environments, *Child Dev.,* 1033–48.
Mitchell, J. V. (1959) Goal setting behaviour as a function of self acceptance, over and under achievement and related personality variables, *J. Educ. Psychol.,* **50,** 93–104.
Moffett, L. (1975) Sex differences in self concept, *Psychol. Rep.,* Aug., 74.
Momberg, A. P. and **Page, H. W.** (1977) Self esteem of coloured and white scholars and students in S. Africa, *J. Soc. Psychol.,* **102,** 179–82.
Monge, R. H. (1973) Developmental trends in factors of adolescent self concept, *Dev. Psychol.,* **8** (3), 382–92.
Morgan, J. B. (1944) Effect of non-rational factors on inductive reasoning, *J. Exp. Psychol.,* **34,** 159–68.
Morse, W. C. (1964) Self concept in a school setting, *Childhood Educ.,* Dec., 195–8.
Mueller, W. J. (1966) Need structure and projection of traits onto parents, *J. Pers. Soc. Psychol.,* **3,** 63–72.
Mulford, H. A. and **Salisbury, W.** (1964) Self conceptions in a general population, *Sociol. Quart,* **5,** 35–46.
Muller, D. G. and **Leonetti, R.** (1972) Primary self concept scale, National Consortia for Bilingual Education, Washington DC: Office of Education (DHEW) mimeo.
Murphy, G. (1947) *Personality. A Bio-Social Approach,* New York: Harper.
Murphy, G., Murphy, L. B. and **Newcomb, T. M.** (1937) *Experimental Social Psychology,* New York: Columbia Univ. Press.
Murray, H. A. (1953) Outline of a conception of personality, in H. A. Murray and C. Kluckhohn (eds), *Personality in Nature, Society and Culture,* New York: Knopf.
Musgrove, F. (1966) The social needs and satisfactions of some young people. Pt. II: At school, *Br. J. Educ. Psychol.,* **36,** 137–49.
Mussen, P. H. (1961) Some antecedents and consequents of masculine sex typing in adolescent boys, *Psychol. Monogr.,* **75,** whole no. 506.
Mussen, P. H. and **Distler, L.** (1959) Masculinity, identification and father–son relationships, *J. Abnorm. Soc. Psychol.,* **59,** 350–6.
Mussen, P. H. and **Jones, M.** (1957) Self conceptions, motivations and interpersonal attitudes of late and early maturing boys, *Child. Dev.,* **28,** 243–56.
Mussen, P. H. and **Kagan, J.** (1958) Group conformity and perception of parents, *Child Dev.,* **29,** 57–60.
Mussen, P., Young, H., Gaddini, R. and **Morante, L.** (1963) The influence of father–son relationships on adolescent personality and attitudes, *J. Child Psychol. Psychiat.,* **4,** 3–16.
Nash, R. (1973) *Classrooms Observed,* London: Routledge and Kegan Paul.
Nichols, K. A. and **Berg, I.** (1970) School phobia and self evaluation, *J. Child Psychol. Psychiat.,* **11,** 133–41.
Nystul, M. S. (1974) The effect of birth order and sex on self concept, *J. Indivl. Psychol.,* **30,** 211–15.
Nystul, M. S. (1976) The effect of birth order and family size on self concept, *Aust. Psychol.,* **11,** 199–201.
Offer, D. (1974) *The Psychological World of the Teenager* (rev. edn), New York: Basic Books.
Olasehinde, M. O. (1972) The development of the ideal self in some Western Nigerian school children, *Educ. Rev.,* **25,** 61–71.
Oles, H. J. (1973) Semantic differential for third through fifth grade students, *Psychol. Rep.,* **33,** 24–6.

Omwake, K. (1954) The relation between acceptance of self and acceptance of others shown by three personality inventories, *J. Consult. Psychol.,* **18** (6), 443–6.

Orne, M. T. (1962) On the social psychology of the psychological experiment, *Amer. Psychol.,* **17**, 776–83.

Osgood, C. E., Suci, G. T. and **Tannenbaum, P. H.** (1957) *The Measurement of Meaning,* Urbana: Univ. of Illinois.

Palfrey, C. F. (1973) Headteachers' expectations and their pupils' self concepts, *Educ. Res.,* **15**, 123–7.

Parker, J. (1966) Relationship of self report to inferred self concept, *Educ. Psychol. Meas.,* **26**, 691–700.

Parlady, M. J. (1969) What teachers believe; what children achieve, *Elem. Sch. J.,* **69**, 370–4.

Parsons, T. (1955) Family structure and the socialisation of the child, in T. Parsons and R. F. Bales (eds), *Family, Socialisation and Interaction Process,* Glencoe: Free Press.

Paschal, B. J. (1968) The role of self concept in achievement, *J. Negro Educ.,* **37**, 392–6.

Patterson, C. H. (1961) The self in recent Rogerian theory, *J. Psychol.,* **17**, 5–11.

Payne, D. A. and **Farquhar, W.** (1962) The dimensions of an objective measure of academic self concept, *J. Educ. Psychol.,* **53**, 116–23.

Payne, D. E. and **Mussen, P. H.** (1956) Parent–child relations and father identification among adolescent boys, *J. Abnorm. Soc. Psychol.,* **52**, 358–62.

Payne, J., Drummond, A. W. and **Lunghi, M.** (1970) Changes in the self concepts of school-leavers who participated in an Arctic expedition, *Br. J. Educ. Psychol.,* **40**, 211–16.

Perkins, H. V. (1958) Factors influencing change in children's self concepts, *Child. Dev.,* **29**, 203–20.

Perlmutter, H. (1954) Relations between self image, image of the foreigner, and the desire to live abroad, *J. Psychol.,* **38**, 131–7.

Peterson, F. T. (1972) Marijuana smokers and non-smokers: a self concept study, *Diss. Abstr.,* **32** (10A), 5619.

Phillips, E. L. (1951) Attitudes towards self and others. *J. Consult. Psychol.,* **15** (1), 79–81.

Piaget, J. (1954) *The Construction of Reality in the Child,* New York: Basic Books.

Pidgeon, D. A. (1970) *Expectation and Pupil Performance,* Slough: NFER.

Piers, E. V. and **Harris, D.** (1964) Age and other correlates of self concept in children, *J. Educ. Psychol.,* **55**, 91–5.

Pigge, F. L. (1970) Children and their self concepts, *Childh. Educ.,* **47**, 107–8.

Purkey, W. W. (1970) *Self Concept and School Achievement,* Englewood Cliffs, NJ: Prentice-Hall.

Purkey, W. W., Graves, W. and **Zelner, M.** (1970) Self perceptions of pupils in an experimental elementary school, *Elem. School. J.,* **71**, 166–71.

Putnam, B. A. and **Hansen, J. C.** (1972) Relationship of self concept and feminine role concept to vocational maturity in young women, *J. Counsel. Psychol.,* **19**, 436–40.

Rabban, M. (1950) Sex role identification in young children in two diverse social groups. *Genet. Psychol. Monogr.,* **42**, 81–158.

Radke, M. J. (1946) *The Relation of Parental Authority to Children's Behaviour and Attitude,* Minneapolis: Univ. Minnesota Press.

Raimy, V. C. (1943) The self concept as a factor in counselling and personality organisation, unpub. Ph.D. thesis, Ohio State Univ.

Raimy, V. C. (1948) Self reference in counselling interviews, *J. Consult. Psychol.,* **12** (3), 153–63.

Rapaport, G. M. (1958) Ideal-self instructions, MMPI profile changes and prediction of clinical improvement, *J. Consult. Psychol.,* **22**, 459–63.

Reckless, W. C., Dinitz, S. and **Murray, E.** (1956) Self concept as an insulator against delinquency. *Amer. Sociol. Rev.,* **21**, 744–6.

Reddy, W. B. (1973) The impact of sensitivity training on self actualisation, *Small Gp Beh.,* **4,** 407–13.

Reed, H. B. (1962) Implications for science education of a teacher competence research, *Sci. Educ.,* **Dec.** 473–86.

Reich, S. and **Geller, A.** (1976a) Self image of nurses, *Psychol. Rep.,* **Oct.,** 401–2.

Reich, S. and **Geller, A.** (1976b) Self image of social workers, *Psychol. Rep.,* **Oct.** 657–8.

Reid, I. (1976) A comparison of four academic self concept scales, unpub. paper, Postgraduate School of Research in Education, Univ. of Bradford.

Renberger, R. N. (1969) An experimental investigation of the relationship between self esteem and academic achievement in a population of disadvantaged adults, *Diss. Abstr.,* **30,** 2318A–2319A.

Richardson, S. A., Hastorf, A. H. and **Dornbusch, S. M.** (1964) The effect of physical disability on a child's description of himself, *Child Dev.,* **35,** 893–907.

Roberts, G. E. (1952) A study of the validity of the index of adjustment and values, *J. Consult. Psychol.,* **16,** 302–4.

Roberts, J. (1972) *Self Image and Delinquency,* Research Series No. 3, Dept. of Justice, Wellington, New Zealand.

Rogers, C. R. (1947) The organisation of personality, *Amer. Psychol.,* **2,** 358–68.

Rogers, C. R. (1951) *Client Centred Therapy,* Boston: Houghton Mifflin.

Rogers, C. R. (1954) The case of Mrs. Oak, in C. R. Rogers, and R. F. Dymond (eds), *Psychotherapy and Personality Change,* Chicago: Univ. of Chicago Press.

Rogers, C. R. (1956) Intellectualised psychotherapy, *Contemp. Psychol.,* **1,** 357–8.

Rogers, C. R. (1959) A theory of therapy, personality and interpersonal relationships as developed in the client-centered framework, in S. Koch (ed.), *Psychology: A Study of a Science,* Vol. 3, New York: McGraw-Hill.

Rogers, C. R. (1961) *On Becoming a Person,* Boston: Houghton Mifflin.

Rogers, C. R. (1963) Towards the science of the person, *J. Hum. Psychol.,* **3,** 72–92.

Rogers, C. R. (1967) The profess of the basic encounter group, in J. F. Bugental (ed.), *Challenges of Humanistic Psychology,* New York: McGraw-Hill.

Rogers, C. R. (1970) *Encounter Groups,* New York: Harper and Row.

Rogers, C. R. and **Dymond, R. F.** (1954) *Psychotherapy and Personality Change,* Chicago: Univ. of Chicago Press.

Rokeach, M. (1968) The nature of attitudes, in *International Encyclopaedia of the Social Sciences,* Vol. 1, London: Macmillan.

Rokeach, M. and **Fruchter, B.** (1956) A Factorial study of dogmatism, *J. Abnorm. Soc. Psychol.,* **53,** 356–60.

Rosen, E. (1956) Self appraisal and perceived desirability of MMPI personality traits, *J. Consult. Psychol.,* **3,** 44–51.

Rosenbaum, M. E. and **Stammers, R. F** (1961) Self esteem, manifest hostility and expression of hostility, *J. Abnorm. Soc. Psychol.,* **63,** 646–9.

Rosenberg, B. G. and **Sutton Smith, B.** (1960) A revised conception of masculine–feminine differences in play activities, *J. Genet. Psychol.,* **96,** 165–70.

Rosenberg, M. (1955) Factors influencing change in occupational choice, in P. F. Lazerfeld and M. Rosenberg (eds), *The Language of Social Research,* New York: Glencoe Free Press, 250–9.

Rosenberg, M. (1965) *Society and the Adolescent Self Image,* Princeton: Princeton Univ. Press.

Rosenberg, M. (1973) Which significant others, *Amer. Beh. Sci.,* **16,** 829–60.

Rosenberg, M. and **Simmons, R.** (1973) *Black and White Self Esteem: The Urban School Child,* Washington DC: Rose Monograph Series, American Sociological Association.

Rosenberg, M. J. (1969) The conditions and consequences of evaluation apprehension, in R. Rosenthal and R. L. Rosnow (eds), *Artifact in Behavioural Research,* New York: Academic Press.

Rosenthal, R. and **Jacobson, L.** (1968) *Pygmalion in the Classroom,* New York: Holt, Rinehart and Winston.

Roth, R. W. (1970) How Negro pupils see Black pride concepts, *Integrated Educ.,* **8,** 24–7.

Rotter, J. B. (1966) Generalised expectancies for internal versus external control of reinforcement, *Psychol. Monogr.,* **80,** Whole No. 609.

Rotter, J., Rafferty, J. and **Schachtitz, E.** (1949) Validation of the Rotter incomplete sentences blank for college screening, *J. Consult. Psychol.,* **13,** 348–56.

Rotter, J. and **Willerman, B.** (1947) The incomplete sentences test as a method of studying personality, *J. Consult. Psychol.* **11,** 43–8.

Rubin, I. (1967a) Increased self acceptance, *J. Pers. Soc. Psychol.,* **5,** 233–8.

Rubin, I. (1976b) The reduction of prejudice through laboratory training, *J. Appl. Beh. Sci.,* **3,** 29–50.

Rubovits, P. C. and **Maehr, M. L.** (1973) Pygmalion black and white, *J. Pers. Soc. Psychol.,* **25,** 210–18.

Ruedi, J. and **West, C. K.** (1973) Pupil self concept in an 'open' school and in a 'traditional' school, *Psychol. in the Schools,* **10,** 48–53.

Rutter, M. (1972) *Maternal Deprivation Reassessed,* London: Penguin.

Ryans, D. G. (1961) Some relationships between pupil behaviour and certain teacher characteristics, *J. Educ. Psychol.,* **52,** 82–90.

Salmon, P. (1963) An investigation of sexual identity, unpub. case study.

Schaeffer, G., Schuckit, M. and **Morrissey, E.** (1976) Correlation between two measures of self esteem and drug use in a college sample, *Psychol. Rep.,* **39,** 915–19.

Schmale, A. H. (1958) Relation of separation and depression to disease, *Psychosom. Med.,* **20,** 259–77.

Schneider, D. J. (1969) Tactical self presentation after success and failure, *J. Pers. Soc. Psychol.,* **13,** 262–8.

Schneider, D. J. and **Turkat, D.** (1975) Self presentation following success or failure, *J. Pers.,* **43,** 127–35.

Schopenhauer, A. (1948) *The World as Will and Idea,* London: Routledge.

Schuer, A. L. (1971) The relationship between personality attributes and effectiveness in teachers of the emotionally disturbed, *Excptl Child.,* **21,** 723–31.

Schuldermann, S. and **Schuldermann, E.** (1969) A note on the use of discrepancy scores in a self concept inventory, *J. Psychol.,* **72,** 33–4.

Scott, I. J. (1969) An analysis of the self concept of seventh grade students in segregated and desegregated schools, unpub. Ph.D., Univ. of Oklahoma, *Diss. Abstr.,* **30,** 1793A.

Sears, R. R. (1970) Relation of early socialisation experiences to self concept and gender role in middle childhood, *Child Dev.,* **41,** 267–89.

Sears, R. R., Maccoby, E. E. and **Levin, H.** (1957) *Patterns of Child Rearing,* Evanston: Row Peterson.

Secord, P. F. and **Jourard, S. M.** (1953) The appraisal of body cathexis: body cathexis and the self, *J. Consult. Psychol.,* **17,** 343–7.

Shaffer, L. F. and **Shoben, E. J.** (1957) *Psychology and Adjustment,* Boston: Houghton Mifflin.

Shaw, H. E. and **Wright, J. M.** (1968) *Scales for Measurement of Attitudes,* New York: McGraw-Hill.

Shaw, M. C. and **Alves, G.** (1962) The self concept of bright academic underachievers, *Pers. Guidance J.,* **42,** 401–3.

Shaw, M. C. and **Dutton, B.** (1962) The use of the parent attitude research inventory with the parents of bright academic underachievers, *J. Educ. Psych.,* **53,** 203–8.

Shaw, M. C., Edson, K. and **Bell, H.** (1960) The self concept of bright under achieving high school students as revealed by an adjective check list, *Pers. Guidance J.,* **42,** 401–3.

Sheerer, E. T. (1949) An analysis of the relationship between acceptance of the respect for self and acceptance of and respect for others, *J. Consult. Psychol.,* **13,** 176–80.

Sheldon, W. H. and Stevens, S. S. (1942) *The Varieties of Temperament,* New York: Harper and Row.

Sherif, M. and Cantril, C. W. (1947) *The Psychology of Ego Involvements,* New York: Wiley.

Sherif, M. and Sherif, C. W. (1956) *An Outline of Social Psychology,* New York: Harper.

Sherriffs, A. C. and McKee, J. P. (1957) Differential evaluation of males and females, *J. Pers.,* **25,** 356–71.

Shore, M. F., Masimo, J. L. and Ricks, D. F. (1965) A factor analytic study of psycho-therapeutic change in delinquent boys, *J. Clin. Psychol.,* **21,** 208–12.

Shostrum, E. L. (1966) *Manual of Personal Orientation Inventory,* San Diego: Educational and Testing Services.

Shrauger, J. S. and Lund, A. K. (1975) Self evaluation and reactions to evaluations from others, *J. Pers.,* **43** (1), 94–108.

Shrauger, J. S. and Patterson, M. (1974) Self evaluation and selection of dimensions for evaluating others, *J. Pers.,* **42,** 569–85.

Sigall, H. and Michela, J. (1976) I bet you say that to all the girls: physical attractiveness and reactions to praise, *J. Pers.,* **44,** 611–26.

Silber, E. and Tippett, J. S. (1965) Self esteem: clinical assessment and measurement validation, *Psychol. Rep.,* **16,** 1017–71.

Simmons, R. G., Rosenberg, F. and Rosenberg, M. (1973) Disturbance in the self image at adolescence. *Amer. Sociol. Rev.,* **38,** 553–68.

Simon, W. E., Primavera, L. H., Simon, M. G. and Orndoff, R. K. (1974) A comparison of marijuana users and non-users on a number of personality variables, *J. Consult. Clin. Psychol.,* **42,** 917–18.

Simon, W. E. and Simon, M. G. (1975) Self esteem, intelligence and standardised academic achievement, *Psychol. Sch.,* **12,** 97–9.

Skinner, B. F. (1938) *The Behaviour of Organisms,* New York: Appleton-Century-Crofts.

Skinner, B. F. (1953) *Science and Human Behaviour,* New York: Macmillan.

Smith, G. M. (1958) Six measures of self concept discrepancy and instability, *J. Consult. Psychol.,* **22,** 101–12.

Smith, G. M. (1969) Personality correlates of academic performance in three dissimilar populations, *Proc. 77th Annual Convention, Amer. Psychol. Assoc.,* Amer. Psychol. Assoc: Washington DC.

Smith, I. D. (1975) Sex differences in the self concepts of primary school children, *Aust. Psychol.,* **10,** 59–63.

Smith, M. B. (1950) The phenomenological approach in personality theory, *J. Abnorm. Soc. Psychol.,* **45,** 516–22.

Smith, P. A. (1962) A comparison of 3 sets of rotated factor analytic solutions of self-concept data, *J. Abnorm. Soc. Psychol.,* **64,** 326–33.

Snadowsky, A. and Belkin, G. (1964) Affecting change in the phenomenal field, *Small Gp Beh.,* **5,** 506–12.

Snygg, D. and Combs, A. W. (1949) *Individual Behaviour: A New Frame of Reference for Psychology,* New York: Harper.

Soares, A. T. and Soares, L. M. (1966) Self description and adjustment correlates of occupational choice, *J. Educ. Res.,* **60,** 27–31.

Soares, A. T. and Soares, L. M. (1969) Self perceptions of culturally disadvantaged children, *Amer. Educ. Res. J.,* **6,** 31–45.

Soares, A. T. and Soares, L. M. (1971) Comparative differences in the self perceptions of disadvantaged and advantaged students, *J. Sch. Psychol.,* **9,** 424–9.

Spaulding, R. (1963) *Achievement, Creativity, and Self Concept Correlates of Teacher–Pupil Transactions in Elementary Schools,* US Office of Education Cooperative Research Project No. 1352.

Spitzer, S. P., Stratton, J. R., Fitzjerald, J. D. and Mach, B. K. (1966) The self concept: test equivalence and perceived validity, *Sociol. Quart.,* **7,** 265–80.

Staffieri, J. (1957) A study of social stereotypes of body image in children, *J. Pers. Soc. Psychol.,* **7,** 101–4.

Staines, J. W. (1954) A psychological and sociological investigation of the self as a significant factor in education, unpub. Ph.D. Thesis, Univ. of London.

Staines, J. W. (1958) The self picture as a factor in the classroom, *Brit. J. Psychol.,* **28** (2), 97–111.

Stanton, H. E. (1975) Change in self insight during an intensive group experience, *Small Gp Beh.,* **6,** 487–93.

Star, S. A. (1950) The screening of psychoneurotics in the army, in S. Stouffer *et al.* (eds), *Measurement and Prediction,* Princeton: Princeton Univ. Press, pp. 486–547.

Stenner, A. J. and **Katzenmeyer, W.** (1976) Self concept, ability and achievement in a sample of 6th grade students, *J. Educ. Res.,* **69,** 270–3.

Stern, G. C. (1942) Measuring non-cognitive variables in research on teaching, in C. L. Gage, (ed.), *Handbook of Research on Teaching,* Skokie: Rand McNally.

Stern, W. (1922) The self concept of teenagers, *Z. Paed. Psychol.,* **23,** 8–15.

Stevenson, W. (1953) *The Study of Behaviour: Q-Technique and its Methodology,* Chicago: Univ. Press.

Stimson, R. (1968) Factor analytic approach to the structural differentiation of description, *J. Counsel. Psychol.,* **15,** 301–7.

Stock, D. (1949) An investigation into the interrelations between the self concept and feelings directed towards other persons and groups, *J. Consult. Psychol.,* **13,** 176–80.

Stotland, E. and **Cottrell, N.** (1961) Self esteem, group interaction and group influence on performance, *J. Pers.,* **29,** 273–84.

Stotland, E. and **Dunn, R. E.** (1962) Identification, opposition, authority, self-esteem and birth order, *Psychol. Monogr.,* **76,** whole No., 609.

Stotland, E. and **Zander, A.** (1958) Effects of public and private failure on self evaluation, *J. Abnorm. Psychol.,* **56,** 223–9.

Stotland, E., Thorley, S., Thomas, E., Cohen, A. R. and **Zander, A.** (1957) The effects of group expectation and self esteem upon self evaluation, *J. Abnorm. Soc. Psychol.,* **54,** 55–63.

Stott, L. H. (1939) Some family life patterns and their relation to personality development in children, *J. Exp. Educ.,* **8,** 148–60.

Strang, R. (1957) *The Adolescent Views Himself,* New York: McGraw-Hill.

Strong, D. J. and **Feder, D.** (1961) Measurement of the self concept: a critique of the literature, *J. Counsel. Psychol.,* **8,** 170–8.

Strong, R. S. and **Gray, B. L.** (1972) Social comparison, self evaluation and influence in counselling, *J. Counsel. Psychol.,* **19,** 178–83.

Sullivan, H. S. (1953) *Interpersonal Theory of Psychiatry,* New York: Norton.

Super, D. E., Stariskevsky, R., Matlin, N. and **Jordaan, J. P.** (1963) *Career Development: Self Concept Theory,* New York: College Entrance Examinations Board.

Symonds, P. M. (1939) *The Psychology of Parent-Child Relationships,* New York: Appleton-Century-Crofts.

Symonds, P. M. (1951) *The Ego and the Self,* New York: Appleton-Century-Crofts.

Tannenbaum, A. J. (1967) Social and psychological considerations in the study of the socially disadvantaged, in P. Witty (ed.), *The Educationally Retarded and Disadvantaged,* 66th Yearbook, Washington DC: National Society for the Study of Education.

Taylor, C. and **Combs, A. W.** (1952) Self acceptance and adjustment, *J. Consult. Psychol.,* **16,** 89–91.

Thomas, J. B. (1974) Research notice, *Educ. for Development,* **3,** 50–1.

Thomas, R. and **Burdick, R.** (1954) Self esteem and interpersonal influence, *J. Pers. Soc. Psychol.,* **51,** 419–26.

Thompson, B. L. (1974) Self concepts among secondary school pupils, *Educ. Res.,* **17,** 41–7.

Thurstone, L. L. (1932) *The Measurement of Social Attitudes,* Chicago: Univ. of Chicago Press.

Todd, A. J. (1916) Primitive notions of the self, *Amer. J. Psychol.,* **27,** 171–203.

Tolor, A., Kelly, B. and **Stebbins, C.** (1976) Assertiveness, sex role stereotyping and self concept, *J. Psychol.*, **93**, 157–68.

Trent, R. D. (1957) The relationship between expressed self acceptance and expressed attitudes to negroes and whites among negro children, *J. Genet. Psychol.*, **91**, 25–31.

Trowbridge, N. T. (1970) Effects of socio-economic class on self concepts of children, *Psychol. in the Schools*, **7**, 304–6.

Trowbridge, N. (1973) Teacher self concept and teaching style; in G. Chanan (ed.), *Towards a Science of Teaching*, Slough: NFER.

Tryon, C. M. (1939) Evaluation of adolescent personality by adolescents, *Monogr. Soc. Res. Child. Dev.*, **4** (4).

Turner, R. H. and **Vanderlippe, R. H.** (1958) Self-ideal congruence as an index of adjustment, *J. Abnorm. Soc. Psychol.*, **57**, 202–6.

Veness, T. (1962) *School Leavers*, London: Methuen.

Verma, G. K. (1973) Self esteem and immigrant pupils in English schools, unpub. paper, Univ. of East Anglia.

Verma, G. K. and **Bagley, C.** (1975) *Race and Education Across Cultures*, Heinemann: London.

Verplanck, W. S. (1954) *Modern Learning Theory: A Critical Analysis*, New York: Appleton Century Crafts.

Vernon, P. E. (1963) *Personality Assessment: A Critical Survey*, London: Methuen.

Videbeck, R. (1960) Self conceptions and the reaction of others, *Sociometry*, **23**, 351–62.

Vidoni, D. O. (1976) Nine-year cross-sectional study of change in self concepts of college freshmen, *Psychol. Rep.*, **Apr.**, **38**, 675–8.

Vinacke, E. W. (1952) *Psychology of Thinking*, New York: McGraw-Hill.

Viney, L. (1969) Self: the history of a concept, *J. Hist. Beh. Sci.*, **5**, 349–59.

Waetjen, W. B. (1963) Self concept as a learner scale. In M. Argyle and V. Lee (eds), *Social Relationships*, Bletchley, Open Univ. Press.

Walker, R. N. (1962) Body build and behaviour in young children, *Monogr. Soc. Res. Child Dev.*, **27** (3).

Walsh, A. M. (1956) *Self concepts of Bright boys with Learning Difficulties*, New York: Teachers College, Columbia Univ.

Walster, E. (1965) The effect of self esteem on romantic liking, *J. Exp. Soc. Psychol.*, **1**, 184–97.

Warehime, R. G. and **Foulds, M. F.** (1971) Perceived locus of control and personal adjustment, *J. Consult. Clin. Psychol.*, **37**, 250–2.

Warr, P. and **Knapper, C.** (1968) *Perception of People and Events*, London: Wiley.

Watkins, D. (1975) Self esteem as a moderator in vocational choice, *Aust. Psychol.*, **10**, 75–80.

Watkins, D. (1976) The antecedents of self esteem in Australian university students, *Aust. Psychol.*, **2**, 169–72.

Watkins, J. T., Noll, G. A. and **Breed, G. R.** (1975) Changes towards self actualisation, *Small Gp Beh.*, **6**, 272–81.

Wattenberg, W. W., and **Clifford, C.** (1964) Relation of self concept to beginning achievement in reading, *Child Dev.*, **35**, 461–7.

Watts, T. W. (1964) *Behaviourism and Phenomenology*, Chicago: Chicago Univ.

Weiner, B. (1971) *Perceiving the Causals of Success and Failure*, New York: General Learning Press.

Weiner, I. B. (1970) *Psychological Disturbance in Adolescence*, New York: Wiley.

Weiner, M., Blumberg, A., Segman, S. and **Cooper, A.** (1959) Judgement of adjustment by psychologists, social workers and college students, *J. Abnorm. Soc. Psychol.*, **59**, 315–21.

White, W. and **Bashaw, W. L.** (1970) Self concept of follow through children, *Annual Rep. of Follow Through*, Atlanta Public School System, Georgia.

White, W. and **Human, S.** (1976) The relationships of self concepts of 3, 4 and 5 year old children with mother, father and teacher percepts, *J. Psychol.*, **92**, 191–4.

White, W. and **Simmons, M.** (1974) First grade readiness predicted by teachers' perception of student maturity and student perception of self, *Percept. and Motor Skills*, **39**, 395–9.

Whiting, J. W. (1960) Resource mediation and learning by identification, in I. Iscoe and H. Stevenson (eds), *Personality Development in Children*, Austin: Univ. of Texas Press.

Willig, C. J. (1973) A study of the relationship between children's academic ability and their constructs of self in school related attitudes, unpub. Ph.D. dissert., Univ. of Surrey.

Wilson, J. P. and **Wilson, S. B.** (1976) Sources of self esteem and the person X situation controversy, *Psychol. Rep.*, Apr., **38**, 355–8.

Wiseman, S. (1973) The educational obstacle race: factors that hinder pupil Progress, *Educ. Res.*, **15**, 87–93.

Witkin, H. A. (1949) Nature and importance of individual differences in perception, *J. Pers.*, **18**, 145–70.

Witkin, H. A. (1965) Psychological differentiation, *J. Abnorm. Soc. Psychol.*, **70**, 317–36.

Wittrock, M. C. and **Husek, T. R.** (1962) Effect of anxiety upon retention of verbal learning, *Psychol. Rep.*, **10**, 78.

Witty, P. (1947) An analysis of the personality traits of the effective teacher, *J. Educ. Res.*, **40**, 662–71.

Wolfenstein, M. (1968) Children's humour, sex names and double meaning, in T. Talbot (ed.), *The World of the Child*, New York: Anchor Books.

Wooster, A. and **Harris, G.** (1973) Concepts of self in highly mobile service boys, *Educ. Res.*, **14**, 195–9.

Worchel, P. (1957) Screening of flying personnel: development of a self concept inventory for predicting maladjustment, *School of Aviation Medicine*, USAF Report No. 56–61.

Wylie, R. (1961) *The Self Concept*, Lincoln: Univ. Nebraska Press.

Wylie, R. (1968) The present status of the self theory, in E. F. Borgatta and W. W. Lambert, *Handbook on Personality*, Ch. 12, Chicago: Rand McNally.

Wylie, R. (1974) *The Self Concept*, Vol. 1, *A Review of Methodological Considerations and Measuring Instruments* (rev. edn), Lincoln: Univ. of Nebraska Press.

Yeatts, P. and **Bentley, E. L.** (1968) The development of a non verbal measure to assess the self concept of young and low verbal children, paper presented at American Educational Research Association New York.

Zelen, S. L. (1954) The relationship of peer acceptance, acceptance of others, and self acceptance, *Iowa Acad. Sci., Proc.*, **61**, 446–9.

Ziller, R. C. (1973) *The Social Self*, New York: Pergamon.

Ziller, R. C., Haley, J., Smith, M. D. and **Long, B. H.** (1969) Self esteem: a self-social construct, *J. Consult. Clin. Psychol.*, **33**, 84–95.

Ziller, R. C. and **Long, B. H.** (1964b) Self-social constructs and geographic mobility, unpub. MS, Univ. of Delaware.

Ziller, R. C., Long, B. H., Remana, K. and **Reddy, V.** (1968) Self–other orientations of Indian and American adolescents, *J. Pers.*, **36**, 315–30.

Ziller, R. C., Megas, J. and **DeCenio, D.** (1964) Self-social constructs of normals and acute neuropsychiatric patients, *J. Consult. Psychol.*, **20**, 50–63.

Zimmer, H. (1954) Self acceptance and its relation to conflict. *J. Consult. Psychol.*, **18**, 447–9.

Zimmer, H. (1956) Motivational factors in dyadic relations, *J. Pers.*, **24**, 251–6.

Zimmerman, I. L. and **Allebrand, G. N.** (1965) Personality characteristics and attitudes towards achievement of good and poor readers, *J. Educ. Res.*, **59**, 28–30.

Zirkel, P. and **Moses, E.** (1971) Self concept and ethnic group membership among public school students, *Am. Ed. Res. J.*, **8**, 253–65.

Zirkel, P. A. and **Greene, J. F.** (1971) The measurement of the self concept of disadvantaged students, unpub. paper presented at National Council on Measurement in Education, New York.

Zuckerman, M., Baer, M. and **Monashkin, I.** (1956) Acceptance of self, parents and people in patients and normals, *J. Clin. Psychol.*, **12**, 327–32.

Name index

Abercrombie, K., 160
Acland, H., 296
Adams, N. M., 144
Adams, S., 40
Adelson, J., 178, 196, 198, 210
Adler, A., 19, 224, 232
Adorno, T. W., 231
Alban Metcalfe, B. M., 178
Allebrand, G. N., 277
Allen, B. P., 133
Allen, F., 225
Allport, G. W., 21, 22–3, 59, 64, 73, 160
Altrochi, J., 250
Alves, G., 276
Angyal, A., 26, 42
Argyle, M., 96, 160
Aronson, E., 268
Ausubel, D. P., 258

Babladelis, G., 40
Back, K. W., 170–1, 266
Backman, C. W., 248
Baer, M., 227
Bakan, D., 194
Ballachey, E. L., 52
Bandura, A., 188–9, 208
Bannister, D., 130
Barker Lunn, J. C., 140, 296–7, 306
Baron, P. H., 243
Bashaw, W. L., 108
Battle, J., 117–19
Bayley, N., 181, 198, 206
Bayne, R., 233
Bedford, A., 270
Behrens, M. L., 201
Belkin, G., 236
Bell, H., 283
Bellak, A. S., 257
Benjamins, J., 249
Bennett, E. M., 194
Bennett, V. D. C., 125–6
Bentley, E. L., 108
Berg, I., 287
Berger, E. M., 123
Bergin, A. E., 251

Bergschied, E., 156
Bertocci, P. A., 21, 22
Bidney, D., 4
Bills, R. E., 80, 84, 85, 86, 108–9
Bledsoe, J. C., 116–17, 197
Block, H. J., 194
Blodgett, H. C., 11
Blumberg, A., 303
Bobele, H. K., 238
Bogo, N., 197
Bond, A., 271
Borislow, B., 278
Borke, H., 162
Boshier, R., 96
Bossom, J., 227
Borhnstedt, G., 156
Bousfield, W. A., 301
Braught, G., 265
Brehm, M. H., 266
Brill, N. Q., 266
Brisset, D., 55
Brodbeck, A., 266
Brodsky, C. M., 152–3
Bromley, D. B., 166–8
Bronfenbrenner, U., 162, 210
Brookover, W. B., 72, 138–9, 278–9,
    280, 282, 289, 293
Broverman, I. K., 194, 195
Bruce, P., 295
Bruch, M., 255
Bruner, J. S., 31
Brudick, R., 247
Bugental, J., 134
Buhler, C., 4
Burke, D. A., 143
Burns, R. B., 13, 124, 127, 130, 194,
    227, 228, 231, 302, 304
Burstall, C., 291
Butler, J. M., 39, 88, 125
Butler, N., 207
Bynner, J., 265

Calden, 156
Caldwell, W., 144
Callison, C. P., 291

Subject index

Material self, 7
Maternal deprivation, 209–10
Mesomorphy, 152–4
Minority groups
Modelling, 188–9, 190

Names, 291
Neo-Freudian theories, 19–21
Nicknames, 155
Non-verbal communication, 160

Observation techniques, 90–3
Occupational choice, 260–5
Oedipus complex, 186–7
Old age, 170–1

Peer interaction, 163–5
Perception score sheet, 100–1
Personal constructs, 45–7
Phenomenal field, 32, 34–5
Phenomenal self, 34
Phenomenology, 30–48
Physical attractiveness, 271–2
Physical handicap, 157
Plurality of self conception, 67–8
Position in class scale, 136
Primary self-concept scale, 106–8
Projective techniques, 89–90
Proprium, 22–3
Puberty, 179–83

Q sort, 84, 88–9, 125–7

Rating scales, 87–8
Reliability, 77–8
Response sets, 82
Role construct repertory technique
    (rep. test), 130–3

Scale for inferring the self concept, 142
School organisation, 296–300
Self actualisation, 25–8, 38
Self-appraisal scale, 136–7
Self as Known, 5, 6, 7, 50–2
Self as Knower, 5, 6, 7, 50–2
Self as Object, 6, 7
Self as Subject, 6, 7
Self attitudes, 52–63
Self comparison, 241–52

Self concept as learner scale, 140–2
Self concept of ability as a worker scale,
    143–5
Self concept of academic ability scale,
    138–9, 277
Self-concept report scale, 101–2
Self-concept scale, 102
Self consistency theory, 242–4
Semantic differential, 127–30
Self esteem, 9, 55–7, 66, 201–9
Self-esteem scale, 103
Self-esteem inventory, 95–6, 277
Self-esteem theory, 242–5
Self image, 55, 66
Self-image questionnaire, 119–20
Self-others questionnaire, 122–3
Self presentation, 16–17, 81
Self regard, 37–8
Self-report techniques, 74–7, 86–90
Self-social symbols task, 96–100
Self theory, 47–8
Semantic differential, 127–30
Sex role identity, 185–200
Sex role standard, 186, 190–2
Smoking, 265
Social desirability, 82–4
Social distance, 228–9
Social learning model of identification,
    188–9
Social self, 7, 64
Somatic apperception test, 144–5
Special schools, 298–300
Spiritual self, 7
Streaming, 296–8
Symbolic interactionism, 12–17

Teacher expectation, 286–94
Teacher feedback, 288–94
Teacher self concept, 300–9
Teaching style, 303–6
Tennessee self-concept scale, 113–15
Transitory self, 64

Validity, 78–81

'Where are you' game, 115–16
'Who am I' test, 133–5, 277

Young children's self-concept
    instrument, 121–2